3317025

WATER RIGHTS AND THE ENVIRONMENT IN THE UNITED STATES

RECENT TITLES IN DOCUMENTARY AND
REFERENCE GUIDES

Immigration: A Documentary and Reference Guide
Thomas Cieslik, David Felsen, and Akis Kalaitzidis

Gun Control: A Documentary and Reference Guide
Robert J. Spitzer

Culture Wars in America: A Documentary and Reference Guide
Glenn H. Utter

Civil Liberties and the State: A Documentary and Reference Guide
Christopher Peter Latimer

The Politics of Sexuality: A Documentary and Reference Guide
Raymond A. Smith

U.S. Election Campaigns: A Documentary and Reference Guide
Thomas J. Baldino and Kyle L. Kreider

U.S. Foreign Policy: A Documentary and Reference Guide
Akis Kalaitzidis and Gregory W. Streich

White-Collar and Corporate Crime: A Documentary and Reference Guide
Gilbert Geis

Homelessness: A Documentary and Reference Guide
Neil Larry Shumsky

Victims' Rights: A Documentary and Reference Guide
Douglas E. Beloof

Substance Abuse in America: A Documentary and Reference Guide
James A. Swartz

The Iraq War: A Documentary and Reference Guide
Thomas R. Mockaitis

Animal Rights and Welfare: A Documentary and Reference Guide
Lawrence W. Baker

WATER RIGHTS AND THE ENVIRONMENT IN THE UNITED STATES

A Documentary and Reference Guide

John R. Burch Jr.

Documentary and Reference Guides

 GREENWOOD™

An Imprint of ABC-CLIO, LLC

Santa Barbara, California • Denver, Colorado

Library of Congress Cataloging-in-Publication Data

Water rights and the environment in the United States : a documentary and reference guide / John R. Burch Jr.

    pages cm. — (Documentary and reference guides)

    Includes bibliographical references and index.

    ISBN 978–1–4408–3802–6 (hard copy : alk. paper) — ISBN 978–1–4408–3803–3 (ebook)

    1. Water—Law and legislation—United States—Sources. I. Burch, John R., 1968– editor.

KF5569.W38 2015

346.7304′691—dc23   2015004980

ISBN: 978–1–4408–3802–6

EISBN: 978–1–4408–3803–3

19 18 17 16 15   1 2 3 4 5

This book is also available on the World Wide Web as an eBook.
Visit www.abc-clio.com for details.

Greenwood
An Imprint of ABC-CLIO, LLC

ABC-CLIO, LLC
130 Cremona Drive, P.O. Box 1911
Santa Barbara, California 93116-1911

This book is printed on acid-free paper ∞

Manufactured in the United States of America

CONTENTS

Contents

Contents

READER'S GUIDE TO RELATED DOCUMENTS AND SIDEBARS

Note: Some documents appear in more than one category.

INTRODUCTION

The development of water policy and politics in the United States has been driven by three factors: the availability of water, the manner in which people could use the commodity to its maximum economic benefit, and governmental control. Access to water is the most important component because it is both a finite resource and necessary to sustain life. Areas that have no water, such as deserts, are incapable of sustaining human populations. Native peoples were the first people on the continent to begin manipulating water resources to meet their needs. When the Spanish arrived in the Southwest, they discovered that Native Americans were already irrigating their crops by diverting water from streams and rivers, thereby making formerly arid lands suitable for agriculture. Over time, the scale of such projects has changed. For instance, today we divert the water from the Colorado River to the states of Arizona, California, Colorado, Nevada, New Mexico, Utah, and Wyoming. Since the amount of water is limited, anytime that water is diverted for use by a person or a specific group of people, the consequence is that somebody else has lost a proportionate share.

Competition for water is thus inevitable, which is why it is the overarching theme of this book. Organized into six parts, this work broadly surveys the development of water politics and policy in the United States from the early nineteenth century to the present day. It is a story told through documents that is wrought with conflict as competing legal rulings and legislation at the state, federal, and international levels have created a morass that pits interest groups against each other. New challenges have also emerged over the centuries that have further complicated matters for the citizenry of the United States. The scale of these new problems, such as climate change, require adjustments that potentially have severe economic costs, which many are unwilling to pay in the short term, but, if ignored, in the long term may bear much more severe consequences. Through these documents, readers learn how our water politics evolved, see how previous generations addressed the challenges that faced them, and have present issues identified with various points of view so that they can consider possible solutions for the future.

Part One: Doctrines and Rights

The first chapter focuses on the initial development of water law in the United States through state judiciaries in the nineteenth century. In the early years of the American republic, the use of water was governed by the riparian rights system that existed in English common law. In a riparian system, all users who owned land along a waterway had an equal right to the water that flowed on their land. This system began to be modified through the 1827 Rhode Island case *Tyler v. Wilkinson*. In his decision on the case, Judge Joseph Story created the reasonable use doctrine, which stated that all landowners utilizing a waterway had the right to use a "reasonable" amount of water. This new doctrine was subsequently adopted by most states in the eastern portion of the United States. It worked well when most of the users along a waterway were engaged in similar practices, most notably agriculture. When industrialization began to impact waterways as people began constructing mills, new legal issues arose.

The second case included in Chapter 1, *William H. Cary v. Albert Daniels*, illustrates the challenges that state courts had in determining what a "reasonable" use of a waterway was. Through the 1844 Massachusetts case, Chief Justice Lemuel Shaw set a precedent when he determined that to allow one user his or her reasonable right of water meant depriving others of theirs. It was thus the needs of the community that determined which individual got his or her reasonable use privileged over another. In his ruling, Shaw unmistakably signaled that industrial uses of water should be favored over that of other uses, such as farming.

As Americans spread west, it quickly became apparent that conditions dictated the need for different water laws. The doctrine of prior appropriation soon came to the fore. Rather than acknowledging that everyone along a waterway had equal rights, the new doctrine favored the person or group that began utilizing the water first. Thus, the person with the oldest claim on the land could use as much water as he or she needed. Once the first user had finished, then the person with the second oldest claim could use whatever he or she required. The process continued in that fashion until all the water was gone. One of the key cases that weighed traditional riparian law against the doctrine of prior appropriation in the West was *Coffin et al. v. Left Hand Ditch Company*. Upon becoming a state, Colorado drafted a constitution that proclaimed that the doctrine of prior appropriation would be used to manage the state's water resources. Since Colorado was the first state to adopt prior appropriation as the law of the land, the concept became known as the "Colorado Doctrine." The constitution was challenged in 1882 by Coffin and other landowners who wanted the state to use traditional riparian doctrine rather than prior appropriation, as they were too far down the queue of the St. Vrain River to be assured of water in times of drought. Their suit proved unsuccessful as the District Court of Boulder County, Colorado, affirmed the state's constitution.

Another important legal decision on prior appropriation was *Lux v. Haggin*. The 1886 California case led the California Supreme Court to definitively determine which form of water law was going to prevail within the state. After exhaustively examining precedents involving the application of both riparian law, as practiced in the eastern part of the country, and prior appropriation doctrine, the justices ultimately determined that prior appropriation was the law within its borders.

Court cases involving water have subsequently resulted in the development of legal statutes that vary from both state to state and from state to federal jurisdictions. Often these are in conflict, as local jurisdictions create statutes that favor their constituencies. Sorting out conflicting priorities has left many issues to be determined by the federal courts, which have made decisions that further complicated matters by bringing in factors that may not otherwise have been considered. Chapter 2 focuses on one of the factors introduced by federal authorities, namely the rights of Native Americans.

In states that utilized prior appropriation, water rights were just about always awarded to the first Euroamerican settler that utilized the water first. The fact that Native Americans were already using the water never factored into the equation until the U.S. Supreme Court determined in the 1908 *Winters v. United States* case that the residents of the Fort Belknap Indian Reservation had a prior appropriation to the waters of the Milk River although American cattlemen claimed their use of the water predated that of the Indians. Since the justices decided the case on a technicality, western states using prior appropriation ignored the 1908 precedent. The Supreme Court would not clearly specify that Native American water rights were established long before white settlers arrived until their decision in *Arizona v. California* in 1963.

The chapter then turns to explorations of the Pacific Northwest fishing rights cases that arose out of the Native American Civil Rights movement. The cases concerned application of Native American treaty rights. Between 1854 and 1856, Governor Isaac Stevens negotiated a series of treaties with Native American groups in present-day Oregon and Washington that divided the anadromous fish runs equally between Native Americans and Euroamerican settlers. At the time the treaties were negotiated, the Native American population in the region was larger than that of the Americans; thus, Stevens had gotten his constituents a disproportionate share of the prodigious salmon runs. When the Native Americans began asserting their treaty rights in the 1960s, the situation had become completely reversed. Officials in what became the states of Oregon and Washington had registered no qualms about the treaties when the terms had greatly benefitted their economic interests, but when they favored the natives, the agreements were considered patently unfair and thus ignored. The Native American peoples of the Pacific Northwest turned first to state courts and then to federal courts to get their treaty rights recognized.

Part One concludes with two federal acts addressing the restoration of fish populations that had been decimated as a result of dam construction. The Truckee-Carson-Pyramid Lake Water Rights Settlement Act made it a federal responsibility to use Nevada's Stampede Reservoir as a fishery to restore the populations of the Pyramid Lake cui-ui and Lahontan cutthroat trout that the Pyramid Lake Paiutes had depended on as a food source and a staple of their economy since time immemorial.

The Elwha River Ecosystem and Fisheries Restoration Act called for a study to determine the most effective method for restoring the Elwha River's once prodigious salmon runs. The researchers in 1995 determined that the best solution was to remove the two dams that had been constructed on the river. After years of planning, work on the Elwha River Restoration Project finally commenced in 2011. The project was notable because it resulted in the largest dams to be voluntarily removed in the history of the United States. Since the dismantling of the dams commenced, the salmon populations in the river have been recovering.

Part Two: Waters of the West

Chapter 3 begins with John Wesley Powell's exploration of the West following the conclusion of the Civil War. In 1878, Powell delivered to the U.S. Congress his *Report on the Lands of the Arid Region of the United States*. Supporters of the expansion of the United States used the report to encourage the migration of Americans West. Ignored was the content of the report, in which Powell warned about settling west of the 100th meridian due to the region's dearth of waterways.

Congress encouraged the states to address the access to water problem by passing the Federal Desert Land Act of 1894, which is better known as the Carey Land Act. It offered a maximum of 1 million acres of land held in the public domain to western states if they reclaimed those lands using irrigation, thus making it suitable for agriculture. The states were not allowed to keep the property, but instead had to sell the land in 160-acre tracts to settlers. The Act proved a disappointment as only Colorado, Idaho, Utah, and Wyoming acquired land. The primary problem was the inability of the states to pay for the water infrastructure required to irrigate such large expanses of land. This led to Congress passing the Reclamation Act of 1902, also known as the Newlands Act. The Act, which created the United States Reclamation Service, transferred the responsibility of constructing dams, canals, and other forms of water infrastructure from the states to the federal government.

During the same period, water conflicts arose between the various states in the West over the ownership and diversion of waterways. In order to address issues arising over the Colorado River, the states of Arizona, California, Colorado, Nevada, Utah, and Wyoming met in Santa Fe, New Mexico, during November 1922 to settle their disagreements. Their participation in the negotiations was encouraged by the federal government, with the promise that a settlement would lead to the construction of dams on the Colorado River. What emerged was the Colorado River Compact of 1922, which equally divided the Colorado's waters between the Upper Basin, which included the states of Colorado, Utah, Wyoming, and part of Nevada, and the Lower Basin, which was comprised of Arizona, California, and a portion of Nevada. Once a majority of the states ratified the Compact, Congress passed the Boulder Canyon Project Act of 1928. The Act resulted in the construction of the Boulder Canyon Dam, later renamed Hoover Dam. Additional infrastructure resulted from the Colorado River Storage Project Act of 1956 for the states of Colorado, New Mexico, Utah, and Wyoming.

Missing from the beneficiaries of the Colorado River Storage Project Act of 1956 were the Lower Basin states of Arizona, California, and Nevada. This was due to the unwillingness of Arizona's legislature to ratify the Colorado River Compact of 1922. Arizonans believed that California was receiving a disproportionate share of the Colorado's water. Arizona thus turned to the federal judicial system to obtain what they believed was their fair share of the water. Decades of legal conflict culminated in the 1963 U.S. Supreme Court landmark decision in *Arizona v. California*. Arizona's victory in the case led to the passage of the Colorado River Basin Act of 1968, which included the final apportionment of the waters of the Colorado River and the construction of the Central Arizona Project, a 336-mile network of aqueducts, canals, and tunnels that transferred water from the Colorado River at Lake Havasu to Pima, Pinal, and Maricopa counties in Arizona.

Part Three: Border Regions

Part Three of this reference focuses on international treaties negotiated between the United States and its neighbors in North America. It starts with a focus on Mexico, beginning with the Rio Grande River Convention of 1906. The treaty was necessary because residents of Texas and Mexico had endured decades of conflict over the use of the Rio Grande River. The Texans believed that Mexico was allowing its citizens to illegally withdraw a disproportionate amount of water from the river in order to irrigate farm land. Regardless of the merit of their claim, the Mexicans were not violating any laws as none existed that regulated the waterway until the 1906 agreement.

The Rio Grande River Convention applied to the segment of the Rio Grande River that began from the river's headwaters in Colorado to its confluence with the Conchos River. Mexico was apportioned 10 percent of the water that flowed down that segment and the United States received the rest. At the time, 10 percent was more than enough water for Mexico since their territory was sparsely populated. The Mexican government was thus satisfied with the terms despite the reality that the United States had negotiated a one-sided agreement. Over time, as the Mexican side became more populated, the inequities in the 1906 agreement became a major issue between the two countries. In order to rectify the problem, the two countries negotiated the United States–Mexico Water Treaty of 1944.

The United States–Mexico Water Treaty of 1944 concerned the management and development of the parts of the Colorado, Rio Grande, and Tijuana rivers shared by the two countries. Once again, the United States held the superior bargaining position between the two parties as Mexico desperately needed access to some of the waters from the Colorado River. Mexico had found itself in severe straits because its water sources along the border were diminishing as the population in the region grew. Mexico had previously been able to depend on water from the Colorado River but that had changed when the United States had begun constructing dams on the river that impounded water instead of allowing it to flow south. The problem was compounded by the many diversions made from the Colorado River downriver of the dams for the irrigation of agricultural lands in the United States. In the treaty, Mexico received an annual allotment of 1.5 million acre feet of water from the Colorado River. In addition, it was allowed to construct the Morelos Dam on the Colorado River in order to impound water for future use.

One issue that has not been adequately addressed between the two countries is the protection of groundwater sources. Mexico has proven reticent to negotiate on the issue because its citizens are heavily tapping the available groundwater along the border and the country surmises that the United States would likely demand that their groundwater use be reduced significantly. Nonetheless, the United States is hopeful that an agreement concerning the protection and use of groundwater can be negotiated. Toward that end, Congress passed the United States–Mexico Transboundary Aquifer Assessment Act of 2006. The Act was designed to study all of the aquifers along the United States–Mexico border. It is notable that the Act contained provisions for Mexican scientists to work on the project in hopes that such collaboration could eventually lead to cooperation on jointly protecting groundwater sources.

In contrast with the relationship with Mexico, the United States and Canada collaborate very closely on the protection of their shared waters. The agreements between the countries do not just cover the portions of rivers and lakes along the border but also address them in their entirety. This is a reflection of the shared belief that what happens in one locale, regardless of which side of the border it is on, affects the entire expanse of a waterway. This commitment to protect their shared resource was evident as early as 1909, when the Boundary Waters Treaty was negotiated by the United States and Great Britain, who was acting on Canada's behalf. That treaty set the foundation for all future negotiations between Canada and the United States.

One of the most important agreements involving Canada and the United States was not even negotiated between the two parties, but instead by the Council of Great Lakes Governors, which included the governors of Illinois, Indiana, Michigan, Minnesota, New York, Ohio, Pennsylvania, and Wisconsin, and the premiers of Ontario and Quebec. They agreed to the Great Lakes Charter, a basinwide agreement that was signed on February 11, 1985. The agreement was intended to establish minimum standards to enhance the water quality of the lakes and to also prevent the transfer of waters from the Great Lakes outside of the Great Lakes states and provinces. Technically the agreement was nonbinding because states are not allowed by the U.S. Constitution to sign international agreements. That problem was addressed by Congress in the Water Resources Development Act of 1986 (included in Chapter 8), which made the terms of the agreement legally binding. Unexpectedly, Congress strengthened the terms of the agreement by essentially making it impossible for water transfers within the basin, even if the transfer never crossed a state or international boundary.

The Great Lakes were also the subject of the Great Lakes Water Quality Protocol of 2012, which was negotiated between the United States and Canada. The first Great Lakes Water Quality Agreement had been negotiated in 1978 and amended in 1987. The primary concerns in both negotiations were the introduction of phosphorous and toxic chemicals in the respective lakes. Despite decades of work, the lakes were continuing to suffer problems from those pollutants, as evidenced in 2014 with the algal bloom in Lake Erie that left residents of Toledo, Ohio, without drinking water for days. The 2012 agreement not only included tougher regulations for polluters but also expanded the scope of the legislation to include issues such as invasive species and climate change. The expansion of cooperation between the countries bodes well for the future as it evidences a shared commitment to protect their shared waters regardless of the future challenges that may emerge.

Part Four: Water Management and Flood Control

Chapter 6 focuses on legislation passed by Congress to address flood control. By no means is it comprehensive, as it includes only three of the many flood control acts that have been enacted. The three that are included had long-term impact on the nation.

The Flood Control Act of 1928 was a reaction by Congress to the massive flooding that inundated the Mississippi River basin in 1927. The floodwaters inundated approximately 15 million acres of land and displaced more than 700,000 people in 10 states. In passing the Act, Congress transferred the responsibility of financing and constructing flood control infrastructure on the Mississippi River from the states to the federal government. The United States Army Corps of Engineers (USACE) was tasked with the actual construction work. Unfortunately, the work conducted proved inadequate to control flooding on the Mississippi River. In truth, the work authorized in 1928 contributed to an even more devastating flood in 1937.

Flooding on the Missouri River in 1943 spurred Congress to pass the Flood Control Act of 1944. It contained the Pick-Sloan Plan, which was a joint effort by the Bureau of Reclamation and the USACE to address the river's constant flooding problem. Their cooperation marked a unique moment that saw the two competitors actually working together. They did so because they wanted to prevent the creation of the proposed Missouri Valley Authority, which was favored by President Franklin Roosevelt, as the agency would have been a new competitor for both in the areas of flood control and dam construction. The Pick-Sloan plan resulted in the construction of 28 dams and more than 40 hydroelectric plants. It also resulted in the construction of a six-foot navigation channel between Sioux City, Iowa, and St. Louis, Missouri.

The chapter concludes with the Flood Control Act of 1962, which was notable for two reasons. First, communities were provided a five-year window from the time they were notified in writing of the beginning of the five years to provide their required contribution to their local water infrastructure project. Depending on the community's contribution, their part might have included easements or other forms of in-kind gifts to help offset construction costs. This requirement helped demonstrate how important a particular project was to the local community. If they were unwilling to help pay for something that they supposedly needed, it demonstrated that their need may not have been as dire as portrayed.

The Act also mandated a change in dam construction. From that point on, all dams authorized by Congress had to be multipurpose. This meant that dams not only be useful for flood control but also be capable of producing hydroelectric power. Congress believed that multipurpose dams represented a better investment of the nation's monies.

Chapter 7 also addresses water infrastructure and flooding, albeit from a different perspective. In 1996, Congress enacted the National Dam Safety Program Act to identify which of the approximately 78,000 dams across the nation were in danger of failing so that they could be repaired. The USACE was responsible for maintaining a database identifying each of the dams and what was the risk they each posed to people and property. The respective federal agencies that managed federally owned dams were responsible for shoring up their properties. Unfortunately, a vast majority of the dams are owned by private interests, and many do not have the funding necessary to repair their dams, even with the federal government providing some grants to offset the costs.

Part Four ends with the conclusion of "A Failure of Initiative: Final Report of the Select Bipartisan Committee to Investigate the Preparation for and Response to Hurricane Katrina." It is a sobering report as to what happens when water infrastructure constructed by the USACE fails. It is also a damning indictment of politicians at all levels who were inadequately prepared to address a disaster that they had forewarning was on its way. The lessons from Hurricane Katrina are necessary to share in order to better prepare for natural catastrophes in the future.

Part Five: Environmental Issues

The Refuse Act of 1899 was technically the first legislation passed by Congress to address water pollution. It banned the dumping of refuse into the nation's waters unless the entity guilty of the dumping had procured a license from the USACE. The law exempted mining operations as long as the waste produced did not interfere with navigation on the nation's waterways.

The first notable legislation addressing the nation's water quality was the Water Pollution Control Act of 1948, which regulated the pollution of surface waters. The 1948 legislation was not very stringent due to the compromises required to get it passed, but environmentalists were able to strengthen its standards and penalties through the Clean Water Restoration Act of 1966. The push for environmental legislation was helped by the reality that most of the country's waterways were obviously horribly polluted. This was reinforced in the public sphere by events such as the Cuyahoga River catching fire in Ohio on June 22, 1969. Congress in 1972 passed the Clean Water Act, which was intended to restore the United States' waterways and protect them into the future. The Act succeeded in its main goals, as today's waters are certainly cleaner than they were in the 1970s, but more work remains to be done. Other notable legislation from that era includes the Water Resources Research Act of 1964; the Water Resources Planning Act of 1965; the Safe Drinking Water Act of 1974; the Surface Mining Control and Reclamation Act of 1977; the Comprehensive Environmental Response, Compensation, and Liability Act of 1980, better known as the "Superfund"; the Water Resources Development Act of 1986; and the Water Quality Act of 1987.

The spate of environmental legislation protecting and improving the nation's waters drew significant legal challenges. The most controversial was *Rapanos et ux., et al. v. United States*. In their decision, the U.S. Supreme Court justices narrowed the definition of "navigable waters," thereby making it more difficult for agencies such as the USACE and the Environmental Protection Agency to apply the Clean Water Act. In response, both agencies are working to once again broaden that definition through their "Proposed Rule: Definition of 'Waters of the United States' Under the Clean Water Act."

Chapter 9 traces the evolution of congressional legislation concerning water habitats. The first document included is the 1871 Joint Resolution for the Protection and Preservation of the Food Fishes of the Coasts of the United States. It created the position of Commissioner of Fish and Fisheries. It also created a commission that was the forbearer of the United States Fish and Wildlife Service.

During the New Deal, Congress passed the Fish and Wildlife Coordination Act of 1934. It was designed to protect the habitats of fish and wildlife that were threatened by the federal government's construction of large dams. Unfortunately, the federal government proved during that era that it put far more importance on the employment benefits of its respective projects than on any potential threats posed to fish and wildlife.

The late 1960s to the 1970s saw Congress pass numerous acts designed to protect fish and wildlife and their habitats. This chapter includes many of the key pieces of legislation, including the Wild and Scenic Rivers Act of 1968; the National Environmental Policy Act of 1969; the Environmental Quality Act of 1970; the Marine Protection, Research, and Sanctuaries Act of 1972; the Endangered Species Act of 1973; and the Soil and Water Conservation Act of 1977. It also includes a similar act from 2000, namely the Estuary Restoration Act.

The chapter includes two documents focusing on threats posed by invasive species, especially those endangering the Great Lakes. The Nonindigenous Aquatic Nuisance Prevention and Control Act of 1990 was intended to prevent the infestations of nonindigenous species in the nation's inland waters. In areas where invasive species had already established themselves, the Act included measure to address the growth of the alien populations.

The FY 2013 Asian Carp Control Strategy Framework is included to illustrate how the federal government is working to prevent five different species of Asian carp already established in the Mississippi River from migrating to the Great Lakes via the Chicago Area Waterway System. Should they find their way into the Great Lakes, they potentially would displace many of the fish species living within those waters, thereby destroying one of the world's most productive fisheries. In order to stop the spread of the carp, the USACE constructed three underwater electrical barriers to block their move into the Chicago Area Waterway System. Another solution to the problem that is being contemplated is the closing of the Chicago canal, thereby disconnecting the Great Lakes from the Mississippi River. All the efforts may be for naught as some scientists claim that some of the carp are already present within some of the Great Lakes.

Part Six: New Threats to Water Supply and Safety

Part Six begins with an examination of oil spills. The first document is the Oil Pollution Act of 1990, which was passed in response to the *Exxon Valdez* disaster of 1989. Among the mandates in the Act were that ships transporting oil be outfitted with a double hull. If the *Exxon Valdez* had contained a double hull, the resulting oil spill would have been reduced by half. The Act also required anyone holding a mariner's license to be subject to alcohol and drug testing, since much of the blame for the accident was placed on *Exxon Valdez*'s captain, who was inebriated at the time of the collision with Alaska's Bligh Reef.

The chapter continues the *Exxon Valdez* discussion with the U.S. Supreme Court majority opinion in *Exxon Shipping Co., et al., Petitioners, v. Grant Baker et al.* In 1991, Exxon was ordered to pay 32,000 plaintiffs $287 million in compensatory damages and $5 billion in punitive damages in a private lawsuit related to the *Exxon Valdez* disaster. This was on top of a settlement that Exxon had made with the U.S. government for violations to the Clean Water Act, the Refuse Act, and the Migratory Bird Treaty Act. Exxon thus went to the U.S. Supreme Court to get the damages reduced. Central to Exxon's argument was that their case should have been judged using maritime law. Secondly, they had already been punished by the federal government so the company should not have to pay another $5 billion in punitive damages. A majority of the Supreme Court justices agreed that maritime law should have been utilized to determine the penalties so the damages were reduced to $507.5 million.

One of the mistakes the federal government made in reacting to the *Exxon Valdez* incident was that all legislation was written to address accidents of that type. The laws were not adequate to address oil spills of the type that occurred in the Gulf of Mexico in 2010. The final document in the chapter, "Deep Water: The Gulf Oil Disaster and the Future of Offshore Drilling: Report to the President," covers the blow-out of the Macondo well, which led to the largest oil spill ever recorded. Known also as the Deepwater Horizon oil spill, it resulted in oil being dispensed into the Gulf of Mexico from April 20 to September 19, 2010. The oil damaged an estimated 65,000 square miles of territory. In an effort to break up the oil, the United States dumped 1.5 million gallons of Corexit oil dispersant into the Gulf of Mexico, which caused further environmental damage. Work continues to clean up the oil that persists in the Gulf, and many lawsuits concerning damages are presently wending their way through the court system.

The next chapter's focus on other forms of chemical pollution begins with the Toxic Substances Control Act of 1976, as amended on December 31, 2002. The Act required the Environmental Protection Agency to test chemicals that were already in use to see if they were harmful to the environment or, more importantly, to humans. This was necessary because synthetic chemicals and heavy metals were already being viewed as culprits in some of the problems that were emerging around the country. Unfortunately, the legislation left it up to the manufacturer of the chemical to determine whether it was safe or not. If they deemed it safe, the Environmental Protection Agency assumed it was safe unless they wanted to prove otherwise. Due to the amount of chemicals in use at the time, it was impossible for the Environmental Protection Agency to test even a small fraction of the chemicals determined to be safe. In order to make regulation manageable, the agency essentially grandfathered all chemicals used before 1976 that were deemed safe by choosing not to test any. Instead the Environmental Protection Agency endeavored to test newly created synthetic chemicals. It was one of these chemicals judged safe in 1976 that was spilled into the Elk River, near Charleston, West Virginia, that rendered local drinking water unsafe from January 9 to 13, 2014.

The next document in the queue, "Consent Agreement and Proposed Final Order to Resolve DuPont's Alleged Failure to Submit Substantial Risk Information Under the Toxic Substance Control Act (TSCA) and Failure to Submit Data Requested Under the Resource Conservation and Recovery Act (RCRA)," concerned the leakage of C8 from DuPont's Washington Works facility near Parkersburg, West Virginia, into local water supplies. The company had become aware in 1984 that their C8 was polluting the local region but did nothing about it. In the late 1990s, a family sued the company over the death of their cattle. At that point, the Environmental Protection Agency began investigating the company. The resulting settlement between the agency and the company resulted in one of the largest fines ever levied against a company for violations of environmental laws.

"Water Quality in the High Plains Aquifer" is an examination of the quality of groundwater contained within the High Plains Aquifer, also known as the Ogallala Aquifer. It underlays portions or all of the states of Colorado, Kansas, Nebraska, New Mexico, Oklahoma, South Dakota, Texas, and Wyoming, and provides not only drinking water but also water for a robust agricultural industry. One of the many concerns identified in the report is the presence of nitrogen and pesticides infiltrating the groundwater from the farms above. It warns that the groundwater on which so many depend is under the threat of being rendered dangerous to humans if the present level of contamination is not abated.

The chapter concludes with an examination of the Elk Creek chemical spill in West Virginia that rendered the local water unusable from January 9 to 13, 2014. Although the chemical that was spilled had been in use for more than 50 years, nobody knew anything about what type of threat it posed to humans. This document shows the results of animal testing that was conducted in the wake of the spill by the Centers of Disease Control and Prevention. It was a rudimentary study that illustrated the weaknesses inherent in the Toxic Substances Act of 1976 and its amendments.

The chapter on Fracking illustrates the conflicts between politics and science within the federal government. In the conclusions for *The Evaluation of Impacts to Underground Sources of Drinking Water by Hydraulic Fracturing of Coalbed Methane Reservoirs*, the Environmental Protection Agency determined that fracking did not pose a threat to the nation's groundwater. The conclusion supported the views of President George W. Bush, who used the study's results in the Energy Policy Act of 2005 to exempt fracking from the provisions of the Safe Drinking Water Act of 1974.

Predictably, a study was commissioned that led the Environmental Protection Agency to revisit the question whether fracking poses a threat to the nation's groundwater. Since the agency is now under the control of appointees of President Barack Obama, many are anticipating that the results from the current study are going to contradict the study done under the second Bush administration. The document included in this chapter is the progress report from 2012 concerning the ongoing study. Republican congressmen are not awaiting the conclusion of the study, as they are anticipating that it will not favor their political views. Through proposed legislation, such as H.R. 2728—Protecting States' Rights to Promote

American Energy Security, they are seeking to ensure that fracking remains beyond the reach of federal regulators before the study is concluded.

Part Six concludes with the topic of climate change. Included are two documents that broadly survey the many ways that the federal government is approaching the related scourges of global warming and climate change. The federal perspective is important to know as our government will be extremely influential in determining how other bodies, most notably the United Nations, choose to address a threat that does not respect territorial borders and thus impacts us all.

Part I

DOCTRINES AND RIGHTS

1

ESTABLISHING WATER LAWS

"He Has a Right to the Use of the Water Flowing over It in Its Natural Current, Without Diminution or Obstruction"

- **Document:** *Tyler v. Wilkinson*, excerpts
- **Date:** June 1827
- **Where:** Circuit Court, Rhode Island District
- **Significance:** *Tyler v. Wilkinson* was the first case decided in the United States on the reasonable use doctrine of riparian rights.

DOCUMENT

Opinion

STORY, Circuit Justice. This is a very important case, complicated in facts, and voluminous in testimony. It will not, however, be necessary to go over the details of the proofs, or even of the arguments, urged at the bar, further than may serve to explain the opinion of the court, and give a clear understanding of the points in controversy.

The river Pawtucket forms a boundary line between the states of Massachusetts and Rhode Island, in that part of its course where it separates the town of North Providence from the town of Seekonk. It is a fresh water river, above the lower falls between these towns, and is unaffected by the ebb or flow of the tide. At these falls there is an ancient dam, called the lower dam, extending quite across the river, and several mills are built near it, as well on the eastern as on the western side of the river. The plaintiffs, together with some of the defendants, are the proprietors in fee of the mils and adjacent land on the eastern bank, and either by themselves or their lessees are occupants of the same. The mills and land adjacent, on the western bank, are owned by some of the defendants. The lower dam was built as early as the year 1718, by the proprietors on both sides of the river, and is indispensable for the use of their mills respectively. There was previously an old dam on the western side, extending about three quarters of the way across the river, and a separate dam for a saw-mill on the east side. The lower dam was a substitute for both. About the year 1714 a canal was dug, or an old channel widened and cleared on the western side of the river, beginning at the river a few rods above the lower dam, and running round the west end thereof, until it emptied into the river about ten rods below the same dam. It has been long known by the name of "Sergeant's Trench," and was originally cut for the passage of fish up and down the river; but having wholly failed for this purpose, about the year 1730 an anchor-mill and dam were built across it by the then proprietors of the land; and between that period and the year 1790, several other dams and mills were built over the same; and since that period more expensive mills have been built there, which are all owned by some of the defendants. About thirty years before the filing of the bill, to wit, in 1792, another dam was built across the river at a place above the head of the trench, and about 20 rods above the lower dam; and the mills on the upper dam, as well as those on Sergeant's trench, are now supplied with water by proper flumes, &c. from the pond formed by the upper dam. The proprietors of this last dam are also made defendants.

Without going into the particulars of the bill (for in consequence of intervening deaths and devises, the cause is not before the court upon a supplemental bill, in the nature of a bill of revivor), it is necessary to state, that the bill charges, that the owners of Sergeant's trench are entitled, as against the owners of the lower dam, only to what is called a wastewater privilege, that is, to a right to use only such surplus water, as is not wanted by the owners of the lower dam and lands for any purposes whatever. In other words, that the right of the owners of Sergeant's trench is a subservient right to that of the plaintiffs, and takes place only as to any water which the plaintiffs may not, from time to time, have any occasion to use for any mills erected, or to be erected, by them. It charges a fraudulent combination between the owners of the upper dam and Sergeant's trench, injuriously to appropriate and use the water, and that the latter appropriate a great deal more water than they are entitled to by ancient usage, and waste the water to the injury of the plaintiffs. The object of the bill is to establish the right of the plaintiffs, and to obtain an injunction and for general relief.

The principal points, which have been discussed at the bar, are, first, what is the nature and extent of the right of the owners of Sergeant's trench; and, secondly, whether that right has been exceeded by them to the injury of the plaintiffs.

Before proceeding to an examination of these points, it may be proper to ascertain the nature and extent of the right, which riparian proprietors generally possess, to the waters of rivers flowing through their lands. Unless I am mistaken, this will relieve us from a great portion of the difficulties which incumber this cause, and lead us to a satisfactory conclusion upon its merits. I shall not attempt to examine the cases at large, or to reconcile the various dicta, which may be found in some of them. The task would be very onerous; and I am not aware that it would be very instructive. I have, however, read over all the cases on this subject, which were cited at the bar, or which are to be found in Mr. Angell's valuable work on water courses, or which my own auxiliary researches have enabled me to reach. The general principles, which they contain and support, I do not say in every particular instance, but with a very strong and controlling current of authority, appear to me to be the following.

Prima facie every proprietor upon each bank of a river is entitled to the land, covered with water, in front of his bank, to the middle thread of the stream, or, as it is commonly expressed, usque ad filum aquae. In virtue of this ownership he has a right to the use of the water flowing over it in its natural current, without diminution or obstruction. But, strictly speaking, he has no property in the water itself; but a simple use of it, while it passes along. The consequence of this principle is, that no proprietor has a right to use the water to the prejudice of another. It is wholly immaterial, whether the party be a proprietor above or below, in the course of the river; the right being common to all the proprietors on the river, no one has a right to diminish the quantity which will, according to the natural current, flow to a proprietor below, or to throw it back upon a proprietor above. This is the necessary result of the perfect equality of right among all the proprietors of that, which is common to all. The natural stream, existing by the county of Providence for the benefit of the land through which it flows, is an incident annexed, by operation of law, to the land itself. When I speak of this common right, I do not mean to be understood, as holding the doctrine, that there can be no diminution whatsoever, and no obstruction or impediment whatsoever, by a riparian proprietor, in the use of the water as it flows; for that would be to deny any valuable use of it. There may be, and there must be allowed of that, which is common to all, a reasonable use. The true test of the principle and extent of the use is, whether it is to the injury of the other proprietors or not. There may be a diminution in quantity, or a retardation or acceleration of the natural current indispensable for the general and valuable use of the water, perfectly consistent with the existence of the common right. The diminution, retardation, or acceleration, not positively and sensibly injurious by diminishing the value of the common right, is an implied element in the right of using the stream at all. The law here, as in many other cases, acts with a reasonable reference to public convenience and general good, and it is not betrayed into a narrow strictness, subversive of common sense, nor into an extravagant looseness, which would destroy private rights. The maxim is applied, "Sic utere tuo, ut non alienum laedas."

But of a thing, common by nature, there may be an appropriation by general consent or grant. Mere priority of appropriation of running water, without such consent or grant, confers no exclusive right. It is not like the case of mere occupancy, where the first occupant takes by force of his priority of occupancy. That supposes no ownership already existing, and no right to the use already acquired. But our law annexes to the riparian proprietors the right to the use in common, as an incident to the land; and whoever seeks to found an exclusive use, must establish a rightful appropriation in some manner known and admitted by the law. Now, this may be, either by a grant from all the proprietors, whose interest is affected by the particular appropriation, or by a long exclusive enjoyment, without interruption, which affords a just presumption of right. By our law, upon principles of public convenience, the term of twenty years of exclusive uninterrupted enjoyment has been held a conclusive presumption of a grant or right. I say of a grant or right; for I very much doubt, whether the principle now acted upon, however in its origin it may have been confined to presumptions of a grant, is now necessarily limited to considerations of this nature. The presumption is applied as a presumption juris et de jure, wherever by possibility a right may be acquired in any manner known to the law. Its operation has never yet been denied in cases where personal disabilities of particular proprietors might have intervened, such as infancy, coverture, and insanity, and where, by the ordinary course of proceeding, grants would not be presumed. In these, and in like cases, there may be an extinguishment of right by positive limitations of time, by estoppels, by statutable compensations and authorities, by elections of other beneficial bequests, by conflicting equities, and by other means. The presumption would be just as operative as to these modes of extinguishment of a common right as to the mode of extinguishment by grant.

. . .

With these principles in view, the general rights of the plaintiffs cannot admit of much controversy. They are riparian proprietors, and, as such, are entitled to the natural flow of the river without diminution to their injury. As owners of the lower dam, and the mills connected therewith, they have no rights beyond those of any other persons, who might have appropriated that portion of the stream to the use of their mills. That is, their rights are to be measured by the extent of their actual appropriation and use of the water for a period, which the law deems a conclusive presumption in favor of rights of this nature. In their character as mill-owners, they have no title to the flow of the stream beyond the water actually and legally appropriated to the mills; but in their character as riparian proprietors, they have annexed to their lands the general flow of the river, so far as it has not been already acquired by some prior and legally operative appropriation. No doubt, then, can exist as to the right of the plaintiffs to the surplus of the natural flow of the stream not yet appropriated. Their rights, as riparian proprietors, are general; and it is incumbent on the parties, who seek to narrow these rights, to establish by competent proofs their own title to divert and use the stream.

. . .

In this view of the matter, the proprietors of Sergeant's trench are entitled to the use of so much of the water of the river as has been accustomed to flow through that trench to and from their mills (whether actually used or necessary for the same mills or not), during the twenty years last before the induring the twenty years last before the institution of this suit, subject only to such qualifications and limitations, as have been acknowledged or rightfully exercised by the plaintiffs as riparian proprietors, or as owners of the lower mill-dam, during that period. But here their right stops; they have no right farther to appropriate any surplus water not already used by the riparian proprietors, upon the notion, that such water is open to the first occupiers. That surplus is the inheritance of the riparian proprietors, and not open to occupancy.

. . .

My opinion accordingly is, that the trench owners have an absolute right to the quantity of water which has usually flowed therein, without any adverse right on the plaintiffs to interrupt that flow in dry seasons, when there is a deficiency of water. But the trench owners have no right to increase that flow; and whatever may be the mills or uses, to which they may apply it, they are limited to the accustomed quantity, and may not exceed it.

. . .

The conclusion, to which my mind has arrived on this point, is that the owners on Sergeant's trench have a right to the flow of the quantity of water which was accustomed to flow therein antecedent to 1796; that this right is general, and not qualified by any preeminent right in the plaintiffs or the other owners of the lower dam, either as riparian proprietors or otherwise, to the use of the water, in case of a deficiency; that, if there be a deficiency, it must be borne by all parties, as a common loss, wherever it may fall, according to existing rights; that the trench proprietors have no right to appropriate more water than belonged to them in 1796, and ought to be restrained from any further appropriation; and that the plaintiffs to this extent are entitled to have their general right established, and an injunction granted.

SOURCE: *Tyler v. Wilkinson*, 24 F. Cas. 472 (D.R.I. 1827). In Story, Joseph. 1827. *Opinion Pronounced by the Hon. Judge Story in the Case of Ebenezer Tyler and Others vs. Abraham Wilkinson and Others: At the Last June Term of the Circuit Court, for the Rhode Island District.* Pawtucket, RI: Randall Meacham.

ANALYSIS

During the colonial period, the English colonies determined water rights according to the English common law. Under that system, men who owned land along a stream or river also owned the right to use the water flowing downriver. This system worked well until citizens of the United States began the process of industrialization. People began making the waters work for them by constructing water-powered mills. The industrial use of water did not conform well to the traditional tenets of English common law; thus, a modified riparian system was needed. Cognizant of this necessity, Judge Story in *Tyler v. Wilkinson* wrote a detailed decision that became a precedent in the eastern part of the United States in subsequent cases dealing with waterways.

As noted by Judge Story, the conflicts involving Ebenezer Tyler and Abraham Wilkinson were quite complicated due to both the history of Sergeant's Trench and the changes of ownership that had taken place over the years in properties adjoining the waterway. Rather than untangle the complicated business relationships and history of land ownership and river use, the judge opted to focus his decision on the basic rights of landowners along a waterway. Story added to the English common law precedents the "reasonable use" *doctrine*. This meant that upriver users had the right to use a reasonable amount of water without impinging on the water rights of downriver users. At the same time, upriver users did not have the right to alter the flow of water because that would deprive downriver users of their water rights. To ensure that access to water was shared fairly between the parties in the case, Judge Story established as the baseline the flow of Seargent's Trench from 20 years earlier. This took any modifications made to the waterway by the respective parties out of the equation.

One area that Judge Story did not address was whether industrial use of water was more important than *natural uses*. Natural uses were generally ascribed to agricultural practices. That was a topic that would be addressed in later cases, most notably in the Massachusetts case *William H. Cary v. Albert Daniels*.

FURTHER READING

Cech, Thomas V. 2010. *Principles of Water Resources: History, Development, Management, and Policy*. 3rd ed. Hoboken, NJ: John Wiley & Sons.

Malone, Patrick M. 2009. *Waterpower in Lowell: Engineering and Industry in Nineteenth-Century America*. Baltimore, MD: Johns Hopkins University Press.

"One of the Beneficial Uses of a Watercourse, and in This Country One of the Most Important, Is Its Application to the Working of Mills and Machinery"

- **Document:** *William H. Cary v. Albert Daniels*
- **Date:** October 1844, decided
- **Where:** Supreme Judicial Court, Norfolk, Massachusetts
- **Significance:** In legal proceedings before this case, water rights cases in the East were determined using the standard of "reasonable use." The decision in this case suggested that the courts give special consideration to the industrial users of water since their activities stood to provide their local communities more benefits than could be provided by other users, such as agriculturalists.

DOCUMENT

William H. Cary vs. Albert Daniels.
SUPREME COURT OF MASSACHUSETTS, NORFOLK
49 Mass. 466
October, 1844, Decided

Opinion

Shaw, C. J. The leading fact in the present case is, that at the time when Hall and others, under whom the defendant claims, conveyed the upper mill to Wilson, under whom the plaintiff claims, they were also the owners of the lower mill, the dam of which is complained of, by the plaintiff in this action, as a nuisance. The complaint is, that the lower dam is so raised as to set back the water and obstruct the free use of the plaintiff's water wheels.

Two questions were made at the trial. 1. Whether, as contended for by the plaintiff, he is not entitled, as against the defendant, to a free and unobstructed use of the stream below his mill, including a right to have the water run off as low as it would run in its natural bed; or whether, as the defendant contends, the plaintiff is entitled to no greater privilege, in this respect, than that which was used for the upper mill against the lower, with the dam raised to the same height to which it was raised when the conveyance was made from the owners of both mills to Wilson. 2. Whether the plaintiff and those under whom he claims, with the conveyance of the upper mill, acquired a right to continue a practice, which had formerly existed when both mills were owned by the same persons, for the occupants of the upper mill, in times of high water, to go down to the middle dam and open the waste gates therein, and by this means relieve the upper mill from back water; and, if so, whether it was a violation of this right, for which the plaintiff can maintain an action, that the defendant had taken away the middle dam, and erected his dam several hundred feet lower down, by means of which, and by the mode of constructing his new dam, he had rendered it impracticable, or more burdensome and expensive, to exercise such right of opening the waste gates and relieving his mill from back water.

On the first point, we are of opinion that the claim cannot be maintained. It is placed on the ground, that the owner of land, through which a stream of water passes, has a right to the run of the water in its natural channel through his land; that a grant of the land, prima facie, and without express reservation, is a grant of such right, and therefore that a grant to Wilson, by Hall and others, who were then owners of both mills, was a grant of an unobstructed flow of the stream below the land granted; and hence, that the grantors could not erect any dam, or maintain any dam already erected, which would in any manner obstruct the flow of the stream in its natural channel, and that the defendant, being privy in estate with those grantors, took the lower mill subject to the same right of the grantee and his assigns. The plaintiff also relies upon the covenants, contained in the deeds of the same grantors to Wilson and his assigns, that the granted premises were free from all incumbrances brought thereon by them, and that, if there was a right to maintain the lower dam, so as in any degree to throw back water upon the plaintiff's mill, it would be an incumbrance.

It is agreed on all hands, that the owner of a parcel of land, through which a stream of water flows, has a right to the use and enjoyment of the benefits to be derived therefrom, as it passes through his own land; but as this right is common to all through whose lands it flows, it follows that no one can wholly destroy or divert it, so as to prevent the water from coming to the proprietor below; nor can a lower proprietor wholly obstruct it, so as to throw it back upon the mills or lands of the proprietor above. We, of course, now speak of rights at common law, independent of any modification thereof by statute. But one of the beneficial uses of a watercourse, and in this country one of the most important, is its application to the working of mills and machinery; a use profitable to the owner, and beneficial to the public. It is therefore held, that each proprietor is entitled to such use of the stream, so far as it is reasonable, conformable to the usages and wants of the community, and having regard to the progress of improvement in hydraulic works, and not inconsistent with a like reasonable use by the other proprietors of land, on the same stream, above and below. This last limitation of the right must be taken with one qualification, growing out of the nature of the case. The usefulness of water for mill purposes depends as well on its fall as its volume. But the fall depends upon the grade of the land over which it runs. The descent may be rapid, in which case there may be fall enough for mill sites at short distances; or the descent may be so gradual as only to admit of mills at considerable distances. In the latter case, the erection of a mill on one proprietor's land may raise and set the water back to such a distance as to prevent the proprietor above from having sufficient fall to erect a mill on his land. It seems to follow, as a necessary consequence from these principles, that in such case, the proprietor who first erects his dam for such a purpose has a right to maintain it, as against the proprietors above and below; and to this extent, prior occupancy gives a prior title to such use. It is a profitable, beneficial, and reasonable use, and therefore one which he has a right to make. If it necessarily occupy so much of the fall as to prevent the proprietor above from placing a dam and mill on his land, it is damnum absque injuria. For the same reason, the proprietor below cannot erect a dam in such a manner as to raise the water and obstruct the wheels of the first occupant. He had an equal right with the proprietor below to a reasonable use of the stream; he had made only a reasonable use of it; his appropriation to that extent, being justifiable and prior in time, necessarily prevents the proprietor below from raising the water, without interfering with a rightful use already made; and it is therefore not an injury to him. Such appears to be the nature and extent of the prior and exclusive right, which one proprietor acquires by a prior reasonable appropriation of the use of the water in its fall; and it results, not from any originally superior legal right, but from a legitimate exercise of his own common right, the effect of which is, de facto, to supersede and prevent a like use by other proprietors originally having the same common right. It is, in this respect, like the right in common, which any individual has, to use a highway; whilst one is reasonably exercising his own right, by a temporary occupation of a particular part of the street with his carriage or team, another cannot occupy the same place at the same time.

But such appropriation of the stream to mill purposes, upon the principles stated, gives the proprietor a prior and exclusive right to such use only so far as it is actual. If, therefore, he has erected his dam and mill, with its waste ways, sluices and other fixtures necessary to command the use of the water to a certain extent, and there is a surplus remaining, the proprietor below may have the benefit of that surplus. If he erects a dam and mills, for the purpose of using and employing such surplus, he is, as to such part of the stream, the first occupant, and makes the first appropriation. As to that, therefore, his right is prior and exclusive. And although the proprietor above might, in the first instance, have raised his dam higher, keeping within the limits of a reasonable use, yet after such appropriation by the proprietor below, he cannot raise his dam and take such surplus; because, as to that, the lower proprietor has acquired a prior right.

So the proprietor above may, in like manner, make any reasonable use of the stream and fall of water which he can do consistently with the previous appropriation of the proprietor below. If, with a view of gaining an advantage to his mill, in low stages of water, which may occur perhaps during the greater part of the year, he places his mill so low that, in high stages of water, the dam below will throw back water on his wheels, he may do so if he choose, because he thereby does no injury to any other proprietor. But if he sustains a damage from such back water, it is a damage resulting from no wrong done by the lower proprietor who had previously established his dam, and it is an inconvenience to which he subjects his mill for the sake of greater advantages; and he has no cause to complain.

Another consequence from this view of the rights of successive proprietors to the use of the fall of water, on their respective lands, is this; that where one has erected a dam and mill on his own land, to a given height, and thereby appropriated as much water as he has occasion for, and there is still a surplus, he has the same right as any other proprietor to appropriate that surplus. If, therefore, before any other person has erected a dam above him or below, so near as to be injured by the change, he elects to appropriate the surplus, or a part of it, he may either raise his dam higher, and thus create a greater head above, or place his wheels lower, so as to discharge the water at the race at a lower level, and thus appropriate to himself such surplus water and power of the stream. In regard to such surplus, he will still be the first occupant.

One other consideration of a general nature, applicable to this subject, it may be proper to advert to. It is obvious that these rights to the use and power of flowing water, whether it be the original right belonging to each successive proprietor to the flow of the water in its natural channel over his own land, or the same right modified by actual appropriation, may be granted away, or acquired, or may be limited, enlarged or qualified, by grant from the proprietor in whom either of them is vested, or by that exclusive, adverse and continued enjoyment which is regarded in law as evidence of a grant. If, therefore, one has enjoyed a particular use of the stream and water, or water power, for a period of twenty years, even though such use would not have been warranted by his original right to the natural flow of the stream—as by diverting it, or raising it unreasonably high, or otherwise—he will be presumed to do it by virtue of a grant from all those whose rights are impaired by such use; and thus his right to continue so to use it will be established. But if he shall thus exceed the equal, common and original right, thus belonging to him as a proprietor, and not justify such use by grant or prescription, it will be deemed a disturbance of the rights of those whose beneficial use and power of the stream are thereby diminished.

Supposing these principles to be well founded, let us proceed to apply them to the present case. The plaintiff is the owner of the upper mill, and he claims it under Wilson, who took it under a deed from Hall and others, who were, at the time, proprietors of the lower mill. It is then argued, that if the proprietors of the lower mill ever had a right to keep up their dam to the height at which it stood at the time of this conveyance, it was an easement; that it was extinguished by unity of ownership; that, consequently, when they conveyed their upper mill, without reserving an easement anew for their lower mill, the easement was gone.

There is some danger of being misled by names, and by analogies between things which are alike in many respects, but not in all. The right to the use of flowing water is, in many respects, like an ordinary easement, but not in all. The right to the use of the flow and fall of the water on the land of the proprietor is not an easement; it is inseparably connected with and inherent in the land, is parcel of the inheritance, and passes with it. The right to have the water flow to one's land over that of the upper proprietor, and to flow from it over the land of the lower proprietor, is more like an easement, because it is a right to some benefit in the estate of another. But it does not necessarily follow that, like a common easement, it is extinguished by unity of ownership between the dominant and the servient tenants. The right to the use of the water is inherent in the land, and in each parcel; but it is a right publici juris, and subject to the rules of law securing to each successive proprietor the like use. If the owner of a large tract, through which a watercourse passes, should sell parcels above and below his own land retained, each grantee would take his parcel with a full right, without special words, to the use of the water flowing on his own land, as parcel, and subject to the right of all other riparian proprietors to have the water flow to and from such parcel. There is no occasion, therefore, for the grantor, in such case, to convey the right of water to the grantee, or reserve the right of water to himself, in express words; because, being inseparable from the land, and parcel of the estate, such right passes with that which is conveyed, and remains with that which is retained. Treating the right as inherent in the land, attaching to each parcel through which the stream passes, and the right to have water run to and from the land of each proprietor, over that of all others, as an easement or service, each parcel is, in turn, a dominant and servient tenement; dominant, to secure the proprietor's own right and servient, to secure the rights of others. If, therefore, such easement is extinguished by unity of ownership, it is created anew by every new division or severance of ownership; and this consequence necessarily results from the nature of their rights. These principles arise from the nature of the inherent and original rights of proprietors to the common and equal use of the flow of a stream; but they apply, with equal force, to the modified rights of owners in the same stream, as acquired and appropriated by actual, prior, reasonable use and enjoyment.

The right, then, which Hall and others, at the time of their conveyance of the upper mill to Wilson, had in the lower mill, and in the flow and fall of the stream, as modified by an appropriation by means of the dam and fixtures then established, was not a mere easement which had been extinguished by unity of ownership, but was parcel of the estate; and no part of it would pass by their deed of the upper estate to Wilson, without express words. The deed from Hall to Wilson—and those of the other tenants in common are substantially like it—is as follows: "One fourth undivided part of a certain tract or parcel of land situated in Medway," (described,) "together with one fourth undivided part of the privilege of water, creek, factory, saw mill, dwelling-houses and other buildings situate on the premises, and of the water wheels, main gears, main drums, connected with the said factory and saw mill, and of all the privileges and appurtenances thereunto belonging."

This deed certainly conveys nothing, in terms, but the mills and mill privileges, and the land over which the stream passes. Does it, by implication, extend further? If we are right in the principles stated, then a deed of land over which a watercourse passes will convey the right of the grantor as it then actually exists. If it be a stream wholly unoccupied, the grantee will take it, with a right to make a reasonable appropriation of the use of the whole stream. If it has been partially appropriated, he will take the land and watercourse, with a right to such use as can be made of it consistently with the right of other riparian proprietors, modified by their prior rightful appropriations. If the stream have been so fully occupied that the grantee cannot raise his dam without throwing back water upon the proprietor above, nor require the proprietor below to remove his dam, or reduce its height, because he has only exercised his just right of appropriation, then the grantee takes the land with the right to the flow and power of the water, as it then exists, on the land conveyed, and no more.

Such appear to us to be the effect and legal operation of the deed above stated, so far as it regards the estate next below, which alone is now in question. The removal or reduction of the grantor's dam below, although it might increase the power and value of that above, was not necessary to the use and beneficial enjoyment of the estate granted; and no implication arises from that consideration. We can see nothing to extend the operation of this deed beyond the plain import of its terms, which was, to carry the land, mills and water power, as it was then modified and appropriated by the dam below.

And we think the same answer applies to the argument drawn from the qualified covenant of warranty, by the grantors, against all incumbrances brought upon the premises by them. The right to the use of the water below the granted premises, as modified by the appropriation previously made for the lower mill, was not, in legal contemplation, an incumbrance, but rather in the nature of parcel of such lower estate. One mode of testing this is, to inquire what would have been the operation of a general covenant of warranty, in this deed, against incumbrances, if the lower mill, with the rights of water appropriated to it by the existing dam, had been owned by a third person. Would the existence of the lower dam, with the existing right of raising water by it to the height at which it then stood, have been an incumbrance for which the grantors would be liable on such covenant? We think it would not. So we think this qualified warranty against incumbrances brought on the estate by themselves was not broken; because their maintaining their lower dam, to the height to which the water had been appropriated for its use, was not an incumbrance upon the estate granted.

The next claim of the plaintiff is this; that he had a right, founded upon the usage and practice of his grantors, to open the waste gates of the middle dam, and thereby relieve his own mill from back water; and that the defendant, by taking down the middle dam, and erecting a new dam further down the stream, had either prevented him from the exercise of this right, or rendered the exercise of it more onerous and expensive. The court are of opinion, that this claim cannot be sustained. At the time of the practice relied on, the grantors were owners of both mills, and might favor one at the expense of the other, as the exigencies of their business might require, or at their own mere pleasure. But no right could be founded on such practice; because it was not adverse. When the estates were severed, and the rights of the respective proprietors became adverse, they stood upon the same footing as if no such usage had existed. The damages, therefore, which were given by the jury, for the violation of this supposed right, must be deducted from the verdict. The removal of the dam of the defendant some hundred feet lower down the stream, if it made the same appropriation of the stream as was made by the mill and dam as they stood before, and no larger, was not an injury to the plaintiff, but was a just exercise of the defendant's own right.

But, for the reasons already given, the court are of opinion, that the defendant had no right to erect his new dam higher than his old one, so as to appropriate an increased portion of the stream to his own use, and thereby set back water upon the mill wheels of the plaintiff. The jury having found that he had so raised his dam, to the injury of the plaintiff, and assessed damages therefor separately, we think the verdict must be amended, so as to stand as a verdict for the latter sum only, and that judgment be rendered thereon for the plaintiff.

SOURCE: *Cary v. Daniels*, 49 Mass. 466 (1844).

ANALYSIS

In the early 1830s, the two mills on the Charles River in Massachusetts that factored into *Cary v. Daniels* were under common ownership. At the bottom mill, there was a gate that was ordinarily closed, thereby damming the water. Whenever the water backed up to the point that it was causing problems at the upper mill, someone would open the gate at the lower mill so that the desired water levels could be restored. This system worked well until the two mills were sold to different entrepreneurs.

In 1837, William H. Cary became the principal owner of the upper mill. He had been one of several owners when both of the mills had been under joint ownership; thus, he was a part of the long-standing practice of opening the lower gate to alleviate water backups. A year later, Albert Daniels became the owner of the lower mill. Soon thereafter, the lower dam failed and had to be rebuilt. Daniels replaced it with a larger dam that caused water levels to rise, thereby negatively affecting Cary's mill. Cary attempted to open the lower dam to drop the water levels upriver but was prevented from doing so by Daniels. Cary responded by suing Daniels. Cary alleged that Daniels had obstructed the operation of his mill. He also charged that Daniels had illegally prevented him from opening the gates on the lower dam, as was customary. In the jury trial, Cary won on both counts. The case then moved to the Supreme Judicial Court of Massachusetts.

Chief Justice Lemuel Shaw recognized that the case brought to the fore new issues that were just emerging at the time. Water law in the East was based on reasonable use doctrine, which provided all users of a waterway an equal right to use the water. This doctrine was not easily applicable in this case as industrialization had changed the nature of water use. To allow one mill owner his or her reasonable use of a waterway might at the same time deprive another mill owner of his or her rightful use of the water. Shaw then posited that it might be in the best interest of the community to consider giving priority to industrial users of waterways over other interests. This form of thinking found many adherents in the judiciary, which ultimately undercut the traditional riparian view that all users had an equal right to the waters flowing along their property.

Ironically, the precedent created in the case had little to do with the actual outcome of the proceedings between Cary and Daniels. Using the principle of prior appropriation, meaning that Cary had gained the right to the water by getting his mill first, the judge ruled that Cary's business interests had been harmed by Daniels's construction of the new dam. Cary had been accustomed to a certain amount of water flow for the operation of his dam. When Daniels built a larger dam, it changed the water flow, thereby depriving Cary of his reasonable use of the water. On the second charge, the judge ruled in favor of Daniels, claiming that Cary did not have the right to trespass on Daniels's property.

FURTHER READING

Cumbler, John T. 2001. *Reasonable Use: The People, the Environment, and the State, New England 1790–1930*. New York: Oxford University Press.

"The First Appropriator of Water from a Natural Stream for a Beneficial Purpose Has, with the Qualifications Contained in the Constitution, a Prior Right Thereto, to the Extent of Such Appropriation"

- **Document:** *Coffin et al. v. Left Hand Ditch Company*
- **Date:** December 1882
- **Where:** Supreme Court of Colorado, Colorado
- **Significance:** Through the decision in this case, Colorado became the first state in the West to adopt prior appropriation as the legal doctrine for managing the use of water.

DOCUMENT

COFFIN ET AL. v. THE LEFT HAND DITCH COMPANY
Supreme Court of Colorado
6 Colo. 443
December, 1882

Opinion

HELM, J. Appellee, who was plaintiff below, claimed to be the owner of certain water by virtue of an appropriation thereof from the south fork of the St. Vrain creek. It appears that such water, after its diversion, is carried by means of a ditch to the James creek, and thence along the bed of the same to Left Hand creek, where it is again diverted by lateral ditches and used to irrigate lands adjacent to the last named stream. Appellants are the owners of lands lying on the margin and in the neighborhood of the St. Vrain below the mouth of said south fork thereof, and naturally irrigated therefrom.

In 1879 there was not a sufficient quantity of water in the St. Vrain to supply the ditch of appellee and also irrigate the said lands of appellant. A portion of appellee's dam was torn out, and its diversion of water thereby seriously interfered with by appellants. The action is brought for damages arising from the trespass, and for injunctive relief to prevent repetitions thereof in the future.

The answer of appellants, who were defendants below, is separated into six divisions.

First. A specific denial of all the material allegations of the complaint.

Second. Allegations concerning an agreement made at the date of the construction of appellee's ditch; by this agreement the parties constructing such ditch were to refrain from the diversion of water therethrough when the quantity in the St. Vrain was only sufficient to supply the settlers thereon.

Third, fourth, fifth and sixth are separate answers by individual defendants, setting up a right to the water diverted, by virtue of ownership of lands along the St. Vrain, and in some instances also by appropriations of water therefrom. But it nowhere appears by sufficient averment that such appropriations of defendants making the same were actually made prior to the diversion of water through appellee's ditch.

Demurrers were sustained to all of the above defenses or answers except the first, and exceptions to the rulings duly preserved; trial was had before a jury upon the issues made by the complaint and answer as it then remained, and verdict and judgment given for appellee. Such recovery was confined, however, to damages for injury to the dam alone, and did not extend to those, if any there were, resulting from the loss of water.

We do not think the court erred in its ruling upon the demurrers, and we believe the verdict and judgment sustained by the pleadings and evidence.

Were we to accept appellants views upon the subject of water rights in this state, it would yet be doubtful if we could justify the trespass. And if the agreement were actually made, as stated in the second defense, that fact would not excuse their act in forcibly destroying appellee's dam without notice or warning. It is sufficient upon this subject for us to say, that even if such agreement were legal and binding, and included subsequent settlers on the St. Vrain, yet appellee was entitled to notice of the insufficiency of water to supply the demands of appellants; it might then, perhaps, have complied with the agreement without serious injury to its property.

But two important questions upon the subject of water rights are fairly presented by the record, and we cannot well avoid resting our decision upon them.

It is contended by counsel for appellants that the common law principles of riparian proprietorship prevailed in Colorado until 1876, and that the doctrine of priority of right to water by priority of appropriation thereof was first recognized and adopted in the constitution. But we think the latter doctrine has existed from the date of the earliest appropriations of water within the boundaries of the state. The climate is dry, and the soil, when moistened only by the usual rainfall, is arid and unproductive; except in a few favored sections, artificial irrigation for agriculture is an absolute necessity. Water in the various streams thus acquires a value unknown in moister climates. Instead of being a mere incident to the soil, it rises, when appropriated, to the dignity of a distinct usufructuary estate, or right of property. It has always been the policy of the national, as well as the territorial and state governments, to encourage the diversion and use of water in this country for agriculture; and vast expenditures of time and money have been made in reclaiming and fertilizing by irrigation portions of our unproductive territory. Houses have been built, and permanent improvements made; the soil has been cultivated, and thousands of acres have been rendered immensely valuable, with the understanding that appropriations of water would be protected. Deny the doctrine of priority or superiority of right by priority of appropriation, and a great part of the value of all this property is at once destroyed.

The right to water in this country, by priority of appropriation thereof, we think it is, and has always been, the duty of the national and state governments to protect. The right itself, and the obligation to protect it, existed prior to legislation on the subject of irrigation. It is entitled to protection as well after patent to a third party of the land over which the natural stream flows, as when such land is a part of the public domain; and it is immaterial whether or not it be mentioned in the patent and expressly excluded from the grant.

The act of congress protecting in patents such right in water appropriated, when recognized by local customs and laws, "was rather a voluntary recognition of a preexisting right of possession, constituting a valid claim to its continued use, than the establishment of a new one." *Broder v. Notoma W. & M. Co.*, 11 Otto, 274.

We conclude, then, that the common law doctrine giving the riparian owner a right to the flow of water in its natural channel upon and over his lands, even though he makes no beneficial use thereof, is inapplicable to Colorado. Imperative necessity, unknown to the countries which gave it birth, compels the recognition of another doctrine in conflict therewith. And we hold that, in the absence of express statutes to the contrary, the first appropriator of water from a natural stream for a beneficial purpose has, with the qualifications contained in the constitution, a prior right thereto, to the extent of such appropriation. See *Schilling v. Rominger*, 4 Col. 103.

The territorial legislature in 1864 expressly recognizes the doctrine. It says: "Nor shall the water of any stream be diverted from its original channel to the detriment of any miner, millmen or others along the line of said stream, who may have a priority of right, and there shall be at all times left sufficient water in said stream for the use of miners and agriculturists along said stream." Session Laws of 1864, p. 68, § 32.

The priority of right mentioned in this section is acquired by priority of appropriation, and the provision declares that appropriations of water shall be subordinate to the use thereof by prior appropriators. This provision remained in force until the adoption of the constitution; it was repealed in 1868, but the repealing act reenacted it verbatim.

But the rights of appellee were acquired, in the first instance, under the acts of 1861 and 1862, and counsel for appellants urge, with no title skill and plausibility, that these statutes are in conflict with our conclusion that priority of right is acquired by priority of appropriation. The only provision, however, which can be construed as referring to this subject is § 4 on page 68, Session Laws of 1861. This section provides for the appointment of commissioners, in times of scarcity, to apportion the stream "in a just and equitable proportion," to the best interests of all parties, "with a due regard to the legal rights of all." What is meant by the concluding phrases of the foregoing statute? What are the legal rights for which the commissioners are enjoined to have a "due regard?" Why this additional limitation upon the powers of such commissioners?

It seems to us a reasonable inference that these phrases had reference to the rights acquired by priority of appropriation. This view is sustained by the universal respect shown at the time said statute was adopted, and subsequently by each person, for the prior appropriations of others, and the corresponding customs existing among settlers with reference thereto. This construction does not, in our judgment, detract from the force or effect of the statute. It was the duty of the commissioners under it to guard against extravagance and waste, and to so divide and distribute the water as most economically to supply all of the earlier appropriators thereof according to their respective appropriations and necessities, to the extent of the amount remaining in the stream.

It appears from the record that the patent under which appellant George W. Coffin holds title was issued prior to the act of congress of 1866, hereinbefore mentioned. That it contained no reservation or exception of vested water rights, and conveyed to Coffin through his grantor the absolute title in fee simple to his land, together with all incidents and appurtenances thereunto belonging; and it is claimed that therefore the doctrine of priority of right by appropriation cannot, at least, apply to him. We have already declared that water appropriated and diverted for a beneficial purpose is, in this country, not necessarily an appurtenance to the soil through which the stream supplying the same naturally flows. If appropriated by one prior to the patenting of such soil by another, it is a vested right entitled to protection, though not mentioned in the patent. But we are relieved from any extended consideration of this subject by the decision in *Broder v. Notoma W. & M. Co.*, supra.

It is urged, however, that even if the doctrine of priority or superiority of right by priority of appropriation be conceded, appellee in this case is not benefited thereby. Appellants claim that they have a better right to the water because their lands lie along the margin and in the neighborhood of the St. Vrain. They assert that, as against them, appellee's diversion of said water to irrigate lands adjacent to Left Hand creek, though prior in time, is unlawful.

In the absence of legislation to the contrary, we think that the right to water acquired by priority of appropriation thereof is not in any way dependent upon the locus of its application to the beneficial use designed. And the disastrous consequences of our adoption of the rule contended for, forbid our giving such a construction to the statutes as will concede the same, if they will properly bear a more reasonable and equitable one.

The doctrine of priority of right by priority of appropriation for agriculture is evoked, as we have seen, by the imperative necessity for artificial irrigation of the soil. And it would be an ungenerous and inequitable rule that would deprive one of its benefit simply because he has, by large expenditure of time and money, carried the water from one stream over an intervening watershed and cultivated land in the valley of another. It might be utterly impossible, owing to the topography of the country, to get water upon his farm from the adjacent stream; or if possible, it might be impracticable on account of the distance from the point where the diversion must take place and the attendant expense; or the quantity of water in such stream might be entirely insufficient to supply his wants. It sometimes happens that the most fertile soil is found along the margin or in the neighborhood of the small rivulet, and sandy and barren land beside the larger stream. To apply the rule contended for would prevent the useful and profitable cultivation of the productive soil, and sanction the waste of water upon the more sterile lands. It would have enabled a party to locate upon a stream in 1875, and destroy the value of thousands of acres, and the improvements thereon, in adjoining valleys, possessed and cultivated for the preceding decade. Under the principle contended for, a party owning land ten miles from the stream, but in the valley thereof, might deprive a prior appropriator of the water diverted therefrom whose lands are within a thousand yards, but just beyond an intervening divide.

We cannot believe that any legislative body within the territory or state of Colorado ever intended these consequences to flow from a statute enacted. Yet two sections are relied upon by counsel as practically producing them. These sections are as follows:

"All persons who claim, own or hold a possessory right or title to any land or parcel of land within the boundary of Colorado territory, . . . when those claims are on the bank, margin or neighborhood of any stream of water, creek or river, shall be entitled to the use of the water of said stream, creek or river for the purposes of irrigation, and making said claims available to the full extent of the soil, for agricultural purposes." Session Laws 1861, p. 67, § 1.

"Nor shall the water of any stream be diverted from its original channel to the detriment of any miner, millmen or others along the line of said stream, and there shall be at all times left sufficient water in said stream for the use of miners and farmers along said stream." Latter part of § 13, p. 48, Session Laws 1862.

The two statutory provisions above quoted must, for the purpose of this discussion, be construed together. The phrase "along said stream," in the latter, is equally comprehensive, as to the extent of territory, with the expression "on the bank, margin or neighborhood," used in the former, and both include all lands in the immediate valley of the stream. The latter provision sanctions the diversion of water from one stream to irrigate lands adjacent to another, provided such diversion is not to the "detriment" of parties along the line of the stream from which the water is taken. If there is any conflict between the statutes in this respect, the latter, of course, must prevail. We think that the "use" and "detriment" spoken of are a use existing at the time of the diversion, and a detriment immediately resulting therefrom. We do not believe that the legislature intended to prohibit the diversion of water to the "detriment" of parties who might at some future period conclude to settle upon the stream; nor do we think that they were legislating with a view to preserving in such stream sufficient water for the "use" of settlers who might never come, and consequently never have use therefor.

But "detriment" at the time of diversion could only exist where the water diverted had been previously appropriated or used; if there had been no previous appropriation or use thereof, there could be no present injury or "detriment."

Our conclusion above as to the intent of the legislature is supported by the fact that the succeeding assembly, in 1864, hastened to insert into the latter statute, without other change or amendment, the cause, "who have a priority of right," in connection with the idea of "detriment" to adjacent owners. This amendment of the statute was simply the acknowledgment by the legislature of a doctrine already existing, under which rights had accrued that were entitled to protection. In the language of Mr. Justice Miller, above quoted, upon a different branch of the same subject, it "was rather a voluntary recognition of a preexisting right constituting a valid claim, than the creation of a new one."

Error is assigned upon alleged defects in the proof of appellee's incorporation.

But this is an action of trespass; the defendants below were, according to the verdict of the jury, and according to the views herein expressed, wrongdoers; and, considering the nature of the action, we think the proof of incorporation sufficient.

The judgment of the court below will be affirmed.

Affirmed.

SOURCE: *Coffin et al. v. Left Hand Ditch Company*, 6 Colo. 443 (1882).

ANALYSIS

Before Colorado became a state, there were already conflicts over the use of water between white settlers. In addressing the problems, it quickly became obvious that the traditional riparian water allocation system that had functioned so well in the East was not suited for application in the West's semi-arid and arid lands. Upon becoming a state, Colorado drafted a constitution that proclaimed that the doctrine of prior appropriation would be used to manage the state's water resources. Since Colorado was the first state to adopt prior appropriation as the law of the land, the concept became known as the *Colorado Doctrine*.

As applied in Colorado, prior appropriation privileged users on the basis of who began using a water source first. The first user of the water established how he/she would utilize the water and then would take out of the water source what was needed. The individual with the second oldest claim would then take his/her share. The process continued until either all users had taken their share or the water ran out. In the latter case, those who did not get any water were simply out of luck. In theory, this system worked fine. In practice, it begat violence as those who did not get water were essentially ruined since they were not capable of growing crops or taking care of livestock.

The legal test for the Colorado Doctrine within Colorado came in 1882 through *Coffin et al. v. Left Hand Ditch Company*. Coffin was one of a number of landholders who owned land along the St. Vrain River and used it to obtain water. During a time of drought, the St. Vrain River ran dry. One of the reasons that water had ceased to flow down the river was that a ditch had been dug upriver on the St. Vrain in 1860 that diverted its waters to Left Hand Ditch Creek for the use of the Left Hand Ditch Company. The company was able to legally divert water from the

St. Vrain because one of its investors had a prior appropriation right to the land where the diversion was dug and had been putting the water to beneficial use for years without complaint from downriver users such as Coffin. After several violent confrontations between the parties, the case moved to the state court.

Coffin and his associates contended that under traditional riparian law, they had an equal right to utilize the waters that flowed through their property. The Left Hand Ditch Company's supporters argued that, according to the state constitution, their right to the water was guaranteed due to prior appropriation. The court agreed with the Left Hand Ditch Company that their water rights had been constitutionally guaranteed. The landmark decision in the case led many states in the West, most notably Alaska, Arizona, Idaho, Montana, Nevada, New Mexico, Utah, and Wyoming, to adopt the Colorado Doctrine as the basis for their water laws.

FURTHER READING

Cech, Thomas V. 2010. *Principles of Water Resources: History, Development, Management, and Policy*. 3rd ed. Hoboken, NJ: John Wiley & Sons.

Kanazawa, Mark T. 1998. "Efficiency in Western Water Law: The Development of the Colorado Doctrine, 1850–1911." *Journal of Legal Studies* 27, no. 1: 159–184.

Pisani, Donald J. 1987. "Enterprise and Equity: A Critique of Western Water Law in the Nineteenth Century." *Western Historical Quarterly* 18, no. 1: 15–37.

Schorr, David B. 2005. "Appropriation as Agrarianism: Distributive Justice in the Creation of Property Rights." *Ecology Law Quarterly* 32, no. 1: 3–71.

"The "Doctrine of Appropriation" Is Not, and Never Was, Applicable to Public Lands"

- **Document:** *Charles Lux et al., Appellants v. James B. Haggin et al. The Kern River Land and Canal Company, Respondent*, excerpts
- **Date:** April 26, 1886
- **Where:** Supreme Court of California
- **Significance:** Prior to this case, water was legally treated as a separate entity from land. This resulted in riparian laws that regulated how individuals or businesses used the water flowing past their property. In this case, which concerned the use of water on agricultural lands, water was treated as a part of land, thus subject to property rights law.

DOCUMENT

CHARLES LUX et al., Appellants, v. JAMES B. HAGGIN et al. THE KERN
RIVER LAND AND CANAL COMPANY, Respondent
Supreme Court of California
69 Cal. 255
April 26, 1886

VIII.

It has never been held by the Supreme Court of the United States, or by the Supreme Court of this state, that an appropriation of the water on the public lands of the United States (made after the act of Congress of July 26, 1866, or the Amendatory Act of 1870) gave to the appropriator the right to the water appropriated, as against a grantee of riparian lands under a grant made or issued prior to the act of 1866; except in a case where the water so subsequently appropriated was reserved by the terms of such grant.

Since, as before, September 28, 1850, the United States has been the owner of lands in California with power to dispose of the same in such manner and on such terms and conditions (not interfering with vested rights derived from the United States) as it deemed proper. But neither the legislation of Congress with respect to the disposition of the public lands, nor its apparent acquiescence in the appropriation by individuals of waters thereon, *subsequent* to the act of September, 1850, granting the swamp lands to the state, can affect the title of the state to lands and waters granted by that act.

Neither the Supreme Court of the United States nor the Supreme Court of California has ever held in opposition to this view.

. . .

IX. *The rights of the state under the grant of September 28, 1850, do not depend upon, nor are they limited by, the decisions of the state courts with respect to controversies upon the public lands of the United States. Those decisions do not enter into nor operate upon the subsequent legislation of Congress in such manner as to require that the legislation (or its affirmance of rights recognized by the state courts as existing between occupants upon the public lands of the United States) must be construed as an attempt to deprive the state of its vested rights.*

If the decisions mentioned can be referred to for any purpose, semble: That the occupant of a tract of riparian land (arable or grazing) on the public domain is by such decisions presumed to have received a grant of the flowing water, to the extent of the common-law right to the use of such water as it flows through the land.

And if the doctrine as to adverse claims upon the public lands as declared by these decisions be extended to lands granted to the state, it cannot affect the title or estate of grantees of the state (the water not being reserved in the grants or in the legislation authorizing the grant). The doctrine is applicable alone to actions in which both parties claim only by possession.

It is insisted that the "doctrine of appropriation" is not, and never was, applicable to public lands—state or United States—in California.

It may be conceded that while lands continue public lands—and in controversies between occupants of land or water thereon—the common-law doctrine of riparian rights has no application.

But where one or both of the parties claim under a grant from the United States (the absolute owner, whose grant includes all the incidents of the land and every part of it), it is difficult to see how a *policy* of the state—or a general practice, or rulings of the state court with reference to adverse occupants on public lands—can be relied on, as limiting the effect of grants of the United States, without asserting that the state, or people of the state, may interfere with "the primary disposal of the public lands."

It has been urged that the courts of this state should adopt the doctrine of *appropriation* as it is accepted in Colorado. But if it be conceded that the Colorado decisions can be sustained on any legal principle, the legal conditions here are different. The sixth and seventh sections of article 16 of the constitution of that state read:—

"Sec. 6. The right to divert the unappropriated waters of any natural stream to beneficial uses shall never be denied. Priority of appropriation shall give the better right as between those using the water for the same purpose; but when the waters of any natural stream are not sufficient for the service of all those desiring the use of the same, those using the water for domestic purposes shall have the preference over those claiming for any other purpose, and those using the water for agricultural purposes shall have preference over those using the same for manufacturing purposes.

"Sec. 7. All persons and corporations shall have the right of way across public, private, and corporate lands for the construction of ditches, canals, and flumes for the purpose of conveying water for domestic purposes, for the irrigation of agricultural lands, and for mining and manufacturing purposes, and for drainage, upon payment of just compensation."

In *Coffin v. Left Hand Company*, 6 Col. 447, *Schilling v. Rominger*, 4 Col. 102, is referred to apparently as authority for the statement that, in the absence of express statute to the contrary, the first appropriator of a natural stream has the better right as against a subsequent patentee of the lands below. But *Schilling v. Rominger*, was a contest between appropriators of land and water on the public lands, none of whom had any title other than possession.

In *Coffin v. Left Hand Company, supra*, both the appropriation of the water and the patent to the riparian land preceded the act of Congress of 1866, and of course the adoption of the state constitution in 1876. The appropriation of the water was prior to the patent. So far as the decision does not depend upon the statutes of the territory of Colorado, it is in conflict with *Vansickle v. Haines*, 7 Nev. 259, the learned court being of the opinion that the Nevada case was overruled by *Broder v. Water Company*. But as we have seen in *Broder v. Water Company, supra*, it was held that in the grant of lands to the railroad company the water was reserved for the benefit of the prior appropriator. And even if the case last mentioned could be held to have decided that the right acquired by one who appropriated water on the public lands *prior* to a grant to another of land over which the stream would flow (made before the act of 1866) was a vested right, protected, although not mentioned nor referred to in the grant, still there is nothing in that case which would give preference to an appropriation of water made (as in the case at bar) long after the grant of the land.

If, by the act of congress admitting Colorado into the Union, with a constitution containing the provisions above recited, the United States *could* abandon the primary disposal of its lands to the extent that not only every subsequent but every prior grant of land would be subject to an appropriation of water made prior to the grant, this would not affect the question as applied to the facts of the case now before us, since our constitution does not contain provisions like those in the constitution of Colorado, and here the grant of the land preceded the appropriation. And so, if the United States is bound by the territorial statutes as construed by the Supreme Court of Colorado.

In *Coffin v. Left Hand Company*, the appropriator was given the preference, by virtue of certain statutes of the territory of Colorado, passed in 1861, 1862, and 1864. It may be that, in interpreting these statutes, the court was somewhat influenced by the general proposition already laid down or assumed in its opinion, that, in the absence of express statute, the prior appropriator of water had the better right as against all the world. But the territorial statutes were so construed *as to give the right* to the prior appropriator.

It would seem clear, however, that the rights of parties who claim title under grant from the United States, of parts of the public domain, must be determined by reference to laws of the United States relating to the disposition of its domain. And this fact is recognized by the Supreme Court of Colorado, which appeals to *Broder v. Water Company* as supporting its interpretation of those laws.

It may be suggested, however, that the rulings of the courts of California, with reference to possessory rights on the public mineral lands, enter into and in some manner limit the effect of grants of land by the government of the United States, made, as is assumed, under statutes enacted in view of the local law, and of the varying rules and regulations of mining districts. The statutes passed long afterwards cannot affect rights acquired by the state by virtue of a grant made in 1850; nor can the subsequent *policy* of the United States (which is supposed to be indicated by a failure, by express laws, to prohibit the occupation of portions of its lands for mining, etc., and by the omission of the executive officers to attempt to remove miners and other occupants by force) be held to affect the rights acquired by the state through the grant of 1850.

The law of California with reference to priority of possession on the public lands has been so long established that we are apt to forget that the whole system was built upon a presumption entertained by the courts, of a permission from the United States to occupy. It was said by Heydenfeldt, J., in 1856: "One of the favorite and much-indulged doctrines of the common law is the doctrine of presumption. Thus, for the purpose of settling men's differences, a presumption is often indulged where the fact presumed cannot have existed. In support of this proposition, I will refer to a few eminent authorities. . . . In these cases, presumptions were indulged against the truth, presumptions of acts of Parliament and grants from the Crown. It is true the basis of the presumption was length of time, but the reason of it was to settle disputes and to quiet the possession. If, then, lapse of time requires the court to raise presumptions, other circumstances which are equally potent and persuasive must have the like effect for the purposes of the desired end; for lapse of time is but a circumstance or fact which calls out the principle, and is not the principle itself.

"Every judge is bound to know the history, and the leading traits which enter into the history, of the country where he presides. This we have held before, and it is also an admitted doctrine of the common law. We must therefore know that this state has a large territory; that upon its acquisition by the United States, from the sparseness of its population, but a small comparative proportion of its land had been granted to private individuals; that the great bulk of it was land of the government; that but little, as yet, has been acquired by individuals by purchase; that our citizens have gone upon the public lands continuously from a period anterior to the organization of the state government to the present time; upon these lands they have dug for gold, excavated mineral rock, constructed ditches, flumes, and canals for conducting water, built mills for sawing lumber and grinding corn, established farms for cultivating the earth, made settlements for the grazing of cattle, laid off towns and villages, felled trees, diverted watercourses; and indeed, have done, in the various enterprises of life, all that is useful and necessary in the high condition of civilized development. All of these are open and notorious facts, charging with notice of them, not only the courts who have to apply the law in reference to them, but also the government of the United States, which claims to be the proprietor of these lands, and the government of the state, within whose sovereign jurisdiction they exist.

"In the face of these notorious facts, the government of the United States has not attempted to assert any right of ownership to any of the large body of lands within the mineral region of the state. The state government has not only looked on quiescently upon this universal appropriation of the public domain for all of these purposes, but has studiously encouraged them in some instances, and recognized them in all.

"Now, can it be said, with any propriety of reason or common sense, that the parties to these acts have acquired no rights? If they have acquired rights, these rights rest upon the presumption of a grant of right arising either from the tacit assent of the sovereign or from expressions of her will in the course of her general legislation, and indeed, from both.

"Possession gives title only by presumption; then, when the possession is shown to be of public land, why may not any one oust the possessor? Why can the latter protect his possession? Only upon the doctrine of presumption, for a license to occupy from the owner will be presumed." (*Conger v. Weaver*, 6 Cal. 556, 557; S. C., 65 Am. Dec. 528).

Both the right to appropriate water on the public lands and that of the occupant of portions of such lands are derived from the implied consent of the owner, and as between the appropriator of land or water the first possessor has the better right. The two rights stand upon an equal footing, and when they conflict they must be decided by the fact of priority. (*Irwin v. Phillips*, 5 Cal. 140; S. C., 73 Am. Dec. 113). Since the United States, the owner of the land and water, is presumed to have permitted the appropriation of both the one and the other, as between themselves the prior possessor must prevail.

None of the early cases intimate that the occupant of land bordering on a stream was presumed to have any less rights in the usufruct of the water than the absolute owner of the land so situated, or that the presumption in his favor was limited to the land without the water, except where the water had been already appropriated.

It was said by Chief Justice Murray, in *Crandall v. Woods*, 8 Cal. 143:—

"If the rule laid down in *Irwin v. Phillips* is correct, as to the location of mining claims and water ditches for mining purposes, and *priority* is to determine the rights of the respective parties, it is difficult to see why the rule should not apply to all other cases where land or water had been appropriated. The simple question was, that as between persons appropriating the same land, or land and water both, as the case might be, that the subsequent appropriator takes subject to the rights of the former.

"But an appropriation of land carries with it the water on the land, or a usufruct in the water; for in such cases the party does not appropriate the water, but the land covered with water. If the owners of the mining claim in the case of *Irwin v. Phillips* had first located along the bed of the stream, they would have been entitled as riparian proprietors to the free and uninterrupted use of the water, without any other or direct act of appropriation of the water as contradistinguished from the soil. If such is the case, why would not the defendant who has appropriated land over which a natural stream flowed be held to have appropriated the water of such stream, as an incident to the soil, as against those who subsequently attempt to divert it from its natural channels for their own purposes?

"One who locates upon public lands with a view of appropriating them to his own use becomes the absolute owner thereof as against everyone but the government, and is entitled to all the privileges and incidents which appertain to the soil, subject to the single exception of rights antecedently acquired. He may admit that he is not the owner in fee, but his possession will be sufficient to protect him as against trespassers. If he admits, however, that he is not the owner of the soil, and the fact is established that he acquired his right subsequent to those of others, then, as both rest for their foundation upon appropriation, the subsequent locator must take subject to the rights of the former, and the rule, *Qui prior est in tempore potior est in jure*, must apply."

The learned judge then proceeds to speak of the alleged evil consequences of the rule he had laid down, saying:—

"Let us examine the effect of such a rule for a moment, and see if the consequences which the respondent predicts, viz., the destruction of the use and value of ditch property in the mines, will necessarily flow from it. A has located mining claims along the bed of a stream, before any water ditch or flume has been constructed: will anyone doubt that he should have the free use of the water, as against subsequent locators of either mining claims or canals? Or suppose he had located a farm, and the water passing through his land was necessary for the purposes of irrigation, is not this purpose just as legitimate as using the water for mining? It may or may not be equally as profitable, but irrigation for agricultural purposes is sometimes necessary to supply natural wants, while gold is not a natural but an artificial want, or a mere stimulant to trade and commerce.

"If it is understood that the location of land carries with it all the incidents belonging to the soil, those who construct water ditches will do so with reference to the appropriations of the public domain that have been previously made and the rights that have been already acquired, with a full knowledge of their own rights as against subsequent locators." (*Crandall v. Woods*, 8 Cal. 143, 144).

Crandall v. Woods, supra, very distinctly decides that, as between an occupant of riparian land (part of the public lands of the United States) and a subsequent appropriator of the waters of the stream, the former may assert the riparian right.

It is claimed, however, that so far as that case decides that the riparian occupant may, under such circumstances, assert a right to the flow of the water, beyond the extent to which he has actually appropriated the same for irrigation or other useful purpose, it has been reversed in later adjudications, if not expressly yet by necessary implication.

In some of the subsequent California cases, where the riparian owner claimed in his pleading, and relied at the trial on, an actual prior appropriation of water, the court confined its inquiry to the existence or non-existence of the facts alleged. Thus in *McDonald v. Bear River etc. Co.*, 13 Cal. 220, one of the parties, although in possession of a tract through which the watercourse ran, claimed an actual prior appropriation of water for turning his mill. It may be observed, however, that at the common law, the extent of the mill-owner's right might depend in part on the actual erection and size of his dam, etc. And since the exercise of the particular right might depend on affirmative acts, the case of water for a mill might differ, perhaps, in its nature, or extent rather, from that of the riparian owner, whose lands are naturally irrigated by the flow. *American Company v. Bradford*, 27 Cal. 360, was an action at law for damages, in which the plaintiff claimed as an appropriator of water through a ditch. The defendants answered, that long prior to the location of plaintiff's ditch and dam, they had located and worked in the creek certain mining claims, whereby they became entitled to the use and possession of the waters of the creek, or so much thereof as might become necessary for their mining claims,—*as prior appropriators of the water*. Moreover, the general verdict in favor of the plaintiff included a finding that the mining claims were not located and worked prior to the plaintiff's appropriation.

In *Yankee Jim Co. v. Crary*, 25 Cal. 504, it was said that the use of a watercourse on the public mineral lands may be held, granted, abandoned, or lost by the same means as a right of the same character *issuing out of lands to which a private title exists*.

In *King v. Hill*, 8 Cal. 336, and *Bear River v. York*, 8 Cal. 339, it was held, that where the constructor of a ditch had diverted water, he could not complain of the muddying of it by the working of a mine above. To permit this, the court said, would be practically to deprive the miner of the use of the water in his business; and any injury from the incidental fouling of the water was *damnum absque injuria*. But in *Hill v. Smith*, 27 Cal. 476, where water was appropriated through a ditch, and a mining claim was afterwards worked above, it was decided that the miner had no right to work his claim in such manner as to mingle mud and sediment with the water so as to fill up the ditch and reservoirs, and thus to lessen their capacity and increase the expense of cleaning them out; that the prior appropriator of the water was entitled to its use and enjoyment *for the purposes for which he claimed it*.

Pope v. Kinman, 54 Cal. 3, was an action to quiet title to the flow of a stream, the plaintiff being the owner of riparian lands by grant from Mexico. Held, that the plaintiff had an interest in the living stream which flowed over his land, called the "riparian right"; and that the defendant, by mere diversion, could not deprive him of that interest or usufruct.

Zimmler v. San Luis Water Co., 57 Cal. 221, not only recognizes the riparian right, the land not being public land, but holds that a recital in a deed that the grantee is about to divert the waters of a certain creek (which flows through the grantor's land), and to appropriate the same, followed by a grant of a right of way to conduct water over the land of the grantor, does not stop the grantor from denying the right of the grantee to divert the water.

As we understand *Ferrea v. Knipe*, 28 Cal. 340, the appellant made the claim that the doctrine of "appropriation," applicable to controversies on the public lands, was also the controlling doctrine in a suit between private owners on the same stream. The court held that the common-law rule obtained, and that the inferior riparian proprietor was entitled to the natural flow, undiminished except by the use of the superior proprietor for domestic purposes and reasonable irrigation.

So far as the cases cited relate to the adverse claims of possessors of land or water on the public lands, no one of them by its terms or by necessary implication overrules *Crandall v. Woods*, 8 Cal. 136.

It is intimated, however, that that case should now be overruled as not in harmony with the reasons which induced the courts to adopt the rule giving the preference to the prior possessor. It is said that the right acquired, with great expenditure of money and labor, by the ditch-owner, *ought not* to be restricted by the occupant of a tract of arable or grazing land. The suggestion repeatedly returns that the amount of money invested by the respective parties should have its influence in determining their rights, or at least in fixing the rule by which their rights are to be determined. The same suggestion (that the amounts expended under the implied license of the United States should control in fixing the rule of right) was urged in the "debris cases," but seems to have received little consideration in the courts of the state or of the United States. In the case of an occupant of land, as in the case of an appropriator of water, the decisions are based on the presumption that the United States has made a grant which in fact it has not made. The effect of the presumed grant of land, over which water flowed, was logically ascertained in *Crandall v. Woods, supra,* by reference to the principles of the common law; according to which every part of the land and all its incidents passed by the grant.

If we were prepared to say that *Crandall v. Woods* was wrongly decided, still there is good reason why, if wrongly decided, it ought not to be overruled in this case. The rulings of the state courts with reference to controversies on the public lands, while they remain such, cannot of themselves operate to deprive the state of the benefit of the grant of the waters of streams flowing over the land granted by the act of September 28, 1850, nor operate upon subsequent legislation of the Congress of the United States so that such legislation shall retroact and deprive the state of its vested rights.

If the decisions referred to are applicable to lands belonging to the state, yet, since they are applicable only to controversies between adverse claimants to the possession, they do not limit the right or title of the grantees of the state. The title of the state's grantees depends upon the state laws providing for the disposition of its lands.

SOURCE: *Charles Lux et al., Appellants v. James B. Haggin et al. The Kern River Land and Canal Company, Respondent,* 69 Cal. 255 (1886).

ANALYSIS

The cause of the conflict between Charles Lux and his business partners and James Ben Ali Haggin and his associates was rooted in the California legislature's adoption of common law in 1850. Under common law, water was governed by the principle that all users had a reasonable use right to the water flowing on or along their property. Nobody paid heed to the law. This was especially true of miners during the gold rush, who were diverting waters from streams and rivers so that they could use them for mining purposes. Constant conflicts over water use resulted in the California legislature in 1872 adopting prior appropriation doctrine, better known as *first in time, first in right,* to settle water conflicts. Unfortunately, when they did so, they did not abrogate the earlier adoption of common law principles. The state thus had two conflicting sets of water laws in place.

Lux v. Haggin essentially asked the California Supreme Court to definitively determine which form of water law was going to prevail within the state. Charles Lux and Henry Miller were cattlemen who had seen their herds perish during a drought because the water that had ordinarily flowed to their property had been diverted by Haggin so that he could irrigate huge swaths of land. They sued Haggin for having cost them their common law right to water that had ordinarily flowed to their property. Haggin, who was favored by local landholders because he was irrigating the entire region, argued for the doctrine of prior appropriation, as he had the earlier claim by three years to the waters in Kern County. He also attacked riparian rights in general, arguing that the common law doctrine was ill-suited for arid regions. To allow common law principles to determine the use of the water would be to allow a handful of agriculturalists to dominate the water due to the location of the property at the expense of the populace as a whole. Haggin won the case because his use of the water benefitted far more people than allowing the cattlemen to use the water for their herds.

The case was appealed to California's Supreme Court, where confusion continued to reign. Three of the seven justices argued that riparian law had never been the law in California although it was found in common law. Another justice claimed that the federal government had done away with reasonable use doctrine when it adopted prior appropriation doctrine on federal lands. The majority of justices ultimately decided that it was vitally important to rely on precedents, and the most important one in this case was that the common law had been adopted in 1850; thus, the cattlemen had a right to the water they had prior to Haggin's diversion. The respect for that principle outweighed the fact that Haggin's use of the water was far more beneficial for the public at large than it was for Lux and Miller. In a 200-page decision, where they weighed the benefits and costs of different forms of water law, they ultimately decided that the water could not be weighed separately from the land, as the value of the land in an arid region was directly tied to the availability of water upon it. With this reality in place, water was not to be legally regulated as a separate entity, but as part of one's real estate.

FURTHER READING

Freyfogle, Eric T. 1986. "Lux v. Haggin and the Common Law Burden of Modern Water Law." *University of Colorado Law Review* 57: 485–525.

Kanazawa, Mark T. 1998. "Efficiency in Western Water Law: The Development of the Colorado Doctrine, 1850–1911." *Journal of Legal Studies* 27, no. 1: 159–184.

Pisani, Donald J. 1984. *From the Family Farm to Agribusiness: The Irrigation Crusade in California and the West, 1850–1931.* Berkeley: University of California Press.

2

NATIVE AMERICAN FISHING AND WATER RIGHTS

"Ambiguities Occurring Will Be Resolved from the Standpoint of the Indians"

- **Document:** *Winters v. United States*, 207 U.S. 564 (1908), excerpt from majority opinion
- **Date:** January 6, 1908
- **Where:** The waters in dispute were from the Milk River, upstream of the Fort Belknap Indian Reservation in Montana.
- **Significance:** In *Winters v. United States*, the U.S. Supreme Court declared that Native Americans had "implied water rights" on their reservations under the doctrine of prior appropriation even if other land users had made claims on the land before the reservation was established by the federal government. Native Americans using the water on lands they owned through treaties with the federal government were privileged over other users because their prior appropriation rights began in time immemorial.

DOCUMENT

The rule which requires the parties to a judgment or decree to join in an appeal or writ of error, or be detached from the right by some proper proceeding, or by their renunciation, is firmly established. But the rule only applies to joint judgments or decrees. In other words, when the interest of a defendant is separate from that of other defendants he may appeal without them. Does the case at bar come within the rule? The bill does not distinguish the acts of the defendants, but it does not necessarily imply that there was between them, in the diversion of the waters of Milk River, concert of action or union of interest. The answer to the bill is joint and several, and in effect avers separate rights, interests and action on the part of the defendants. In other words, whatever rights were asserted or admission of acts done by any one defendant had no dependence upon or relation to the acts of any other defendant in the appropriation or diversion of the water. If trespassers at all, they were separate trespassers. Joinder in one suit did not necessarily identify them. Besides, the defendants other than appellants defaulted. A decree *pro confesso* was entered against them, and thereafter, according to Equity Rule 19, the cause was required to proceed *ex parte* and the matter of the bill decreed by the court. *Thomson v. Wooster, 114 U.S. 104*. The decree was in due course made absolute, and granting that it might have been appealed from by the defaulting defendants, they would have been, as said in *Thomson v. Wooster*, absolutely barred and precluded from questioning its correctness, unless on the face of the bill it appeared manifest that it was erroneous and improperly granted. Their rights, therefore, were entirely different from those of the appellants; they were naked trespassers, and conceded by their default the rights of the United States and the Indians, and were in no position to resist the prayer of the bill. But the appellants justified by counter rights and submitted those rights for Judgment. There is nothing, therefore, in common between appellants and the other defendants. The motion to dismiss is denied and we proceed to the merits.

The case, as we view it, turns on the agreement of May, 1888, resulting in the creation of Fort Belknap Reservation. In the construction of this agreement there are certain elements to be considered that are prominent and significant. The reservation was a part of a very much larger tract which the Indians had the right to occupy and use and which was adequate for the habits and wants of a nomadic and uncivilized people. It was the policy of the Government, it was the desire of the Indians, to change those habits and to become a pastoral and civilized people. If they should become such the original tract was too extensive, but a smaller tract would be inadequate without a change of conditions. The lands were arid and, without irrigation, were practically valueless. And yet, it is contended, the means of irrigation were deliberately given up by the Indians and deliberately accepted by the Government. The lands ceded were, it is true, also arid; and some argument may be urged, and is urged, that with their cession there was the cession of the waters, without which they would be valueless, and "civilized communities could not be established thereon." And this, it is further contended, the Indians knew, and yet made no reservation of the waters. We realize that there is a conflict of implications, but that which makes for the retention of the waters is of greater force than that which makes for their cession. The Indians had command of the lands and the waters—command of all their beneficial use, whether kept for hunting, "and grazing roving herds of stock," or turned to agriculture and the arts of civilization. Did they give up all this? Did they reduce the area of their occupation and give up the waters which made it valuable or adequate? And, even regarding the allegation of the answer as true, that there are springs and streams on the reservation flowing about 2,900 inches of water, the inquiries are pertinent. If it were possible to believe affirmative answers, we might also believe that the Indians were awed by the power of the Government or deceived by its negotiators. Neither view is possible. The Government is asserting the rights of the Indians. But extremes need not be taken into account. By a rule of interpretation of agreements and treaties with the Indians, ambiguities occurring will be resolved from the standpoint of the Indians. And the rule should certainly be applied to determine between two inferences, one of which would support the purpose of the agreement and the other impair or defeat it. On account of their relations to the Government, it cannot be supposed that the Indians were alert to exclude by formal words every inference which might militate against or defeat the declared purpose of themselves and the Government, even if it could be supposed that they had the intelligence to foresee the "double sense" which might sometime be urged against them.

Another contention of appellants is that if it be conceded that there was a reservation of the waters of Milk River by the agreement of 1888, yet the reservation was repealed by the admission of Montana into the Union, February 22, 1889, c. 180, 25 Stat. 676, "upon an equal footing with the original States." The language of counsel is that "any reservation in the agreement with the Indians, expressed or implied, whereby the waters of Milk River were not to be subject of appropriation by the citizens and inhabitants of said State, was repealed by the act of admission." But to establish the repeal counsel rely substantially upon the same argument that they advance against the intention of the agreement to reserve the waters. The power of the Government to reserve the waters and exempt them from appropriation under the state laws is not denied, and could not be. *The United States v. The Rio Grande Ditch & Irrigation Co.*, 174 U.S. 690, 702; *United States v. Winans*, 198 U.S. 371. That the Government did reserve them we have decided, and for a use which would be necessarily continued through years. This was done May 1, 1888, and it would be extreme to believe that within a year Congress destroyed the reservation and took from the Indians the consideration of their grant, leaving them a barren waste— took from them the means of continuing their old habits, yet did not leave them the power to change to new ones.

Appellants argument upon the incidental repeal of the agreement by the admission of Montana into the Union and the power over the waters of Milk River which the State thereby acquired to dispose of them under its laws, is elaborate and able, but our construction of the agreement and its effect make it unnecessary to answer the argument in detail. For the same reason we have not discussed the doctrine of riparian rights urged by the Government.
Decree affirmed.

SOURCE: *Winters v. United States*, 207 U.S. 564 (1908).

ANALYSIS

Winters v. United States was a landmark 1908 U.S. Supreme Court case that ostensibly determined how the federal government viewed Native American water rights in the West. Although the Supreme Court reaffirmed the stance it took in *Winters v.*

United States in its 1939 decision in *United States v. Powers*, western interests, including states, opted to ignore the decision. They did not believe that the *Winters* decision could be widely applied because, in their view, it was decided on a technicality. The justices never issued a ruling based on the arguments posed by the respective litigants. It was not until the 1963 decision in *Arizona v. California* that the U.S. Supreme Court unambiguously affirmed its ruling in *Winters v. United States.*

Before Montana became a state, water rights were gained through the principle of prior appropriation, which was widely interpreted as "first in time, first in right." Those users who made their claims to local waters first got priority to use whatever amount of water they could put to "beneficial" use before other users could utilize any water. The water conflict at the heart of *Winters v. United States* had its origins in 1888 when the federal government created the Fort Belknap Indian Reservation in Montana for the Gros Ventre and the Assiniboine. At that time, there was sufficient water in the Milk River to meet everyone's needs. The native groups used the water to irrigate lands on their reservation so that they could raise crops and herds of animals. Gradually, the Gros Ventre and the Assiniboine developed such proficient agricultural operations that their water needs grew significantly. Upriver, due to the Homestead and Desert Land Acts, several companies began establishing claims to the Milk River, most notably Henry Winters's Empire Cattle Company. Winters quickly bought out his competitors and began posting required notices of his intent to utilize the waters of the Milk River. Once the legal requirements were met, he began constructing dams and ditches to impound the Milk River's waters for his company's use. Since the Empire Cattle Company's activities were denying the Indians the waters that they required, the federal government sued the Empire Cattle Company and its leaders on behalf of the Gros Ventre and Assiniboine.

At the Federal District Court level, Judge William H. Hunt ruled in favor of the United States because, in his opinion, the 1888 treaty that created the Fort Belknap Indian Reservation reserved water rights for the native groups as part of the agreement because, without water, the land found therein was essentially useless for agricultural purposes. Winters and his associates appealed the decision to the U.S. Supreme Court. The Supreme Court justices affirmed the lower court decision without ruling on the specific merits of the case. In what is known as the "Winters Doctrine," the justices created an "implied water right" for Native American groups on reservations. This meant that when Native American groups exchanged their former lands for reservations, they received lands that were guaranteed to be useful to them in the future. This included an implied right to the waters they required to irrigate the land on the reservation. As part of their ruling, the justices provided native peoples on reservations the earliest possible priority date for water claims since they had been putting the water to beneficial use since "time immemorial." With water rights that extended before any nonnative was in the region, the Gros Ventre and Assiniboine were able to once again use whatever waters they required from the Milk River. Since the Supreme Court's decision was not based on the actions of the Empire Cattle Company, it gave western interests the ability to ignore the ramifications of *Winters v. United States* for decades.

FURTHER READING

Colby, Bonnie G., et al. 2005. *Negotiating Tribal Water Rights: Fulfilling Promises in the Arid West*. Tucson: University of Arizona Press.

Cosens, Barbara, and Judith V. Royster, eds. 2012. *The Future of Indian and Federal Reserved Water Rights: The Winters Centennial*. Albuquerque: University of New Mexico Press.

Hundley, Norris, Jr. 1982. "The Winters Decision and Indian Water Rights: A Mystery Reexamined." *The Western Historical Quarterly* 13, no. 1: 17–42.

McCool, Daniel. 2002. *Native Waters: Contemporary Indian Water Settlements and the Second Treaty Era*. Tucson: University of Arizona Press.

Shurts, John. 2000. *Indian Reserved Water Rights: The Winters Doctrine in Its Social and Legal Context, 1880s-1930s*. Norman: University of Oklahoma Press.

"The United States Did Reserve the Water Rights for the Indians"

- **Document:** *Arizona v. California*, 373 U.S. 546 (1963), excerpt from majority opinion
- **Date:** The case was first argued on January 8–11, 1962. It was reargued on November 13–14, 1962. The ruling was released on June 3, 1963.
- **Where:** Washington, DC
- **Significance:** The Supreme Court clarified the legal interpretation of *Winters v. United States* (1908), so that it was unambiguous that the waters contained on American Indian reservations were the permanent property of the natives who owned the reservation since it was legally impossible for a nonnative to have a claim on the water that predated the claim of the region's native peoples.

DOCUMENT

V.

Claims Of The United States.

In these proceedings, the United States has asserted claims to waters in the main river and in some of the tributaries for use on Indian Reservations, National Forests, Recreational and Wildlife Areas and other government lands and works. While the Master passed upon some of these claims, he declined to reach others, particularly those relating to tributaries. We approve his decision as to which claims required adjudication, and likewise we approve the decree he recommended for the

DID YOU KNOW?

The Cornplanter Tract and the Kinzua Dam

Cornplanter, born to a Dutch trader named John O'Bail and a Seneca woman named Gahhononeh, was a prominent Seneca war chief who lived from ca. 1740 to 1836. During the American Revolution, he initially opted for neutrality but eventually allied himself with Great Britain. In 1777, he helped besiege Fort Stanwix. Three years later, he helped lead Iroquois warriors in raids within New York's Mohawk and Schoharie Valleys. After the war concluded, Cornplanter became an advocate of accommodation with the United States. He was a signatory to the 1784 Treaty of Fort Stanwix, the Treaty of Buffalo Creek in 1788, and the 1789 Treaty of Fort Harmar. Each of the treaties required the Seneca to make land cessions, which resulted in a steady decline of his standing among his people. Due to his service to the United States, he was awarded 10,000 acres of land in the 1794 Treaty of Canandaigua. Known as the Cornplanter Tract, ownership of the land was guaranteed in perpetuity to the Allegheny Seneca. The federal government honored the terms of the Treaty of Canandaigua until the construction of the Kinzua Dam.

The impetus for the construction of the Kinzua Dam on the Allegheny River was the need to control flooding in Pittsburgh, Pennsylvania. An added bonus was the generation of hydroelectric power. Flood control advocates had proposed constructing a dam on the Allegheny River as early as the first decade of the twentieth century, but none had ever moved beyond the initial planning stages. In the 1950s, the Kinzua Dam went from an initial proposal to construction in just a few years. The Seneca were left unaware of the dam until the United States Corps of Engineers was actively appropriating the necessary property in Pennsylvania to begin construction. By then it was too late to effectively combat the threat to their homeland. Kinzua Dam was constructed between 1956 and 1966. The reservoir behind the dam flooded significant portions of the land occupied by the Allegheny Seneca in present-day Pennsylvania and New York. Locales sacred to the Seneca, most notably the Cold Spring Longhouse, were forever lost. Less than 70 acres of the original Cornplanter Tract escaped inundation. To compensate the Seneca for their losses, the federal government provided them $15 million.

FURTHER READING

Bilharz, Joy A. 1998. *The Allegheny Seneca and the Kinzua Dam: Forced Relocation through Two Generations*. Lincoln, NE: University of Nebraska Press.

government claims he did decide. We shall discuss only the claims of the United States on behalf of the Indian Reservations.

The Government, on behalf of five Indian Reservations in Arizona, California, and Nevada, asserted rights to water in the mainstream of the Colorado River. The Colorado River Reservation, located partly in Arizona and partly in California, is the largest. It was originally created by an Act of Congress in 1865, but its area was later increased by Executive Order. Other reservations were created by Executive Orders and amendments to them, ranging in dates from 1870 to 1907. The Master found both as a matter of fact and law that when the United States created these reservations or added to them, it reserved not only land but also the use of enough water from the Colorado to irrigate the irrigable portions of the reserved lands. The aggregate quantity of water which the Master held was reserved for all the reservations is about 1,000,000 acre-feet, to be used on around 135,000 irrigable acres of land. Here, as before the Master, Arizona argues that the United States had no power to make a reservation of navigable waters after Arizona became a State; that navigable waters could not be reserved by Executive Orders; that the United States did not intend to reserve water for the Indian Reservations; that the amount of water reserved should be measured by the reasonably foreseeable needs of the Indians living on the reservation rather than by the number of irrigable acres; and, finally, that the judicial doctrine of equitable apportionment should be used to divide the water between the Indians and the other people in the State of Arizona.

The last argument is easily answered. The doctrine of equitable apportionment is a method of resolving water disputes between States. It was created by this Court in the exercise of its original jurisdiction over controversies in which States are parties. An Indian Reservation is not a State. And while Congress has sometimes left Indian Reservations considerable power to manage their own affairs, we are not convinced by Arizona's argument that each reservation is so much like a State that its rights to water should be determined by the doctrine of equitable apportionment. Moreover, even were we to treat an Indian

Reservation like a State, equitable apportionment would still not control since, under our view, the Indian claims here are governed by the statutes and Executive Orders creating the reservations.

Arizona's contention that the Federal Government had no power, after Arizona became a State, to reserve waters for the use and benefit of federally reserved lands rests largely upon statements in *Pollard's Lessee v. Hagan*, 3 How. 212 (1845), and *Shively v. Bowlby*, 152 U. S. 1 (1894). Those cases and others that followed them gave rise to the doctrine that lands underlying navigable waters within territory acquired by the Government are held in trust for future States and that title to such lands is automatically vested in the States upon admission to the Union. But those cases involved only the shores of and lands beneath navigable waters. They do not determine the problem before us and cannot be accepted as limiting the broad powers of the United States to regulate navigable waters under the Commerce Clause and to regulate government lands under Art. IV, § 3, of the Constitution. We have no doubt about the power of the United States under these clauses to reserve water rights for its reservations and its property.

Arizona also argues that, in any event, water rights cannot be reserved by Executive Order. Some of the reservations of Indian lands here involved were made almost 100 years ago, and all of them were made over 45 years ago. In our view, these reservations, like those created directly by Congress, were not limited to land, but included waters as well. Congress and the Executive have ever since recognized these as Indian Reservations. Numerous appropriations, including appropriations for irrigation projects, have been made by Congress. They have been uniformly and universally treated as reservations by map makers, surveyors, and the public. We can give but short shrift at this late date to the argument that the reservations either of land or water are invalid because they were originally set apart by the Executive.

Arizona also challenges the Master's holding as to the Indian Reservations on two other grounds: first, that there is a lack of evidence showing that the United States in establishing the reservations intended to reserve water for them; second, that even if water was meant to be reserved the Master has awarded too much water. We reject both of these contentions. Most of the land in these reservations is and always has been arid. If the water necessary to sustain life is to be had, it must come from the Colorado River or its tributaries. It can be said without overstatement that when the Indians were put on these reservations they were not considered to be located in the most desirable area of the Nation. It is impossible to believe that when Congress created the great Colorado River Indian Reservation and when the Executive Department of this Nation created the other reservations they were unaware that most of the lands were of the desert kind—hot, scorching sands— and that water from the river would be essential to the life of the Indian people and to the animals they hunted and the crops they raised. In the debate leading to approval of the first congressional appropriation for irrigation of the Colorado River Indian Reservation, the delegate from the Territory of Arizona made this statement:

Hauptman, Laurence M. 2013. *In the Shadow of Kinzua: The Seneca Nation of Indians Since World War II.* Syracuse, NY: Syracuse University Press.

Purcell, Aaron D. 1997. "The Engineering of Forever: Arthur E. Morgan, the Seneca Indians, and the Kinzua Dam." *New York History* 78, no. 3: 309–336.

"Irrigating canals are essential to the prosperity of these Indians. Without water there can be no production, no life; and all they ask of you is to give them a few agricultural implements to enable them to dig an irrigating canal by which their lands may be watered and their fields irrigated, so that they may enjoy the means of existence. You must provide these Indians with the means of subsistence or they will take by robbery from those who have. During the last year I have seen a number of these Indians starved to death for want of food." Cong. Globe, 38th Cong., 2d Sess. 1321 (1865).

The question of the Government's implied reservation of water rights upon the creation of an Indian Reservation was before this Court in *Winters v. United States*, 207 U. S. 564, decided in 1908. Much the same argument made to us was made in *Winters* to persuade the Court to hold that Congress had created an Indian Reservation without intending to reserve waters necessary to make the reservation livable. The Court rejected all of the arguments. As to whether water was intended to be reserved, the Court said, at p. 576:

"The lands were arid and, without irrigation, were practically valueless. And yet, it is contended, the means of irrigation were deliberately given up by the Indians and deliberately accepted by the Government. The lands ceded were, it is true, also arid; and some argument may be urged, and is urged, that with their cession there was the cession of the waters, without which they would be valueless, and 'civilized communities could not be established thereon'. And this, it is further contended, the Indians knew, and yet made no reservation of the waters. We realize that there is a conflict of implications, but that which makes for the retention of the waters is of greater force than that which makes for their cession."

The Court in *Winters* concluded that the Government, when it created that Indian Reservation, intended to deal fairly with the Indians by reserving for them the waters without which their lands would have been useless. *Winters* has been followed by this Court as recently as 1939 in *United States v. Powers*, 305 U. S. 527. We follow it now and agree that the United States did reserve the water rights for the Indians effective as of the time the Indian Reservations were created. This means, as the Master held, that these water rights, having vested before the Act became effective on June 25, 1929, are "present perfected rights" and as such are entitled to priority under the Act.

We also agree with the Master's conclusion as to the quantity of water intended to be reserved. He found that the water was intended to satisfy the future as well as the present needs of the Indian Reservations and ruled that enough water was reserved to irrigate all the practicably irrigable acreage on the reservations. Arizona, on the other hand, contends that the quantity of water reserved should be measured by the Indians' "reasonably foreseeable needs," which, in fact, means by the number of Indians. How many Indians there will be and what their future needs will be can only be guessed. We have concluded, as did the Master, that the only feasible and fair way by which reserved water for the reservations can be measured is irrigable acreage. The various acreages of irrigable land which the Master found to be on the different reservations we find to be reasonable.

SOURCE: *Arizona v. California*, 373 U.S. 546 (1963).

ANALYSIS

During the legal process that led to the decision in *Arizona v. California*, the federal government asserted that the native peoples residing on five reservations, located in the states of Arizona, California, and Nevada, had a legal right to the water they required to irrigate the lands on which they resided. The states, most notably Arizona, disagreed with the federal government's position because any of the Colorado River's water that was reserved for the use of American Indians was water that was unavailable for the needs of the respective states. In advance of the decision, a special master appointed by the justices of the U.S. Supreme Court, whose duties included collecting evidence and identifying legal precedents, determined that Native Americans residing on the reservations had a reserved right to waters from the main stem of the Colorado River that had existed from the time that the reservations had been established. His reasoning was that the federal government would not have placed the natives on reservations where the land was uninhabitable due to a lack of water. Thus, the right to the waters the Indians required to irrigate their land was implicitly part of the agreement that led to them residing on the reservation in the first place.

There was also a legal precedent in place that also guaranteed that the natives had a priority claim on the water from the Colorado River. In the 1908 U.S. Supreme Court case *United States v. Winters*, the justices had created an implied reserved right to the water required by Native American groups on reservations that prioritized them over other landholders. The move was justified by the treaty process, which saw Native American groups yield large amounts of land in exchange for reservation lands that were provided for their present and future use. As part of the agreement between the federal government and the respective native groups, the justices determined that the Native Americans retained all rights of land owners not specifically addressed within the treaty's documentation. Since most western states apportioned water based on when a user established his or her claim to the water, the justices prioritized Native Americans over all users under the determination that their claim was made in "time immemorial."

Although *United States v. Winters* was confirmed as a legal precedent by the U.S. Supreme Court in *United States v. Powers* in 1939, it was largely ignored in the West. This was due to the mistaken interpretation that *United States v. Winters* was decided on a technicality; thus, it had only narrow legal applicability. In the majority opinion for *Arizona v. California*, the justices agreed with most of the special master's suggestions and unambiguously affirmed the original decision in *United States v.*

Winters. The confirmation that Native Americans had a reserved right to waters that served their needs on reservations led to a spate of lawsuits that saw Native Americans successfully acquire waters that should have been theirs for decades.

FURTHER READING

Burton, Lloyd. 1991. *American Indian Water Rights and the Limits of Law.* Lawrence: University Press of Kansas.

Fradkin, Philip L. 1995. *A River No More: The Colorado River and the West.* Expanded and updated ed. Berkeley: University of California Press.

McCool, Daniel. 1987. *Command of the Waters: Iron Triangles, Federal Water Development, and Indian Water.* Berkeley: University of California Press.

McCool, Daniel. 2002. *Native Waters: Contemporary Indian Water Settlement and the Second Treaty Era.* Tucson: University of Arizona Press.

Wilkinson, Charles F. 1987. *American Indians, Time, and the Law: Native Societies in a Modern Constitutional Democracy.* New Haven, CT: Yale University Press.

"An Almost Total Lack of Meaningful Communication on Problems of Treaty Right Fishing"

- **Document:** *United States of America, Plaintiff, Quinault Tribe of Indians on its own behalf and on Behalf of the Queets Band of Indians, et al., Intervenor-Plaintiffs, v. State of Washington, Defendant, Thor C. Tollefson, Director, Washington State Department of Fisheries, et al., Intervenor and Defendants,* excerpts
- **Date:** February 12, 1974
- **Where:** U.S. District Court, Western District, Tacoma, Washington
- **Significance:** More commonly known as either *United States v. Washington* (1974) or the "Boldt Decision," this case was a landmark decision on the rights of the native peoples of the Pacific Northwest to fish at their traditional sites as their ancestors had done since time immemorial.

DOCUMENT

STATEMENT OF THE CASE

BOLDT, Senior District Judge.

In September, 1970 the United States, on its own behalf and as trustee for several Western Washington Indian Tribes, later joined as intervenor plaintiffs by additional tribes, filed the complaint initiating this action against the State of Washington. Shortly later the State Department of Fisheries (Fisheries) and the State Game Commission (Game), their respective directors, and the Washington Reef Net

Owners Association (Reef Net Owners) were included as defendants. By state statute Fisheries is charged with exercising regulatory authority over fishing for all anadromous food fish. Regulation of anadromous steelhead trout is vested in Game. Plaintiffs seek a declaratory judgment pursuant to 28 U.S.C. §§ 2201 and 2202 concerning off reservation treaty right fishing within the case area by plaintiff tribes, which long has been and now is in controversy, and for injunctive relief to provide enforcement of those fishing rights as they previously have been or herein may be judicially determined. The case area is that portion of the State of Washington west of the Cascade Mountains and north of the Columbia River drainage area, and includes the American portion of the Puget Sound watershed, the watersheds of the Olympic Peninsula north of the Grays Harbor watershed, and the offshore waters adjacent to those areas.

Plaintiffs also assert claims for relief concerning alleged destruction or impairment of treaty right fishing due to state authorization of, or failure to prevent, logging and other industrial pollution and obstruction of treaty right fishing streams. Separation of those claims for pretrial and trial after trial of the issues determined in this decision was stipulated and approved by the court.

. . .

Fisheries contends the Muckleshoot, Stillaguamish and Upper Skagit tribes do not hold a special treaty status to harvest anadromous fish. Game joins in this contention and makes the same contention regarding the Sauk-Suiattle Tribe. These contentions are considered and denied in the written Findings of Fact and Conclusions of Law.

. . .

More than a century of frequent and often violent controversy between Indians and non-Indians over treaty right fishing has resulted in deep distrust and animosity on both sides. This has been inflamed by provocative, sometimes illegal, conduct of extremists on both sides and by irresponsible demonstrations instigated by nonresident opportunists.

To this court the evidence clearly shows that, in the past, root causes of treaty right dissension have been an almost total lack of meaningful communication on problems of treaty right fishing between state, commercial and sport fishing officials and non-Indian fishermen on one side and tribal representatives and members on the other side, and the failure of many of them to speak to each other and act as fellow citizens of equal standing as far as treaty right fishing is concerned. Some commendable improvement in both respects has developed in recent years but this court believes high priority should be given to further improvement in communication and in the attitude of every Indian and non-Indian who as a fisherman or in any capacity has responsibility for treaty right fishing practices or regulation. Hopefully that will be expedited by some of the measures required by this decision.

The ultimate objective of this decision is to determine every issue of fact and law presented and, at long last, thereby finally settle, either in this decision or on appeal thereof, as many as possible of the divisive problems of treaty right fishing which for so long have plagued all of the citizens of this area, and still do.

I. ESTABLISHED BASIC FACTS AND LAW

. . .

In the mid-1850's the United States treated with the unlettered Northwest Tribes to acquire great expanses of land. Reluctant to be confined to small reservation bases, the Indian negotiators insisted that their people continue to fish as they had beyond the reservation boundaries. There is no indication that the Indians intended or understood the language "in common with all citizens of the Territory" to limit their right to fish in any way. For many years following the treaties the Indians continued to fish in their customary manner and places, and although non-Indians also fished, there was no need for any restrictions on fishing.

. . .

III. STATE REGULATION OF OFF RESERVATION TREATY RIGHT FISHING

There is neither mention nor slightest intimation in the treaties themselves, in any of the treaty negotiation records or in any other credible evidence, that the Indians who represented the tribes in the making of the treaties, at that time or any time afterward, understood or intended that the fishing rights reserved by the tribes as recorded in the above quoted language would, or ever could, authorize the "citizens of the territory" or their successors, either individually or through their territorial or state government, to qualify, restrict or in any way interfere with the full *exercise* of those rights. All of the evidence is overwhelmingly to the contrary, particularly in the vivid showing in the record that the treaty Indians pleaded for and insisted upon retaining the *exercise* of those rights as essential to their survival. They were given unqualified assurance of that by Governor Stevens himself without any suggestion that the Indians *exercise* of those rights might someday, without authorization of Congress, be subjected to regulation by non-Indian citizens through their territorial or state government.

For several decades following negotiation and ratification of the treaties all of the tribes extensively exercised their treaty rights by fishing as freely in time, place and manner as they had at treaty time, totally without regulation or any restraint whatever, excepting only by the tribes themselves in strictly enforcing tribal customs and practices which, during that period and for innumerable prior generations, had so successfully assured perpetuation of all fish species in copious volume. The first other than naturally caused threat to volume or species came from non-Indian population growth and non-Indian industrial development in the rapid westward advance of civilization.

. . .

It also appears that the United States Supreme Court has exercised a prerogative specifically reserved by and to Congress in the treaties. Congress has never exercised its prerogative to either limit or abolish Indian treaty right fishing. In recent years it declined to do the latter by three times failing to enact proposed legislation for the termination of Indian treaty fishing rights. It may be that the refusal or failure of Congress to exercise a specific prerogative, by enactment of legislation, would legally justify judicial exercise of that particular prerogative. If so, it has never been stated or indicated in any United States Supreme Court decision as the basis or source of authority for the federal judicial decisions authorizing state regulation of off reservation treaty fishing rights.

. . .

IV. RULINGS ON MAJOR ISSUES IN THIS CASE

1. In the detailed Findings of Fact and Conclusions of Law on file herein this court has found and held and hereby reaffirms that each of plaintiff tribes in this case, including each of the tribes whose status as such was challenged by some or all defendants, has established its status as an Indian tribe recognized as such by the federal government and therefore is entitled to maintain this action for relief based on a treaty of the United States negotiated by and for the tribe, its members at that time and their descendants.

An appeal from a district court decision holding that the Puyallup reservation no longer exists has not yet been determined. However, in *Menominee* (1968) the United States Supreme Court held that termination of a tribal reservation established pursuant to a treaty did not extinguish hunting and fishing rights, reserved in the treaty by implication, or impair the exercise of such rights within the area of the terminated reservation. In the opinion of this court, treaty right fishing within the area of a former Indian reservation cannot be *exclusive* when that reservation no longer exists, but such fishing must be "in common with" non-treaty right fishermen. It is so found and held and hereby shall be applicable to any plaintiff tribe, the reservation of which has been or hereafter may be terminated.

2. Ever since the first Indian treaties were confirmed by the Senate, Congress has recognized that those treaties established self-government by treaty tribes, excepting only as limited in the treaties, judicial interpretation thereof or by Congress. This basic principle was confirmed in the first United States Supreme Court decision dealing with such a treaty and has always been expressly or impliedly reaffirmed when applicable in every succeeding decision of that court. There was a period during which Congress enacted legislation limiting the exercise of tribal autonomy in various particulars. However, in the last decade Congressional legislation has definitely been in the contrary direction, notably in the so called "Indian Civil Rights Act." Among other measures in that Act encouraging the exercise of tribal autonomy are those providing for enlarged jurisdiction of tribal courts, pursuant to which special training of tribal judges and other court personnel has been in progress for some time and still continues.

These measures and others make plain the intent and philosophy of Congress to increase rather than diminish or limit the exercise of tribal self-government.

. . .

FINDINGS OF FACT AND CONCLUSIONS OF LAW

This case came on regularly for trial on August 27, 1973, upon the basis of a final pretrial order entered August 24, 1973, and the presentation of evidence concluded September 18, 1973. Counsel for all parties appeared and presented nearly 50 witnesses, whose testimony was reported in 4,600 pages of trial transcript, more than 350 exhibits, pretrial briefs, final oral argument 12/9-10/73 and post-trial briefs. In addition to consideration of the above evidence and material by the court, more than 500 proposed findings of fact and conclusions of law, submitted by counsel and annotated to the record, have been checked to determine the accuracy of every citation made by any counsel alleged to support a proposed finding or conclusion. Many of the proposed findings and conclusions were modified and many of the supporting citations were corrected, and additional findings and conclusions not proposed by any party were developed. The court has also read and examined, individually and in relation to one another, every case cited by any party as possible authority concerning any issue in this case, as well as other cases not cited by the parties.

Based upon this exhaustive examination of the controlling law, the briefs and oral argument of counsel and upon a preponderance of the evidence found credible and inferences reasonably drawn therefrom, the court now makes the following Findings of Fact and Conclusions of Law:

TREATY STATUS

1. The United States has entered into treaties with each of the following Indian tribes or bands (herein collectively referred to as "Plaintiff tribes" and individually by the shorter name set out after each such tribe), or with their predecessors in interest:

Hoh Indian Tribe ("Hoh Tribe")	Treaty with the Quinaeilt, et al. (Treaty of Olympia), July 1, 1855, and January 25, 1856, ratified March 8, 1859, and proclaimed April 11, 1859, 12 Stat. 971.
Lummi Tribe of Indians ("Lummi Tribe")	Treaty of Point Elliott, January 22, 1855, ratified March 8, 1859, and proclaimed April 11, 1859, 12 Stat. 927.
Makah Indian Tribe	Treaty with the Makah (Treaty of Neah Bay), January 31, 1855, ratified March 8, 1859, and proclaimed April 18, 1859, 12 Stat. 939.
Muckleshoot Indian Tribe ("Muckleshoot Tribe")	Treaty of Point Elliott, *supra*, and also Treaty of Medicine Creek, December 26, 1854, ratified March 3, 1855, and proclaimed April 10, 1855, 10 Stat. 1132.
Nisqually Indian Community of the Nisqually Reservation ("Nisqually Tribe")	Treaty of Medicine Creek, *supra*.
Puyallup Tribe of the Puyallup Reservation ("Puyallup Tribe")	Treaty of Medicine Creek, *supra*.
Quileute Tribe of the Quileute Reservation ("Quileute Tribe")	Treaty with the Quinaeilt, et al., *supra*.
Quinault Tribe of Indians ("Quinault Tribe")	Treaty with the Quinaeilt, et al., *supra*.
Sauk-Suiattle Indian Tribe ("Sauk-Suiattle Tribe")	Treaty of Point Elliott, *supra*.
Skokomish Indian Tribe ("Skokomish Tribe")	Treaty of Point No Point, January 26, 1855, ratified March 8, 1859, and proclaimed April 29, 1859, 12 Stat. 933.

(*Continued*)

Squaxin Island Tribe of Indians ("Squaxin Island Tribe")	Treaty of Medicine Creek, *supra*.
Stillaguamish Indian Tribe ("Stillaguamish Tribe")	Treaty of Point Elliott, *supra*.
Upper Skagit River Tribe ("Upper Skagit Tribe")	Treaty of Point Elliott, *supra*.
Confederated Tribes and Bands of the Yakima Indian Nation ("Yakima Nation")	Treaty with the Yakimas, June 9, 1855, ratified March 8, 1859, and proclaimed April 18, 1859, 12 Stat.

Each of said treaties contains a provision securing to the Indians certain off-reservation fishing rights. The following provision from the Treaty of Medicine Creek is typical of these treaty provisions:

"The right of taking fish, at all usual and accustomed grounds and stations, is further secured to said Indians, in common with all citizens of the Territory, and of erecting temporary houses for the purpose of curing,. . . ."

NEGOTIATION AND EXECUTION OF THE TREATIES

19. The principal purposes of the treaties were to extinguish Indian claims to the land in Washington Territory and provide for peaceful and compatible coexistence of Indians and non-Indians in the area. The United States was concerned with forestalling friction between Indians and settlers and between settlers and the government. The Indians had received constant assurances from settlers and government representatives that they would be compensated for lands which were being settled by United States citizens. Settlers had taken up land claims under the Donation Act even though the Indian rights had not yet been extinguished by treaties as required by the act creating the Oregon Territory. [FPTO § 3-35; Ex. USA-20, p. 24] Governor Stevens and the treaty commissioners were not authorized to grant to the Indians or treat away on behalf of the United States any governmental authority of the United States. . . .

20. At the treaty negotiations, a primary concern of the Indians whose way of life was so heavily dependent upon harvesting anadromous fish, was that they have freedom to move about to gather food, particularly salmon, (which both Indians and non-Indians meant to include steelhead), at their usual and accustomed fishing places. . . . The Indians were assured by Governor Stevens and the treaty commissioners that they would be allowed to fish, but that the white man also would be allowed to fish. [Ex. PL-17c, p. 1e] In 1856, it was felt that the development of the non-Indian fisheries in the case area would not interfere with the subsistence of the Indians.

. . .

POST-TREATY INDIAN FISHING

29. Fish continue to provide a vital component of many Indians' diet. For others it may remain an important food in a symbolic sense—analogous to Thanksgiving turkey. Few habits are stronger than dietary habits and their persistence is usually a

matter of emotional preference rather than a nutritional need. For some Indians, fishing is also economically important. Fishing is also important for some non-Indians.

. . .

31. Subsequent to the execution of the treaties and in reliance thereon, the members of the Plaintiff tribes have continued to fish for subsistence, sport and commercial purposes at their usual and accustomed places. Such fishing provided and still provides an important part of their livelihood, subsistence and cultural identity. . . . The Indian cultural identification with fishing is primarily dietary, related to the subsistence fishery, and secondarily associated with religious ceremonies and commercial fishing. Indian commercial fishermen share the same economic motivation as non-Indian commercial fishermen to maximize their harvest and fishing opportunities. . . . Indians allow non-Indians to fish on their reservation in sport fisheries for which Indians serve as guides and charge a license fee.

. . .

DECLARATORY JUDGMENT AND DECREE

This judgment and decree is based upon the Findings of Fact, Agreed Facts, Conclusions of Law and Decision of the Court entered in this case, all of which by this reference are hereby made a part hereof as though set forth in full herein, and close and detailed consideration by the Court. No language herein shall be interpreted as superseding the Decision of the Court, which shall control if in any respect it appears to be in conflict with any Finding herein.

In order clearly to delineate the off-reservation fishing rights held by certain Indian entities in this district under treaties made with the United States, it is hereby ordered, adjudged and decreed that the right of each of the plaintiff tribes in this case to harvest anadromous fish in waters within the Western District of Washington, outside the boundaries of Indian reservations and areas of exclusive *federal jurisdiction,* is declared to be as follows:

A. *Definitions*

All definitions contained in the Glossary of Terms of the Joint Biological Statement (Exhibit JX-2a) are hereby incorporated by reference. In addition and specifically for the purposes of interpreting all provisions of this decree, the following definitions shall be controlling:

1. *Anadromous fish*: Any fish which spawns or is artificially produced in freshwater, reaches mature size while rearing in saltwater and returns to freshwater to reproduce, and which spends any portion of its life cycle in waters within the Western District of Washington.

2. *Adequate production escapement*: In an approximate number of anadromous fish, that level of escapement from each fishery which will produce viable offspring in numbers to fully utilize all natural spawning grounds and propagation facilities reasonable and necessary for conservation of the resource, as defined in the Decision of the court.

3. *Harvestable stock*: The approximate number of anadromous fish which is surplus beyond adequate production escapement and Indian needs as defined in the Decision; that is, the number remaining when the adequate production escapement and Indian needs are subtracted from the run size.

4. *To preserve and maintain the resource*: Upon a full consideration of (a) the history of State anadromous fish management, (b) the level of catch within the Western District of Washington in recent years, (c) the quality of freshwater and artificial production environments, (d) the most recent facts and data concerning anadromous fish production potential, (e) the potential for interspecific competition, and (f) the prospects for improvement of anadromous fish production, to perpetuate the runs of anadromous fish at least at their current level.

5. *Run*: A group of anadromous fish on its return migration, identified by species, race and water of origin.

6. *State*: The State of Washington, its agents, officers, agencies, assigns and subdivisions.

7. *Stevens treaties*: Those treaties identified in the Findings of Fact and Conclusions of Law as having been negotiated between Isaac I. Stevens, for the United States, and certain Indian tribes and bands who lived in Washington Territory during the 1850's.

8. *Treaty Tribe*: One of the Indian entities described in paragraph 10 below, or any other entity entitled to exercise treaty fishing rights under the treaties construed herein within the Western District of Washington.

9. *Usual and accustomed places*: Those areas in, on and around the freshwater and saltwater areas within the Western District of Washington, which were understood by the Indian parties to the Stevens' treaties to be embraced within the treaty terms "usual and accustomed" "grounds," "stations" and "places."

B. *Treaty Fishing Rights*

10. Each of the plaintiff tribes listed below is a Treaty Tribe. The list given below is a declaration only as to those 14 Indian entities which have been represented on the plaintiff side in this case. A Treaty Tribe occupies the status of a party to one or more of the Stevens' treaties and therefore holds for the benefit of its members a reserved right to harvest anadromous fish at all usual and accustomed places outside reservation boundaries, in common with others:

Hoh Tribe of Indians;
Lummi Indian Tribe;
Makah Indian Tribe;
Muckleshoot Indian Tribe;
Nisqually Indian Community of the Nisqually Reservation;
Puyallup Tribe of the Puyallup Reservation;
Quileute Indian Tribe;
Quinault Tribe of Indians;

Sauk-Suiattle Indian Tribe;
Skokomish Indian Tribe;
Squaxin Island Tribe of Indians;
Stillaguamish Tribe of Indians;
Upper Skagit River Tribe;
Confederated Tribes and Bands of the Yakima Indian Nation

11. The right of a Treaty Tribe to harvest anadromous fish outside reservation boundaries arises from a provision which appears in each of the Stevens' treaties and which, with immaterial variations, states:

The right of taking fish, at all usual and accustomed grounds and stations, is further secured to said Indians, in common with all citizens of the Territory. . . .

12. It is the responsibility of all citizens to see that the terms of the Stevens' treaties are carried out, so far as possible, in accordance with the meaning they were understood to have by the tribal representatives at the councils, and in a spirit which generously recognizes the full obligation of this nation to protect the interests of a dependent people.

13. From the earliest known times, up to and beyond the time of the Stevens' treaties, the Indians comprising each of the treating tribes and bands were primarily a fishing, hunting and gathering people dependent almost entirely upon the natural animal and vegetative resources of the region for their subsistence and culture. They were heavily dependent upon anadromous fish for their subsistence and for trade with other tribes and later with the settlers. Anadromous fish was the great staple of their diet and livelihood. They cured and dried large quantities for year around use, both for themselves and for others through sale, trade, barter and employment. With the advent of canning technology in the latter half of the 19th Century the commercial exploitation of the anadromous fish resources by non-Indians increased tremendously. Indians, fishing under their treaty-secured rights, also participated in this expanded commercial fishery and sold many fish to non-Indian packers and dealers.

14. The taking of anadromous fish from usual and accustomed places, the right to which was secured to the Treaty Tribes in the Stevens' treaties, constituted both the means of economic livelihood and the foundation of native culture. Reservation of the right to gather food in this fashion protected the Indians' right to maintain essential elements of their way of life, as a complement to the life defined by the permanent homes, allotted farm lands, compulsory education, technical assistance and pecuniary rewards offered in the treaties. Settlement of the West and the rise of industrial America have significantly circumscribed the opportunities of members of the Treaty Tribes to fish for subsistence and commerce and to maintain tribal traditions. But the mere passage of time has not eroded, and cannot erode, the rights guaranteed by solemn treaties that both sides pledged on their honor to uphold.

15. The treaty-secured rights to resort to the usual and accustomed places to fish were a part of larger rights possessed by the treating Indians, upon the exercise of which there was not a shadow of impediment, and which were not much less necessary to their existence than the atmosphere they breathed. The treaty was not a grant of rights to the treating Indians, but a grant of rights from them, and a

reservation of those not granted. In the Stevens' treaties, such reservations were not of particular parcels of land, and could not be expressed in deeds, as dealings between private individuals. The reservations were in large areas of territory, and the negotiations were with the tribes. The treaties reserved rights, however, to every individual Indian, as though described therein. There was an exclusive right of fishing reserved within certain boundaries. There was a right outside of those boundaries reserved for exercise "in common with citizens of the Territory."

16. The Stevens' treaties do not reserve to the Treaty Tribes any specific manner, method or purpose of taking fish; nor do the treaties prohibit any specific manner, method or purpose. Just as non-Indians may continue to take advantage of improvements in fishing techniques, the Treaty Tribes may, in exercising their rights to take anadromous fish, utilize improvements in traditional fishing methods, such for example as nylon nets and steel hooks.

17. The exercise of a Treaty Tribe's right to take anadromous fish outside of reservation boundaries is limited only by geographical extent of the usual and accustomed places, the limits of the harvestable stock and the number of fish which non-treaty fishermen shall have an opportunity to catch, as provided in the Decision of the Court.

18. Because the right of each Treaty Tribe to take anadromous fish arises from a treaty with the United States, that right is preserved and protected under the supreme law of the land, does not depend on State law, is distinct from rights or privileges held by others, and may not be qualified by any action of the State.

19. The treaty phrase "in common with" does not secure any treaty right or privilege to anyone other than the Treaty Tribes, nor does that phrase qualify any Indian's treaty right to fish, except as provided in the Decision of the Court.

20. Except for tribes now or hereafter entitled to self-regulation of tribal fishing, as provided in the Decision of the Court, the right of a Treaty Tribe to take anadromous fish may be regulated by an appropriate exercise of State power. To be appropriate, such regulation must:

a. Not discriminate against the Treaty Tribe's reserved right to fish;

b. Meet appropriate standards of substantive and procedural due process; and

c. Be shown by the State to be both reasonable and necessary to preserve and maintain the resource. When State law or regulations affect the volume of anadromous fish available for harvest by a Treaty Tribe at usual and accustomed places, such regulations must be designed so as to carry out the purposes of the treaty provision securing to the Tribe the right to take fish.

21. If any person shows identification, as provided in the Decision of the Court, that he is exercising the fishing rights of a Treaty Tribe and if he is fishing in a usual and accustomed place, he is protected under federal law against any State action which affects the time, place, manner, purpose or volume of his harvest of anadromous fish, unless the State has previously established that such action is an appropriate exercise of its power.

22. The application of currently effective laws and regulations of the State of Washington specified in the Conclusions of Law which affect the time, place, manner and volume of off-reservation harvest of anadromous fish by Treaty Tribes is unlawful for the reasons also stated in the Conclusions of Law.

23. All Findings of Fact and Conclusions of Law pertinent to the nature, scope and effect of the fishing rights of the Treaty Tribes are specifically incorporated by reference herein.

24. The court retains jurisdiction of this case for the life of this decree to take evidence, to make rulings and to issue such orders as may be just and proper upon the facts and law and in implementation of this decree.

25. Appointment of a Master, technical experts and an Advisory Committee on Treaty Right Fishing will be considered and determined as provided in the Decision of the court.

26. Plaintiffs' application for an injunction will be considered and determined upon hearing thereof at the earliest practicable date following entry of this judgment and decree.

SOURCE: *United States v. State of Washington*, 384 F. Supp. 312—District Court, Western District, Washington (1974).

ANALYSIS

United States v. Washington (1974), or the "Boldt Decision," was a landmark ruling that has subsequently become the most important Native American fishing rights case ever litigated. The decision by the United States to sue Washington on behalf of the 14 native nations named in the suit had its origins in the 1960s when Native American activists began asserting their treaty rights dating back to the 1850s by conducting fish-ins at their traditional accustomed locations. Some of these locales were off of the reservation, thus putting them directly into conflict with nonnatives. Sporadic violence on both sides soon ensued. To reestablish control, Washington began pursuing some of the natives as instigators despite the fact that they were not breaking any laws due to the long-ignored treaties. Washington's attempts to impinge on the rights of the natives forced the United States to turn to the court for redress.

Washington based its defense in the case on the claim that the native groups that signed the treaties with Governor Isaac Stevens between 1854 and 1856 no longer existed. The absence of the native nations meant that none of the treaties were still in force. Through the use of expert testimony, all 14 of the native nations that were plaintiffs in the case were able to prove that they had remained a distinct political entity through all of the years that had passed since the signing of the treaties. This was an important part of the case because this affirmed their continued federal recognition status, which gave them the legal standing to pursue the case.

Judge George Boldt in his ruling determined that, according to the treaties, the fishing rights of the respective native groups extended beyond their reservations to areas where their ancestors had customarily fished. More importantly, he determined that the natives together had a right to an equal share of the anadromous fish runs in Washington, and by extension Oregon, due to the treaty terms. This meant that the respective native nations, in the eyes of the state, had gotten the right to a disproportionate share of fish since they comprised a small segment of the states' population. They conveniently ignored the fact that when the treaties had been negotiated, the U.S. citizens, who were the minority, received a similar disproportionate share and had no qualms about the very same agreements that greatly benefitted their economic interests.

Although Judge Boldt's decision was later affirmed by the U.S. Supreme Court, Washington refused to accept defeat. Fishing rights cases based on Governor Stevens's negotiations would continue first at the state level, and eventually to the federal courts.

FURTHER READING

Deloria, Vine, Jr., et al. 2011. "The Boldt Decision: A Roundtable Discussion." *Journal of Northwest Anthropology* 45, no. 1: 111–122.

Harmon, Alexandra. 1998. *Indians in the Making: Ethnic Relations and Indian Identities Around Puget Sound.* Berkeley: University of California Press.

Harmon, Alexandra, ed. 2008. *The Power of Promises: Rethinking Indian Treaties in the Pacific Northwest.* Seattle: University of Washington Press.

Ulrich, Roberta. 2007. *Empty Nets: Indians, Dams, and the Columbia River.* 2nd ed. Corvallis: Oregon State University Press.

"The Congress Has Not Authorized the Taking of Indian Fishing Rights for the Catherine Creek Project"

- **Document:** *Confederated Tribes of the Umatilla Indian Reservation, Plaintiff, v. Clifford L. Alexander, Jr., Secretary of the Army of the United States, Lt. Gen. John W. Morris, Chief of Engineers, United States Army Corps of Engineers, Christopher J. Allaire, District Engineer, United States Army Corps of Engineers, Walla Walla District, Defendants*
- **Date:** November 10, 1977
- **Where:** U.S. District Court, Oregon
- **Significance:** The Confederated Tribes of the Umatilla Indian Reservation contended that the construction of the Catherine Creek Dam by the United States Army Corps of Engineers (USACE) would violate their reserved fishing rights by destroying the habitats on which the salmon and steelhead trout depended on for spawning.

DOCUMENT

440 F.Supp. 553 (1977)
CONFEDERATED TRIBES OF the UMATILLA INDIAN RESERVATION,
Plaintiff, Clifford L. ALEXANDER, Jr., Secretary of the Army of the United
States, Lt. Gen. John W. Morris, Chief of Engineers, United States Army Corps
of Engineers, Christopher J. Allaire, District Engineer, United States Army
Corps of Engineers, Walla Walla District, Defendants.

Civ. No. 74-991.
United States District Court, D. Oregon.
November 10, 1977.

Opinion

BELLONI, District Judge:

The United States Army Corps of Engineers plans to dam Catherine Creek, in Northeastern Oregon, for flood control, irrigation and recreation purposes. Plaintiff Confederated Tribes of the Umatilla Indian Reservation seek to enjoin construction of the dam, contending that it will infringe fishing rights guaranteed to them by the treaty of 1855 by which they ceded the bulk of their aboriginal lands to white settlers. Plaintiffs recognize that Congress has power to take such fishing rights. They maintain, however, that Congress has not exercised that power in this case. The government replies that no treaty fishing rights exist on the relevant segment of Catherine Creek and that, even if such rights can be found, the Chinook hatchery planned as part of the project will sufficiently mitigate any adverse effects by increasing fish populations.

The controlling treaty language is similar to that found in most Northwest Indian treaties of the middle nineteenth century:

... the exclusive right of taking fish in the streams running through and bordering said reservation is hereby secured to said Indians, and at all other usual and accustomed stations ...

Treaty of June 9, 1855, 12 Stat. 945. The significant difference between this and other similar treaties is that the off-reservation right to fish is secured only at "stations", not "grounds and stations". "Grounds" and "stations" have been held to convey distinct meanings as used in these treaties, the former including large areas where Indians had traditionally fished, the latter restricted to "fixed locations such as the site of a fish weir or a fishing platform or some other narrowly limited area;" *United States v. Washington*, 384 F.Supp. 312, 332 (W.D.Wash.1974), *aff'd* 520 F.2d 676 (9th Cir. 1975), *cert. denied* 423 U.S. 1086, 96 S.Ct. 877, 47 L.Ed.2d 97, *reh. denied* 424 U.S. 978, 96 S.Ct. 1487, 47 L.Ed.2d 750 (1976).

In applying this definition of fishing stations to the facts of a particular case, the manner of fishing used by the Indians at the time of the treaty necessarily determines the extent and location of fishing stations. The evidence is clear in this case that the primary method of Indian fishing on Catherine Creek before 1855 was by spear or gaff. The fishermen would locate a hole, usually 30 or 40 feet long, in which salmon were likely to be found. Those wielding spears or gaffs would be stationed at one or both ends of such a hole while the others in the fishing party beat the banks so as to drive the salmon toward the shallow ends of the hole where they would be speared or gaffed.

The Indians camped at various sites along Catherine Creek and ranged up and down its length, fishing wherever they found holes which were likely to harbor salmon or steelhead. Certainly changes in the creekbed due to erosion and rockfall would alter the size, shape and location of such holes.

The passage of time and the changed conditions affecting the water courses and the fishery resources in the case area have not eroded and cannot erode the right secured by the treaties . . .

United States v. Washington, supra at 401. Catherine Creek is particularly susceptible to natural changes in its bed. Amounts of water in the creek vary widely, depending mainly on the accumulation of snow available for melting. During Catherine Creek's 65 year recorded history, streamflows have fluctuated from five cubic feet per second (cfs) to 1740 cfs. In 1970 alone, flows ranged from about 40 cfs to over 800 cfs. Such conditions make the course of the creek and the topography of its bed unpredictable. Indeed it is partly for this reason that the Corps of Engineers project was authorized.

Given the evidence of these natural factors and the mobile character of the traditional Indian fishing on Catherine Creek, it is far more likely than not that pretreaty fishing holes were located on the creek at places which the dam's 2½ mile reservoir will flood. I find that these holes were fishing stations, and treaty rights in them will be destroyed by the project.

Further, while the 1855 treaty spoke only of "stations", it is clear that the government and the Indians intended that all Northwest tribes should reserve the same fishing rights.

It is designed to make the same provision for all the tribes and for each Indian of every tribe. The people of one tribe are as much the people of the Great Father as the people of another tribe; the red men are as much his children as the white men.

Isaac Stevens, Governor and Superintendent of Indian Affairs for the Washington Territory, in Treaty Minutes of June 5, 1855, *quoted in* E. G. Swindell, Report of Source, Nature & Extent of the Fishing, Hunting and Miscellaneous Related Rights of Certain Indian Tribes in Washington and Oregon 423 (1942). The fishing locations specifically found above are "stations", as distinguished from "grounds". If the evidence had not warranted a finding of fishing stations, it would have been appropriate to consider whether fishing *grounds* existed on the relevant sections of Catherine Creek. The proof at trial established, and I find, that the term "stations" in this particular treaty was intended to designate the same kinds of fishing locations as the phrase "grounds and stations" in the other Northwest Indian treaties.

Some of the Indian fishing stations on Catherine Creek will be inundated by the reservoir which the dam will create. These stations will be covered by as much as 200 feet of water. Such a flooding will deprive the Indians of their right to occupy the fishing stations and of their right to access for that purpose. *Cf. United States v. Winans,* 198 U.S. 371, 381, 25 S.Ct. 662, 49 L.Ed. 1089 (1905). I find unpersuasive the government's argument that 200 feet of water will not impair access to these traditional stations. The dam will also prevent all wild fish from swimming upstream. Chinook will be trapped and hauled above the dam to mitigate the loss, but the steelhead run will be eliminated entirely at all stations upstream from the dam. Whatever the merits of the government's mitigation program, the treaty right to fish at all usual and accustomed stations will be destroyed as to those stations within the reservoir.

In order to nullify treaty rights in this way, Congress must act expressly and specifically. *Menominee Tribe v. United States,* 391 U.S. 404, 413, 88 S.Ct. 1705,

20 L.Ed.2d 697 (1968). The right to destroy Indian rights will not be inferred from a general project authorization such as that for this dam. Congress authorized this project in 1965 without knowing that the dam would affect treaty rights. The Corps of Engineers first knowledge of the existence of fishing rights in the area came in 1972. Therefore, the Congress has not authorized the taking of Indian fishing rights for the Catherine Creek Project.

Since the dam would take treaty rights without proper authorization, plaintiffs are entitled to relief. They ask declaratory judgment and injunction. According to the evidence, actual construction of the dam, hence the actual taking of Indian fishing rights, is not planned for another two to three years. The situation thus appears to lack the urgency which ordinarily demands the drastic remedy of injunction. I therefore find it appropriate to issue a declaratory judgment in the following terms: Plaintiff Indians have usual and accustomed fishing stations on Catherine Creek. Some of these will be flooded, thus destroyed, by the construction of defendant's dam. The steelhead fishery above the dam will be destroyed. Specific congressional authority is required for such action by defendants, and none now exists.

It is expected that, without injunction, the Corps of Engineers will seek proper authority for their project.

The above constitutes findings of fact and conclusions of law in accordance with Fed.R.Civ.P. 52(a).

SOURCE: *Confederated Tribes, etc. v. Alexander*, 440 F. Supp. 553—District Court, D. Oregon (1977).

ANALYSIS

In 1965, Congress authorized the USACE to construct a dam on Oregon's Catherine Creek for the purpose of flood control, irrigation, and recreation. In 1972, the USACE discovered during the preconstruction planning process that there was a potential problem with the fishing rights of the Confederated Tribes of the Umatilla Indian Reservation. Rather than returning to Congress to determine whether they intended to abrogate the fishing rights of the natives at the time they authorized the dam, the USACE continued preparation for dam construction. The Confederated Tribes of the Umatilla Indian Reservation turned to the courts to stop the USACE from building the Catherine Creek Dam.

The Confederated Tribes of the Umatilla Indian Reservation contended that their reserved fishing rights had been guaranteed through the treaty that they negotiated with the federal government in 1855. The treaty terms would be broached if the Catherine Creek Dam was constructed because it would have flooded their traditional places to fish. It would also have negatively impacted the fish, most notably the salmon and steelhead trout, because it would have permanently altered the habitats on which they depended. Judge Belloni agreed with the Confederated Tribes of the Umatilla Indian Reservation and ruled in their favor. He first noted that there was no indication that Congress had ever intended to abrogate the fishing rights of any native group when they authorized the damming of Catherine Creek. From a practical standpoint, he also observed that the dam would have prevented all wild fish from swimming upstream of it, thus denying the Confederated Tribes of the Umatilla Indian Reservation their guaranteed fishing rights.

FURTHER READING

Harmon, Alexandra, ed. 2008. *The Power of Promises: Rethinking Indian Treaties in the Pacific Northwest.* Seattle: University of Washington Press.

Lewis, O. Yale, III. 2002/2003. "Treaty Fishing Rights: A Habitat Right as Part of the Trinity of Rights Implied by the Fishing Clause of the Stevens Treaties." *American Indian Law Review* 27, no. 1: 281–311.

Ulrich, Roberta. 2007. *Empty Nets: Indians, Dams, and the Columbia River.* 2nd ed. Corvallis: Oregon State University Press.

Wilson, Rollie. 1999/2000. "Removing Dam Development to Recover Columbia Basin Treaty Protected Salmon Economies." *American Indian Law Review* 24, no. 2: 357–419.

"The Right of Taking Fish, at All Usual and Accustomed Grounds and Stations, Is Further Secured to Said Indians, in Common with All Citizens of the Territory"

- *Document:* United States of America, et al., Plaintiffs, v. State of Washington et al., Defendants, 506 F. Supp. 187 (1980), excerpts from majority opinion
- *Date:* September 26, 1980
- *Where:* U.S. District Court, Western District, Washington
- *Significance:* The federal case affirmed that Native American peoples in Washington had a right to approximately 50 percent of the fish harvest in areas where those rights were guaranteed through treaties negotiated by Governor Isaac Stevens between 1854 and 1856.

DOCUMENT

This opinion constitutes but the most recent link in a long chain of opinions construing the following 27 words:

"The right of taking fish, at all usual and accustomed grounds and stations, is further secured to said Indians, in common with all citizens of the Territory,...."

The quoted clause appears in six treaties negotiated between the United States and several Pacific Northwest Indian tribes in 1854 and 1855. The Indians traded their interest in the land west of the Cascade Mountains and north of the Columbia River for the exclusive use of small land parcels (reservations), cash payments, and various guarantees, including, of prime importance in 1854-1855 as well as today, the right to continue fishing. In each of the seven cases where the Supreme Court has directly addressed the scope of the fishing clause in these treaties, it has "placed a relatively broad gloss on the Indians' fishing rights." *Washington v. Washington State Commercial Passenger Fishing Vessel Ass'n*, 443 U.S. 658, 679, 99 S.Ct. 3055, 3071, 61 L.Ed.2d 823 (1979).

This complex case, which was commenced in 1970 by the United States on its own behalf and as trustee of seven Indian tribes, involves three key issues: (1) whether the treaties fishing clause entitles the Indians to a specific allocation of the salmon and steelhead trout in the "case area"; (2) if such allocation is required, whether hatchery-bred and artificially-propagated fish are included in the allocable fish population; and (3) whether the right of taking fish incorporates the right to have treaty fish protected from environmental degradation.

. . .

I

The treaties in question were negotiated between Isaac Stevens, the first Governor and first Superintendent of Indian Affairs of the Washington Territory, and tribal representatives. Few contemporaneous documents explicate the parties intentions regarding the scope of and limitations on the tribes' fishing right. For the simple reason that fish were plentiful in 1854-1855 but have since become relatively scarce, the allocation, hatchery and environmental issues which all arise from the fact of scarcity were not addressed. However, the extensive record developed in connection with this litigation and recounted in the many opinions issued to date provides considerable insight into the treaty negotiations. Preceding opinions have spelled out in impressive detail the parties intentions and the surrounding circumstances, as well as relevant subsequent events; only a capsule summary is necessary here.

When the treaties were negotiated, fish were the mainstay of the Indians economy and the focal point of their culture. "All of [the otherwise-diverse tribes] shared a vital and unifying dependence on anadromous fish." . . . An essential element of consideration for which the Indians bargained was the right to continue fishing as they had always done. "It is perfectly clear . . . that they were invited by the white negotiators to rely and in fact did rely heavily on the good faith of the United States to protect that right." *Id.* at 667, 99 S.Ct. at 3065.

In 1854-1855, Indians constituted approximately 75 percent of the 10,000-person case area population and accounted for most of the fishing activity. In 1974, Indians represented approximately 10.8 percent of case area's commercial fishermen and they netted 2.4 percent of the commercial catch. The dramatic decline in the Indians case-area fishing activity is attributable to such factors as the settlement of the West by predominantly non-Indians and the industrialization of fishing and related activities, acculturation of Indians into non-Indian forms of employment, belated access of Indian fishermen to the salmon runs by virtue of the location of Indians fishing sites, and the discriminatory manner in which state officials have applied fishing laws and regulations to Indian fishermen.

The most salient effect of Phase I was to reverse this trend and place Indian fishermen on an equal footing with non-Indians. In February, 1974, following a month-long trial and several months of post-trial briefing and argument, Judge Boldt held that the treaty language securing to the Indians "the right of taking fish ... in common with all citizens" entitles them to up to 50 percent of the harvestable fish passing through the tribes' usual and accustomed fishing grounds. *Final Decision I, supra*, 384 F.Supp. at 343-344. The quantity of harvestable fish subject to the 50/50 allocation between Indians and non-Indians was to be computed by subtracting the following categories of fish from all those within the case area: (1) fish taken on, rather than off of, Indian reservations; (2) fish taken at off-reservation sites other than the tribes usual and accustomed fishing grounds; (3) fish taken by the tribes for ceremonial and subsistence needs; and (4) fish not to be taken at all but to "escape" for spawning or conservation purposes. In addition, Judge Boldt called for an equitable adjustment augmenting the tribes share because non-Indians take a "substantially disproportionate" number of the fish caught offshore that would otherwise have passed through the tribes fishing grounds. *Id.* at 344. Finally, Judge Boldt abstained from deciding whether hatchery-bred fish should be excluded from the allocable fish population. *Id.* at 344-345. The Ninth Circuit affirmed Judge Boldt's allocation in all significant respects, modifying only the formula for computing the equitable adjustment. *United States v. State of Washington, supra*, 520 F.2d 676. Initially, the Supreme Court denied *certiorari*. 423 U.S. 1086, 96 S.Ct. 877, 47 L.Ed. 2d 97. However, the Court later reviewed Judge Boldt's rulings when a conflict arose between the Washington state courts, which enjoined the State's Department of Fisheries ("Fisheries") from enforcing regulations designed to implement the allocation decision, and the federal courts, which had decreed and undertook directly to implement the treaty-based allocation. The Court consolidated the state and federal court proceedings, affirmed and adopted Judge Boldt's construction of the treaties, and upheld, with slight modification, his allocation decision. *Washington—Phase I, supra*. The Court affirmed the Ninth Circuit's modification of the equitable adjustment formula, and further modified the computation of allocable fish by including: (1) fish taken on-reservation as well as those taken off-reservation; (2) fish taken off-reservation at sites other than the tribes usual and accustomed fishing sites; (3) fish taken by the tribes for ceremonial and subsistence needs. *Id.*, 443 U.S. at 687-688, 99 S.Ct. at 3075-3076. The Court amplified the 50/50 allocation ruling by emphasizing that the crucial determinant of the tribes treaty share is that quantity of fish sufficient to provide a moderate standard of living, subject to a ceiling of 50 percent of the harvestable fish.

> "[T]he 50% figure imposes a maximum but not a minimum allocation. ... [T]he central principle here must be that Indian treaty rights to a natural resource that once was thoroughly and exclusively exploited by the Indians secures so much as, but no more than, is necessary to provide the Indians with a livelihood—that is to say, a moderate living." *Id.* at 686, 99 S.Ct. at 3075.

. . .

In August, 1976, several months after the Supreme Court denied *certiorari* in the first round of Phase I, the plaintiffs formally commenced Phase II by filing amended and supplemental complaints. The State responded with an answer and counterclaim. The issues were further refined through joint and separate statements of the issues to be resolved in Phase II. After considerable discovery and pretrial preparation, the plaintiffs moved for partial summary judgment on the issue "whether the federal treaty fishing right reserves to treaty tribes a right to have the fishery resource protected from adverse environmental actions or inactions of the State of Washington." Excluded from the scope of the plaintiffs motion, and not yet presented to the Court for resolution, are two subsidiary environmental issues: (1) whether, if such right exists, the State has violated it; and (2) what remedies, if any, are appropriate. After extensive briefing by all parties, the Court heard oral argument on May 11, 1979. The Supreme Court's opinion in the second round of Phase I was handed down two months thereafter, and the parties submitted additional briefs regarding the significance of that opinion in relation to the pending environmental issue.

Following a status conference in September, 1979, the parties filed cross-motions for summary judgment on the issue "whether the federal treaty fishing right includes all, some or no artificially-reared fish released into public waters." Each party supported its motion with statements of facts and legal contentions, briefs, and affidavits in accordance with the procedures outlined in Section 3.30 of the Manual for Complex Litigation. Oral argument took place on April 10, 1980, and, after the parties filed supplementary factual material, both the hatchery and the environmental issues were deemed submitted.

II

In analyzing the allocation issue in Phase I, it was possible to rely on the express language of the treaties, as well as the parties intentions and surrounding circumstances, in construing the treaties fishing clause. In particular, the 50/50 allocation between treaty and nontreaty fishermen was derived from the "in common with" provision in that clause. . . . However, none of the express terms in the fishing clause pertain to the hatchery or environmental issues. Canons of interpreting Indian treaties accordingly assume especial significance in ascertaining the treaties implicit meaning with respect to those issues.

Indian treaties must be interpreted so as to promote their central purposes. *United States v. Winans*, 198 U.S. 371, 381, 25 S.Ct. 662, 664, 49 L.Ed. 1089 (1905). They must be read "in light of the common notions of the day and the assumptions of those who drafted them." *Oliphant v. Suquamish Indian Tribe*, 435 U.S. 191, 206, 98 S.Ct. 1011, 1020, 55 L.Ed.2d 209 (1978). The Supreme Court has been notably attentive to the intentions and assumptions of the Indians as they entered into the treaties.

"[T]he United States, as the party with the presumptively superior negotiating skills and superior knowledge of the language in which the treaty is recorded, has a responsibility to avoid taking advantage of the other side. '[T]he treaty must therefore be construed, not according to the technical meaning of its words to learned lawyers, but in the sense in which they would naturally be understood by the Indians.'" *Washington—Phase I, supra,* 443 U.S. at 675-676, 99 S.Ct. at 3069-3070, *quoting in part from Jones v. Meehan,* 175 U.S. 1, 11, 20 S.Ct. 1, 5, 44 L.Ed. 49 (1899).

... Any ambiguities must be resolved in the Indians' favor; "the wording of treaties ... with the Indians is not to be construed to their prejudice." *Antoine v. Washington*, 420 U.S. 194, 199, 95 S.Ct. 944, 948, 43 L.Ed.2d 129 (1975). ... The Supreme Court has repeatedly relied on the rule of attending to the Indians common-sense understanding of the treaties "in broadly interpreting these very treaties in the Indians favor." *Washington—Phase I, supra*, 443 U.S. at 676, 99 S.Ct. at 3070.

III

A

Prior to 1973, the State had never drawn a distinction in either its legal arguments or its fisheries programs between natural and hatchery-bred fish. The State initially proposed that distinction in oral argument before the Supreme Court in a case involving discriminatory state regulation of steelhead trout fishing in the Puyallup River. In the course of striking down the state regulation as impermissible infringement upon the Puyallup Tribe's treaty-based fishing right, the Supreme Court expressly reserved ruling on whether the existence of a license fee-funded hatchery program should affect the allocation of steelhead trout under the fishing clause. *Department of Game v. Puyallup Tribe*, 414 U.S. 44, 48, 94 S.Ct. 330, 333, 38 L.Ed.2d 254 (1973) ("*Puyallup II*"). In a concurring opinion, three Justices suggested that the Indians treaty right should not extend to hatchery fish subsidized by non-Indian sport fishermen. *Id.* at 49-50, 94 S.Ct. at 333-334.

On remand, the State courts converted that suggestion into a ruling. *Department of Game v. Puyallup Tribe*, No. 158069 (Super.Ct.1975), *aff'd* 86 Wash.2d 664, 548 P.2d 1058 (1976). Although the *Puyallup* litigation involved fishing by the Puyallup Tribe (but not the other 20 tribes that are parties to this litigation) for steelhead trout (but not the other five species of salmon that are the subject of this litigation) in the Puyallup River (but not the entire case area), the State moved to exclude all hatchery fish from the 50 percent treaty share to which Judge Boldt had declared all of the Indians in this case to be entitled. Judge Boldt then enjoined the State from extending the State court's holding beyond the *Puyallup* parties and subject matter. ... Throughout Phase I, which was litigated concurrently with *Puyallup II and III*, hatchery fish have been legally indistinguishable from natural fish.

B

Although the legal status of hatchery fish did not assume significance until 1973, the State's hatchery program has been in existence since 1895. The hatchery activities of the Fisheries and Game Departments have steadily increased since that time, particularly in the more recent years. ...

An estimated 371,000,000 salmon and 8,755,000 steelhead trout were released into the State's waters from federal, State, tribal, and all other hatcheries during the 1978-1979 season (*i.e.*, July 1978-June 1979). Hatchery fish presently account for 60 percent of the steelhead and 17 percent of the salmon in the case area. ... Because salmon return to their native streams to spawn, the placement of hatcheries has a tremendous impact on the proportion of propagated and natural fish in each geographically distinct population.

...

In its motion for summary judgment, the State seeks to exclude from the population of allocable fish the "first generation" of hatchery-produced fish. Subsequent generations, who spend their entire life cycle in the natural environment, are undisputedly included in the tribes treaty share.

C

The Court concludes that all hatchery fish must be included in the computation of the tribes treaty share in order to effectuate the parties intent and the purposes of the fishing clause. The Supreme Court's recent reaffirmation of the longstanding view that the treaties were designed to guarantee the tribes an adequate supply of fish goes far toward resolving the hatchery issue.

"Governor Stevens and his associates were well aware of the 'sense' in which the Indians were likely to view assurances of their fishing rights. During the negotiations, the vital importance of the fish to the Indians was repeatedly emphasized by both sides, and the Governor's promises that the treaties would protect the source of food and commerce were crucial in obtaining the Indians' assent. It is absolutely clear, as Governor Stevens himself said, that neither he nor the Indians' intended that the latter should be excluded from their ancient fisheries,' and it is accordingly inconceivable that either party deliberately agreed to authorize future settlers to crowd the Indians out of any meaningful use of their accustomed places to fish." *Washington—Phase I, supra,* 443 U.S. at 676, 99 S.Ct. at 3070 (citations omitted).

The only express limitation on the tribes' right of taking fish is the requirement to share the harvest "in common with" non-Indians. The only implicit limitations on that right are the tribes moderate living needs, the State's power to impose conservation measures necessary to preserve the resource, and the physical availability of fish.
. . .
The inescapable conclusion is that if hatchery fish were to be excluded from the allocation, the Indians' treaty-secured right to an adequate supply of fish—the right for which they traded millions of acres of valuable land and resources—would be placed in jeopardy. The tribes' share would steadily dwindle and the paramount purpose of the treaties would be subverted. Contrary to what the Supreme Court held to be the parties' intentions, nontreaty fishermen would ultimately "crowd the Indians out of any meaningful use of their accustomed places to fish." *Washington—Phase I, supra,* 443 U.S. at 676-677, 99 S.Ct. at 3070.

D
. . .
The record establishes that the Indians recognized exclusive property interests in land and in sedentary resources. However, the Indians viewed migratory fish and animals differently from stationary ones. The right to take fish existed when, and only when, the fish were within or passing through a tribe's particular territory. Indians attempted to "enhance" their fish supply by religious means, but there is no

evidence that those who participated in enhancement activities attained any superior or exclusive interests in the fish for whose arrival they had prayed.

. . .

Ultimately, the State is asserting an ownership interest in hatchery fish. This argument must fail as a matter of law. As the State concedes, the Supreme Court has flatly rejected the notion that a state owns fish swimming within its waters.

> " '[T]o put the claim of the State upon title is,' in Mr. Justice Holmes' words, 'to lean upon a slender reed.' A State does not stand in the same position as the owner of a private game preserve and it is pure fantasy to talk of 'owning' wild fish, birds, or animals. Neither the State nor the Federal Government, any more than a hopeful fisherman or hunter, has title to these creatures until they are reduced to possession by skillful capture." *Douglas v. Seacoast Products, Inc.*, 431 U.S. 265, 284, 97 S.Ct. 1740, 1751, 52 L.Ed.2d 304 (1977) (citations omitted).

. . .

Whatever merit the State's argument might have when applied to fish confined within hatchery facilities, it has no logical application to harvestable fish that have been released from such facilities and are freely swimming alongside naturally-bred fish in the State's rivers, streams, and bays. The State acknowledges that private hatchery owners have no ownership interest in fish released into public waters. . . .

IV

A

From the numerous opinions rendered in Phase I, and the application of the principles enunciated therein to the hatchery issue, flows the resolution of the remaining issue in Phase II—the environmental issue. As previously noted, the only aspect of this issue presently before the Court is the legal question whether the tribes' fishing right includes the right to have treaty fish protected from environmental degradation. . . .

At the outset, the Court holds that implicitly incorporated in the treaties' fishing clause is the right to have the fishery habitat protected from man-made despoliation. Virtually every case construing this fishing clause has recognized it to be the cornerstone of the treaties and has emphasized its overriding importance to the tribes. *See Washington—Phase I, supra,* 443 U.S. at 664-667, 675-681, 99 S.Ct. at 3063-3065, 3069-3072, and cases cited therein. The Indians understood, and were led by Governor Stevens to believe, that the treaties entitled them to continue fishing in perpetuity and that the settlers would not qualify, restrict, or interfere with their right to take fish. *Final Decision I, supra,* 384 F.Supp. at 334, 355-357.

The most fundamental prerequisite to exercising the right to take fish is the existence of fish to be taken. In order for salmon and steelhead trout to survive, specific environmental conditions must be present. A fisheries study prepared jointly by the State and the federal government identifies at least five such conditions: "(1) access to and from the sea, (2) an adequate supply of good-quality water, (3) a sufficient amount of suitable gravel for spawning and egg incubation, (4) an ample supply of food, and (5) sufficient shelter." It is undisputed that "alteration of even one of these essential, finely-balanced requirements will affect the production potential." It is also undisputed that these conditions have been altered and that human activities have seriously degraded the quality of the fishery habitat.

"Over the years, there has been a gradual deterioration and loss of natural fish production habitat in Washington State streams. Although there are many individual factors contributing to this, the general trend toward reduced production habitat is more the result of a combination of activities performed by man— activities which alter and destroy one or more habitat conditions required for successful fish production. Generally, these factors can be categorized under the broad headings of watershed alterations, water storage dams, industrial developments, stream channel alterations, and residential developments.

. . .

A century ago, salmon abounded in the Pacific Northwest. Almost every accessible area, even in the deep interior, nurtured crops of salmon which renewed themselves as they had for millennia. However, in the Twentieth Century the urbanization and intensive settlement of the area, the rapid development of water power, lumbering and irrigation and the pollution of the watersheds reduced the quality and amount of accessible spawning grounds. These activities also reduced the rearing capacity of the streams."

Were this trend to continue, the right to take fish would eventually be reduced to the right to dip one's net into the water . . . and bring it out empty. Such result would render nugatory the nine-year effort in Phase I, sanctioned by this Court, the Ninth Circuit, and the Supreme Court, to enforce the treaties reservation to the tribes of a sufficient quantity of fish to meet their fair needs. The Supreme Court all but resolved the environmental issue when it expressly rejected the State's contention, initially reiterated on this motion, that the treaty right is but an equal opportunity to try to catch fish. Rather, the Court held that the treaty assures the tribes something considerably more tangible than "merely the chance . . . occasionally to dip their nets into the territorial waters." *Washington—Phase I, supra,* 443 U.S. at 679, 99 S.Ct. at 3071.

. . .

The conclusion that the treaty-secured fishing right incorporates an environmental right is consonant with the implied-reservation-of-water doctrine that is often employed in the construction of Indian treaties. In *Winters v. United States,* 207 U.S. 564, 28 S.Ct. 207, 52 L.Ed. 340 (1908), the seminal case in this area, the Supreme Court held that when the treaty creating the Fort Belknap Indian Reservation was signed, the parties impliedly reserved a sufficient quantity of water to irrigate the arid reservation land. Without that water, the purpose of creating the Reservation—to enable the tribe to give up its nomadic existence and sustain itself on a relatively small tract of land—would be incapable of fulfillment. *Id.* at 576, 28 S.Ct. at 211.

. . .

In this case, there can be no doubt that one of the paramount purposes of the treaties in question was to reserve to the tribes the right to continue fishing as an economic and cultural way of life. It is equally beyond doubt that the existence of an environmentally-acceptable habitat is essential to the survival of the fish, without which the expressly-reserved right to take fish would be meaningless and valueless. Thus, it is necessary to recognize an implied environmental right in order to fulfill the purposes of the fishing clause.

. . .

C

The more difficult issues pertaining to the State's duty involve its nature and scope. Several guiding considerations emerge from the numerous cases involving disputes between states and treaty tribes. First, the treaty-secured right to take fish at usual and accustomed places may not be qualified or conditioned by the State. . . . Second, the State may not subordinate the fishing right to any other objectives or purposes it may prefer.

"It [the state] may not force treaty Indians to yield their own protected interests in order to promote the welfare of the state's other citizens." *United States v. State of Washington, supra*, 520 F.2d at 686.

. . . Third, the State may affirmatively regulate treaty fishing solely for the purpose of conserving the resource. . . . It would virtually obliterate these narrowly-drawn limitations on the State's authority were this Court to rule, by denying plaintiffs' pending motion, that the State may now regulate treaty fishing for two purposes: to conserve the resource *or* to destroy it.

. . .

The treaties reserve to the tribes a sufficient quantity of fish to satisfy their moderate living needs, subject to a ceiling of 50 percent of the harvestable run. *Washington—Phase I, supra*, 443 U.S. at 686-687, 99 S.Ct. at 3075. That is the minimal need which gives rise to an implied right to environmental protection of the fish habitat. Therefore, the correlative duty imposed upon the State (as well as the United States and third parties) is to refrain from degrading the fish habitat to an extent that would deprive the tribes of their moderate living needs.

SOURCE: U.S. District Court for the Western District of Washington. *United States of America, et al., Plaintiffs, v. State of Washington et al., Defendants*, 506 F. Supp. 187 (1980).

ANALYSIS

United States of America, et al., Plaintiffs, v. State of Washington et al., Defendants was the culmination of more than a decade of legal conflicts between various Native American groups and Washington. At issue were six separate treaties negotiated by Governor Isaac Stevens between 1854 and 1856 with a number of native groups that essentially split the anadromous fish harvest equally between Native Americans and

U.S. citizens. The exact wording that appeared in the respective treaties at the time was as follows: "The right of taking fish, at all usual and accustomed grounds and stations, is further secured to said Indians, in common with all citizens of the Territory, ..." At the time that the respective treaties were negotiated, Native Americans outnumbered U.S. citizens so the treaty terms were quite advantageous to the new arrivals in the region. By the mid-twentieth century, the situation had reversed. Native peoples comprised only a small fraction of the total population of the state. Although by treaty they still had a right to half of the salmon passing through their territories, the state opted to ignore its responsibilities and allowed nonnative fisherman to harvest more than their share of anadromous fish. In order to stop Washington's inattention to the treaty violations, the United States sued the state on behalf of several native nations to have their fishing rights respected. The United States ultimately won the landmark 1974 case *United States v. Washington*, better known as the "Boldt Decision." Despite the loss, Washington continued to litigate the issues in several cases decided at the state and federal levels. Predictably, the federal government had to revisit Boldt's decision in *United States of America, et al., Plaintiffs, v. State of Washington et al., Defendants.*

In the majority decision of the 1980 case, the federal judges upheld the original Boldt decision. In essence, Governor Isaac had promised the Native Americans he negotiated with that they could fish in their accustomed places as they had since time immemorial. Although Washington asserted that the fish should not be divided equally on native lands because natives comprised a significant minority of the general population, the court determined that Isaac was not concerned about equity due to population at the time he was negotiating because he acquired for nonnative peoples a disproportionate share of the fish. The fact that the demographics had completely changed over time did not negate the original agreement.

Washington also attempted to change the way the share of fish was determined by exempting from the treaty terms fish that had been raised in hatcheries. The state claimed that fish raised in that manner were not considered by the parties in the mid-1850s, thus fell outside of the purview of the respective treaties. Noting that hatchery-raised fish were basically indistinguishable from wild fish and, once released, lived as wild fish, the court determined that they were included in the terms of the treaty. The overwhelming victory by the United States on behalf of the various native nations had a profound relationship between the natives and state officials. Today, native groups are working with the state to manage their waters so that the salmon and other anadromous fish runs are restored to their former glory of the mid-1850s. Some of these native groups are also managing their own fish hatcheries, which benefit not only them but also nonnative fishermen.

FURTHER READING

Deloria, Vine, Jr., et al. 2011. "The Boldt Decision: A Roundtable Discussion." *Journal of Northwest Anthropology* 45, no. 1: 111–122.
Harmon, Alexandra. 1998. *Indians in the Making: Ethnic Relations and Indian Identities Around Puget Sound*. Berkeley: University of California Press.

Harmon, Alexandra, ed. 2008. *The Power of Promises: Rethinking Indian Treaties in the Pacific Northwest*. Seattle: University of Washington Press.

Ulrich, Roberta. 2007. *Empty Nets: Indians, Dams, and the Columbia River*. 2nd ed. Corvallis: Oregon State University Press.

"Provides for the Acquisition of Water and Rights to Assist the Conservation and Recovery of the Pyramid Lake Fishery"

- *Document:* The Truckee-Carson-Pyramid Lake Water Rights Settlement Act, excerpts
- *Date:* November 16, 1990
- *Where:* Pyramid Lake is located approximately 30 miles north of Reno, Nevada. The Act was passed in Washington, DC
- *Significance:* The Act made it a federal responsibility to use the Stampede Reservoir as a fishery to restore the populations of the Pyramid Lake cui-ui and Lahontan cutthroat trout that the Pyramid Lake Paiutes had depended on as a food source and a staple of their economy since time immemorial.

DOCUMENT

Title II: Truckee-Carson-Pyramid Lake Water Settlement—Truckee-Carson-Pyramid Lake Water Rights Settlement Act—Confirms the interstate allocation of waters of the Carson River and its tributaries pursuant to a specified court decree.

States that such confirmed allocations shall not be construed as precluding, foreclosing, or limiting the assertion of any additional right to the waters of the River or its tributaries which were in existence under applicable law as of January 1, 1989, but are not recognized in such court decree. Prohibits any increase in diversions from the Carson River or its tributaries beyond those in existence on December 31, 1992.

. . .

Confirms the right to water use on the Pyramid Lake Indian Reservation with respect to certain claims of the Orr Ditch decree.

. . .

Directs the Secretary to implement the Preliminary Settlement Agreement as modified by the Ratification Agreement, and to implement the Operating Agreement, including entering into contracts for the use of space in Truckee River reservoirs to store and exchange water, subject to certain preconditions.

States that firm and non-firm municipal and industrial credit water, and a certain amount of fishery credit water in Stampede Reservoir available under worse than critical drought conditions, shall be used only to supply municipal and industrial needs when drought conditions or emergency or repair conditions exist, or as required to be converted to fishery credit water.

Requires that all of the fishery credit water established shall be used by the United States solely for the benefit of the Pyramid Lake fishery, subject to the terms and conditions of the Preliminary Settlement Agreement as modified by the Ratification Agreement.

. . .

Requires that payments received by the Secretary for such uses be credited annually first to pay the operation and maintenance costs of Stampede Reservoir, then covered into the Lahontan Valley and Pyramid Lake Fish and Wildlife Fund created by this Title, with excessive funds credited to the Reclamation Fund.

Authorizes the Secretary to enter into an interim agreement with the Sierra Pacific Power Company and Pyramid Lake Tribe to store water owned by the Company in Stampede Reservoir except that: (1) the amount of such Storage shall not exceed a specified acre-feet on September 1 of any year; and (2) such agreement shall be superseded by the Preliminary Settlement as modified by the Ratification Agreement and the Operating Agreement, upon the entry into effect of those agreements.

. . .

Directs the Secretary to revise, update, and implement plans for the conservation and recovery of the cui-ui and Lahontan cutthroat trout, pursuant to the Endangered Species Act, as amended.

Directs the Secretary of the Army to incorporate into its ongoing reconnaissance level study of the Truckee River a study of the rehabilitation of the lower Truckee River to Pyramid Lake, for the benefit of the Pyramid Lake fishery. Authorizes appropriations. Provides for the acquisition of water and rights to assist the conservation and recovery of the Pyramid Lake fishery.

Requires the Secretary to use the United States' right to store water in Stampede Reservoir and Prosser Creek Reservoir for the benefit of the Pyramid Lake fishery, subject to certain agreements.

Establishes the Pyramid Lake Paiute Fisheries Fund, and the Pyramid Lake Paiute Economic Development Fund in the Treasury.

Authorizes appropriations to the Pyramid Lake Paiute Fisheries Fund. Provides that interest from such Fund shall be used by the Pyramid Lake Tribe for operation and maintenance of fishery facilities at Pyramid Lake (excluding Marble Bluff Dam and Fishway), and for conservation of the Pyramid Lake fishery.

Prohibits the Secretaries from disbursing any monies from the Fund unless certain specified conditions are met, including release by the Pyramid Lake Tribe of specified claims against the United States.

Authorizes appropriations for FY 1993 through 1997 to the Pyramid Lake Paiute Economic Development Fund for tribal economic development.

Gives the Tribe complete discretion to invest and manage the Fund, except that no portion of the principal shall be used to develop, operate, or finance any form of gaming or gambling, except as provided by the Indian Gaming Regulatory Act.

Prohibits the Secretaries from disbursing any monies to the Tribe unless it adopts and submits an economic development plan to the Secretary.

Disallows distribution of such Fund to members of the Pyramid Lake Tribe on a per capita basis.

. . .

Grants the Pyramid Lake Tribe the sole and exclusive authority to establish rules and regulations for hunting, fishing, boating, and all forms of recreation on all Reservation lands except fee-patented land. Consents to negotiation and execution of an agreement between Nevada and the Tribe for enforcement of such rules and regulations, including fee-patented lands.

Declares that, between August 26, 1935, and enactment of this Title, there was no construction within the meaning of the Federal Power Act at the four run-of-river hydroelectric project works on the Truckee River owned by Sierra Pacific Power Company. States that development of additional generating capacity shall also not be construction under such Act.

Authorizes the Secretary to exchange surveyed public land in Nevada for rights and interests in lands within the Reservation.

Authorizes appropriations.

SOURCE: Title II of P.L. 101-618, signed into law on November 9, 1990; 104 Stat. 3289.

ANALYSIS

The path to the Truckee-Carson-Pyramid Lake Water Rights Settlement Act, which was Title II of the Fallon Paiute Shoshone Indian Tribes Water Rights Settlement Act of 1990, had its origin with the passage of the Reclamation Act of 1902, better known as the Newlands Act. The first project undertaken under the Reclamation Act was the construction of Derby Dam, on the Truckee River in Nevada. Constructed by the U.S. Reclamation Service between 1902 and 1905, Derby Dam diverted the river's waters through a canal to the Carson River, where it was collected for use in irrigating the arid lands in the region.

The damming of the Truckee River reduced the flow of water from the river to Pyramid Lake by approximately half. Over time, this led the lake level to drop significantly, which severely impacted the Pyramid Lake Paiutes. The decline in the water level, combined with the lack of access to their spawning grounds due to Derby Dam, resulted in a drastic drop in the populations of Pyramid Lake cui-ui and Lahontan cutthroat trout, two species that the Pyramid Lake Paiutes depended on for sustenance. In response to the needs of the Paiutes, the Reclamation Service constructed fish ladders around Derby Dam, but they failed to stem the population decline.

For decades, the Pyramid Lake Paiutes actively sought a measure to reduce, if not completely stop, the diversions from the Truckee River so that Pyramid Lake could be restored to its former glory. In 1973, it appeared that such a solution had been attained through the U.S. District Court decision in *Pyramid Lake Paiute Tribe v. Morton*. Unfortunately, while the amount of water diverted from the Truckee River was reduced, the heightened flow increased the transfer of toxins originating from agricultural operations upriver to Pyramid Lake.

An opportunity to address the state of Pyramid Lake emerged when California and Nevada in 1971 agreed on the apportionment of waters emanating from Lake Tahoe and the Carson, Truckee, and Walker River Basins. The agreement between the states ignored the needs of the region's native peoples, which led Congress to refuse to ratify the agreement. During this period, Congress did fund two projects to help the Pyramid Lake Paiutes. The Marble Bluff Dam was built approximately 3.5 miles upriver of Pyramid Lake to stem the flow of silt downriver. Also constructed was the Pyramid Lake Fishway, which helped the lake's fish travel upriver to spawn. Although those measures represented progress, much more was required to meet the long-term needs of the affected Paiutes. Congress thus determined that the solution was not waiting for California and Nevada to negotiate an agreement; instead, the federal government should craft a solution that was fair to all. The result was the Truckee-Carson-Pyramid Lake Water Rights Settlement Act.

In the act, the waters from Lake Tahoe and the Carson and Truckee River Basins were apportioned between Nevada and California. The federal government also addressed the needs of the Pyramid Lake Paiutes by promising to revive the ecosystems in and around Pyramid Lake as well as those in the neighboring Lahontan Valley wetlands. As part of the settlement, the federal government allocated $65 million to rebuild the local fish populations. The effort included using Stampede Reservoir as a fishery to propagate the Pyramid Lake cui-ui and Lahontan cutthroat trout populations. Another $43 million was provided to the Pyramid Lake Paiutes to better protect their land and water holdings for the future.

The efforts undertaken to restore the respective fish populations have proven quite successful. Part of the success can be attributed not only to the Pyramid Lake Fishway but also to the Marble Bluff Fish Passage Facility, part of the Marble Bluff Dam complex, which aid fish in their spawning efforts. The Lahontan cutthroat trout population has grown substantially since the settlement was put into place in 1990. Although the number of Pyramid Lake cui-ui has also increased significantly, the species is on the endangered species list.

FURTHER READING

Fixico, Donald L. 1998. *The Invasion of Indian Country in the Twentieth Century: American Capitalism and Tribal Natural Resources*. Niwot: University Press of Colorado.

Pisani, Donald J. 2002. *Water and American Government: The Reclamation Bureau, National Water Policy, and the West, 1902–1935*. Berkeley: University of California Press.

Seney, Donald B. 2002. "The Changing Political Fortunes of the Truckee Carson Irrigation District." *Agricultural History* 76, no. 2: 220–231.

"The Restoration of the Elwha River Ecosystem and the Native Anadromous Fisheries"

- *Document:* The Elwha River Ecosystem and Fisheries Restoration Act, excerpts
- *Date:* October 24, 1992
- *Where:* Olympic Peninsula, Washington
- *Significance:* The Act resulted in the largest dams ever removed from a waterway within the United States.

DOCUMENT

An Act to Restore Olympic National Park and the Elwha River Ecosystem and Fisheries
In the State of Washington.
Be it enacted by the Senate and House of Representatives of the United States of America in Congress assembled,

SECTION 1. SHORT TITLE.

This Act may be referred to as the "Elwha River Ecosystem and Fisheries Restoration Act."

SEC. 2. DEFINITIONS.

. . .

SEC. 3. ACQUISITION OF PROJECTS.

(a) Effective sixty days after submission to the Congress of the report referred to in section 3(c), the Secretary is authorized to acquire the Elwha and Glines Canyon

Projects, and all rights of the owner and local industrial consumer therein, subject to the appropriation of funds therefor: *Provided*, That the Secretary shall not acquire the projects unless he has determined pursuant to subsection (c) that removal of the Project dams is necessary for the full restoration of the Elwha River ecosystem and native anadromous fisheries and that funds for that purpose will be available for such removal within two years *after* acquisition.

(b) The consideration for acquisition of the Projects shall be $29.5 million and no more, to be paid by the Secretary to the owner and local industrial consumer at the time of acquisition, and shall be conditioned on a release of liability providing that all obligations and liabilities of the owner and the local industrial consumer to the United States arising from the Projects, based upon ownership, license, permit, contract, or other authority, including, but not limited to, project removal and any ecosystem, fish and wildlife mitigation or restoration obligations, shall, from the moment of title transfer, be deemed to have been satisfied: *Provided*, That the United States may not assume or satisfy any liability, if any, of the owner or local industrial consumer to any federally recognized Indian Tribe nor shall such liability to the Tribe, if any, be deemed satisfied without the consent of such Tribe.

(c) The Secretary shall prepare a report on the acquisition of the Projects and his plans for the full restoration of the Elwha River ecosystem and the native anadromous fisheries and submit such report on or before January 31, 1994, to the Appropriations Committees of the United States Senate and the United States House of Representatives, as well as to the Committee on Energy and Natural Resources of the Senate and the Committees on Energy and Commerce, Interior and Insular Affairs, and Merchant Marine and Fisheries of the United States House of Representatives. The report shall contain, without limitation:

(1) The precise terms of acquisition of the Projects, with an analysis of the costs, in addition to the consideration set out in section 3(b), and potential liabilities and benefits, if any, to the Federal Government resulting from the acquisition and all other actions authorized under this Act;

(2) Alternatives, in lieu of dam removal, for the restoration of the Elwha River ecosystem and the native anadromous fisheries and wildlife of the Elwha River Basin, consistent with the management plan of the Park, the rights of any Indian tribe secured by treaty or other Federal law, and applicable State law. The report shall include feasibility studies for each alternative considered and a definite plan for removal. Such definite plan shall include the timetable after conveyance for removal of the dams and the plans for removal and disposal of sediment, debris, and other materials consistent with all applicable environmental laws and a detailed explanation of all costs of removal. In conducting the feasibility studies and in the preparation of the definite plan, the Secretary is authorized to use the services of any Federal agency on a reimbursable basis and the heads of all Federal agencies are authorized to provide such technical and other assistance as the Secretary may request. For each alternative considered, the Secretary shall estimate total costs, environmental risks and benefits, the potential for full restoration of the Elwha River ecosystem and native anadromous fisheries, and the effect on natural and historic resources (together with any comments made by the Advisory Council on Historic Preservation for any properties which are listed, or eligible for listing, on the National Register of Historic Places).

(3) Specific proposals for management of all lands or interests therein acquired pursuant to this Act which are located outside the exterior boundaries of the Olympic National Park. The Secretary shall specifically address the suitability of such lands, or portions thereof, for addition to the National Wildlife Refuge System; National Park System; transfer to the Lower Elwha Klallam Tribe in trust for tribal housing, cultural, or economic development purposes in accordance with a plan developed by the Lower Elwha Klallam Tribe in consultation with the Secretary; and development and use by the State. Upon acquisition, all lands and interests therein within the exterior boundaries of the Park shall be managed pursuant to authorities otherwise applicable to the Park. For the purposes of protecting the Federal investment in restoration, that portion of the river outside the Park on which the Federal Government will acquire both banks shall, upon such acquisition, be managed in accordance with the declared policy of section 1(b) of Public Law 90-542, except that modifications necessary to restore, protect, and enhance fish resources and to protect the existing quality of water supplied from the river are hereby authorized.

(4) Specific proposals and any Federal funding and the availability of that funding that may be necessary to protect the existing quality and availability of water from the Elwha River for municipal and industrial use from possible adverse impacts of dam removal.

(5) Identification of any non-Federal parties or entities, excluding Federally recognized Indian tribes, which would directly benefit from the commercial, recreational, and ecological values that would be enhanced by the restoration of the Elwha River ecosystem and fisheries, if the Secretary believes that such parties or entities should assume some portion of the cost involved in the restoration, together with the specific cost-share provisions which the Secretory deems necessary and reasonable.

(d) In preparing his report, the Secretary shall consult with appropriate State and local officials, affected Indian tribes, the Commission, the Environmental Protection Agency, the Secretary of Energy, the Administrator, the Pacific Northwest Power Planning Council, the Secretary of Commerce, and of the Advisory Council on Historic Preservation, as well as interested members of the public. In addition, the Secretary shall afford an opportunity for public comment on the report prior to its submission to the Congress.

(e) Upon the appropriation of the sum provided for in section 3(b) for the acquisition of the Projects and the determination that dam removal is necessary, the owner and local industrial consumer shall convey to the United States, through the Secretary, title to the Projects, including all property and all other rights and interests. Upon such conveyance and payment of the consideration as provided in section 3(b), and without further action by the United States, title shall transfer and vest in the United States, the owner *and* local industrial consumer shall be released from any further liability to the United States, as provided in section 3(b), and the acquisition from the owner and local industrial consumer shall be deemed to be completed.

SEC. 4. ECOSYSTEM AND FISHERIES RESTORATION.

(a) Effective sixty days after submission of the report referred to in section 3(c) and following the conveyance in section 3(e), the Secretary is authorized and directed, subject to the appropriation of funds therefore, to take such actions as are necessary to implement—

(1) the definite plan referred to in section 3(cX2) for the removal of the dams and full restoration of the Elwha River ecosystem and native anadromous fisheries;

(2) management of lands acquired pursuant to this Act which are located outside the exterior boundaries of the Park; and

(3) protection of the existing quality and availability of water from the Elwha River for municipal and industrial uses from possible adverse impacts of dam removal.

(b) The definite plan referred to section 3(cX2) must include all actions reasonably necessary to maintain and protect existing water quality for the City of Port Angeles, Dry Creek Water Association, and the industrial users of Elwha River water against adverse impacts of dam removal. The cost of such actions, which may include as determined by the Secretary, if reasonably necessary, design, construction, operation and maintenance of water treatment or related facilities, shall be borne by the Secretary. Funds may not be appropriated for removal of the dams, unless, at the same time, funds are appropriated for actions necessary to protect existing water quality.

(c) Nothing in this section shall be construed as an entitlement for which a claim against the United States may be made under the Tucker Act.

SOURCE: The Elwha River Ecosystem and Fisheries Restoration Act, Public Law 102-495 (1992).

ANALYSIS

For millennia, the Elwha River's prodigious anadromous fish populations had provided for the sustenance needs of the Lower Elwha Klallam Tribe. The fish populations on which the natives depended were devastated in 1914 with the construction of the Elwha Dam, which blocked the ability of the fish to reach the waterways they used to spawn. The problem was compounded with the building of the Glines Canyon Dam in 1927. The resulting drop in the fish populations hurt the Lower Elwha Klallam economically because they were guaranteed by treaty half of the river's fish harvest. Culturally, the reservoirs created by the dams inundated both places where the natives had fished for centuries and numerous sacred locales.

At the time the dams were constructed, the Lower Elwha Klallam had no ability to challenge their construction because they were not viewed as American citizens. By the late 1970s, the legal landscape had changed. Both at the state and the federal level, Native Americans were winning landmark legal cases enforcing their treaty rights to fish. The Lower Elwha Klallam Tribe, joined by numerous environmental groups, began campaigning not only to have their fishing rights honored but also to have their fishery rebuilt to its former levels. Decades of discord and negotiation ultimately resulted in the passage of the "Elwha River Ecosystem and Fisheries Restoration Act of 1992." In that legislation, the U.S. Congress pledged to explore how the fishery could be rebuilt for the benefit of all. Surprisingly, the legislation even allowed for the possibility that the two dams on the river could be removed if that was deemed the only way to restore the Elwha River to its past glory. After years of study, it was determined in 1995 that dam removal was the necessary course to follow.

After years of planning, work on the Elwha River Restoration Project finally commenced in 2011. The project was notable because it resulted in the largest dams to be voluntarily removed in the history of the United States. The Elwha Dam was completely dismantled during 2013. With the destruction of the final part of the Glines Canyon Dam on August 26, 2013, the Elwha was once again a free-flowing river. Since 2011, when the dismantling of the dams commenced, the anadromous fish populations in the river have been recovering.

FURTHER READING

Brenkman, S. J., et al. 2012. "A Riverscape Perspective of Pacific Salmonids and Aquatic Habitats Prior to Large-Scale Dam Removal in the Elwha River, Washington, USA." *Fisheries Management & Ecology* 19, no. 1: 36–53.

Crane, Jeff. 2011. *Finding the River: An Environmental History of the Elwha*. Corvallis: Oregon State University Press.

Lowry, William R. 2003. *Dam Politics: Restoring America's Rivers*. Washington, DC: Georgetown University Press.

Nicole, Wendee. 2012. "Lessons of the Elwha River: Managing Health Hazards During Dam Removal." *Environmental Health Perspectives* 120, no. 11: A430–A435.

Stokes, Dale. 2014. *The Fish in the Forest: Salmon and the Web of Life*. Berkeley: University of California Press.

Part II

WATERS OF THE WEST

3

WATERS OF THE WEST

"The Arable Lands Are Much Greater Than the Irrigable"

- **Document:** *Report on the Lands of the Arid Region of the United States, with a More Detailed Account of the Lands of Utah. With Maps.* 2nd ed., excerpt from Chapter 5
- **Date:** 1879
- **Where:** The Rocky Mountains and lands west of the 100th meridian
- **Significance:** John Wesley Powell's best known publication encouraged many settlers to move to the West.

DOCUMENT

CERTAIN IMPORTANT QUESTIONS RELATING TO IRRIGABLE LANDS.

THE UNIT OF WATER USED IN IRRIGATION.

The unit of water employed in mining as well as manufacturing enterprises in the west is usually the inch, meaning, thereby the amount of water which will flow through an orifice one inch square. But in practice this quantity is very indefinite, due to the "head" or amount of pressure from above. In some districts this latter is taken at six inches. Another source of uncertainty exists in the fact that increase in the size of the orifice and increase in the amount of flow do not progress in the same ratio. An orifice of one square inch will not admit of a discharge one-tenth as great as an orifice of ten square inches. An inch of water, therefore, is variable with the size of the stream as well as with the head or pressure. For these reasons it seemed better to take a more definite quantity of water, and for this purpose the *second-foot* has been adopted. By its use the volume of a stream will be given by stating the number of cubic feet which the stream will deliver per second.

THE QUANTITATIVE VALUE OF WATER IN IRRIGATION.

In general, throughout the Arid Region the extent of the irrigable land is limited by the water supply; the arable lands are much greater than the irrigable. Hence it becomes necessary, in determining the amount of irrigable lands with reasonably approximate accuracy, to determine the value of water in irrigation; that is, the amount of land which a given amount of water will serve.

All questions of concrete or applied science are more or less complex by reason of the multifarious conditions found in nature, and this is eminently true of the problem we are now to solve, namely, how much water must an acre of land receive by irrigation to render agriculture, thereon most successful; or, how much land will a given amount of water adequately supply. This will be affected by the following general conditions, namely, the amount of water that will be furnished by rainfall, for if there is rainfall in the season of growing crops, irrigation is necessary only to supply the deficiency; second, the character of the soil and subsoil.

If the conditions of soil are unfavorable, the water supply may be speedily evaporated on the one hand, or quickly lost by subterranean drainage on the other; but if there be a soil permitting the proper permeation of water downward and upward, and an impervious subsoil, the amount furnished by artificial irrigation will be held in such a manner as to serve the soil bearing crops to the greatest extent; and, lastly, there is a great difference in the amount of water needed for different crops, some requiring less, others more.

Under these heads come the general complicating conditions. In the mountainous country the areal distribution of rainfall is preeminently variable, as the currents of air which carry the water are deflected in various ways by diverse topographic inequalities. The rainfall is also exceedingly irregular, varying from year to year, and again from season to season.

But in all these varying conditions of time and space there is one fact which must control our conclusions in considering most of the lands of the Arid Region, namely: any district of country which we may be studying is liable for many seasons in a long series to be without rainfall, when the whole supply must be received from irrigation. Safety in agricultural operations will be secured by neglecting the rainfall and considering only the supply of water to be furnished by artificial methods; the less favorable seasons must be considered; in the more favorable there will be a surplus. In general, this statement applies throughout the Arid Region, but there are some limited localities where a small amount of rainfall in the season of growing crops seems to be constant from year to year. In such districts irrigation will only be used to supply deficiencies.

The complicating conditions arising from soil and subsoil are many. Experience has already shown that there are occasional conditions of soil and subsoil so favorable that the water may be supplied before the growing season, and the subsoil will hold it for weeks, or even months, and gradually yield the moisture to the overlying soil by slow upward percolation or capillary attraction during the season when growing crops require its fertilizing effect. When such conditions of soil and subsoil obtain, the construction of reservoirs is unnecessary, and the whole annual supply of the streams may be utilized. On the other hand, there are extremely pervious soils underlaid by sands and gravels, which speedily carry away the water by a natural under drainage. Here a maximum supply by irrigation is necessary, as the soils must be kept moist by frequent flowing. Under such conditions the amount of water to be supplied is many fold greater than under the conditions previously mentioned, and between these extremes almost infinite variety prevails.

SOURCE: Powell, J. W. 1879. *Report on the Lands of the Arid Region of the United States, with a More Detailed Account of the Lands of Utah. With Maps.* http://pubs.usgs.gov/unnumbered/70039240/report.pdf (accessed August 20, 2014).

ANALYSIS

John Wesley Powell was a self-trained naturalist with particular interests in botany, zoology, and geology. During the 1850s, he began exploring the environs of the Illinois, Mississippi, and Ohio rivers. His travels were interrupted by the Civil War, where he served in the Union army.

After the war concluded, Powell began exploring Colorado's Rocky Mountain region. On one of his trips in 1869, Powell and nine companions traveled approximately 900 miles down the Green and Colorado rivers. In 1875, Powell published his account of the trip in *Explorations of the Colorado River of the West and Its Tributaries*. His most influential work was submitted to the U.S. Congress in 1878, namely the *Report on the Lands of the Arid Region of the United States*. Supporters of the expansion of the United States, especially the political and financial backers of the railroad companies, used the report to tout the benefits of using their railroads to move people to the West. Ignored was the content of the report, in which Powell warned about settling west of the 100th meridian due to the region's dearth of waterways. Also disregarded were his suggestions concerning needed changes to the country's existing homestead laws. He proposed that homesteaders be allowed to settle only where they had ready access to irrigable farmland. His concerns were suppressed because they would have led settlers to stay in the East, which was not the desire of the railroad companies or their influential supporters in Congress.

FURTHER READING

Fowler, Don D., ed. 2012. *Cleaving an Unknown World: The Powell Expeditions and the Scientific Exploration of the Colorado Plateau.* Salt Lake City, UT: University of Utah Press.

Powell, John Wesley. 2004. *The Arid Lands.* Wallace Stegner, ed. Lincoln, NE: University of Nebraska Press.

Stegner, Wallace. 1954. *Beyond the Hundredth Meridian: John Wesley Powell and the Second Opening of the West.* New York: Penguin.

Worster, Donald. 2001. *A River Running West: The Life of John Wesley Powell.* New York: Oxford University Press.

"To Aid the Public Land States in the Reclamation of the Desert Lands Therein"

- *Document:* The Federal Desert Land Act of 1894, also known as the Carey Land Act
- *Date:* August 18, 1894
- *Where:* Washington, DC
- *Significance:* The act offered the transfer of public lands owned by the United States to states in the West under the condition that the lands be irrigated.

DOCUMENT

Sec. 4. That to aid the public land States in the reclamation of the desert lands therein, and the settlement, cultivation and sale thereof in small tracts to actual settlers, the Secretary of the Interior with the approval of the President, be, and hereby is, authorized and empowered, upon proper application of the State to contract and agree, from time to time, with each of the States in which there may be situated desert lands as defined by the Act entitled "An Act to provide for the sale of desert land in certain States and Territories," approved March third, eighteen hundred and seventy-seven, and the Act amendatory thereof, approved March third, eighteen hundred and ninety-one, binding the United States to donate, grant and patent to the State free of cost for survey or price such desert lands, not exceeding one million acres in each state, as the State may cause to be irrigated, reclaimed, occupied, and not less than twenty acres of each one hundred and sixty-acre tract cultivated by actual settlers, within ten years next after the passage of this Act, as thoroughly as is required of citizens who may enter under said desert land law.

Before the application of any State is allowed or any contract or agreement is executed or any segregation of any of the land from the public domain is ordered by the Secretary of the Interior, the State shall file a map of the said land proposed to be irrigated which shall exhibit a plan showing the mode of the contemplated irrigation and which plan shall be sufficient to thoroughly irrigate and reclaim said land and prepare it to raise ordinary agricultural crops and shall also show the source of the water to be used for irrigation and reclamation, and the Secretary of the Interior may make necessary regulations for the reservation of the lands applied for by the States to date from the date of the filing of the map and plan of irrigation, but such reservation shall be of no force whatever if such map and plan of irrigation shall not be approved. That any State contracting under this section is hereby authorized to make all necessary contracts to cause the said lands to be reclaimed, and to induce their settlement and cultivation in accordance with and subject to the provisions of this section; but the State shall not be authorized to lease any of said lands or to use or dispose of the same in any way whatever, except to secure their reclamation, cultivation and settlement.

As fast as any State may furnish satisfactory proof according to such rules and regulations as may be prescribed by the Secretary of the Interior, that any of said lands are irrigated, reclaimed and occupied by actual settlers, patents shall be issued to the State or its assigns for said lands to be reclaimed and settled: *Provided*, That said States shall not sell or dispose of more than one hundred and sixty acres of said lands to any one person, and any surplus of money derived by any State from the sale of said lands in excess of the cost of their reclamation, shall be held as a trust fund for and be applied to the reclamation of other desert lands in such State. That to enable the Secretary of the Interior to examine any of the lands that may be selected under the provisions of this section, there is hereby appropriated out of the moneys in the Treasury, not otherwise appropriated, one thousand dollars.

Approved, August 18, 1894.

SOURCE: U.S. Congress. 1895. *The Statutes at Large of the United States of America, from August 1893, to March, 1895, and Recent Treaties, Conventions, and Executive Proclamations.* Vol XXVIII. Washington: Government Printing Office. http://www.loc.gov/law/help/statutes-at-large/53rd-congress/c53.pdf (accessed November 5, 2014).

ANALYSIS

The Federal Desert Land Act of 1894 (FDLA), also known as the Carey Land Act, was section 4 of the Civil Appropriations Bill of 1894. It was proposed by U.S. Senator Joseph M. Carey of Wyoming to encourage the settlement of sparsely populated western states by improving the region's semi-arid lands through irrigation. It was viewed as the replacement for the Desert Land Act of 1877, which was repealed in 1891. The FDLA offered a maximum of 1 million acres of land held in the public domain to western states if they reclaimed those lands using irrigation, thus making it suitable for agriculture. The states were not allowed to keep the land, but instead were to sell the land in 160-acre tracts to settlers at a cost of 50 cents an acre. At the time of the initial transaction, settlers had to agree to pay an annual fee for the water the state was providing to their tract of land. Furthermore, under the terms of the act, the settlers were required to irrigate 1/16th of their land within one year of the time that the state made water available to them. By the end of the second year, another 1/16th of the land had to be irrigated. During the third year, assuming the requirements for the previous years had been met and all fees were paid, the settlers had to be living on their homestead and cultivating crops in order to receive a deed to their property.

Although many of the FDLAs are in force today, the law was a great disappointment to its proponents as it failed to stimulate mass migration to the West's semi-arid expanses. This was due to the inability of the states to meet the terms set forth in the legislation for the land. Only Colorado, Idaho, Utah, and Wyoming received land through the FDLA. Of those states, only Idaho and Wyoming really benefitted from its provisions. The FDLA proved extremely valuable in demonstrating that the states were unable on their own to construct the water infrastructure required to make semi-arid and arid lands suitable for human habitation. Beginning with the Reclamation Act of 1902, better known as the Newlands Act, the federal government took responsibility for constructing the necessary infrastructure.

FURTHER READING

Pisani, Donald J. 1992. *To Reclaim a Divided West: Water, Law, and Public Policy, 1848–1902.* Albuquerque: University of New Mexico Press.

Pisani, Donald J. 2002. *Water and the American Government: The Reclamation Bureau, National Water Policy, and the West, 1902–1935.* Berkeley: University of California Press.

Worster, Donald. 1985. *Rivers of Empire: Water, Aridity, and the Growth of the American West.* New York: Oxford University Press.

"The Construction and Maintenance of Irrigation Works for the Storage, Diversion, and Development of Waters for the Reclamation of Arid and Semiarid Lands"

- *Document:* The Reclamation Act of 1902
- *Date:* June 17, 1902
- *Where:* Washington, DC
- *Significance:* The act created the U.S. Reclamation Service, later renamed the U.S. Bureau of Reclamation.

DOCUMENT

CHAP. 1093.—An Act Appropriating the receipts from the sale and disposal of public lands in certain States and Territories to the construction of irrigation works for the reclamation of arid lands.

Be it enacted by the Senate and House of Representatives of the United States of America in Congress assembled, That all moneys received from the sale and disposal of public lands in Arizona, California, Colorado, Idaho, Kansas, Montana, Nebraska, Nevada, New Mexico, North Dakota, Oklahoma, Oregon, South Dakota, Utah, Washington, and Wyoming, beginning with the fiscal year ending June thirtieth, nineteen hundred and one, including the surplus of fees and commissions in excess of allowances to registers and receivers, and excepting the five per centum of the proceeds of the sales of public lands in the above States set aside by law for educational and other purposes, shall be, and the same are hereby, reserved set aside, and appropriated as a special fund in the Treasury to be known as the "reclamation fund," to be used in the examination and survey for and the construction and maintenance of irrigation works for the storage, diversion, and development of waters for the reclamation of arid and semiarid lands in the said States and Territories, and for the payment of all other expenditures provided for in this Act: Provided, That in case the receipts from the sale and disposal of public lands other than those realized from the sale and disposal of lands referred to in this section are insufficient to meet the requirements for the support of agricultural colleges in the several States and Territories, under the Act of August thirtieth, eighteen hundred and ninety, entitled "An Act to apply a portion of the proceeds of the public lands to the more complete endowment and support of the colleges for the benefit of agriculture and the mechanic arts, established under the provisions of an Act of Congress approved July second, eighteen hundred and sixty-two," the deficiency, if any, in the sum necessary for the support of the said colleges shall be provided for from any moneys in the Treasury not otherwise appropriated.

SEC. 2. That the Secretary of the Interior is hereby authorized and directed to make examinations and surveys for, and to locate and construct, as herein provided, irrigation works for the storage, diversion, and development of waters, including artesian wells, and to report to Congress at the beginning of each regular session as to the results of such examinations and surveys, giving estimates of cost of all contemplated works, the quantity and location of the lands which can be irrigated therefrom, and all facts relative to the practicability of each irrigation project; also the cost of works in process of construction as well as of those which have been completed.

SEC. 3. That the Secretary of the Interior shall, before giving the public notice provided for in section four of this Act, withdraw from public entry the lands required for any irrigation works contemplated under the provisions of this Act, and shall restore to public entry any of the lands so withdrawn when, in his judgment, such lands are not required for the purposes of this Act; and the Secretary of the Interior is hereby authorized, at or immediately prior to the time of beginning the surveys for any contemplated irrigation works, to withdraw from entry, except under the homestead laws, any public lands believed to be susceptible of irrigation from said works: Provided, That all lands entered and entries made under the homestead laws within areas so withdrawn during such withdrawal shall be subject to all the provisions, limitations, charges, terms, and conditions of this Act; that said surveys shall be prosecuted diligently to completion, and upon the completion thereof, and of the necessary maps, plans, and estimates of cost, the Secretary of interior shall determine whether or not said project is practicable and advisable, and if determined to be impracticable or unadvisable he shall thereupon restore said lands to entry; that public lands which it is proposed to irrigate by means of any contemplated works shall be subject to entry only under the provisions of the homestead laws in tracts of not less than forty nor more than one hundred and sixty acres, and shall be subject to the limitations, charges, terms, and conditions herein provided: Provided, That the commutation provisions of the homestead laws shall not apply to entries made under this Act.

SEC 4. That upon the determination by the Secretary of the Interior that any irrigation project is practicable, he may cause to be let contracts for the construction of the same, in such portions or sections are available in the reclamation fund, and irrigable under such project, and limit of area per entry which limit shall represent the acreage which, in the opinion of the Secretary, may be reasonably required for the support of a family upon the lands in question; also of the charges which shall be made per acre upon the said entries, and upon lands in private ownership which may be irrigated by the waters of the said irrigation project, and the number of annual installments, not exceeding ten, in which such charges shall be paid and the time when such payments shall commence. The said charges shall be determined with a view of returning to the reclamation fund the estimated cost of construction of the project, and shall be apportioned equitably: Provided, That in all construction work eight hours shall constitute a day's work, and no Mongolian labor shall be employed thereon.

SEC 5. That the entryman upon lands to be irrigated by such works shall, in addition to compliance with the homestead laws, reclaim at least one-half of the total irrigable area of his entry for agricultural purposes, and before receiving patent for the lands covered by his entry shall pay to the Government the charges apportioned against such tract, as provided in section four. No right to the use of water for land in private ownership shall be sold for a tract exceeding one hundred and sixty acres to any one landowner, and no such sale shall be made to any landowner unless he be an actual bona fide resident on such land, or occupant thereof residing in the neighborhood of said land, and no such right shall permanently attach until all payments therefor are made. The annual installments shall be paid to the receiver of the local land office of the district in which the land is situated, and a failure to make any two payments when due shall render the entry subject to cancellation, with the forfeiture of all rights under this Act, as well as of any moneys already paid thereon. All moneys received from the above sources shall be paid into the reclamation fund. Registers and receivers shall be allowed the usual commissions on all moneys paid for lands entered under this Act.

SEC 6. That the Secretary of the Interior is hereby authorized and directed to use the reclamation fund for the operation and maintenance of all reservoirs and irrigation works constructed under the provisions of this Act: Provided, That when the payments required by this Act are made for the major portion of the lands irrigated from the waters of any of the works herein provided for, then the management and operation of such irrigation works shall pass to the owners of the lands irrigated thereby, to be maintained at their expense under such form of organization and under such rules and regulations as may be acceptable to the Secretary of the Interior: Provided, That the title to and the management and operation of the reservoirs and the the works necessary for their protection and operation shall remain in the Government until otherwise provided by Congress.

SEC 7. That where in carrying out the provisions of this Act it becomes necessary to acquire any rights or property, the Secretary of the Interior is hereby authorized to acquire the same for the United States by purchase or by condemnation under judicial process, and to pay from the reclamation fund the sums which may be needed for that purpose, and it shall be the duty of the Attorney-General of the United States upon every application of the Secretary of the Interior, under this Act, to cause proceedings to be commenced for condemnation within thirty days from the receipt of the application at the Department of Justice.

SEC 8. That nothing in this Act shall be construed as affecting or intended to affect or to in any way interfere with the laws of any State or Territory relating to the control, appropriation, use, or distribution of water used in irrigation, or any vested right acquired thereunder, and the Secretary of the Interior, in carrying out the provisions of this Act, shall proceed in conformity with such laws, and nothing herein shall in any way affect any right of any State or of the Federal Government or of any landowner, appropriator, or user of water in, to, or from any interstate stream or the waters thereof: Provided, That the right of the use of water acquired under the provisions of this Act shall be appurtenant to the land irrigated, and beneficial use shall be the basis, the measure, and the limit of the right.

SEC 9. That it is hereby declared to be the duty of the Secretary of the Interior in carrying out the provisions of this Act, so far as the same may be practicable and subject to the existence of feasible irrigation projects, to expend the major portion of the funds arising from the sale of public lands within each State and Territory hereinbefore named for the benefit of arid and semiarid lands within the limits of such State or Territory: Provided, That the Secretary may temporarily use such portion of said funds for the benefit of arid or semiarid lands in any particular State or Territory herein before named as he may deem advisable, but when so used the excess shall be restored to the fund as soon as practicable, to the end that ultimately, and in any event, within each ten-year period after the passage of this Act, the expenditures for The benefit of the said States and Territories shall be equalized according to the proportions and subject to the conditions as to practicability and feasibility aforesaid.

SEC 10. That the Secretary of the Interior is hereby authorized to perform any and all acts and to make such rules and regulations as may be necessary and proper for the purpose of carrying the provisions of this Act into full force and effect.

Approved, June 17, 1902.

SOURCE: Reclamation Act of 1902 (Pub.L. 57–161).

ANALYSIS

Commonly known as the Newlands Act, in honor of Nevada Senator Francis G. Newlands, the Reclamation Act of 1902 transferred the responsibility of constructing dams, canals, and other forms of water infrastructure from the states to the federal government. The effort was initiated by congressmen of western states in order to tap the federal budget for the funds required to irrigate the arid lands of the West. Irrigation was required in order to make the land suitable for agricultural purposes. It did not represent the states ceding their authority to the federal government as the legislation included terminology requiring federal officials to acquiesce to local laws and the desires of state authorities.

The act created the Reclamation Fund, which was partially funded by the sale of public lands in the western states. Other funding came from water users that benefitted from the respective projects. The monies were designated for use by the Secretary of the Interior to study potential water projects or fund their actual construction.

Central to the Reclamation Act was the creation of the U.S. Reclamation Service, later renamed the U.S. Bureau of Reclamation (BOR). Its purpose was to provide a trained cadre of engineers to oversee the irrigation of the West. Its role would subsequently expand to include the construction of many of the West's largest dams and associated water delivery systems. Today the BOR is responsible for approximately 10 million acres of irrigated lands in the West.

FURTHER READING

Pisani, Donald J. 1984. *From the Family Farm to Agribusiness: The Irrigation Crusade in California and the West, 1850–1931*. Berkeley: University of California Press.

Pisani, Donald J. 1992. *To Reclaim a Divided West: Water, Law, and Public Policy, 1848–1902*. Albuquerque: University of New Mexico Press.

Pisani, Donald J. 2002. *Water and American Government: The Reclamation Bureau, National Water Policy, and the West, 1902–1935*. Berkeley: University of California Press.

Reisner, Marc. 1986. *Cadillac Desert: The American West and Its Disappearing Water*. New York: Viking.

"The Equitable Division and Apportionment of the Use of the Waters of the Colorado River System"

- *Document:* The Colorado River Compact of 1922
- *Date:* November 24, 1922
- *Where:* Santa Fe, New Mexico
- *Significance:* The agreement apportioned the waters of the Colorado River between the Upper Basin and Lower Basin states.

DOCUMENT

Colorado River Compact, 1922

The States of Arizona, California, Colorado, Nevada, New Mexico, Utah, and Wyoming, having resolved to enter into a compact under the Act of the Congress of the United States of America approved August 19, 1921 ...

ARTICLE I

The major purposes of this compact are to provide for the equitable division and apportionment of the use of the waters of the Colorado River System; to establish the relative importance of different beneficial uses of water, to promote interstate comity; to remove causes of present and future controversies; and to secure the expeditious agricultural and industrial development of the Colorado River Basin, the storage of its waters, and the protection of life and property from floods. To these ends the Colorado River Basin is divided into two Basins, and an apportionment of the use of part of the water of the Colorado River System is made to each of them with the provision that further equitable apportionments may be made.

ARTICLE II

As used in this compact-

(a) The term "Colorado River System" means that portion of the Colorado River and its tributaries within the United States of America.

(b) the term "Colorado River Basin" means all of the drainage area of the Colorado River System and all other territory within the United States of America to which the waters of the Colorado River System shall be beneficially applied.

(c) The term "States of the Upper Division" means the States of Colorado, New Mexico, Utah, and Wyoming.

(d) The term "States of the Lower Division" means the States of Arizona, California, and Nevada.

(e) The term "Lee Ferry" means a point in the main stream of the Colorado River one mile below the mouth of the Paria River.

(f) The term "Upper Basin" means those parts of the States of Arizona, Colorado, New Mexico, Utah, and Wyoming within and from which waters naturally drain into the Colorado River System above Lee Ferry, and also all parts of said States located without the drainage area of the Colorado River System which are now or shall hereafter be beneficially served by waters diverted from the System above Lee Ferry.

(g) The term "Lower Basin" means those parts of the States of Arizona, California, Nevada, New Mexico, and Utah within and from which waters naturally drain into the Colorado River System below Lee Ferry, and also all parts of said States located without the drainage area of the Colorado River System which are now or shall hereafter be beneficially served by waters diverted from the System below Lee Ferry.

(h) The term "domestic use" shall include the use of water for household, stock, municipal, mining, milling, industrial, and other like purposes, but shall exclude the generation of electrical power.

ARTICLE III

(a) There is hereby apportioned from the Colorado River System in perpetuity to the Upper Basin and to the Lower Basin, respectively, the exclusive beneficial consumptive use of 7,500,000 acre-feet of water per annum, which shall include all water necessary for the supply of any rights which may now exist.

(b) In addition to the apportionment in paragraph (a), the Lower Basin is hereby given the right to increase its beneficial consumptive use of such waters by one million acre-feet per annum.

(c) If, as a matter of international comity, the United States of America shall hereafter recognize in the United States of Mexico any right to the use of any waters of the Colorado River System, such waters shall be supplied first from the waters which are surplus over and above the aggregate of the quantities specified in paragraphs (a) and (b); and if such surplus shall prove insufficient for this purpose, then, the burden of such deficiency shall be equally borne by the Upper Basin and the Lower Basin, and whenever necessary the States of the Upper Division shall deliver at Lee Ferry water to supply one-half of the deficiency so recognized in addition to that provided in paragraph (d).

(d) The States of the Upper Division will not cause the flow of the river at Lee Ferry to be depleted below an aggregate of 75,000,000 acre-feet for any period of ten consecutive years reckoned in continuing progressive series beginning with the first day of October next succeeding the ratification of this compact.

(e) The States of the Upper Division shall not withhold water, and the States of the Lower Division shall not require the delivery of water, which cannot reasonably be applied to domestic and agricultural uses.

(f) Further equitable apportionment of the beneficial uses of the waters of the Colorado River System unapportioned by paragraphs (a), (b), and (c) may be made in the manner provided in paragraph (g) at any time after October first, 1963, if and when either Basin shall have reached its total beneficial consumptive use as set out in paragraphs (a) and (b).

(g) In the event of a desire for a further apportionment as provided in paragraph (f) any two signatory States, acting through their Governors, may give joint notice of such desire to the Governors of the other signatory States and to The President of the United States of America, and it shall be the duty of the Governors of the signatory States and of The President of the United States of America forthwith to appoint representatives, whose duty it shall be to divide and apportion equitably between the Upper Basin and Lower Basin the beneficial use of the unapportioned water of the Colorado River System as mentioned in paragraph (f), subject to the legislative ratification of the signatory States and the Congress of the United States of America.

ARTICLE IV

(a) Inasmuch as the Colorado River has ceased to be navigable for commerce and the reservation of its waters for navigation would seriously limit the development of its Basin, the use of its waters for purposes of navigation shall be subservient to the uses of such waters for domestic, agricultural, and power purposes. If the Congress shall not consent to this paragraph, the other provisions of this compact shall nevertheless remain binding.

(b) Subject to the provisions of this compact, water of the Colorado River System may be impounded and used for the generation of electrical power, but such impounding and use shall be subservient to the use and consumption of such water for agricultural and domestic purposes and shall not interfere with or prevent use for such dominant purposes.

(c) The provisions of this article shall not apply to or interfere with the regulation and control by any State within its boundaries of the appropriation, use, and distribution of water.

ARTICLE V

The chief official of each signatory State charged with the administration of water rights, together with the Director of the United States Reclamation Service and the Director of the United States Geological Survey shall cooperate, ex-officio:

(a) To promote the systematic determination and coordination of the facts as to flow, appropriation, consumption, and use of water in the Colorado River Basin, and the interchange of available information in such matters.

(b) To secure the ascertainment and publication of the annual flow of the Colorado River at Lee Ferry.

(c) To perform such other duties as may be assigned by mutual consent of the signatories from time to time.

ARTICLE VI

Should any claim or controversy arise between any two or more of the signatory States: (a) with respect to the waters of the Colorado River System not covered by the terms of this compact; (b) over the meaning or performance of any of the terms of this compact; (c) as to the allocation of the burdens incident to the performance of any article of this compact or the delivery of waters as herein provided; (d) as to the construction or operation of works within the Colorado River Basin to be situated in two or more States, or to be constructed in one State for the benefit of another State; or (e) as to the diversion of water in one State for the benefit of another State; the Governors of the States affected, upon the request of one of them, shall forthwith appoint Commissioners with power to consider and adjust such claim or controversy, subject to ratification by the Legislatures of the States so affected. Nothing herein contained shall prevent the adjustment of any such claim or controversy by any present method or by direct future legislative action of the interested States.

ARTICLE VII

Nothing in this compact shall be construed as affecting the obligations of the United States of America to Indian tribes.

ARTICLE VIII

Present perfected rights to the beneficial use of waters of the Colorado River System are unimpaired by this compact. Whenever storage capacity of 5,000,000 acre-feet shall have been provided on the main Colorado River within or for the benefit of the Lower Basin, then claims of such rights, if any, by appropriators or users of water in the Lower Basin against appropriators or users of water in the Upper Basin shall attach to and be satisfied from water that may be stored not in conflict with Article III.

All other rights to beneficial use of waters of the Colorado River System shall be satisfied solely from the water apportioned to that Basin in which they are situate.

ARTICLE IX

Nothing in this compact shall be construed to limit or prevent any State from instituting or maintaining any action or proceeding, legal or equitable, for the protection of any right under this compact or the enforcement of any of its provisions.

ARTICLE X

This compact may be terminated at any time by the unanimous agreement of the signatory States. In the event of such termination all rights established under it shall continue unimpaired.

ARTICLE XI

This compact shall become binding and obligatory when it shall have been approved by the Legislatures of each of the signatory States and by the Congress of the United States. Notice of approval by the Legislatures shall be given by the Governor of each signatory State to the Governors of the other signatory States and to the President of the United States, and the President of the United States is requested to give notice to the Governors of the signatory States of approval by the Congress of the United States.

IN WITNESS WHEREOF, the Commissioners have signed this compact in a single original, which shall be deposited in the archives of the Department of State of the United States of America and of which a duly certified copy shall be forwarded to the Governor of each of the signatory States.

DONE at the City of Santa Fe, New Mexico, this twenty-fourth day of November, A.D. One Thousand Nine Hundred and Twenty-two. . . .

SOURCE: U.S. Department of the Interior, Bureau of Reclamation. n.d. *Colorado River Compact of 1922.* http://www.usbr.gov/lc/region/g1000/pdfiles/crcompct.pdf (accessed August 23, 2014).

ANALYSIS

During the early decades of the twentieth century, water conflicts arose between the various states in the West over the ownership and diversion of waterways. In order to address issues arising over the Colorado River, the states of Arizona, California, Colorado, Nevada, Utah, and Wyoming met in Santa Fe, New Mexico, during November 1922 to settle their disagreements. Their participation in the negotiations was encouraged by the federal government, with the promise that a settlement would lead to the construction of dams on the Colorado River.

In the Compact, the states agreed to equally divide the Colorado's waters between the Upper Basin, which included the states of Colorado, Utah, Wyoming, and part of Nevada, and the Lower Basin, which was comprised of Arizona, California, and a portion of Nevada, with each receiving 7.5 million acre-feet of water. The dividing point between the basins was determined to be Lees Ferry, near Page, Arizona. The distribution of the waters within the respective basins was left to the affected states to negotiate among themselves.

The Colorado River Compact of 1922 paved the way for the federal government to begin extensive restructuring of the Colorado River. Following the Compact's ratification, Congress passed the Boulder Canyon Act of 1928, which authorized the construction of what became the Hoover Dam. On the heels of the Hoover Dam came others, including Davis and Parker dams.

Unfortunately, the Colorado River Compact failed to end conflicts over the apportionment of the Colorado River's waters as Arizona refused to ratify the document. The problem was that Arizona claimed that California was using far more than its fair share of the Lower Basin states' allocation. Congress attempted to no avail to address Arizona's concerns in the Boulder Canyon Act of 1928. Arizona subsequently made three unsuccessful attempts at the U.S. Supreme Court to get a greater share of the water through the Compact but was rebuffed because the state's failure to ratify the agreement meant that they were not being harmed by the enforcement of the document. Arizona agreed to the Compact in 1944 in order to continue its legal challenges to the agreement. Arizona ultimately emerged victorious in the landmark 1963 Supreme Court case *Arizona v. California.*

FURTHER READING

Fradkin, Philip L. 1995. *A River No More: The Colorado River and the West.* Expanded and updated ed. Berkeley: University of California Press.

Hundley, Norris, Jr. 2001. *The Great Thirst: Californians and Water: A History.* Rev. ed. Berkeley: University of California Press.

Hundley, Norris, Jr. 2009. *Water and the West: The Colorado River Compact and the Politics of Water in the American West.* 2nd ed. Berkeley: University of California Press.

Worster, Donald. 1985. *Rivers of Empire: Water, Aridity, and the Growth of the American West.* New York: Oxford University Press.

"For the Approval of the Colorado River Compact"

- **Document:** The Boulder Canyon Project Act, excerpts
- **Date:** December 21, 1928
- **Where:** Washington, DC
- **Significance:** The act promised the construction of the Boulder Canyon Dam, later renamed Hoover Dam, provided that at least six of the seven states that were parties to the Colorado River Compact ratified the 1922 agreement.

DOCUMENT

BOULDER CANYON PROJECT ACT

. . .

AN ACT To provide for the construction of works for the protection and development of the Colorado River Basin, for the approval of the Colorado River compact, and for other purposes.

Be it enacted by the Senate and House of Representatives of the United States of America in Congress assembled, That for the purpose of controlling the floods, improving navigation and regulating the flow of the Colorado River, providing for storage and for the delivery of the stored waters thereof for reclamation of public lands and other beneficial uses exclusively within the United States, and for the generation of electrical energy as a means of making the project herein authorized a self-supporting and financially solvent undertaking, the Secretary of the Interior, subject to the terms of the Colorado River compact hereinafter mentioned, is hereby authorized to construct, operate, and maintain a dam and incidental works in the main stream of the Colorado River at Black Canyon or Boulder Canyon adequate to create a storage reservoir of a capacity of not less than twenty million acre-feet of water and a main canal and appurtenant structures located entirely within the United States connecting the Laguna Dam, or other suitable diversion dam, which the Secretary of the Interior is hereby authorized to construct if deemed necessary or advisable by him upon engineering or economic considerations, with the Imperial and Coachella Valleys in California, the expenditures for said main canal and appurtenant structures to be reimbursable, as provided in the reclamation law, and shall not be paid out of revenues derived from the sale or disposal of water power or electric energy at the dam authorized to be constructed at said Black Canyon or Boulder Canyon, or for water for potable purposes outside of the Imperial and Coachella Valleys: *Provided, however*, That no charge shall be made for water or for the use, storage, or delivery of water for irrigation or water for potable purposes in the Imperial or Coachella Valleys; also to construct and equip, operate, and maintain at or near said dam, or cause to be constructed, a complete plant and incidental structures suitable for the fullest economic development of electrical energy from the water discharged from said reservoir; and to acquire by proceedings in eminent domain, or otherwise all lands, rights-of-way, and other property necessary for said purposes.

. . .

SEC. 4. (a) This Act shall not take effect and no authority shall be exercised hereunder and no work shall be begun and no moneys expended on or in connection with the works or structures provided for in this Act, and no water rights shall be claimed or initiated hereunder, and no steps shall be taken by the United States or by others to initiate or perfect any claims to the use of water pertinent to such works or structures unless and until (1) the States of Arizona, California, Colorado, Nevada, New Mexico, Utah, and Wyoming shall have ratified the Colorado River compact, mentioned in section 13 hereof, and the President by public proclamation shall have so declared, or (2) if said States fail to ratify the said compact within six months from the date of the passage of this Act then, until six of said States, including the State of California, shall ratify said compact and shall consent to waive the provisions of the first paragraph of Article XI of said compact, which makes the same binding and obligatory only when approved by each of the seven States signatory thereto, and shall have approved said compact without conditions, save that of such six-State approval, and the President by public proclamation shall have so declared, and, further, until the State of California, by act of its legislature, shall agree irrevocably and unconditionally with the United States and for the benefit of the States of Arizona, Colorado, Nevada, New Mexico, Utah, and Wyoming, as an express covenant and in consideration of the passage of this Act, that the aggregate annual consumptive use (diversions less returns to the river) of water of and from the Colorado River for use in the State of California, including all uses under contracts made under the provisions of this Act and all water necessary for the supply of any rights which may now exist, shall not exceed four million four hundred thousand acre-feet of the waters apportioned to the lower basin States by paragraph (a) of Article III of the Colorado River compact, plus not more than one-half of any excess or surplus waters unapportioned by said compact, such uses always to be subject to the terms of said compact.

The States of Arizona, California, and Nevada are authorized to enter into an agreement which shall provide (1) that of the 7,500,000 acre-feet annually apportioned to the lower basin by paragraph (a) of Article III of the Colorado River compact, there shall be apportioned to the State of Nevada 300,000 acre-feet and to the State of Arizona 2,800,000 acre-feet for exclusive beneficial consumptive use in perpetuity, and (2) that the State of Arizona may annually use one-half of the excess or surplus waters unapportioned by the Colorado River compact, and (3) that the State of Arizona shall have the exclusive beneficial consumptive use of the Gila River and its tributaries within the boundaries of said State, and (4) that the waters of the Gila River and its tributaries, except return flow after the same enters the Colorado River, shall never be subject to any diminution whatever by any allowance of water which may be made by treaty or otherwise to the United States of Mexico but if, as provided in paragraph (c) of Article III of the Colorado River compact, it shall become necessary to supply water to the United States of Mexico from waters over and above the quantities which are surplus as defined by said compact, then the State of California shall and will mutually agree with the State of Arizona to supply, out of the main stream of the Colorado River, one-half of any deficiency which must be supplied to Mexico by the lower basin, and (5) that the State of California shall and will further mutually agree with the States of Arizona and Nevada that none of said three States shall withhold water and none shall require the delivery of water, which cannot reasonably be applied to domestic and agricultural uses, and (6) that all of the provisions of said tri-State agreement shall be subject in all particulars to the provisions of the Colorado River compact, and (7) said agreement to take effect upon the ratification of the Colorado River compact by Arizona, California, and Nevada.

. . .

SEC. 8. (a) The United States, its permittees, licensees, and contractees, and all users and appropriators of water stored, diverted, carried, and/or distributed by the reservoir, canals, and other works herein authorized, shall observe and be subject to and controlled by said Colorado River compact in the construction, management, and operation of said reservoir, canals, and other works and the storage, diversion, delivery, and use of water for the generation of power, irrigation, and other purposes, anything in this Act to the contrary notwithstanding, and all permits, licenses, and contracts shall so provide.

(b) Also the United States, in constructing, managing, and operating the dam, reservoir,

canals, and other works herein authorized, including the appropriation, delivery, and use of water for the generation of power, irrigation, or other uses, and all users of water thus delivered and all users and appropriators of waters stored by said reservoir and/or carried by said canal, including all permittees and licensees of the United States or any of its agencies, shall observe and be subject to and controlled, anything to the contrary herein notwithstanding, by the terms of such compact, if any, between the States of Arizona, California, and Nevada, or any two thereof, for the equitable division of the benefits, including power, arising from the use of water accruing to said States, subsidiary to and consistent with said Colorado River compact, which may be negotiated and approved by said States and to which

Congress shall give its consent and approval on or before January 1, 1929; and the terms of any such compact concluded between said States and approved and consented to by Congress after said date: *Provided*, That in the latter case such compact shall be subject to all contracts, if any, made by the Secretary of the Interior under section 5 hereof prior to the date of such approval and consent by Congress.

. . .

SEC. 13. (a) The Colorado River compact signed at Santa Fe, New Mexico, November 24, 1922, pursuant to Act of Congress approved August 19, 1921, entitled "An Act to permit a compact or agreement between the States of Arizona, California, Colorado, Nevada, New Mexico, Utah, and Wyoming respecting the disposition and apportionment of the waters of the Colorado River, and for other purposes," is hereby approved by the Congress of the United States, and the provisions of the first paragraph of article II of the said Colorado River compact, making said compact binding and obligatory when it shall have been approved by the legislature of each of the signatory States, are hereby waived, and this approval shall become effective when the State of California and at least five of the other States mentioned, shall have approved or may hereafter approve said compact as aforesaid and shall consent to such waiver, as herein provided.

(b) The rights of the United States in or to waters of the Colorado River and its tributaries howsoever claimed or acquired, as well as the rights of those claiming under the United States, shall be subject to and controlled by said Colorado River compact.

(c) Also all patents, grants, contracts, concessions, leases, permits, licenses, rights-of-way, or other privileges from the United States or under its authority, necessary or convenient for the use of waters of the Colorado River or its tributaries, or for the generation or transmission of electrical energy generated by means of the waters of said river or its tributaries, whether under this Act, the Federal Water Power Act, or otherwise, shall be upon the express condition and with the express covenant that the rights of the recipients or holders thereof to waters of the river or its tributaries, for the use of which the same are necessary, convenient, or incidental, and the use of the same shall likewise be subject to and controlled by said Colorado River compact.

(d) The conditions and covenants referred to herein shall be deemed to run with the land and the right, interest, or privilege therein and water right, and shall attach as a matter of law, whether set out or referred to in the instrument evidencing any such patent, grant, contract, concession, lease, permit, license, right-of-way, or other privilege from the United States or under its authority, or not, and shall be deemed to be for the benefit of and be available to the States of Arizona, California, Colorado, Nevada, New Mexico, Utah, and Wyoming, and the users of water therein or thereunder, by way of suit, defense, or otherwise, in any litigation respecting the waters of the Colorado River or its tributaries.

. . .

SEC. 17. Claims of the United States arising out of any contract authorized by this Act shall have priority over all others, secured or unsecured.

SEC. 18. Nothing herein shall be construed as interfering with such rights as the States now have either to the waters within their borders or to adopt such policies and enact such laws as they may deem necessary with respect to the appropriation, control, and use of waters within their borders, except as modified by the Colorado River compact or other interstate agreement.

SEC. 19. That the consent of Congress is hereby given to the States of Arizona, California, Colorado, Nevada, New Mexico, Utah, and Wyoming to negotiate and enter into compacts or agreements, supplemental to and in conformity with the Colorado River compact and consistent with this Act for a comprehensive plan for the development of the Colorado River and providing for the storage, diversion, and use of the waters of said river. Any such compact or agreement may provide for the construction of dams, headworks, and other diversion works or structures for flood control, reclamation, improvement of navigation, division of water, or other purposes and/or the construction of power houses or other structures for the purpose of the development of water power and the financing of the same; and for such purposes may authorize the creation of interstate commissions and/or the creation of corporations, authorities, or other instrumentalities.

(a) Such consent is given upon condition that a representative of the United States, to be appointed by the President, shall participate in the negotiations and shall make report to Congress of the proceedings and of any compact or agreement entered into.

(b) No such compact or agreement shall be binding or obligatory upon any of such States unless and until it has been approved by the legislature of each of such States and by the Congress of the United States.

SEC. 20. Nothing in this Act shall be construed as a denial or recognition of any rights, if any, in Mexico to the use of the waters of the Colorado River system.

SEC. 21. That the short title of this Act shall be "Boulder Canyon Project Act." Approved, December 21, 1928.

SOURCE: U.S. Department of the Interior, Bureau of Reclamation. n.d. *Boulder Canyon Project Act.* http://www.usbr.gov/lc/region/g1000/pdfiles/bcpact.pdf (accessed October 24, 2014).

ANALYSIS

In the early 1920s, U.S. Commerce Secretary Herbert Hoover began exploring the construction of a dam on the Colorado River in Boulder Canyon, in the vicinity of the Arizona–Nevada border. The dam and its reservoir offered numerous benefits to the general populace, including flood control, water for irrigation, and the generation of hydroelectric power. Despite its promise, the dam was not approved for construction at the time due to conflicts between the states of Arizona, California, Colorado, Nevada, New Mexico, Utah, and Wyoming over the allocation of water and hydroelectric power. Legislators from the respective states were generally unwilling to make concessions to get the needed dam constructed unless they received guarantees that privileged their state over those of the other six states.

It was hoped that the differences between the states would be settled through the Colorado River Compact of 1922. Although the compact was agreed to in principle, some of the state legislatures refused to ratify the agreement.

The Boulder Canyon Project Act was designed to entice the states to ratify the Colorado River Compact. It was targeted primarily toward Arizona and California, as Colorado, Nevada, New Mexico, Utah, and Wyoming had ratified the 1922 compact. Six states were required to get the Boulder Dam constructed, but if all seven ratified the agreement, the federal government promised to deliver even more benefits from the dam to the respective states. California ultimately opted to ratify the agreement, which cleared the way for the construction of the Boulder Dam. By that time, the Boulder Canyon site had been abandoned in favor of Black Canyon, a site just downriver from the original location. The Boulder Dam was constructed between 1931 and 1936. It was renamed in honor of Herbert Hoover, who by that time had become president of the United States. The Hoover Dam proved instrumental to California, as it brought significant amounts of hydroelectric power to the state and also provided much needed water for the Imperial Valley, which subsequently transformed into one of the country's richest agricultural areas.

Rather than benefitting from the dam, Arizona turned to the U.S. Supreme Court in 1931 claiming that the Boulder Canyon Project Act was unconstitutional. Arizona's claim was rejected by the justices. The state tried two more times over the next five years to get the U.S. Supreme Court to reverse their decision but was unsuccessful. Arizona finally ratified the Colorado River Compact of 1922 in 1944. They did so not to settle their disagreements with the other states, most notably California, but instead to continue the legal process in the federal courts.

FURTHER READING

Billington, David P., and Donald C. Jackson. 2006. *Big Dams of the New Deal Era: A Confluence of Engineering and Politics.* Norman: University of Oklahoma Press.

Dunar, Andrew J., and Dennis McBride. 1993. *Building Hoover Dam: An Oral History of the Great Depression.* New York: Twayne Publishers.

Hundley, Norris, Jr. 2009. *Water and the West: The Colorado River Compact and the Politics of Water in the American West.* 2nd ed. Berkeley: University of California Press.

"To Initiate the Comprehensive Development of the Water Resources of the Upper Colorado River Basin"

- **Document:** The Colorado River Storage Project Act, excerpts
- **Date:** April 11, 1956
- **Where:** Washington, DC
- **Significance:** The act authorized the construction of dams and other water infrastructure on the Colorado River in the states of Colorado, New Mexico, Utah, and Wyoming.

DOCUMENT

CHAPTER 203-PUBLIC LAW 485
[S. 500]

An Act to authorize the Secretary of the Interior to construct, operate, and maintain the Colorado River storage project and participating projects, and for other purposes.

Be it enacted by the Senate and House of Representatives of the United States of America in Congress assembled, That:

In order to initiate the comprehensive development of the water resources of the Upper Colorado River Basin, for the purposes, among others, of regulating the flow of the Colorado River, storing water for beneficial consumptive use, making it possible for the States of the Upper Basin to utilize, consistently with the provisions of the Colorado River Compact, the apportionments made to and among them in the Colorado River Compact and the Upper Colorado River Basin Compact, respectively, providing for the reclamation of arid and semiarid land, for the control of floods, and for the generation of hydroelectric power, as an incident of the foregoing purposes, the Secretary of the Interior is hereby authorized (1) to construct, operate, and maintain the following initial units of the Colorado River storage project, consisting of dams, reservoirs, powerplants, transmission facilities and appurtenant works: Curecanti, Flaming Gorge, Navajo (dam and reservoir only), and Glen Canyon: *Provided*, That the Curecanti Dam shall be constructed to a height which will impound not less than nine hundred and forty thousand acre-feet of water or will create a reservoir of such greater capacity as can be obtained by a high waterline located at seven thousand five hundred and twenty feet above mean sea level, and that construction thereof shall not be undertaken until the Secretary has on the basis of further engineering and economic investigations, reexamined the economic justification of such unit and, accompanied by appropriate documentation in the form of a supplemental report, has certified to the Congress and to the President that, in his judgment, the benefits of such unit will exceed its costs; and (2) to construct, operate, and maintain the following additional reclamation projects (including power-generating and transmission facilities related thereto), hereinafter referred to as participating projects: Central Utah (initial phase); . . . *Provided further*, That as part of the Glen Canyon Unit the Secretary of the Interior shall take adequate protective measures to preclude impairment of the Rainbow Bridge National Monument.

Sec. 2. In carrying out further investigations of projects under the Federal reclamation laws in the Upper Colorado River Basin, the Secretary shall give priority to completion of planning reports on the Gooseberry, San Juan-Chama, Navajo, Parshall, Troublesome, Rabbit Ear, Eagle Divide, San Miguel, West Divide, Bluestone, Battlement Mesa, Tomichi Creek, East River, Ohio Creek, Fruitland Mesa, Bostwick Park, Grand Mesa, Dallas Creek, Savery-Pot Hook, Dolores, Fruit Growers Extension, Animas- La Plata, Yellow Jacket, and Sublette participating projects. Said reports shall be completed as expeditiously as funds are made available therefor and shall be submitted promptly to the affected States, which in the case of the San Juan-Chama project shall include the State of Texas, and thereafter to the President and the Congress: *Provided*, That with reference to the plans and specifications for the San Juan-Chama project, the storage for control and regulation of water imported from the San Juan River shall (1) be limited to a single offstream dam and reservoir on a tributary of the Chama River, (2) be used solely for control and regulation and no power facilities shall be established, installed or operated thereat, and (3) be operated at all times by the Bureau of Reclamation of the Department of the Interior in strict compliance with the Rio Grande Compact as administered by the Rio Grande Compact Commission. The preparation of detailed designs and specifications for the works proposed to be constructed in connection with projects shall be carried as far forward as the investigations thereof indicate is reasonable in the circumstances.

The Secretary, concurrently with the investigations directed by the preceding paragraph, shall also give priority to completion of a planning report on the Juniper project.

Sec. 3. It is not the intention of Congress, in authorizing only those projects designated in section1 of this Act, and in authorizing priority in planning only those additional projects designated in section 2 of this Act, to limit, restrict, or otherwise interfere with such comprehensive development as will provide for the consumptive use by States of the Upper Colorado River Basin of waters, the use of which is apportioned to the Upper Colorado River Basin by the Colorado River Compact and to each State thereof by the Upper Colorado River Basin Compact, nor to preclude consideration and authorization by the Congress of additional projects under the allocations in the compacts as additional needs are indicated. It is the intention of Congress that no dam or reservoir constructed under the authorization of this Act shall be within any national park or monument.

. . .

Sec. 9. Nothing contained in this Act shall be construed to alter, amend, repeal, construe, interpret, modify, or be in conflict with the provisions of the Boulder Canyon Project Act (45 Stat. 1057), the Boulder Canyon Project Adjustment Act (54 Stat. 774), the Colorado River Compact, the Upper Colorado River Basin Compact, the Rio Grande Compact of 1938, or the Treaty with the United Mexican States (Treaty Series 994).

. . .

Sec. 14. In the operation and maintenance of all facilities, authorized by Federal law and under the jurisdiction and supervision of the Secretary of the Interior, in the basin of the Colorado River, the Secretary of the Interior is directed to comply with the applicable provisions of the Colorado River Compact, the Upper Colorado River Basin Compact, the Boulder Canyon Project Act, the Boulder Canyon Project Adjustment Act, and the Treaty with the United Mexican States, in the storage and release of water from reservoirs in the Colorado River Basin. In the event of the failure of the Secretary of the Interior to so comply, any State of the Colorado River Basin may maintain an action in the Supreme Court of the United States to enforce the provisions of this section, and consent is given to the joinder of the United States as a party in such suit or suits, as a defendant or otherwise.

SOURCE: U.S. Department of the Interior, Bureau of Reclamation. n.d. *Colorado River Storage Project*. http://www.usbr.gov/lc/region/g1000/pdfiles/crspuc.pdf (accessed August 23, 2014).

ANALYSIS

The Colorado River Storage Project Act (CRSP) provided for the construction of dams and other types of water infrastructure in Colorado, New Mexico, Utah, and Wyoming. The legislation had its origin in the Colorado River Compact of 1922. The respective states were all part of the Upper Basin, which according to the compact meant that they shared 7.5 million acre-feet of water annually from the Colorado River. Congress had signaled to the states that once they allotted the water in a manner that satisfied all the parties, they would be rewarded with water infrastructure projects that they desired. In 1948 the respective states agreed to share the water according to percentages: Colorado received 51.75 percent, New Mexico got 11.25 percent, Utah's share was 23 percent, with the remaining 14 percent belonging to Wyoming. Congress responded to the settlement with the CRSP in 1956.

The CRSP would have probably emerged several years earlier had it not been for the proposed Echo Park Dam in Dinosaur National Park, located just east of the Utah–Colorado border. An earlier version of the CRSP in 1953 included the Echo Park Dam and was met with intense opposition. A deal was made between congressmen and environmental activists that paved the way for the CRSP. The Echo Park Dam was dropped from the legislation and the environmentalists, in exchange, agreed not to oppose its replacement in the legislation, the Glen Canyon Dam. The environmentalists knew little about Arizona's Glen Canyon at the time and learned of its scenic beauty only after it was too late to save. Many environmental groups today advocate for the decommissioning of the Glen Canyon Dam.

Three of the dams included in the CRSP were under construction by the end of the 1950s: Flaming Gorge, Glen Canyon, and Navajo. The three dams included in the Curecanti Unit, namely Crystal, Mesa, and Morrow Point, did not begin the construction process until 1964, with work on them continuing into the late 1970s.

While the CRSP reflected progress growing out of the Colorado River Compact of 1922, it also reflected the continuing political difficulties that emerged from the compact. The CRSP legislation repeatedly made mention of all the agreements in force at the time concerning the Colorado River, including the Colorado River Compact, the Upper Colorado River Basin Compact, the Boulder Canyon Project Act, the Boulder Canyon Project Adjustment Act, and the Treaty with the United Mexican States to ensure that none of the terms of the respective agreements were broached. This was of concern due to the judicial proceedings that were engulfing the Lower Basin states, most notably Arizona and California, which ultimately culminated in the landmark 1963 U.S. Supreme Court decision in *Arizona v. California*.

FURTHER READING

Farmer, Jared. 1999. *Glen Canyon Dammed: Inventing Lake Powell & the Canyon Country.* Tucson: University of Arizona Press.

Fradkin, Philip L. 1995. *A River No More: The Colorado River and the West.* Expanded and updated ed. Berkeley: University of California Press.

Harvey, Mark W. T. 2000. *A Symbol of Wilderness: Echo Park and the American Conservation Movement.* Seattle: University of Washington Press.

Summitt, April R. 2013. *Contested Waters: An Environmental History of the Colorado River.* Boulder: University Press of Colorado.

"The Government's Construction, Ownership, Operation, and Maintenance of the Vast Colorado River"

- *Document:* Arizona v. California, 373 U.S. 546 (1963), excerpts from majority opinion
- *Date:* The case was first argued on January 8–11, 1962. It was reargued on November 13–14, 1962. The decision was released on June 3, 1963.
- *Where:* Washington, DC
- *Significance:* The case definitively gave the federal government the authority to supervise how the waters of the Colorado River would be divided among the states of Arizona, California, Colorado, Nevada, New Mexico, Utah, and Wyoming.

DOCUMENT

I.

ALLOCATION OF WATER AMONG THE STATES AND DISTRIBUTION TO USERS.

We have concluded, for reasons to be stated, that Congress in passing the Project Act intended to and did create its own comprehensive scheme for the apportionment among California, Arizona, and Nevada of the Lower Basin's share of the mainstream waters of the Colorado River, leaving each State its tributaries. Congress decided that a fair division of the first 7,500,000 acre-feet of such mainstream waters would give 4,400,000 acre-feet to California, 2,800,000 to Arizona, and 300,000 to Nevada; Arizona and California would each get one-half of any surplus. Prior approval was therefore given in the Act for a tri-state compact to incorporate these terms. The States, subject to subsequent congressional approval, were also permitted to agree on a compact with different terms. Division of the water did not, however, depend on the States agreeing to a compact, for Congress gave the Secretary of the Interior adequate authority to accomplish the division. Congress did this by giving the Secretary power to make contracts for the delivery of water and by providing that no person could have water without a contract.

. . .

C. *The Project Act's Apportionment and Distribution Scheme.*—The legislative history, the language of the Act, and the scheme established by the Act for the storage and delivery of water convince us also that Congress intended to provide its own method for a complete apportionment of the mainstream water among Arizona, California, and Nevada.

First, the legislative history. In hearings on the House bill that became the Project Act, Congressman Arentz of Nevada, apparently impatient with the delay of this much needed project, told the committee on January 6, 1928, that if the States could not themselves allocate the water, "there must be some power which will say to California You cannot take any more than this amount and the balance is allocated to the other States.' " Later, May 25, 1928, the House passed the bill, but it did not contain any allocation scheme. When the Senate took up that bill in December, pressure mounted swiftly for amendments that would provide a workable method for apportioning the waters among the Lower Basin States and distributing them to users in the States. The session convened on December 3, 1928, on the fifth the Senate took up the bill, nine days later the bill with significant amendments passed the Senate, four days after that the House concurred in the Senate's action, and on the twenty-first the President signed the bill. When the bill first reached the Senate floor, it had a provision, added in committee, limiting California to 4,600,000 acre-feet, and Senator Hayden on December 6 proposed reducing that share to 4,200,000. The next day, December 7, Mr. Pittman, senior Senator from Nevada, vigorously argued that Congress should settle the matter without delay. He said,

> "What is the difficulty? We have only minor questions involved here. There is practically nothing involved except a dispute between the States of Arizona and California with regard to the division of the increased water that will be impounded behind the proposed dam; that is all. . . . Of the 7,500,000 acre-feet of water let down that river they have gotten together within 400,000 acre-feet. They have got to get together, and if they do not get together Congress should bring them together."

The day after that, December 8, New Mexico's Senator Bratton suggested an amendment splitting the difference between the demands of Arizona and California by limiting California to 4,400,000 acre-feet. On the tenth, reflecting the prevailing sense of urgency for decisive action. Senator Bratton emphasized that this was not a dispute limited simply to two States:

"The two States have exchanged views, they have negotiated, they have en-deavored to reach an agreement, and until now have been unable to do so. This controversy does not affect those two States alone. It affects other States in the Union and the Government as well.

"Without undertaking to express my views either way upon the subject, I do think that if the two States are unable to agree upon a figure then that we, as a disinterested and friendly agency, should pass a bill which, according to our combined judgment, will justly and equitably settle the controversy. I suggested 4,400,000 acre-feet with that in view. I still hold to the belief that somewhere between the two figures we must fix the amount, and that this difference of 400,000 acre-feet should not be allowed to bar and preclude the passage of this important measure dealing with the enormous quantity of 15,000,000 acre-feet of water and involving seven States as well as the Government."

The very next day, December 11, this crucial amendment was adopted, and on the twelfth Senator Hayden pointed out that the bill settled the dispute over Lower Basin waters by giving 4,400,000 acre-feet to California and 2,800,000 to Arizona:

"One [dispute] is how the seven and a half million acre-feet shall be divided in the lower basin. The Senate has settled that by a vote—that California may have 4,400,000 acre-feet of that water. It follows logically that if that demand is to be conceded, as everybody agrees, the remainder is 2,800,000 acre-feet for Arizona. That settles that part of the controversy."

On the same day, Senator Pittman, intimately familiar with the whole water problem, summed up the feeling of the Senate that the bill fixed a limit on Califor-nia and "practically allocated" to Arizona her share of the water:

"The Senate has already determined upon the division of water between those States. How? It has determined how much water California may use, and the rest of it is subject to use by Nevada and Arizona. Nevada has already admitted that it can use only an insignificant quantity, 300,000 acre-feet. That leaves the rest of it to Arizona. As the bill now stands it is just as much divided as if they had mentioned Arizona and Nevada and the amounts they are to get. . . ."

. . .

"As I understand this amendment, Arizona to-day has practically allocated to it 2,800,000 acre-feet of water in the main Colorado River."

The Senator went on to explain why the Senate had found it necessary to set up its own plan for allocating the water:

"Why do we not leave it to California to say how much water she shall take out of the river or leave it to Arizona to say how much water she shall take out of the river? It is because it happens to become a duty of the United States Senate to settle this matter, and that is the reason."

Not only do the closing days of the debate show that Congress intended an apportionment among the States but also provisions of the Act create machinery plainly adequate to accomplish this purpose, whatever contingencies might occur. As one alternative of the congressional scheme, § 4 (a) of the Act invited Arizona, California, and Nevada to adopt a compact dividing the waters along the identical lines that had formed the basis for the congressional discussions of the Act: 4,400,000 acre-feet to California, 300,000 to Nevada, and 2,800,000 to Arizona. Section 8 (b) gave the States power to agree upon some other division, which would have to be approved by Congress. Congress made sure, however, that if the States did not agree on any compact the objects of the Act would be carried out, for the Secretary would then proceed, by making contracts, to apportion water among the States and to allocate the water among users within each State.

In the first section of the Act, the Secretary was authorized to "construct, operate, and maintain a dam and incidental works . . . adequate to create a storage reservoir of a capacity of not less than twenty million acre-feet of water . . ." for the stated purpose of "controlling the floods, improving navigation and regulating the flow of the Colorado River, providing for storage and for the delivery of the stored waters thereof for reclamation of public lands and other beneficial uses . . .," and generating electrical power. The whole point of the Act was to replace the erratic, undependable, often destructive natural flow of the Colorado with the regular, dependable release of waters conserved and stored by the project. Having undertaken this beneficial project, Congress, in several provisions of the Act, made it clear that no one should use mainstream waters save in strict compliance with the scheme set up by the Act. Section 5 authorized the Secretary "under such general regulations as he may prescribe, to contract for the storage of water in said reservoir and for the delivery thereof at such points on the river . . . as may be agreed upon, for irrigation and domestic uses. . . ." To emphasize that water could be obtained from the Secretary alone, § 5 further declared, "No person shall have or be entitled to have the use for any purpose of the water stored as aforesaid except by contract made as herein stated." The supremacy given the Secretary's contracts was made clear in § 8 (b) of the Act, which provided that, while the Lower Basin States were free to negotiate a compact dividing the waters, such a compact if made and approved after January 1, 1929, was to be "subject to all contracts, if any, made by the Secretary of the Interior under section 5" before Congress approved the compact.

These several provisions, even without legislative history, are persuasive that Congress intended the Secretary of the Interior, through his § 5 contracts, both to carry out the allocation of the waters of the main Colorado River among the Lower Basin States and to decide which users within each State would get water. The general authority to make contracts normally includes the power to choose with whom and upon what terms the contracts will be made. When Congress in an Act grants authority to contract, that authority is no less than the general authority, unless Congress has placed some limit on it. In this respect it is of interest that in an earlier version the bill did limit the Secretary's contract power by making the contracts "subject to rights of prior appropriators." But that restriction, which preserved the law of prior appropriation, did not survive. It was stricken from the bill when the requirement that every water user have a contract was added to § 5. Significantly, no phrase or provision indicating that the Secretary's contract power was to be controlled by the law of prior appropriation was substituted either then or at any other time before passage of the Act, and we are persuaded that had Congress intended so to fetter the Secretary's discretion, it would have done so in clear and unequivocal terms, as it did in recognizing "present perfected rights" in § 6.

That the bill was giving the Secretary sufficient power to carry out an allocation of the waters among the States and among the users within each State without regard to the law of prior appropriation was brought out in a colloquy between Montana's Senator Walsh and California's Senator Johnson, whose State had at least as much reason as any other State to bind the Secretary by state laws. Senator Walsh, who was thoroughly versed in western water law and also had previously argued before this Court in a leading case involving the doctrine of prior appropriation, made clear what would follow from the Government's impounding of the Colorado River waters when he said, "I always understood that the interest that stores the water has a right superior to prior appropriations that do not store." He sought Senator Johnson's views on what rights the City of Los Angeles, which had filed claims to large quantities of Colorado River water, would have after the Government had built the dam and impounded the waters. In reply to Senator Walsh's specific question whether the Government might "dispose of the stored water as it sees fit," Senator Johnson said. "Yes; under the terms of this bill." Senator Johnson added that "everything in this scheme, plan, or design" was "dependent upon the Secretary of the Interior contracting with those who desire to obtain the benefit of the construction. . . ." He admitted that it was possible that the Secretary could "utterly ignore" Los Angeles appropriations.

In this same discussion, Senator Hayden emphasized the Secretary's power to allocate the water by making contracts with users. After Senator Walsh said that he understood Senator Johnson to be arguing that the Secretary must satisfy Los Angeles appropriations, Senator Hayden corrected him, pointing out that Senator Johnson had qualified his statement by saying that "after all, the Secretary of the Interior could allow the city of Los Angeles to have such quantity of water as might be determined by contract." Senator Hayden went on to say that, where domestic and irrigation needs conflicted, "the Secretary of the Interior will naturally decide as between applicants, one who desires to use the water for potable purposes in the city and another who desires to use it for irrigation, if there is not enough water to go around, that the city shall have the preference." It is also significant that two vigorous opponents of the bill, Arizona's Representative Douglas and Utah's Representative Colton, criticized the bill because it gave the Secretary of the Interior "absolute control" over the disposition of the stored waters.

The argument that Congress would not have delegated to the Secretary so much power to apportion and distribute the water overlooks the ways in which his power is limited and channeled by standards in the Project Act. In particular, the Secretary is bound to observe the Act's limitation of 4,400,000 acre-feet on California's consumptive uses out of the first 7,500,000 acre-feet of mainstream water. This necessarily leaves the remaining 3,100,000 acre-feet for the use of Arizona and Nevada, since they are the only other States with access to the main Colorado River. Nevada consistently took the position, accepted by the other States throughout the debates, that her conceivable needs would not exceed 300,000 acre-feet, which, of course, left 2,800,000 acre-feet for Arizona's use. Moreover, Congress indicated that it thought this a proper division of the waters when in the second paragraph of § 4 (a) it gave advance consent to a tri-state compact adopting such division. While no such compact was ever entered into, the Secretary by his contracts has apportioned the water in the approved amounts and thereby followed the guidelines set down by Congress. And, as the Master pointed out, Congress set up other standards and placed other significant limitations upon the Secretary's power to distribute the stored waters. It specifically set out in order the purposes for which the Secretary must use the dam and the reservoir:

> "First, for river regulation, improvement of navigation, and flood control; second, for irrigation and domestic uses and satisfaction of present perfected rights in pursuance of Article VIII of said Colorado River compact; and third, for power." § 6.

The Act further requires the Secretary to make revenue provisions in his contracts adequate to ensure the recovery of the expenses of construction, operation, and maintenance of the dam and other works within 50 years after their construction.§ 4 (b). The Secretary is directed to make water contracts for irrigation and domestic uses only for "permanent service."§ 5. He and his permittees, licensees, and contractees are subject to the Colorado River Compact, § 8 (a), and therefore can do nothing to upset or encroach upon the Compact's allocation of Colorado River water between the Upper and Lower Basins. In the construction, operation, and management of the works, the Secretary is subject to the provisions of the reclamation law, except as the Act otherwise provides. § 14. One of the most significant limitations in the Act is that the Secretary is required to satisfy present perfected rights, a matter of intense importance to those who had reduced their water rights to actual beneficial use at the time the Act became effective. § 6. And, of course, all of the powers granted by the Act are exercised by the Secretary and his well-established executive department, responsible to Congress and the President and subject to judicial review.

Notwithstanding the Government's construction, ownership, operation, and maintenance of the vast Colorado River works that conserve and store the river's waters and the broad power given by Congress to the Secretary of the Interior to make contracts for the distribution of the water, it is argued that Congress in §§ 14 and 18 of the Act took away practically all the Secretary's power by permitting the States to determine with whom and on what terms the Secretary would make water contracts. Section 18 states:

> "Nothing herein shall be construed as interfering with such rights as the States now have either to the waters within their borders or to adopt such policies and enact such laws as they may deem necessary with respect to the appropriation, control, and use of waters within their borders. . . ."

Section 14 provides that the reclamation law, to which the Act is made a supplement, shall govern the management of the works except as otherwise provided, and

§ 8 of the Reclamation Act, much like § 18 of the Project Act, provides that it is not to be construed as affecting or interfering with state laws "relating to the control, appropriation, use, or distribution of water used in irrigation. . . ." In our view, nothing in any of these provisions affects our decision, stated earlier, that it is the Act and the Secretary's contracts, not the law of prior appropriation, that control the apportionment of water among the States. Moreover, contrary to the Master's conclusion, we hold that the Secretary in choosing between users within each State and in settling the terms of his contracts is not bound by these sections to follow state law.

. . .

III.

APPORTIONMENT AND CONTRACTS IN TIME OF SHORTAGE.

We have agreed with the Master that the Secretary's contracts with Arizona for 2,800,000 acre-feet of water and with Nevada for 300,000, together with the limitation of California to 4,400,000 acre-feet, effect a valid apportionment of the first 7,500,000 acre-feet of mainstream water in the Lower Basin. There remains the question of what shall be done in time of shortage. The Master, while declining to make any findings as to what future supply might be expected, nevertheless decided that the Project Act and the Secretary's contracts require the Secretary in case of shortage to divide the burden among the three States in this proportion: California 4.4/7.5; Arizona 2.8/7.5; Nevada .3/7.5. While pro rata sharing of water shortages seems equitable on its face, more considered judgment may demonstrate quite the contrary. Certainly we should not bind the Secretary to this formula. We have held that the Secretary is vested with considerable control over the apportionment of Colorado River waters. And neither the Project Act nor the water contracts require the use of any particular formula for apportioning shortages. While the Secretary must follow the standards set out in the Act, he nevertheless is free to choose among the recognized methods of apportionment or to devise reasonable methods of his own. This choice, as we see it, is primarily his, not the Master's or even ours. And the Secretary may or may not conclude that a pro rata division is the best solution.

It must be remembered that the Secretary's decision may have an effect not only on irrigation uses but also on other important functions for which Congress brought this great project into being—flood control, improvement of navigation, regulation of flow, and generation and distribution of electric power. Requiring the Secretary to prorate shortages would strip him of the very power of choice which we think Congress, for reasons satisfactory to it, vested in him and which we should not impair or take away from him. For the same reasons we cannot accept California's contention that in case of shortage each State's share of water should be determined by the judicial doctrine of equitable apportionment or by the law of prior appropriation. These principles, while they may provide some guidance, are not binding upon the Secretary where, as here, Congress, with full power to do so, has provided that the waters of a navigable stream shall be harnessed, conserved, stored, and distributed through a government agency under a statutory scheme.

None of this is to say that in case of shortage, the Secretary cannot adopt a method of proration or that he may not lay stress upon priority of use, local laws and customs, or any other factors that might be helpful in reaching an informed judgment in harmony with the Act, the best interests of the Basin States, and the welfare of the Nation. It will be time enough for the courts to intervene when and if the Secretary, in making apportionments or contracts, deviates from the standards Congress has set for him to follow, including his obligation to respect "present perfected rights" as of the date the Act was passed. At this time the Secretary has made no decision at all based on an actual or anticipated shortage of water, and so there is no action of his in this respect for us to review. Finally, as the Master pointed out, Congress still has broad powers over this navigable international stream. Congress can undoubtedly reduce or enlarge the Secretary's power if it wishes. Unless and until it does, we leave in the hands of the Secretary, where Congress placed it, full power to control, manage, and operate the Government's Colorado River works and to make contracts for the sale and delivery of water on such terms as are not prohibited by the Project Act.

SOURCE: *Arizona v. California*, 373 U.S. 546 (1963).

ANALYSIS

Arizona v. California was the culmination of interstate battles over the waters of the Colorado River that began in the early years of the twentieth century. The first major attempt to settle the water issues was the Colorado River Compact of 1922. Although the compact was agreed to by the states of California, Colorado, Nevada, New Mexico, Utah, and Wyoming, Arizona was unhappy with the terms and refused to ratify the document.

The Boulder Canyon Project Act of 1928 soon followed, and it included a proposed apportionment of 7,500,000 acre-feet of water from the Colorado River for the states of Arizona, California, and Nevada. Arizona was to receive 2,800,000 acre-feet, Nevada 300,000, and California's share was 4,400,000. Rather than accept their apportionment, Arizona filed suit in 1928 and took the case to the U.S. Supreme Court, where they argued the act was unconstitutional. The Supreme Court rejected Arizona's argument in 1931. Arizona returned to the Supreme Court in 1934 with a different argument. The state claimed that it had a right to the 1 million acre-feet of the Colorado River's waters that it was guaranteed in the Colorado River Compact of 1922. That argument also failed since Arizona had refused to ratify the agreement. In 1936, Arizona once again appeared before the justices. They had apparently lost patience with the state and noted that Arizona was not being harmed by any parties using the river because unused water flowed down to its terminus every year unused. The justices also noted that Arizona's legal claims concerning the river had been consistently flawed because the state continuously failed to make the United States a party to their lawsuits. Duly chastised, Arizona finally ratified the 1922 Colorado River Compact in 1944.

Arizona's congressional delegation took the lead in the mid-1940s in addressing Arizona's water needs. Senator Carl Hayden in 1947 got the U.S. Senate to approve the construction of the Central Arizona Project (CAP), which was intended to build aqueducts, canals, and water impoundment structures for the benefit of Arizona. It failed in the House of Representatives due to the actions of California's delegation, which claimed that not enough water was available in the Colorado River to support the CAP. Every subsequent year that CAP was introduced, it passed in the Senate but not the House of Representatives. Due to the California delegation's intransigence in the House of Representatives, Arizona once again turned to the courts in 1952 and filed suit against California and seven of its public utilities. Over the course of the lawsuit, *Arizona v. California*, Nevada, New Mexico, the United States, and Utah also became parties to the case.

Before the U.S. Supreme Court in 1962, Arizona claimed that California used far more of the Colorado River's waters than it was due. That assertion led to the Supreme Court justices hearing arguments on the case on two occasions and appointing a special master to research the history of the dispute and identify relevant legal precedents that would assist in settling the case. Ultimately, the special master recommended, and the justices agreed, that the fair way to divide the waters of the Colorado River was to use the apportionment made by the U.S. Congress in the Boulder Canyon Act of 1928; namely, that Arizona's share was 2,800,000 acre-feet, Nevada's 300,000, and California's 4,400,000.

In order to ensure that interstate conflicts over the Colorado River's waters did not continue, the justices charged the Secretary of the Interior with the responsibility of ensuring that all parties honored the terms of the Supreme Court decision. The secretary was also empowered to make any adjustments to the apportionment of the waters that were found necessary by the federal government in the future, with or without the consent of the respective states. This power is necessary since one of the claimants to the river's waters is Mexico. Its rights are guaranteed in international treaties negotiated with the United States.

In the majority decision, the justices had the foresight to also address how the Colorado River's waters were to be divided in times when the river did not have enough water available to meet each party's apportionment. Since the case was settled in the fall of 2014, the Colorado River has been able to meet most, if not all, of the needs of the states and Native American groups that have rights to its waters. Unfortunately, the river is fast losing the ability to continue providing the many claimants the waters that they require. Since the dawn of the twenty-first century, the West as a whole has been gripped by one of its driest periods in recorded history. This has led many of the reservoirs on the Colorado River to shrink drastically as their waters have either evaporated or been used. For instance, at the end of summer 2014, Lake Mead, which is the reservoir behind Hoover Dam, was filled to approximately 38 percent of its capacity. The pending shortages portend reductions in the amounts that the respective states and holders of senior water rights receive from the river. The results will potentially prove catastrophic to many as even areas that have not suffered water shortages of any type will be impacted as their share of water is reduced in order to meet the needs of areas that are extremely dry.

FURTHER READING

August, Jack L., Jr. 2007. *Dividing Western Waters: Mark Wilmer and Arizona v. California.* Fort Worth: Texas Christian University Press.

Fradkin, Philip L. 1995. *A River No More: The Colorado River and the West.* Expanded and updated ed. Berkeley: University of California Press.

Hundley, Norris, Jr. 2001. *The Great Thirst: Californians and Water: A History.* Rev. ed. Berkeley: University of California Press.

"A Program for the Further Comprehensive Development of the Water Resources of the Colorado River Basin"

- **Document:** Colorado River Basin Act of 1968, excerpts
- **Date:** September 30, 1968
- **Where:** Washington, DC
- **Significance:** The act settled decades of political and legal discord between Arizona and California, which allowed for the final apportionment of the waters of the Colorado River.

DOCUMENT

Public Law 90-537
90th Congress, S. 1004
September 30, 1968
An Act

To authorize the construction, operation, and maintenance of the Colorado River Basin project, and for other purposes.

Be it enacted by the Senate and House of Representative of the United States of America in Congress assembled,

TITLE 1 – COLORADO RIVER BASIN PROJECT; OBJECTIVES
    SEC. 101. That this Act may be cited as the "Colorado River Basin Project Act".
    SEC. 102 (a) It is the object of this Act to provide a program for the further comprehensive development of the water resources of the Colorado River Basin and for

the provision of additional and adequate water supplies for use in the upper as well as in the lower Colorado River Basin. This program is declared to be for the purposes, among others, of regulating the flow of the Colorado River; controlling floods; improving navigation; providing for the storage and delivery of the waters of the Colorado River for reclamation of lands, including supplemental water supplies, and for municipal, industrial, and other beneficial purposes; improving water quality; providing for basic public outdoor recreation facilities; improving conditions for fish and wildlife, and for the generation and sale of electrical power as an incident of the foregoing purposes.

(b) It is the policy of the Congress that the Secretary of the Interior (hereinafter referred to as the "Secretary") shall continue to develop, after consultation with affected States and appropriate Federal agencies, a regional water plan, consistent with the provisions of this Act and with future authorizations, to serve as the framework under which projects in the Colorado River Basin may be coordinated and constructed with proper timing to the end that an adequate supply of water may be made available for such projects, whether heretofore, herein, or hereafter authorized.

TITLE II – INVESTIGATIONS AND PLANNING
SEC. 201. . . .
SEC. 202. The Congress declares that the satisfaction of the requirements of the Mexican Water Treaty from the Colorado River constitutes a national obligation which shall be the first obligation of any water augmentation project planned pursuant to section 201 of this Act, and authorized by the Congress. Accordingly, the States of the Upper Division (Colorado, New Mexico, Utah, and Wyoming) and the States of the Lower Division (Arizona, California, and Nevada) shall be relieved from all obligations which may have been imposed upon them by article III(c) of the Colorado River Compact so long as the Secretary shall determine and proclaim that means are available and in operation which augment the water supply of the Colorado River system in such quantity as to satisfy the requirements of the Mexican Water Treaty together with any losses of water associated with the performance of that treaty; *Provided,* That the satisfaction of the requirements of the Mexican Water Treaty (Treaty Series 994, 50 Stat. 1219), shall be from the waters of the Colorado River pursuant to the treaties, laws, and compacts presently relating thereto, until such time as a feasible plan showing the most economical means of augmenting the water supply available in the Colorado River below Lee Ferry by two and one-half million acre-feet shall be authorized by the Congress and is in operation as provided in this Act.

. . .

TITLE III–AUTHORIZED UNITS: PROTECTION OF EXISTING USES
SEC., 301 (a) For the purposes of furnishing irrigation water and municipal water supplies to the water-deficient areas of Arizona and western New Mexico through direct diversion or exchange of water, control of floods, conservation and development of fish and wildlife resources, enhancement of recreation opportunities, and for other purposes, the Secretary shall construct, operate, and maintain the Central Arizona Project, consisting of the following principal works: (1) a system of main

conduits and canals, including a main canal and pumping plants (Granite Reef aqueduct and pumping plants), for diverting and carrying water from Lake Havasu to Orme Dam or suitable alternative which system may have a capacity of 3,000 cubic feet per second or whatever lesser capacity is found to be feasible: *Provided,* That any capacity in the Granite Reef aqueduct in excess of 2,500 cubic feet per second shall be utilized for the conveyance of Colorado River water only when Lake Powell is full or releases of water are made from Lake Powell to prevent the reservoir from exceeding elevation 3,700 feet above mean sea level or when releases are made pursuant to the proviso in section 602 (a) (3) of this Act: *Provided further,* That the costs of providing any capacity in excess of 2,500 cubic feet per second shall be repaid by those funds available to Arizona pursuant to the provision of subsection 403 (f) of this Act, or by funds from sources other than the development fund; (2) Orme Dam and Reservoir and power-pumping plant or suitable alternative; (3) Buttes Dam and Reservoir, which shall be so operated as not to prejudice the rights of any user in and to the waters of the Gila River as those rights are set forth in the decree entered by the United States District Court for the District of Arizona on June 29, 1935, in United States against Gila Valley Irrigation District and others (Globe Equity Numbered 59); (4) Hooker Dam and Reservoir or suitable alternative, which shall be constructed in such a manner as to give effect to the provisions of subsection (f) of section 304; (5) Charleston Dam and Reservoir; (6) Tucson aqueduct and pumping plants; (7) Salt-Gila aqueducts; (8) related canals, regulating facilities, hydroelectric power plants, and electrical transmission facilities required for the operation of said principal works; (9) related water distribution and drainage works; and (10) appurtenant works.

(b) Article II (B) (3) of the decree of the Supreme Court of the United States in Arizona against California (376 U.S. 340) shall be so administered that in any year in which, as determined by the Secretary, there is insufficient main stream Colorado River water available for release to satisfy annual consumptive use of seven million five hundred thousand acre-feet in Arizona, California, and Nevada, diversions from the main stream for the Central Arizona Project shall be so limited as to assure the availability of water in quantities sufficient to provide for the aggregate annual consumptive use by holders of present perfected rights, by other users in the State of California served under existing contracts with the United States by diversion works heretofore constructed, and by other existing Federal reservations in that State, of four million four hundred thousand acre-feet of mainstream water, and by users of the same character in Arizona and Nevada. Water users in the State of Nevada shall not be required to bear shortages in any proportion greater than would have been imposed in the absence of this subsection 301(b). This subsection shall not affect the relative priorities, among themselves, of water users in Arizona, Nevada, and California which are senior to diversions for the Central Arizona Project, or amend any provisions of said decree.

(c) The limitation stated in subsection (b) of this section shall not apply so long as the Secretary shall determine and proclaim that means are available and in operation which augment the water supply of the Colorado River system in such quantity as to make sufficient mainstream water available for release to satisfy annual consumptive use of seven million five hundred thousand acre-feet in Arizona, California, and Nevada.

SOURCE: Colorado River Basin Act, Public Law 90-537 (1968). U.S. Department of the Interior, Bureau of Reclamation. n.d. *Colorado River Basin Project.* http://www.usbr.gov/lc/region/g1000/pdfiles/crbproj.pdf (accessed August 23, 2014).

ANALYSIS

Following Arizona's victory in the 1963 landmark case *Arizona v. California*, new legislation from the U.S. Congress was required to apportion the remaining waters of the Colorado River that were in dispute. Although California had lost before the Supreme Court, it still had the votes to complicate matters for Arizona within Congress. Legislators from the two states thus negotiated among themselves much of the language that would subsequently appear in the Colorado River Basin Act of 1968 (CRBA).

For decades, Arizona legislators had dreamed of the Central Arizona Project (CAP). They envisioned a network of different types of water infrastructure that would transfer water from the Colorado River to both Phoenix and Tucson. Their ambitions had been blocked by California's legislators who feared that water transferred to Arizona was water lost by their state. With the passage of the CRBA, the CAP was finally a reality. Construction began in 1973 and was completed 20 years later. Arizona ultimately received a 336-mile network of aqueducts, canals, and tunnels that transferred water from the Colorado River at Lake Havasu to the Arizona counties of Pima, Pinal, and Maricopa.

The political and economic cost borne by Arizona for the CAP was significant. In exchange for the votes of the other states that relied on the Colorado River's waters, Arizona agreed to a significant and disproportionate reduction in the amount of water it received during times that the Colorado River was unable to provide each state's allotment. This means that in times of severe drought, Arizona's citizens are in far more danger of losing their water source than their counterparts in other states.

To compound matters, section 202 privileges Mexico's water needs above all other users. It is clearly stated in that section that the United States will meet its international obligations with Mexico regardless of the amount of water flowing in the Colorado River. Since Mexico is guaranteed not to suffer a drop in its share of the Colorado River's waters, it puts the states, especially Arizona, in a precarious position when water is scarce in a waterway that is over-allocated for the amount of water that actually flows in it in the best of times.

FURTHER READING

August, Jack L., Jr. 1999. *Vision in the Desert: Carl Hayden and Hydropolitics in the American Southwest.* Fort Worth: Texas Christian University Press.

Fradkin, Philip L. 1995. *A River No More: The Colorado River and the West.* Expanded and updated ed. Berkeley: University of California Press.

Schulte, Steven C. 2002. *Wayne Aspinall and the Shaping of the American West*. Boulder: University of Colorado Press.

Sturgeon, Stephen Craig. 2002. *The Politics of Western Water: The Congressional Career of Wayne Aspinall*. Tucson: University of Arizona Press.

Part III

BORDER REGIONS

4

WATER AND MEXICO

"To Remove All Causes of Controversy Between Them"

- *Document:* The Rio Grande River Convention of 1906, excerpt
- *Date:* Signed at Washington, DC, on May 21, 1906. Ratified by the president of the United States on December 26, 1906; ratified by Mexico on January 5, 1907; proclaimed, January 16, 1907
- *Where:* Washington, DC
- *Significance:* The Rio Grande River Convention of 1906 was the first agreement negotiated by Mexico and United States concerning the apportionment of waters from a river shared by the respective countries.

DOCUMENT

Equitable Distribution of the Waters of the Rio Grande

. . .

A. PROCLAMATION

Whereas a Convention between the United States of America and the United States of Mexico, providing for the equitable distribution of the waters of the Rio Grande for irrigation purposes, and to remove all causes of controversy between them in respect thereto, was concluded and signed by their respective Plenipotentiaries at Washington on the twenty-first day of May, one thousand nine hundred and six, the original of which Convention being in the English and Spanish languages, is word for word as follows:

The United States of America and the United States of Mexico being desirous to provide for the equitable distribution of the waters of the Rio Grande for irrigation purposes, and to remove all causes of controversy between them in respect thereto, and being moved by considerations of international comity, have resolved to conclude a Convention for these purposes and have named as their Plenipotentiaries:

The President of the United States Of America, Elihu Root Secretary of State of the United States; and The President of the United Sates of Mexico, His Excellency Señor Don Joaquin D. Casasus, Ambassador Extraordinary and Plenipotentiary of the United States Of Mexico at Washington; who, after having exhibited their respective full powers, which were found to be in good and due form, have agreed upon the following articles:

Article I.

After the completion of the proposed storage dam near Engle, New Mexico, and the distributing system auxiliary thereto, and as soon as water shall be available in said system for the purpose, the United States shall deliver to Mexico a total of 60,000 acre-feet of water annually in the bed of the Rio Grande at the point where the head works of the Acequia Madre, known as the Old Mexican Canal, now exist above the city of Juarez, Mexico

Article II.

The delivery of the said amount of water shall be assured by the United States and shall be distributed through the year in the same proportions as the water supply proposed to be furnished from the said irrigation system to lands in the United States in the vicinity of El Paso, Texas, according to the following schedule, as nearly as may be possible:

In case, however, of extraordinary drought or serious accident to the irrigation system in the United States, the amount delivered to the Mexican Canal shall be

The Monthly Delivery Schedule of Water Provided by the United States to Mexico in the Bed of the Rio Grande River

	Acre-feet per month	Corresponding cubic feet of water
January	0	0
February	1,090	47,480,400
March	5,460	237,837,000
April	12,000	522,720,000
May	12,000	522,720,000
June	12,000	522,720,000
July	8,180	356,320,800
August	4,370	190,357,200
September	3,270	142,441,200
October	1,090	47,480,400
November	540	23,522,400
December	0	0
	60,000	

diminished in the same proportion as the water delivered to lands under said irrigation system in the United States.

Article III.

The said delivery shall be made without cost to Mexico, and the United States agrees to pay the whole cost of storing the said quantity of water to be delivered to Mexico, of conveying the same to the international line, of measuring the said water, and of delivering it in the river bed above the head of the Mexican Canal. It is understood that the United States assumes no obligation beyond the delivering of the water in the bed of the river above the head of the Mexican Canal.

Article IV.

The delivery of water as herein provided is not to be construed as a recognition by the United States of any claim on the part of Mexico to the said waters; and it is agreed that in consideration of such delivery of water, Mexico waives any and all claims to the waters of the Rio Grande for any purpose whatever between the head of the present Mexican Canal and Fort Quitman, Texas, and also declares fully settled and disposed of, and hereby waives, all claims heretofore asserted or existing, or that may hereafter arise, or be asserted, against the United States on account of any damages alleged to have been sustained by the owners of land in Mexico, by reason of the diversion by citizens of the United States of waters of the Rio Grande.

Article V.

The United States, in entering into this treaty, does not thereby concede, expressly or by implication, any legal basis for any claims heretofore asserted or which may be hereafter asserted by reason of any losses incurred by the owners of land in Mexico due or alleged to be due to the diversion of the waters of the Rio Grande within the United States; nor does the United States in anyway concede the establishment of any general principle or precedent by the concluding of this treaty. The understanding of both parties is that the arrangement contemplated by this treaty extends only to the portion of the Rio Grande which forms the international boundary, from the head of the Mexican Canal down to Fort Quitman, Texas, and in no other case.

Article VI.

The present Convention shall be ratified by both contracting parties in accordance with their constitutional procedure, and the ratifications shall be exchanged at Washington as soon as possible.

In witness whereof, the respective Plenipotentiaries have signed the Convention both in the English and Spanish languages and have thereunto affixed their seals. Done in duplicate at the City of Washington, this 21st day of May, one thousand nine hundred and six.

Elihu Root [SEAL.] Joaquin D Casasus [SEAL.]

And whereas the said Convention has been duly ratified on both parts, and the ratifications of the two governments were exchanged in the City of Washington, on the sixteenth day of January, one thousand nine hundred and seven;

Now, therefore, be it known that I, Theodore Roosevelt, President of the United States of America, have caused the said Convention to be made public, to the end that the same and every article and clause thereof may be observed and fulfilled with good faith by the United States and the citizens thereof.

SOURCE: Convention Between the United States and Mexico: Equitable Distribution of the Waters of the Rio Grande. 1919. Treaty Series, No. 455. Washington, DC: Government Printing Office.

ANALYSIS

The Rio Grande Water Convention of 1906 was a landmark agreement that marked the first occasion in North America where neighboring countries agreed to apportion the waters of a shared river. The agreement was necessitated by decades of conflict over the use of Rio Grande River's waters between residents of Texas and Mexico.

Disagreements began in the 1870s as Texans alleged that Mexicans residing in the Juarez Valley were illegally diverting water from the Rio Grande to irrigate their agricultural lands. Mexico, on behalf of its citizens, denied that there were any illegal withdrawals. In truth, there were no precedents as to the legality of how the waters were to be utilized since that issue had never been addressed in either the 1848 Treaty of Guadalupe Hidalgo or the Gadsden Treaty of 1853. Tensions smoldered for years but did not reach a crisis point until the late-1880s when a serious drought gripped the region. The Texans turned to Anson Mills, a military engineer, who wrote a report endorsing the claims of the Texans, which was subsequently shared with members of the U.S. Congress. Congress opted to begin negotiations with the Mexican government to come to an equitable solution. Mexico took the negotiating stance that the shortage of water to meet the needs of Texas was not the fault of Mexico, but instead that of the United States, which allowed excessive withdrawals of the Rio Grande's headwaters in Colorado. The United States responded with the famous "Harmon Doctrine," in which U.S. Attorney General Judson Harmon determined that the United States did not need to negotiate an international agreement concerning the Rio Grande River because south of El Paso, the river was not navigable. Without a navigable river, there were no commercial relationships being impacted between the respective countries. Under Harmon's reasoning, Mexico should be happy with whatever the United States chose to share with it because the United States was not under any legal obligation to give any of the Rio Grande's water to Mexico. Despite their initial bargaining stances, the two countries were able to come to a mutually acceptable agreement in 1906.

The agreement itself was fairly straightforward. The treaty governs the waters of the Rio Grande River from its headwaters in Colorado to its confluence with the Conchos River near Fort Quitman, Texas. Of the amount that naturally flows down that section of the river, Mexico was awarded 60,000 acre-feet of water, which translated to less than 10 percent of the available water. At the time the treaty was negotiated, that was more than enough water to meet Mexico's needs since the region was sparsely populated. Unfortunately for Mexico, provisions were not made to adjust the apportionment should the population grow, which it did. There was language inserted to protect the interests of the United States should water flows decrease due to drought or other unforeseen calamity. If reductions were made, each country would see the same percentage drop in their allocation. Many of the inequities evident in the agreement would be addressed by Mexico during the negotiation of the United States—Mexico Water Treaty of 1944.

FURTHER READING

Hundley, Norris, Jr. 1966. *Dividing the Waters: A Century of Controversy Between the United States and Mexico*. Berkeley: University of California Press.
Littlefield, Douglas R. 2008. *Conflict on the Rio Grande: Water and the Law, 1879–1939*. Norman: University of Oklahoma Press.

"To Avoid Difficulties Occasioned by Reason of the Changes Which Take Place in the Beds of the Rio Grande (Rio Bravo) and the Colorado River"

- *Document:* The United States–Mexico Water Treaty, excerpt
- *Date:* Signed on February 3, 1944. Ratified by the U.S. Senate on April 18, 1945. Ratified by Mexico on October 6, 1945. Ratified by the President of the United States on November 1, 1945. The treaty was effective on November 8, 1945.
- *Where:* Washington, DC
- *Significance:* The treaty established how Mexico and the United States would manage and develop the portions of the Colorado, Rio Grande, and Tijuana rivers that they shared. The two countries also more clearly defined the role that the International Boundary and Water Commission would play in resolving conflicts over the shared surface waters that would inevitably develop.

DOCUMENT

UTILIZATION OF WATERS
OF THE COLORADO AND TIJUANA RIVERS
AND OF THE RIO GRANDE
TREATY BETWEEN THE UNITED STATES OF AMERICA AND MEXICO
Signed at Washington February 3, 1944.
AND PROTOCOL

. . .

Article 2

The International Boundary Commission established pursuant to the provisions of the Convention between the United States and Mexico signed in Washington March 1, 1889 to facilitate the carrying out of the principles contained in the Treaty of November 12, 1884 and to avoid difficulties occasioned by reason of the changes which take place in the beds of the Rio Grande (Rio Bravo) and the Colorado River shall hereafter be known as the International Boundary and Water Commission, United States and Mexico, which shall continue to function for the entire period during which the present Treaty shall continue in force. Accordingly, the term of the Convention of March 1, 1889 shall be considered to be indefinitely extended, and the Convention of November 21, 1900 between the United States and Mexico regarding that Convention shall be considered completely terminated.

The application of the present Treaty, the regulation and exercise of the rights and obligations which the two Governments assume thereunder, and the settlement of all disputes to which its observance and execution may give rise are hereby entrusted the International Boundary and Water Commission, which shall function in conformity with the powers and limitations set forth in this treaty.

The Commission shall in all respects have the status of an international body, and shall consist of a United States Section and a Mexican Section. The head of each Section shall be an Engineer Commissioner. Wherever there are provisions in this Treaty for joint action or joint agreement by the two Governments, or for the furnishing of reports, studies or plans to the two Governments, or similar provisions, it shall be understood that the particular matter in question shall be handled by or through the Department of State of the United States and the Ministry of Foreign Relations of Mexico.

The Commission or either of its two Sections may employ such assistants and engineering and legal advisers as it may deem necessary. Each government shall accord diplomatic status to the Commissioner, designated by the other Government. The Commissioner, two principal engineers, a legal adviser, and a secretary, designated by each Government as members of its Section of the Commission, shall be entitled in the territory of the other country to the privileges and immunities appertaining to diplomatic officers. The Commission and its personnel may freely carry out their observations, studies and field work in the territory of either country.

The jurisdiction of the Commission shall extend to the limitrophe parts of the Rio Grande (Rio Bravo) and the Colorado River, to the land boundary between the two countries, and to works located upon their common boundary, each Section of the Commission retaining jurisdiction over that part of the works located within the limits of its own country. Neither Section shall assume jurisdiction or control over works located within the limits of the country of the other without the express consent of the Government of the latter. The works constructed, acquired or used in fulfillment of the provisions of this Treaty and located wholly within the territorial limits of either country, although these works may be international in character, shall remain, except as herein otherwise specifically provided, under the exclusive jurisdiction and control of the Section of the Commission in whose country the works may be situated.

The duties and powers vested in the Commission by the Treaty shall be in addition to those vested in the International Boundary Commission by the Convention of March 1, 1889 and other pertinent treaties and agreements in force between the two countries except as the provisions of any of them may be modified by the present Treaty.

Each Government shall bear the expenses incurred in the maintenance of its Section of the Commission. The joint expenses, which may be incurred as agreed upon by the Commission, shall be borne equally by the two Governments.

Article 3

In matters in which the Commission may be called upon to make provision for the joint use of international waters, the following order of preferences shall serve as a guide:

1. Domestic and municipal uses.
2. Agriculture and stock-raising.
3. Electric Power.
4. Other industrial uses.
5. Navigation.
6. Fishing and hunting.
7. Any other beneficial uses which may be determined by the Commission.

All of the foregoing uses shall be subject to any sanitary measures or works which may be mutually agreed upon by the two Governments, which hereby agree to give preferential attention to the solution of all border sanitation problems.

SOURCE: International Boundary and Water Commission, United States and Mexico, U.S. Section. n.d. *Utilization of Waters of the Colorado and Tijuana River and of the Rio Grande.* http://www.ibwc.gov/Files/1944Treaty.pdf (accessed August 23, 2014).

ANALYSIS

The United States–Mexico Water Treaty of 1944 determined how Mexico and the United States would protect, develop, and distribute the waters on the portions of the Colorado and Tijuana rivers, along with the Rio Grande, which they share. Both countries were motivated to make the agreement due to local political needs. Mexico desired the agreement because its population was growing along the border, but the water sources they depended on were diminishing at the same time. A significant source of the problem was the Colorado River, whose waters were being diverted to irrigate large portions of the western United States. The flow was also being reduced by the construction of dams along its length, which were impounding the water instead of allowing it to flow freely. An agreement that provided Mexico with a guaranteed amount of water from the Colorado was thus desperately needed by the country. The United States was amenable to an agreement because they wanted to shore up diplomatic relations between the two countries to ensure that Mexico supported U.S. interests during the ongoing World War II. Both countries thus benefitted from the resulting treaty.

While the treaty apportioned the waters of three rivers between the two countries, Mexico was particularly pleased with being guaranteed 1.5 million acre-feet of water from the Colorado River annually. Much of that amount was provided to Mexicali. Mexico was also allowed to construct the Morelos Dam, which made the country less dependent on the United States for its water supply. One group dissatisfied with the agreement in the United States was California's congressional delegation. The state and its congressmen unsuccessfully attempted to block the treaty's ratification in Congress because they believed that the water needs of their state outweighed those of a neighboring country. In short, any water sent to Mexico was water denied to California's residents.

Title II of the agreement has particularly proven noteworthy as it redefined the function of the International Boundary and Water Commission (IBWC). The IBWC replaced the International Boundary Commission, which was created between the two countries in 1889. The IBWC was charged as both an administrative and a diplomatic agency to manage the shared rivers and settle disputes that arise. The organization has become a model for other international agencies, as the Mexican and American parts of the organization have successfully worked on issues such as the improvement of the water quality and setting minimal water standards that apply equally to both sides of the border.

FURTHER READING

Mumme, Stephen P. 2008. "The Liquid Frontier: Water and Sustainable Development on the U.S.–Mexico Border." *Journal of the West* 47, no. 3: 56–64.
Sánchez, Anabel. 2006. "1944 Water Treaty Between Mexico and the United States: Present Situation and Future Potential." *Frontera Norte* 18, no. 36: 125–144.

"To Characterize, Map, and Model Priority Transboundary Aquifers"

- *Document:* The United States–Mexico Transboundary Aquifer Assessment Act, excerpts
- *Date:* December 22, 2006
- *Where:* Washington, DC
- *Significance:* The act funded 10 years of research on the aquifers straddling the border between the United States and Mexico.

DOCUMENT

An Act

To authorize the Secretary of the Interior to cooperate with the States on the border with Mexico and other appropriate entities in conducting a hydrogeologic characterization, mapping, and modeling program for priority Transboundary aquifers, and for other purposes.

Be it enacted by the Senate and House of Representatives of the United States of America in Congress assembled,

SECTION 1. SHORT TITLE.

This Act may be cited as the "United States-Mexico Transboundary Aquifer Assessment Act."

SEC. 2. PURPOSE.

The purpose of this Act is to direct the Secretary of the Interior to establish a United States-Mexico transboundary aquifer assessment program to systematically assess priority Transboundary aquifers.

. . .

SEC. 4. ESTABLISHMENT OF PROGRAM.

(a) IN GENERAL.—The Secretary, in consultation and cooperation with the Participating States, the water resources research institutes, Sandia National Laboratories, and other appropriate entities in the United States and Mexico, and the IBWC, as appropriate, shall carry out the United States-Mexico Transboundary aquifer assessment program to characterize, map, and model priority transboundary aquifers along the United States-Mexico border at a level of detail determined to be appropriate for the particular aquifer.

(b) OBJECTIVES.—The objectives of the program are to—

1. develop and implement an integrated scientific approach to identify and assess priority transboundary aquifers, including—

   (A) for purposes of subsection (c)(2), specifying priority transboundary aquifers for further analysis by assessing—

      (i) the proximity of a proposed priority transboundary aquifer to areas of high population density;

      (ii) the extent to which a proposed priority transboundary aquifer would be used;

      (iii) the susceptibility of a proposed priority transboundary aquifer to contamination; and

      (iv) any other relevant criteria;

   (B) evaluating all available data and publications as part of the development of study plans for each priority transboundary aquifer;

   (C) creating a new, or enhancing an existing, geographic information system database to characterize the spatial and temporal aspects of each priority Transboundary aquifer; and

   (D) using field studies, including support for and expansion of ongoing monitoring and metering efforts, to develop—

      (i) the additional data necessary to adequately define aquifer characteristics; and

      (ii) scientifically sound groundwater flow models to assist with State and local water management and administration, including modeling of relevant groundwater and surface water interactions;

2. consider the expansion or modification of existing agreements, as appropriate, between the United States Geological Survey, the Participating States, the water resources research institutes, and appropriate authorities in the United States and Mexico, to—

144

(A) conduct joint scientific investigations;

(B) archive and share relevant data; and

(C) carry out any other activities consistent with the program; and

3. produce scientific products for each priority transboundary aquifer that—

(A) are capable of being broadly distributed; and

(B) provide the scientific information needed by water managers and natural resource agencies on both sides of the United States-Mexico border to effectively accomplish the missions of the managers and agencies.

(C) DESIGNATION OF PRIORITY TRANSBOUNDARY AQUIFERS.—

1. IN GENERAL.—For purposes of the program, the Secretary shall designate as priority transboundary aquifers—

(A) the Hueco Bolson and Mesilla aquifers underlying parts of Texas, New Mexico, and Mexico;

(B) the Santa Cruz River Valley aquifers underlying Arizona and Sonora, Mexico; and

(C) the San Pedro aquifers underlying Arizona and Sonora, Mexico.

2. ADDITIONAL AQUIFERS.—The Secretary may, using the criteria under subsection (b)(1)(A), evaluate and designate additional priority transboundary aquifers which underlie New Mexico or Texas.

(D) COOPERATION WITH MEXICO.—To ensure a comprehensive assessment of priority transboundary aquifers, the Secretary shall, to the maximum extent practicable, work with appropriate Federal agencies and other organizations to develop partnerships with, and receive input from, relevant organizations in Mexico to carry out the program.

(E) GRANTS AND COOPERATIVE AGREEMENTS.—The Secretary may provide grants or enter into cooperative agreements and other agreements with the water resources research institutes and other Participating State entities to carry out the program.

SEC. 5. IMPLEMENTATION OF PROGRAM.

(a) COORDINATION WITH STATES, TRIBES, AND OTHER ENTITIES.—
The Secretary shall coordinate the activities carried out under the program with—

(1) the appropriate water resource agencies in the Participating States;

(2) any affected Indian tribes;

(3) any other appropriate entities that are conducting monitoring and metering activity with respect to a priority transboundary aquifer; and

(4) the IBWC, as appropriate.

(b) NEW ACTIVITY.—After the date of enactment of this Act, the Secretary shall not initiate any new field studies or analyses under the program before consulting with, and coordinating the activity with, any Participating State water resource agencies that have jurisdiction over the aquifer.

(c) STUDY PLANS; COST ESTIMATES.—

    (1) IN GENERAL.—The Secretary shall work closely with appropriate Participating State water resource agencies, water resources research institutes, and other relevant entities to develop a study plan, timeline, and cost estimate for each priority transboundary aquifer to be studied under the program.

    (2) REQUIREMENTS.—A study plan developed under paragraph (1) shall, to the maximum extent practicable—

        (A) integrate existing data collection and analyses conducted with respect to the priority transboundary aquifer;

        (B) if applicable, improve and strengthen existing groundwater flow models developed for the priority transboundary aquifer; and

        (C) be consistent with appropriate State guidelines and goals.

SEC. 6. EFFECT.

(a) IN GENERAL.—Nothing in this Act affects—

    (1) the jurisdiction or responsibility of a Participating State with respect to managing surface or groundwater resources in the Participating State;

    (2) the water rights of any person or entity using water from a transboundary aquifer; or

    (3) State water law, or an interstate compact or international treaty governing water.

(b) TREATY.—Nothing in this Act shall delay or alter the implementation or operation of any works constructed, modified, acquired, or used within the territorial limits of the United States relating to the waters governed by the Treaty Between the United States and Mexico Regarding Utilization of Waters of the Colorado and Tijuana Rivers and of the Rio Grande, Treaty Series 994(59 Stat. 1219).

SEC. 7. REPORTS.

Not later than 5 years after the date of enactment of this Act, and on completion of the program in fiscal year 2016, the Secretary shall submit to the appropriate water resource agency in the Participating States, an interim and final report, respectively, that describes—

    (1) any activities carried out under the program;

    (2) any conclusions of the Secretary relating to the status of priority transboundary aquifers; and

    (3) the level of participation in the program of entities in Mexico.

SEC. 8. AUTHORIZATION OF APPROPRIATIONS.

(a) IN GENERAL.—There are authorized to be appropriated to carry out this Act $50,000,000 for the period of fiscal years 2007 through 2016.

    . . .

SEC. 9. SUNSET OF AUTHORITY.

The authority of the Secretary to carry out any provisions of this Act shall terminate 10 years after the date of enactment of this Act.

Approved December 22, 2006.

SOURCE: 109th Congress. 2006. *Public Law 109-448.* http://www.gpo.gov/fdsys/pkg/ STATUTE-120/pdf/STATUTE-120-Pg3328.pdf (accessed August 21, 2014).

ANALYSIS

Although the United States and Mexico had negotiated international agreements concerning shared surface waters, most notably the United States–Mexico Water Treaty of 1944, no agreements had been made concerning groundwater. There were two reasons why neither country had discussed the issue with the other. First, much of the water usage into the latter portion of the twentieth century involved shared rivers and streams. Secondly, the scientific data concerning the groundwater sources was very limited. The research that had been conducted on some of the aquifers by groups such as the United States Geological Survey and the International Boundary and Water Commission and by scientists at research universities had tended to be narrowly focused. The importance of groundwater increased as the population boomed on both sides of the border. Gradually, it became increasingly difficult for the region's surface waters to meet everyone's needs. Many began tapping groundwater sources to augment their supply of surface water.

Recognizing that better information was required on the estimated 20 aquifers shared by the United States and Mexico, Congress passed the United States–Mexico Transboundary Aquifer Assessment Act of 2006. The research initiative was not just for federal agencies and officials but also included researchers at the state level and in Mexico. The participation of Mexican officials was vitally important due to the need for consensus on both sides of the border on how to manage the shared resources. The research, which is ongoing until 2016, represents the first step between Mexico and the United States in reaching an accord affecting their shared groundwater that reaches the scope of the amended United States–Mexico Water Treaty of 1944.

FURTHER READING

Eckstein, Gabriel E. 2011. "Buried Treasure of Buried Hope? The Status of Mexico–U.S. Transboundary Aquifers Under International Law." *International Community Law Review* 13, no. 3: 273–290.

Hathaway, Deborah L. 2011. "Transboundary Water Policy: Developing Approaches in the Western and Southwestern United States." *Journal of the American Water Resources Association* 47, no. 1: 103–113.

Sanchez-Munguia, Vicente. 2011. "The US–Mexico Border: Conflict and Co-operation in Water Management." *International Journal of Water Resources Development* 27, no. 3: 577–593.

Sandoval-Solis, Samuel, et al. 2011. "Groundwater Banking in the Rio Grande Basin." *Journal of Water Resources Planning & Management* 137, no. 1: 62–71.

5

WATER AND CANADA

"All Navigable Boundary Waters Shall Forever Continue Free and Open"

- *Document:* The Boundary Waters Treaty of 1909, excerpt
- *Date:* Agreed to on January 11, 1909. Final ratification by all parties on May 5, 1910
- *Where:* Washington, DC
- *Significance:* The Boundary Waters Treaty of 1909 defined how the waters shared by the United States and Canada, represented by Great Britain, would be managed.

DOCUMENT

TREATY BETWEEN THE UNITED STATES AND GREAT BRITAIN RELATING TO BOUNDARY WATERS, AND QUESTIONS ARISING BETWEEN THE UNITED STATES AND CANADA

. . .

PRELIMINARY ARTICLE

For the purpose of this treaty boundary waters are defined as the waters from main shore to main shore of the lakes and rivers and connecting waterways, or the portions thereof, along which the international boundary between the United States and the Dominion of Canada passes, including all bays, arms, and inlets thereof, but not including tributary waters which in their natural channels would flow into such lakes, rivers, and waterways, or waters flowing from such lakes, rivers, and waterways, or the waters of rivers flowing across the boundary.

ARTICLE I

The High Contracting Parties agree that the navigation of all navigable boundary waters shall forever continue free and open for the purposes of commerce to the inhabitants and to the ships, vessels, and boats of both countries equally, subject, however, to any laws and regulations of either country, within its own territory, not inconsistent with such privilege of free navigation and applying equally and without discrimination to the inhabitants, ships, vessels, and boats of both countries.

It is further agreed that so long as this treaty shall remain in force, this same right of navigation shall extend to the waters of Lake Michigan and to all canals connecting boundary waters, and now existing or which may hereafter be constructed on either side of the line. Either of the High Contracting Parties may adopt rules and regulations governing the use of such canals within its own territory and may charge tolls for the use thereof, but all such rules and regulations and all tolls charged shall apply alike to the subjects or citizens of the High Contracting Parties and the ships, vessels, and boats of both of the High Contracting Parties, and they shall be placed on terms of equality in the use thereof.

ARTICLE II

Each of the High Contracting Parties reserves to itself or to the several State Governments on the one side and the Dominion or Provincial Governments on the other as the case may be, subject to any treaty provisions now existing with respect thereto, the exclusive jurisdiction and control over the use and diversion, whether temporary or permanent, of all waters on its own side of the line which in their natural channels would flow across the boundary or into boundary waters; but it is agreed that any interference with or diversion from their natural channel of such waters on either side of the boundary, resulting in any injury on the other side of the boundary, shall give rise to the same rights and entitle the injured parties to the same legal remedies as if such injury took place in the country where such diversion or interference occurs; but this provision shall not apply to cases already existing or to cases expressly covered by special agreement between the parties hereto. It is understood however, that neither of the High Contracting Parties intends by the foregoing provision to surrender any right, which it may have, to object to any interference with or diversions of waters on the other side of the boundary the effect of which would be productive of material injury to the navigation interests on its own side of the boundary.

ARTICLE III

It is agreed that, in addition to the uses, obstructions, and diversions heretofore permitted or hereafter provided for by special agreement between the Parties hereto, no further or other uses or obstructions or diversions, whether temporary or permanent, of boundary waters on either side of the line, affecting the natural level or flow of boundary waters on the other side of the line shall be made except by authority of the United States or the Dominion of Canada within their respective jurisdictions and with the approval, as hereinafter provided, of a joint commission, to be known as the International Joint Commission.

The foregoing provisions are not intended to limit or interfere with the existing rights of the Government of the United States on the one side and the Government of the Dominion of Canada on the other, to undertake and carry on governmental works in boundary waters for the deepening of channels, the construction of break-waters, the improvement of harbours, and other governmental works for the benefit of commerce and navigation, provided that such works are wholly on its own side of the line and do not materially affect the level or flow of the boundary waters on the other, nor are such provisions intended to interfere with the ordinary use of such waters for domestic and sanitary purposes.

ARTICLE IV

The High Contracting Parties agree that, except in cases provided for by special agreement between them, they will not permit the construction or maintenance on their respective sides of the boundary of any remedial or protective works or any dams or other obstructions in waters flowing from boundary waters or in waters at a lower level than the boundary in rivers flowing across the boundary, the effect of which is to raise the natural level of waters on the other side of the boundary unless the construction or maintenance thereof is approved by the aforesaid International Joint Commission.

It is further agreed that the waters herein defined as boundary waters and waters flowing across the boundary shall not be polluted on either side to the injury of health or property on the other.

ARTICLE V

The High Contracting Parties agree that it is expedient to limit the diversion of waters from the Niagara River so that the level of Lake Erie and the flow of the stream shall not be appreciably affected. It is the desire of both Parties to accomplish this object with the least possible injury to investments which have already been made in the construction of power plants on the United States side of the river under grants of authority from State of New York, and on the Canadian side of the river under licences authorized by the Dominion of Canada and the Province of Ontario.

So long as this treaty shall remain in force, no diversion of the waters of the Niagara River above the Falls from the natural course and stream thereof shall be permitted except for the purposes and to the extent hereinafter provided.

- The United States may authorize and permit the diversion within the State of New York of the waters of said river above the Falls of Niagara, for power purposes, not exceeding in the aggregate a daily diversion at the rate of twenty thousand cubic feet of water per second.
- The United Kingdom, by the Dominion of Canada, or the Province of Ontario, may authorize and permit the diversion within the Province of Ontario of the waters of said rive above the Falls of Niagara, for the power purposes, not exceeding in the aggregate a daily diversion at the rate of thirty-six thousand cubic feet of water per second.

- The prohibitions of this article shall not apply to the diversion of water for sanitary or domestic purposes, or for the service of canals for the purposes of navigation.

Note: The third, fourth and fifth paragraphs of Article V were terminated by the Canada-United States Treaty of February 27, 1950 concerning the diversion of the Niagara River.

ARTICLE VI

The High Contracting Parties agree that the St. Mary and Milk Rivers and their tributaries (in the State of Montana and the Provinces of Alberta and Saskatchewan) are to be treated as one stream for the purposes of irrigation and power, and the waters thereof shall be apportioned equally between the two countries, but in making such equal apportionment more than half may be taken from one river and less than half from the other by either country so as to afford a more beneficial use to each. It is further agreed that in the division of such waters during the irrigation season, between the 1st of April and 31st of October, inclusive, annually, the United States is entitled to a prior appropriation of 500 cubic feet per second of the waters of the Milk River, or so much of such amount as constitutes three-fourths of its natural flow, and that Canada is entitled to a prior appropriation of 500 cubic feet per second of the flow of St. Mary River, or so much of such amount as constitutes three-fourths of its natural flow.

The channel of the Milk River in Canada may be used at the convenience of the United States for the conveyance, while passing through Canadian territory, of waters diverted from the St. Mary River. The provisions of Article II of this treaty shall apply to any injury resulting to property in Canada from the conveyance of such waters through the Milk River.

The measurement and apportionment of the water to be used by each country shall from time to time be made jointly by the properly constituted reclamation officers of the United States and the properly constituted irrigation officers of His Majesty under the direction of the International Joint Commission.

ARTICLE VII

The High Contracting Parties agree to establish and maintain an International Joint Commission of the United States and Canada composed of six commissioners, three on the part of the United States appointed by the President thereof, and three on the part of the United Kingdom appointed by His Majesty on the recommendation of the Governor in Council of the Dominion of Canada.

ARTICLE VIII

This International Joint Commission shall have jurisdiction over and shall pass upon all cases involving the use or obstruction or diversion of the waters with respect to which under Article III or IV of this Treaty the approval shall be governed by the following rules of principles which are adopted by the High Contracting Parties for this purpose: The High Contracting Parties shall have, each on its own side of the boundary, equal and similar rights in the use of the waters hereinbefore defined as boundary waters.

The following order of precedence shall be observed among the various uses enumerated hereinafter for these waters, and no use shall be permitted which tends materially to conflict with or restrain any other use which is given preference over it in this order of precedence:

1. Uses for domestic and sanitary purposes;
2. Uses for navigation, including the service of canals for the purposes of navigation;
3. Uses for power and for irrigation purposes.

The foregoing provisions shall not apply to or disturb any existing uses of boundary waters on either side of the boundary. The requirement for an equal division may in the discretion of the Commission be suspended in cases of temporary diversions along boundary waters at points where such equal division can not be made advantageously on account of local conditions, and where such diversion does not diminish elsewhere the amount available for use on the other side.

The Commission in its discretion may make its approval in any case conditional upon the construction of remedial or protective works to compensate so far as possible for the particular use or diversion proposed, and in such cases may require that suitable and adequate provision, approved by the Commission, be made for the protection and indemnity against injury of all interests on the other side of the line which may be injured thereby.

In cases involving the elevation of the natural level of waters on either side of the line as a result of the construction or maintenance on the other side of remedial or protective works or dams or other obstructions in boundary waters flowing there from or in waters below the boundary in rivers flowing across the boundary, the Commission shall require, as a condition of its approval thereof, that suitable and adequate provision, approved by it, be made for the protection and indemnity of all interests on the other side of the line which may be injured thereby.

The majority of the Commissioners shall have power to render a decision. In case the Commission is evenly divided upon any question or matter presented to it for decision, separate reports shall be made by the Commissioners on each side to their own Government. The High Contracting Parties shall thereupon endeavour to agree upon an adjustment of the question or matter of difference, and if an agreement is reached between them, it shall be reduced to writing in the form of a protocol, and shall be communicated to the Commissioners, who shall take such further proceedings as may be necessary to carry out such agreement.

ARTICLE IX

The High Contracting Parties further agree that any other questions or matters of difference arising between them involving the rights, obligations, or interests of either in relation to the other or to the inhabitants of the other, along the common frontier between the United States and the Dominion of Canada, shall be referred from time to time to the International Joint Commission for examination and report, whenever either the Government of the United States or the Government of the Dominion of Canada shall request that such questions or matters of difference be so referred.

The International Joint Commission is authorized in each case so referred to examine into and report upon the facts and circumstances of the particular questions and matters referred, together with such conclusions and recommendations as may be appropriate, subject, however, to any restrictions or exceptions which may be imposed with respect thereto by the terms of the reference.

Such reports of the Commission shall not be regarded as decisions of the questions or matters so submitted either on the facts or the law, and shall in no way have the character of an arbitral award.

The Commission shall make a joint report to both Governments in all cases in which all or a majority of the Commissioners agree, and in case of disagreement the minority may make a joint report to both Governments, or separate reports to their respective Governments.

In case the Commission is evenly divided upon any question or matter referred to it for report, separate reports shall be made by the Commissioners on each side to their own Government.

ARTICLE X

Any questions or matters of difference arising between the High Contracting Parties involving the rights, obligations, or interests of the United States or of the Dominion of Canada either in relation to each other or to their respective inhabitants, may be referred for decision to the International Joint Commission by the consent of the two Parties, it being understood that on the part of the United States any such action will be by and with the advice and consent of the Senate, and on the part of His Majesty's Government with the consent of the Governor General in Council. In each case so referred, the said Commission is authorized to examine into and report upon the facts and circumstances of the particular questions any matters referred, together with such conclusions and recommendations as may be appropriate, subject, however, to any restrictions or exceptions which may be imposed with respect thereto by the terms of the reference.

A majority of the said Commission shall have power to render a decision or finding upon any of the questions or matters so referred.

If the said Commission is equally divided or otherwise unable to render a decision or finding as to any questions or matters so referred, it shall be the duty of the Commissioners to make a joint report to both Governments, or separate reports to their respective Governments, showing the different conclusions arrived at with regard to the matters or questions referred, which questions or matters shall thereupon be referred for decision by the High Contracting Parties to an umpire chosen in accordance with the procedure prescribed in the fourth, fifth and sixth paragraphs of Article XLV of the Hague Convention for the pacific settlement of international disputes, dated October 18, 1907. Such umpire shall have power to render a final decision with respect to those matters and questions so referred on which the Commission fail to agree.

ARTICLE XI

A duplicate original of all decisions rendered and joint reports made by the Commission shall be transmitted to and filed with the Secretary of State of the United States and the Governor General of the Dominion of Canada, and to them shall be addressed all communications of the Commission.

ARTICLE XII

The International Joint Commission shall meet and organize at Washington promptly after the members thereof are appointed, and when organized the Commission may fix such times and places for its meetings as may be necessary, subject at all times to special call or direction by the two Governments. Each Commissioner upon the first joint meeting of the Commission after his appointment, shall, before proceeding with the work of the Commission, make and subscribe a solemn declaration in writing that he will faithfully and impartially perform the duties imposed upon him under this treaty, and such declaration shall be entered on the records of the proceedings of the Commission.

The United States and Canadian sections of the Commission may each appoint a secretary, and these shall act as joint secretaries of the Commission at its joint sessions, and the Commission may employ engineers and clerical assistants from time to time as it may deem advisable. The salaries and personal expenses of the Commission and of the secretaries shall be paid by their respective Governments, and all reasonable and necessary joint expenses of the Commission, incurred by it, shall be paid in equal moieties by the High Contracting Parties.

The Commission shall have power to administer oaths to witnesses, and to take evidence on oath whenever deemed necessary in any proceeding, or inquiry, or matter within its jurisdiction under this treaty, and all parties interested therein shall be given convenient opportunity to be heard, and the High Contracting Parties agree to adopt such legislation as may be appropriate and necessary to give the Commission the powers above mentioned on each side of the boundary, and to provide for the issue of subpoenas and for compelling the attendance of witnesses in proceedings before the Commission before the Commission. The Commission may adopt such rules of procedure as shall be in accordance with justice and equity, and may make such examination in person and through agents or employees as may be deemed advisable.

ARTICLE XIII

In all cases where special agreements between the High Contracting Parties hereto are referred to in the foregoing articles, such agreements are understood and intended to include not only direct agreements between the High Contracting Parties, but also any mutual arrangement between the United States and the Dominion of Canada expressed by concurrent or reciprocal legislation on the part of Congress and the Parliament of the Dominion.

ARTICLE XIV

The present treaty shall be ratified by the President of the United States of America, by and with the advice and consent of the Senate, thereof, and by His

Britannic Majesty. The ratifications shall be exchanged at Washington as soon as possible and the treaty shall take effect on the date of the exchange of its ratifications. It shall remain in force for five years, dating from the day of exchange of ratifications, and thereafter until terminated by twelve months written notice given by either High Contracting Party to the other.

SOURCE: *Treaty Between the United States and Great Britain Relating to Boundary Waters, and Questions Arising Between the United States and Canada.* January 11, 1909. United States Treaties and Other International Agreements. Washington, DC: Government Printing Office, 2607.

ANALYSIS

The Boundary Waters Treaty of 1909 (BWT) was an agreement between the United States and Great Britain on how the freshwater sources shared by both countries would be utilized and protected. Unlike the Rio Grande Water Convention of 1906 between the United States and Mexico, which applied only to the portions of the respective waterways on the border, the BWT applied from "main shore to main shore of the lakes and rivers and connecting waterways, or the portions thereof, along which the international boundary between the United States and the Dominion of Canada passes, including all bays, arms, and inlets thereof." This meant that regulations established to protect waters on the border could be applied to waterways that extended far into the interior of the respective countries.

An impetus for the treaty negotiations were conflicts between American and Canadian interests over several waterways. In one case, Canada was diverting water from the Niagara River that would have otherwise gone into Lake Erie. The United States wanted the diversions stopped in order to protect Lake Erie's water levels into the future. The BWT resolved the conflict with Canada agreeing to stop diverting the waters from the Niagara River. The other problem resolved by the BWT involved how waters from the Milk and St. Mary rivers were being distributed between users along the border of Alberta and Montana. The BWT addressed the problems by distributing the waters equally between users on both sides of the border.

To ensure that sovereign interests were protected, the United States and Great Britain created the International Joint Commission (IJC), which included three representatives from each of the countries. These six individuals initially worked to mediate conflicts between citizens of the respective countries. As such, they essentially worked as an international court. Over time, the dependence on legal precedence faded as scientific concerns began to factor more into the IJC's work. This is reflected in the organization of the IJC today, as the six representatives are advised by 27 water boards, each with equal representation from the respective countries.

FURTHER READING

Dorsey, Kurkpatrick. 1998. *The Dawn of Conservation Diplomacy: U.S.—Canadian Wildlife Protection Treaties of the Progressive Era.* Seattle: University of Washington Press.

International Joint Commission (IJC). 2014. "IJC—Protecting Shared Waters." http://www.ijc.org/en_/.

Klein, K. K., Danny G. Le Roy, and Tatiana Cook. 2012. "International Water Sharing: Examining the Montana—Alberta Dispute in the Context of the Century-old Boundary Waters Treaty." *Water Policy* 14, no. 2: 358–370.

Spencer, Robert Allan, John J. Kirton, and Kim Richard Nossal, eds. 1981. *The International Joint Commission Seventy Years On.* Toronto: Centre for International Studies, University of Toronto.

"The Great Lakes Are Valuable Regional, National and International Resources"

- *Document:* The Great Lakes Charter, excerpt
- *Date:* February 11, 1985
- *Where:* Milwaukee, Wisconsin
- *Significance:* The purpose of the Great Lakes Charter was to prevent the transfer of waters from the respective lakes outside of the Great Lakes region.

DOCUMENT

THE GREAT LAKES CHARTER

Principles for the Management of Great Lakes Water Resources

FINDINGS

The Governors and Premiers of the Great Lakes States and Provinces jointly find and declare that:

The water resources of the Great Lakes Basin are precious public natural resources, shared and held in trust by the Great Lakes States and Provinces.

The Great Lakes are valuable regional, national and international resources for which the federal governments of the United States and Canada and the International Joint Commission have, in partnership with the States and Provinces, and important, continuing and abiding role and responsibility.

The Waters of the Great Lakes Basin are interconnected and part of a single hydrologic system. The multiple uses of these resources for municipal, industrial and agricultural water supply; mining; navigation; hydroelectric power and energy

DID YOU KNOW?

North American Water and Power Alliance

Daniel McCord Baker, an engineer for the Los Angeles Department of Water and Power, began in the early 1950s to promote a water development project that encompassed all of North America that he called the North American Water and Power Alliance (NAWAPA). His plan called for the creation of a network of interconnected rivers and reservoirs that extended from Alaska to Mexico. Included in the plan was the construction of the Canadian-Great Lakes Waterway, which was intended to connect the water network to both the Great Lakes and the Mississippi River. In total, the water scheme would have redistributed more than 35 trillion gallons of water between seven of Canada's provinces, 33 states in the United States, and parts of Northern Mexico.

The proposal was initially very popular in the western parts of the United States. Its supporters at the federal level included Congressman Stewart Udall of Arizona, the U.S. Army Corps of Engineers, and the Bureau of Reclamation. Support from the latter two was not surprising as the proposal promised decades of construction projects for them. Environmentalists opposed the plan by exposing its environmental costs. For example, the plan would have drastically altered both the Columbia and Fraser Rivers, two of the largest rivers on the continent, by combining them through what was dubbed the Columbia–Fraser Interchange. All the Great Lakes would have grown in size, because they were going to be used to store water until it was needed elsewhere. In fact, millions of acres of land throughout Canada and the United States would have been flooded if the plan had ever been implemented.

Although preliminary discussions about NAWAPA were held between U.S. Secretary of State Dean Rusk and his counterpart in Canada, the proposal never moved beyond the discussion stage. Canadians simply saw very little benefit for their country for participating in the water transfers, especially considering that Canada would have borne the brunt of the environmental impacts.

FURTHER READING

Burch, John R., Jr. 2011. "North American Water and Power Alliance." In *Encyclopedia of Water Politics and Policy in the United States*, ed. Steven Danver and John R. Burch Jr. Washington, DC: Congressional Quarterly Press.

production; recreation; and the maintenance of fish and wildlife habitat and a balanced ecosystem are interdependent.

Studies conducted by the International Joint Commission, the Great Lakes States and Provinces, and other agencies have found that without careful and prudent management, the future development of diversions and consumptive uses of the water resources of the Great Lakes Basin may have significant adverse impacts on the environment, economy, and welfare of the Great Lakes region.

As trustees of the Basin's natural resources, the Great Lakes States and Provinces have a shared duty to protect, conserve, and manage the renewable but finite waters of the Great Lakes Basin for the use, benefit, and enjoyment of all their citizens, including generations yet to come. The most effective means of protecting, conserving and managing the water resources of the Great Lakes is through the joint pursuit of unified and cooperative principles, policies and programs mutually agreed upon, enacted and adhered to by each and every Great Lakes State and Province.

Management of the water resources of the Basin is subject to the jurisdiction, rights and responsibilities of the signatory States and Provinces. Effective management of the water resources of the Great Lakes requires the exercise of such jurisdiction, rights, and responsibilities in the interest of all the people of the Great Lakes Region, acting in a continuing spirit of comity and mutual cooperation. The Great Lakes States and Provinces reaffirm the mutual rights and obligations of all Basin jurisdictions to use, conserve, and protect Basin water resources, as expressed in the Boundary Waters Treaty of 1909, the Great Lakes Water Quality Agreement, of 1978, and the principles of other applicable international agreements.

PURPOSE

The purposes of this Charter are to conserve the levels and flows of the Great Lakes and their tributary and connecting waters; to protect and conserve the environmental balance of the Great Lakes Basin ecosystem; to provide for cooperative programs and management of the water resources of the Great Lakes Basin by the signatory States and Provinces; to make secure and protect present developments within the region; and to provide a secure foundation for future investment and development within the region.

McCool, Daniel. 1994. *Command of the Waters: Iron Triangles, Federal Water Development, and Indian Waters*. Tucson: University of Arizona Press.
Reisner, Marc. 1986. *Cadillac Desert: The American West and Its Disappearing Water*. New York: Viking.

PRINCIPLES FOR THE MANAGEMENT OF GREAT LAKES WATER RESOURCES

In order to achieve the purposes of this Charter, the Governors and Premiers of the Great Lakes States and Provinces agree to the following principles.

Principle I

Integrity of the Great Lakes Basin

The planning and management of the water resources of the Great Lakes Basin should recognize and be founded upon the integrity of the natural resources and ecosystem of the Great Lakes Basin. The water resources of the Basin transcend political boundaries within the Basin, and should be recognized and treated as a single hydrologic system. In managing Great Lakes Basin waters, the natural resources and ecosystem of the Basin should be considered as a unified whole.

Principle II

Cooperation Among Jurisdictions

The signatory States and Provinces recognize and commit to a spirit of cooperation among local, state, and provincial agencies, the federal governments of Canada and the United States, and the International Joint Commission in the study, monitoring, planning, and conservation of the water resources of the Great Lakes Basin.

Principle III

Protection of the Water Resources of the Great Lakes

The signatory States and Provinces agree that new or increased diversions and consumptive uses of Great Lakes Basin water resources are of serious concern. In recognition of their shared responsibility to conserve and protect the water resources of the Great Lakes Basin for the use, benefit, and enjoyment of all their citizens, the States and Provinces agree to seek (where necessary) and to implement legislation establishing programs to manage and regulate the diversion and consumptive use of Basin water resources. It is the intent of the signatory states and provinces that diversions of Basin water resources will not be allowed if individually or cumulatively they would have any significant adverse impacts on lake levels, in-basin uses, and the Great Lakes Ecosystem.

Principle IV

Prior Notice and Consultation

It is the intent of the signatory States and Provinces that no Great Lakes State or Province will approve or permit any major new or increased diversion or consumptive use of the water resources of the Great Lakes Basin without notifying and consulting with and seeking the consent and concurrence of all affected Great Lakes States and Provinces.

Principle V

Cooperative Programs and Practices
The Governors and Premieres of the Great Lakes States and Provinces commit to pursue the development and maintenance of a common base of data and information regarding the use and management of the Basin water resources, to the establishment of a systematic arrangements for the exchange of water data and information, to the creation of a Water Resources Management Committee, to the development of a Great Lakes Water Resources Management Program, and to additional and concerted and coordinated research efforts to provide improved information for future water planning and management decisions.

IMPLEMENTATION OF PRINCIPLES

Common Base of Data
The Great Lakes States and Provinces will pursue the development and maintenance of a common base of data and information regarding the use and management of Basin water resources and the establishment of systematic arrangements for the exchange of water data and information. The common base of data will include the following:

1. Each State and Province will collect and maintain, in comparable form, data regarding the location, type, and qualities of water use, diversion, and consumptive use, and information regarding projections of current and future needs.
2. In order to provide accurate information as a basis for future water resources planning and management, each State and Province will establish and maintain a system for the collection of data on major water uses, diversions, and consumptive uses in the Basin. The States and Provinces, in cooperation with the Federal Governments of Canada and the United States and the International Joint Commission, will seek appropriate vehicles and institutions to assure responsibility for coordinated collation, analysis, and dissemination of data and information.
3. The Great Lakes States and Provinces will exchange on a regular basis plans, data, and other information on water use, conservation, and development, and will consult with each other in the development of programs and plans to carry out these provisions.

Water Resources Management Committee
A Water Resources Management Committee will be formed, composed of representatives appointed by the Governors and Premiers of each of the Great Lakes States and Provinces.

Appropriate agencies of the federal governments, the International Joint Commission, and other interested and expert organizations will be invited to participate in discussions of the Committee.

The Committee will be charged with responsibility to identify specific common water data needs; to develop and design a system for the collection and exchange of comparable water resources management data; to recommend institutional arrangements to facilitate the exchange and maintenance of such information; and to develop procedures to implement the prior notice and consultation process established in this Charter. The Committee will report its findings to the Governors and Premiers of the Great Lakes States and Provinces within 15 months of the appointment of the Committee.

Consultation Procedures

The principle of prior notice and consultation will apply to any new or increased diversion or consumptive use of the water resources of the Great Lakes Basin which exceeds 5,000,000 gallons (19 million litres) per day average in any 30-day period.

The consultation process will include the following procedures:

1. The State or Province with responsibility for issuing the approval or permit, after receiving an application for such diversion or consumptive use, will notify the Offices of the Governors and Premiers of the respective Great Lakes States and Provinces, the appropriate water management agencies of the Great Lakes States and Provinces and, where appropriate, the International Joint Commission.

2. The permitting State or Province will solicit and carefully consider the comments and concerns of the other Great Lakes States and Provinces, and where applicable the International Joint Commission, prior to rendering a decision on an application.

3. Any State or Province which believes itself to be affected may file a written objection to the proposed diversion or consumptive use. Notice of such objection stating the reasons therefore will be given to the permitting State or Province and all other Great Lakes States and Provinces.

4. In the event of an objection to a proposed diversion or consumptive use, the permitting State or Province will convene a consultation process of the affected Great Lakes States and Provinces to investigate and consider the issues involved, and to seek and provide mutually agreeable recommendations to the permitting State or Province.

5. The permitting State or Province will carefully consider the concerns and objections expressed by other Great Lakes States and Provinces, and the recommendations of any consultation process convened under this Charter.

6. The permitting State or Province will have lead responsibility for resolution of water management permit issues. The permitting State or Province will notify each affected Great Lakes State or Province of its final decision to issue, issue with conditions, or deny a permit.

The prior notice and consultation process will be formally initiated following the development of procedures by the Water Resources Management Committee and approval of those procedures by the Governors and Premiers. During the interim period prior to approval of formal procedures, any State or Province may voluntarily undertake the notice and consultation procedures as it deems appropriate.

Basin Water Resources Management Program

In order to guide the future development, management, and conservation of the water resources of the Great Lakes Basin, the signatory States and Provinces commit to the development of a cooperative water resources management program for the Great Lakes Basin.

Such a program should include consideration of the following elements:

1. An inventory of the Basin's surface and groundwater resources;
2. An identification and assessment of existing and future demands for diversions, into as well as out of the Basin, withdrawals, and consumptive uses for municipal, domestic, agricultural, manufacturing, mining, navigation, power production, recreation, fish and wildlife, and other uses and ecological considerations;
3. The development of cooperative policies and practices to minimize the consumptive use of the Basin's water resources; and
4. Recommended policies to guide the coordinated conservation, development, protection, use, and management of the water resources of the Great Lakes Basin.

Research Program

The Great Lakes States and Provinces recognize the need for and support additional research in the area of flows and lake levels required to protect fisheries and wildlife, a balanced aquatic environment, navigation, important recreational uses, and the assimilative capacity of the Great Lakes system. Through appropriate state, provincial, federal and international agencies and other institutions, the Great Lakes States and Provinces will encourage coordinated and concerted research efforts in these areas, in order to provide improved information for future water planning and management decisions.

PROGRESS TOWARD IMPLEMENTATION

The Governors and Premiers of the Great Lakes States and Provinces commit to the coordinated implementation of this Charter. To this end, the Governors and Premiers shall, no less than once per year, review progress toward implementation of this Charter and advise one another on actions taken to carry out the principles of the Charter together with recommendations for further action or improvements to the management of the Great Lakes Basin water resources.

The signatory States and Provinces consider each of the principles and implementing provisions of this Charter to be material and interdependent. The rights of each State and Province under this Charter are mutually dependent upon the good faith performance by each State and Province of its commitments and obligations under the Charter.

The following sequence will be adhered to by the Great Lakes States and Provinces in implementing the provisions of this Charter:

1. The Water Resources Management Committee will be appointed by the Governors and Premiers within 60 days of the effective date of this Charter and will submit its recommendations to the Governors and Premiers of the Great Lakes States and Provinces within 15 months of the appointment of the Committee.

2. Upon the signing of the Charter, and concurrent with the activities of the Water Resources Management Committee, the Great Lakes States and Provinces will commence collecting and assembling existing Great Lakes water use data and information. The water use data collected and assembled by the States and Provinces will include, but not be limited to, the data and information specified under the "Common Base of Data" provisions of the Charter.

   Copies of the data and information collected and assembled by the States and Provinces will be submitted to the Water Resources Management Committee. The Great Lakes States and Provinces will pursue: the collection of data and information on the use and management of Basin water resources; the establishment of systematic arrangements for the exchange of water data and information on a continuing basis as enabled by existing state and provincial data collection and regulatory programs; and where necessary, the enactment of water withdrawal registration and diversion and consumptive use management and regulatory programs pursuant to the provisions of the Charter.

3. To assist in the ongoing collection of Great Lakes water use data and information, and in the development of the Basin Water Resources Management Program, States and Provinces will pursue the enactment of legislation where it is needed for the purpose of gathering accurate and comparable information on any new or increased withdrawal of Great Lakes Basin water resources in excess of 100,000 gallons (380,000 litres) per day average in any 30-day period.

4. The prior notice and consultation process will be formally initiated following the development of procedures by the Water Resources Management Committee and approval of those procedures by the Governors and Premiers. Any State or Province may voluntarily undertake additional notice and consultation procedures as it deems appropriate. However, the right of any individual State or Province to participate in the prior notice and consultation process, either before or after approval of formal procedures by the Governors and Premiers, is contingent upon its ability to provide accurate and comparable information on water withdrawals in excess of 100,000 gallons (380,000 litres) per day average in any 30-day period and its authority to manage and regulate water withdrawals involving a total diversion or

consumptive use of Great Lakes Basin water resources in excess of 2,000,000 gallons (7,600,000 litres) per day average in any 30-day period.

5. Development of the Basin Water Resources Management Program will commence upon receipt and formal approval by the Great Lakes Governors and Premiers of the recommendations of the Water Resources Management Committee.

RESERVATION OF RIGHTS

The Great Lakes States and Provinces mutually recognize the rights and standing of all Great Lakes States and Provinces to represent and protect the rights and interests of their respective jurisdictions and citizens in the shared water and other natural resources of the Great Lakes region.

Each Great Lakes State and Province reserves and retains all rights and authority to seek, in any state, provincial, federal, or other appropriate court or forum, adjudication or protection of their respective rights in and to Basin water resources, in such manner as may now or hereafter be provided by law.

In entering into this Charter, no Great Lakes State or Province shall be deemed to imply its consent to any diversion or consumptive use of Great Lakes Basin water resources now or in the future.

SOURCE: The Council of Great Lakes Governors. n.d. *The Great Lakes Charter.* http:// www.cglg.org/projects/water/docs/GreatLakesCharter.pdf (accessed August 21, 2014).

ANALYSIS

Lakes Erie, Huron, Michigan, Ontario, and Superior, collectively known as the Great Lakes, combine to form the largest source of freshwater in the world. They contain approximately 84 percent of the available freshwater in North America. Not surprisingly, residents in other parts of the United States who desire more water have looked hungrily toward the lakes for decades as a potential water source. The scale of some of the schemes that have been envisioned are almost beyond comprehension.

In the 1950s, Donald McCord Baker proposed the North American Water and Power Alliance (NAWAPA). He envisioned a water development project to connect rivers and reservoirs from Alaska to northern Mexico. In total, the project would have impacted 33 states in the United States, seven Canadian provinces, and parts of northern Mexico. If constructed, NAWAPA would have used the Great Lakes to store water until it was required in another part of the United States. Although widely discussed, primarily in the United States' arid west where its proponents resided, NAWAPA never stood a chance of being constructed because Canadians correctly surmised that the project would not have benefitted them at all, but would have required the country to endure severe environmental costs.

Another proposed water transfer that startled residents of the Great Lakes region occurred in 1981. A coal mining operation in Wyoming wanted to construct a roughly 1,900-mile pipeline to obtain water from Lake Superior so that it could make coal slurry. Due to the unwillingness of the U.S. Congress to grant the coal company the necessary eminent domain legislation to build the pipeline, the project was ultimately abandoned. The audacity of the proposal, and its many predecessors, convinced politicians in the states and provinces around the Great Lakes that they had to find a way to protect their water.

Through the Council of Great Lakes Governors, the governors of Illinois, Indiana, Michigan, Minnesota, New York, Ohio, Pennsylvania, and Wisconsin, and the premiers of Ontario and Quebec, began working together in 1983 to write a basinwide water policy. They determined that the Great Lakes were a shared resource; thus, any harm that came to the water levels in the respective lakes affected them all. Such an agreement required the establishment of basinwide standards, which required some of the states to strengthen their environmental standards. After two years of work, the Great Lakes Charter was signed on February 11, 1985.

While the Great Lakes Charter was greatly needed, the agreement was legally nonbinding since the U.S. Constitution does not grant states the ability to negotiate international agreements. That power is reserved for the federal government. The governors opted to request that Congress pass legislation to make the Great Lakes Charter binding. It proved a miscalculation as the charter was drastically revised. The original agreement was intended to prevent transfers outside of the Great Lakes Basin. In what became the Water Resources Development Act of 1986, the transfer prohibition was expanded to include water transfers within the basin. The prohibition even included transfers that never crossed a state boundary, which was justified by the claim in the Great Lakes Charter that all of the waters were a shared resource.

FURTHER READING

Annin, Peter. 2006. *The Great Lakes Water Wars*. Washington, DC: Island Press.

Burch, John R., Jr. 2011. "Great Lakes Charter (1985)." In *Encyclopedia of Water Politics and Policy in the United States*, ed. Steven L. Danver and John R. Burch Jr.. Washington, DC: Congressional Quarterly Press, 282–283.

Glass, Charles F., Jr. 2003. "Enforcing Great Lakes Water Export Restrictions Under the Water Resources Development Act of 1986." *Columbia Law Review* 103, no. 6: 1503–1537.

Heinmiller, B. Timothy. 2007. "Do Intergovernmental Institutions Matter? The Case of Water Diversion Regulation in the Great Lakes Basin." *Governance* 20, no. 4: 655–674.

Reisner, Marc. 1986. *Cadillac Desert: The American West and Its Disappearing Water*. New York: Viking.

"To Preserve the Great Lakes Basin Ecosystem"

- *Document:* The Great Lakes Water Quality Protocol of 2012, excerpts
- *Date:* September 7, 2012
- *Where:* Washington, DC
- *Significance:* The protocol, which amended the Great Lakes Water Quality Agreement of 1978, defined how the United States and Canada would work together to improve the water quality in the Great Lakes and the St. Lawrence River through the International Joint Commission.

DOCUMENT

PROTOCOL AMENDING THE AGREEMENT BETWEEN CANADA AND THE UNITED STATES OF AMERICA ON GREAT LAKES WATER QUALITY, 1978, AS AMENDED ON OCTOBER 16, 1983 AND ON NOVEMBER 18, 1987 THE GOVERNMENT OF CANADA AND THE GOVERNMENT OF THE UNITED STATES OF AMERICA (the "Parties"),

RECOGNIZING that the *Agreement between Canada and the United States of America on Great Lakes Water Quality, 1978*, done at Ottawa on 22 November 1978, as amended on October 16, 1983 and on November 18, 1987 (the "1978 Agreement") and its predecessor, the *Agreement between Canada and the United States of America on Great Lakes Water Quality*, done at Ottawa on 15 April 1972, provide a vital framework for binational consultation and cooperative action to restore, protect and enhance the water quality of the Great Lakes to promote the ecological health of the Great Lakes basin;

REAFFIRMING their commitment to achieve the goals and objectives of the 1978 Agreement, as amended on 16 October, 1983 and 18 November, 1987, as well as those of its 1972 predecessor agreement;

RECOGNIZING the need to update and strengthen the 1978 Agreement to address current impacts on the quality of the Waters of the Great Lakes, and anticipate and prevent emerging threats to the quality of the Waters of the Great Lakes,

HAVE AGREED as follows:

ARTICLE 1
This Protocol shall be referred to as the Great Lakes Water Quality Protocol of 2012.

ARTICLE 2
The title, preamble, article and annexes of the 1978 Agreement are amended to read as set forth in the Appendix to this Protocol.

ARTICLE 3
This Protocol shall enter into force on the date of the last notification in an Exchange of Notes by the Parties indicating that each Party has completed its domestic processes for approval.

. . .

AGREEMENT BETWEEN CANADA AND THE UNITED STATES OF AMERICA ON GREAT LAKES WATER QUALITY, 2012

THE GOVERNMENT OF CANADA AND THE GOVERNMENT OF THE UNITED STATES OF AMERICA (the Parties),

ACKNOWLEDGING the vital importance of the Great Lakes to the social and economic well-being of both countries, the close connection between quality of the Waters of the Great Lakes and the environment and human health, as well as the need to address the risks to human health posed by environmental degradation;

REAFFIRMING their determination to protect, restore, and enhance water quality of the Waters of the Great Lakes and their intention to prevent further pollution and degradation of the Great Lakes Basin Ecosystem;

REAFFIRMING, in a spirit of friendship and cooperation, the rights and obligations of both countries under the *Treaty relating to the Boundary Waters and Questions arising along the Boundary between Canada, and the United States* done at Washington on 11 January 1909 (Boundary Waters Treaty) and, in particular, the obligation not to pollute boundary waters;

EMPHASIZING the need to strengthen efforts to address new and continuing threats to the quality of the Waters of the Great Lakes, including aquatic invasive species, nutrients, chemical substances, discharge from vessels, the climate change impacts, and the loss of habitats and species;

ACKNOWLEDGING that pollutants may enter the Waters of the Great Lakes from air, surface water, groundwater, sediment, runoff from non-point sources, direct discharges and other sources;

RECOGNIZING that restoration and enhancement of the Waters of the Great Lakes cannot be achieved by addressing individual threats in isolation, but rather depend upon the application of an ecosystem approach to the management of water quality that addresses individually and cumulatively all sources of stress to the Great Lakes Basin Ecosystem;

RECOGNIZING that nearshore areas must be restored and protected because they are the major source of drinking water for communities within the basin, are where most human commerce and recreation occurs, and are the critical ecological link between watersheds and the open waters of the Great Lakes;

ACKNOWLEDGING that the quality of the Waters of the Great Lakes may affect the quality of the waters of the St. Lawrence River downstream of the international boundary;

CONCLUDING that the best means to preserve the Great Lakes Basin Ecosystem and to improve the quality of the Waters of the Great Lakes is to adopt common objectives, develop and implement cooperative programs and other compatible measures, and assign special responsibilities and functions to the International Joint Commission;

RECOGNIZING that, while the Parties are responsible for decision-making under this Agreement, the involvement and participation of State and Provincial Governments, Tribal Governments, First Nations, Métis, Municipal Governments, watershed management agencies, local public agencies, and the Public are essential to achieve the objectives of this Agreement;

DETERMINED to improve management processes for the implementation of measures necessary to achieve the objectives of this Agreement,

HAVE AGREED as follows:

. . .

ARTICLE 2
Purpose, Principles and Approaches

PURPOSE

1. The purpose of this Agreement is to restore and maintain the chemical, physical, and biological integrity of the Waters of the Great Lakes. To achieve this purpose, the Parties agree to maximize their efforts to:

(a) cooperate and collaborate;

(b) develop programs, practices and technology necessary for a better understanding of the Great Lakes Basin Ecosystem; and

(c) eliminate or reduce, to the maximum extent practicable, environmental threats to the Waters of the Great Lakes.

2. The Parties, recognizing the inherent natural value of the Great Lakes Basin Ecosystem, are guided by a shared vision of a healthy and prosperous Great Lakes region in which the Waters of the Great Lakes, through sound management, use and enjoyment, will benefit present and future generations of Canadians and Americans.

3. The Parties recognize that it is necessary to take action to resolve existing environmental problems, as well as to anticipate and prevent environmental problems,

by implementing measures that are sufficiently protective to achieve the purpose of this Agreement.

PRINCIPLES AND APPROACHES

4. The Parties shall be guided by the following principles and approaches in order to achieve the purpose of this Agreement:

(a) accountability – establishing clear objectives, regular reporting made available to the Public on progress, and transparently evaluating the effectiveness of work undertaken to achieve the objectives of this Agreement;

(b) adaptive management – implementing a systematic process by which the Parties assess effectiveness of actions and adjust future actions to achieve the objectives of this Agreement, as outcomes and ecosystem processes become better understood;

(c) adequate treatment – treating wastewater without relying on flow augmentation to achieve applicable water quality standards;

(d) anti-degradation – implementing all reasonable and practicable measures to maintain or improve the existing water quality in the areas of the Waters of the Great Lakes that meet or exceed the General Objectives or Specific Objectives of this Agreement, as well as in areas that have outstanding natural resource value;

(e) coordination – developing and implementing coordinated planning processes and best management practices by the Parties, as well as among State and Provincial Governments, Tribal Governments, First Nations, Métis, Municipal Governments, watershed management agencies, and local public agencies;

(f) ecosystem approach – taking management actions that integrate the interacting components of air, land, water, and living organisms, including humans;

(g) innovation – considering and applying advanced and environmentally-friendly ideas, methods and efforts;

(h) "polluter pays" – incorporating the "polluter pays" principle, as set forth in the *Rio Declaration on Environment and Development*, "that the polluter should, in principle, bear the cost of pollution;"

(i) precaution – incorporating the precautionary approach, as set forth in the *Rio Declaration on Environment and Development*, the Parties intend that, "Where there are threats of serious or irreversible damage, lack of full scientific certainty shall not be used as a reason for postponing cost-effective measures to prevent environmental degradation;"

(j) prevention – anticipating and preventing pollution and other threats to the quality of the Waters of the Great Lakes to reduce overall risks to the environment and human health;

(k) Public engagement – incorporating Public opinion and advice, as appropriate, and providing information and opportunities for the Public to participate in activities that contribute to the achievement of the objectives of this Agreement;

(l) science-based management – implementing management decisions, policies and programs that are based on best available science, research and knowledge, as well as traditional ecological knowledge, when available;

(m) sustainability – considering social, economic and environmental factors and incorporating a multi-generational standard of care to address current needs, while enhancing the ability of future generations to meet their needs;

(n) tributary management – restoring and maintaining surface waters that flow into and impact the quality of the Waters of the Great Lakes;

(o) virtual elimination – adopting the principle of virtual elimination for elimination of releases of chemicals of mutual concern, as appropriate; and

(p) zero discharge – adopting the philosophy of zero discharge for control of releases of chemicals of mutual concern, as appropriate.

ARTICLE 3

General and Specific Objectives

1. The Parties, in achieving the purpose of this Agreement, shall work to attain the following General and Specific Objectives, and are guided by the Principles and Approaches identified in Article 2:

(a) GENERAL OBJECTIVES

The Parties adopt the following General Objectives. The Waters of the Great Lakes should:

(i) be a source of safe, high-quality drinking water;

(ii) allow for swimming and other recreational use, unrestricted by environmental quality concerns;

(iii) allow for human consumption of fish and wildlife unrestricted by concerns due to harmful pollutants;

(iv) be free from pollutants in quantities or concentrations that could be harmful to human health, wildlife, or aquatic organisms, through direct exposure or indirect exposure through the food chain;

(v) support healthy and productive wetlands and other habitats to sustain resilient populations of native species;

(vi) be free from nutrients that directly or indirectly enter the water as a result of human activity, in amounts that promote growth of algae and cyanobacteria that interfere with aquatic ecosystem health, or human use of the ecosystem;

(vii) be free from the introduction and spread of aquatic invasive species and free from the introduction and spread of terrestrial invasive species that adversely impact the quality of the Waters of the Great Lakes;

(viii) be free from the harmful impact of contaminated groundwater; and

(ix) be free from other substances, materials or conditions that may negatively impact the chemical, physical or biological integrity of the Waters of the Great Lakes;

(b) SPECIFIC OBJECTIVES

The Parties, to help achieve the General Objectives, shall, in cooperation and consultation with State and Provincial Governments, Tribal Governments, First Nations, Métis, Municipal Governments, watershed management agencies, other local public agencies, downstream jurisdictions, and the Public, identify and work to attain Specific Objectives for the Waters of the Great Lakes, including:

(i) LAKE ECOSYSTEM OBJECTIVES

Lake Ecosystem Objectives shall be established for each Great Lake, including its connecting river systems, that:

(A) are binational, except for Lake Michigan, where the Government of the United States shall have sole responsibility;

(B) specify interim or long term ecological conditions necessary to achieve the General Objectives of this Agreement;

(C) may be narrative or numeric in nature;

(D) will be developed in recognition of the complexities of large, dynamic ecosystems; and

(E) may be developed for temperature, pH, total dissolved solids, dissolved oxygen, settleable, and suspended solids, light transmission, and other physical parameters; and levels of plankton, **benthos**, microbial organisms, aquatic plants, fish or other **biota**; or other parameters, as appropriate;

(ii) SUBSTANCE OBJECTIVES

Substance Objectives are numeric targets that may be established binationally by the Parties, except where specific to Lake Michigan, to further direct actions to manage the level of a substance or combination of substances to reduce threats to human health and the environment in the Great Lakes Basin Ecosystem. The Parties shall identify Substance Objectives, where deemed essential to achieve the General Objectives and Lake Ecosystem Objectives of this Agreement.

SOURCE: International Joint Commission. 2012. *Great Lakes Water Quality Agreement 2012.* http://www.ijc.org/en_/Great_Lakes_Water_Quality (accessed October 16, 2014).

ANALYSIS

In 1972, the United States and Canada negotiated the first Great Lakes Water Quality Agreement (GLWQA). It was a response to both the fires on the Cuyahoga River and the severe eutrophication that was evident within Lake Erie. In the agreement, the two countries agreed to reduce the amount of phosphorous being introduced into the lakes by 50 percent, require sewage treatment plants to filter substances such as nitrogen and phosphorous out of the waste they were dumping into the lakes to reduce algal growth, and reduce the level of toxic chemicals in the lakes. The agreement was a tentative step in the right direction, as it identified issues that needed to be addressed. The failing was that specific standards were not established.

Six years later, the countries passed the GLWQA of 1978. Like its predecessor, the agreement focused primarily on the regulation of phosphorous and toxic chemicals, as those substances were blamed for the continuing eutrophication of Lake Erie. Toward that end, strict regulations were passed to ensure that municipal sewage and solid waste plants significantly reduced the waste introduced into the ecosystems impacting the respective lakes. The definition of what constituted a toxic substance was broadened from the 1972 version, which required more chemicals to be identified and regulated. These included heavy metals, pesticides, and polychlorinated biphenyls.

The first amendment to the GLWQA of 1978 was signed on November 18, 1987. Instead of focusing on the Great Lakes as a whole, the 1987 amendment required the establishment of lake management plans for each of the Great Lakes. This was an important step as it acknowledged that the challenges facing the respective lakes differed. Another change was that the focus on pollutants went from point sources, which were specific locations where pollutants were entering the waters (such as factories and sewage plants), to nonpoint sources, where the point of origin could not be definitively determined. This included air pollution, water run-off, and pollutants introduced into the Great Lakes by groundwater.

The 2012 amendments broadened the scope of the GLWQA of 1978. Up to that point the primary concern was water quality since a significant number of people used water from the Great Lakes for drinking. While that focus remained, the threats of invasive species and the impacts of climate change were added to the portfolio.

While the introduction of new concerns bodes well for the effectiveness of the GLWQA going forward, it is important for the two countries to continue to work on the issues that originally led to the 1972 agreement. This was driven home in 2014 when an algal bloom fueled by phosphorous in Lake Erie led to people in the environs of Toledo, Ohio, unable to drink their tap water for days.

FURTHER READING

Annin, Peter. 2006. *Great Lakes Water Wars*. Washington, DC: Island Press.

Hall, Noah, Murray Clamen, and Lorne Thomas. 2010. "Great Lakes Emerging Legal Issues Regarding the International Boundary Waters Treaty and the Great Lakes Water Quality Agreement." *Canada–United States Law Journal* 34, no. 2: 193–235.

Rodriguez, Carleigh Trappe. 2012. "Assessing and Mending the Great Lakes: A Call for Transboundary Environmental Impact Assessment in the Amended Great Lakes Quality Agreement." *Georgetown International Environmental Law Review* 24, no. 4: 559–589.

Part IV

WATER MANAGEMENT AND
FLOOD CONTROL

6

FLOOD CONTROL LEGISLATION

"No Local Contribution to the Project Herein Adopted Is Required"

- *Document:* Flood Control Act of 1928, excerpts
- *Date:* May 15, 1928
- *Where:* Washington, DC
- *Significance:* The act gave the federal government the responsibility for the financing, planning, and construction of flood prevention infrastructure on the Mississippi River.

DOCUMENT

Be it enacted by the Senate and House of Representatives of the United States of America in Congress assembled, That the project for the flood control of the Mississippi River in its alluvial valley and for its improvement from the Head of Passes to Cape Girardeau, Missouri, in accordance with the engineering plan set forth and recommended in the report submitted by the Chief of Engineers to the Secretary of War dated December 1, 1927, and printed in House Document Numbered 90, Seventieth Congress, first session, is hereby adopted and authorized to be prosecuted under the direction of the Secretary of War and the supervision of the Chief of Engineers: Provided, That a board to consist of the Chief of Engineers, the president of the Mississippi River Commission, and a civil engineer chosen from civil life to be appointed by the President, by and with the advice and consent of the Senate, whose compensation shall be fixed by the President and be paid out of the appropriations made to carry on this project, is hereby created; and such board is authorized and directed to consider the engineering differences between the adopted project and the plans recommended by the Mississippi River Commission in its special report dated November 28, 1927, and after such study and such further surveys as may be necessary, to recommend to the President such action as it may deem necessary to be taken in respect to such engineering differences and the decision of the President upon all recommendations or questions submitted to him by such board shall be followed in carrying out the project herein adopted. The board shall not have any power or authority in respect to such project except as hereinbefore provided. Such project and the changes therein, if any, shall be executed in accordance with the provisions of section 8 of this Act. Such surveys shall be made between Baton Rouge, Louisiana, and Cape Girardeau, Missouri, as the board may deem necessary to enable it to ascertain and determine the best method of securing flood relief in addition to levees, before any flood-control works other than levees and revetments are undertaken on that portion of the river: Provided, That all diversion works and outlets constructed under the provisions of this Act shall be built in a manner and of a character which will fully and amply protect the adjacent lands: Provided further, That pending completion of any floodway, spillway, or diversion channel, the areas within the same shall be given the same degree of protection as is afforded by levees on the west side of the river contiguous to the levee at the head of said floodway, but nothing herein shall prevent, postpone, delay, or in anywise interfere with the execution of that part of the project on the east side of the river, including raising, strengthening, and enlarging the levees on the east side of the river. The sum of $325,000,000 is hereby authorized to be appropriated for this purpose.

All unexpended balances of appropriations heretofore made for prosecuting work of flood control on the Mississippi River in accordance with the provisions of the Flood Control Acts approved March 1, 1917, and March 4, 1923, are hereby made available for expenditure under the provisions of this Act, except section 13.

Sec. 2. That it is hereby declared to be the sense of Congress that the principle of local contribution toward the cost of flood-control work, which has been incorporated in all previous national legislation on the subject, is sound, as recognizing the special interest of the local population in its own protection, and as a means of preventing inordinate requests for unjustified items of work having no material national interest. As a full compliance with this principle in view of the great expenditure estimated at approximately $292,000,000, heretofore made by the local interests in the alluvial valley of the Mississippi River for protection against the floods of that river; in view of the extent of national concern in the control of these floods in the interests of national prosperity, the flow of interstate commerce, and the movement of the United States mails; and, in view of the gigantic scale of the project, involving flood waters of a volume and flowing from a drainage area largely outside the States most affected, and far exceeding those of any other river in the United States, no local contribution to the project herein adopted is required.

Sec. 3. Except when authorized by the Secretary of War upon the recommendation of the Chief of Engineers, no money appropriated under authority of this Act shall be expended on the construction of any item of the project until the States or levee districts have given assurances satisfactory to the Secretary of War that they will (a) maintain all flood-control works after their completion, except controlling and regulating spillway structures, including special relief levees; maintenance includes normally such matters as cutting grass, removal of weeds, local drainage, and minor repairs of main river levees; (b) agree to accept land turned over to them under the provisions of section 4; (c) provide without cost to the United States, all rights of way for levee foundations and levees on the main stem of the Mississippi River between Cape Girardeau, Missouri, and the Head of Passes.

No liability of any kind shall attach to or rest upon the United States for any damage from or by floods or flood waters at any place: Provided, however, That if in carrying out the purposes of this Act it shall be found that upon any stretch of the banks of the Mississippi River it is impracticable to construct levees, either because such construction is not economically justified or because such construction would unreasonably restrict the flood channel, and lands in such stretch of the river are subjected to overflow and damage which are not now overflowed or damaged by reason of the construction of levees on the opposite banks of the river it shall be the duty of the Secretary of War and the Chief of Engineers to institute proceedings on behalf of the United States Government to acquire either the absolute ownership of the lands so subjected to overflow and damage or floodage rights over such lands.

Sec. 4. The United States shall provide flowage rights for additional destructive flood waters that will pass by reason of diversions from the main channel of the Mississippi River: Provided, That in all cases where the execution of the flood-control plan herein adopted results in benefits to property such benefits shall be taken into consideration by way of reducing the amount of compensation to be paid.

The Secretary of War may cause proceedings to be instituted for the acquirement by condemnation of any lands, easements, or rights of way which, in the opinion of the Secretary of War and the Chief of Engineers, are needed in carrying out this project, the said proceedings to be instituted in the United States district court for the district in which the land, easement, or right of way is located. In all such proceedings the court, for the purpose of ascertaining the value of the property and assessing the compensation to be paid, shall appoint three commissioners, whose award, when confirmed by the court, shall be final. When the owner of any land, easement, or right of way shall fix a price for the same which, in the opinion of the Secretary of War is reasonable, he may purchase the same at such price; and the Secretary of War is also authorized to accept donations of lands, easements, and rights of way required for this project. The provisions of sections 5 and 6 of the River and Harbor Act of July 18, 1918, are hereby made applicable to the acquisition of lands, easements, or rights of way needed for works of flood control: Provided That any land acquired under the provisions of this section shall be turned over without cost to the ownership of States or local interests.

Sec. 5. Subject to the approval of the heads of the several executive departments concerned, the Secretary of War, on the recommendation of the Chief of Engineers, may engage the services and assistance of the Coast and Geodetic Survey, the Geological Survey, or other mapping agencies of the Government, in the preparation of maps required in furtherance of this project, and funds to pay for such services may be allotted from appropriations made under authority of this Act.

Sec. 6. Funds appropriated under authority of section 1 of this Act may be expended for the prosecution of such works for the control of the floods of the Mississippi River as have heretofore been authorized and are not included in the present project, including levee work on the Mississippi River between Rock Island, Illinois, and Cape Girardeau, Missouri, and on the outlets and tributaries of the Mississippi River between Rock Island and Head of Passes in so far as such outlets or tributaries are affected by the backwaters of the Mississippi: Provided, That for such work on the Mississippi River between Rock Island, Illinois, and Cape Girardeau, Missouri, and on such tributaries, the States or levee districts shall provide rights of way without cost to the United States, contribute 331/3 per centum of the costs of the works, and maintain them after completion: And provided further, That not more than $10,000,000 of the sums authorized in section 1 of this Act, shall be expended under the provisions of this section.

In an emergency, funds appropriated under authority of section 1 of this Act may be expended for the maintenance of any levee when it is demonstrated to the satisfaction of the Secretary of War that the levee cannot be adequately maintained by the State or levee district.

Sec. 7. That the sum of $5,000,000 is authorized to be appropriated as an emergency fund to be allotted by the Secretary of War on the recommendation of the Chief of Engineers, in rescue work or in the repair or maintenance of any flood-control work on any tributaries of the Mississippi River threatened or destroyed by flood including the flood of 1927.

Sec. 8. The project herein authorized shall be prosecuted by the Mississippi River Commission under the direction of the Secretary of War and supervision of the Chief of Engineers and subject to the provisions of this Act. It shall perform such functions and through such agencies as they shall designate after consultation and discussion with the president of the commission. For all other purposes the existing laws governing the constitution and activities of the commission shall remain unchanged. . . .

Sec. 10. That it is the sense of Congress that the surveys of the Mississippi River and its tributaries, authorized pursuant to the Act of January 21, 1927, and House Document Numbered 308, Sixty-ninth Congress, first session, be prosecuted as speedily as practicable, and the Secretary of War, through the Corps of Engineers, United States Army, is directed to prepare and submit to Congress at the earliest practicable date projects for flood control on all tributary streams of the Mississippi River system subject to destructive floods which shall include: The Red River and tributaries, the Yazoo River and tributaries, the White River and tributaries, the Saint Francis River and tributaries, the Arkansas River and tributaries, the Ohio River and tributaries, the Missouri River and tributaries, and the Illinois River and tributaries; and the reports thereon, in addition to the surveys provided by said House Document 308, Sixty-ninth Congress, first session, shall include the effect on the subject of further flood control of the lower Mississippi River to be attained through the control of the flood waters in the drainage basins of the tributaries by the establishment of a reservoir system; the benefits that will accrue to navigation and agriculture from the prevention of erosion and siltage entering the stream; a determination of the capacity of the soils of the district to receive and hold waters from such reservoirs; the prospective income from the disposal of reservoir waters; the extent to which reservoir waters may be made available for public and private uses; and inquiry as to the return flow of waters placed in the soils from reservoirs, and as to their stabilizing effect on stream flow as a means of preventing erosion, siltage, and improving navigation: Provided, That before transmitting such reports to Congress the same shall be presented to the Mississippi River Commission, and its conclusions and recommendations thereon shall be transmitted to Congress by the Secretary of War with his report.

The sum of $5,000,000 is hereby authorized to be used out of the appropriation herein authorized in section 1 of this Act, in addition to amounts authorized in the River and Harbor Act of January 21, 1927, to be expended under the direction of the Secretary of War and the supervision of the Chief of Engineers for the preparation of the flood-control projects authorized to be submitted to Congress under this section: Provided further, That the flood surveys herein provided for shall be made simultaneously with the flood-control work on the Mississippi River provided for in this Act: And provided further, That the President shall proceed to ascertain through the Secretary of Agriculture and such other agencies as he may deem proper, the extent to and manner in which the floods in the Mississippi Valley may be controlled by proper forestry practice.

Sec. 11. That the Secretary of War shall cause the Mississippi River Commission to make an examination and survey of the Mississippi River below Cape Girardeau, Missouri, (a) at places where levees have heretofore been constructed on one side of the river and the lands on the opposite side have been thereby subjected to greater overflow, and where, without unreasonably restricting the flood channel, levees can be constructed to reduce the extent of this overflow, and where the construction of such levees is economically justified, and report thereon to the Congress as soon as practicable with such recommendations as the commission may deem advisable; (b) with a view to determining the estimated effects, if any, upon lands lying between the river and adjacent hills by reason of overflow of such lands caused by the construction of levees at other points along the Mississippi River, and determining the equities of the owners of such lands and the value of the same, and the commission shall report thereon to the Congress as soon as practicable with such recommendation as it may deem advisable: Provided, That inasmuch as the Mississippi River Commission made a report on the 26th day of October, 1912, recommending a levee to be built from Tiptonville, Tennessee, to the Obion River in Tennessee, the said Mississippi River Commission is authorized to make a resurvey of said proposed levee and a relocation of the same if necessary, and if such levee is found feasible, and is approved by the board created in section 1 of this Act, and by the President the same shall be built out of appropriations hereafter to be made.

ANALYSIS

During the summer of 1926, the Upper Midwest began to suffer unseasonably heavy rains. In a short amount of time, the South began to suffer the same fate. This resulted in a substantial part of the country becoming heavily saturated with rainwater. By April of the following year, the constant rainfall resulted in the Mississippi River and many of its tributaries flooding. The floodwaters impacted the states of Arkansas, Kansas, Kentucky, Illinois, Louisiana, Mississippi, Missouri, Oklahoma, Tennessee, and Texas. Approximately 15 million acres of land was under water. More than 700,000 people were displaced and 246 lost their lives. The flooded rivers did not return to their normal state until the fall of 1927. In total the Mississippi River flood of 1927 resulted in approximately $400 million in damages.

Despite the catastrophe, there was no real effort by the federal government to address the flooding problem as President Calvin Coolidge did not believe it was the responsibility of the federal government to pay for flood control projects. He believed that it was a state responsibility. The head of the U.S. Army Corps of Engineers (USACE), Edgar Jadwin, concurred with Coolidge, noting that states should fund any flood control measures that were desired. Unfortunately for them, many congressmen demanded action. Recognizing that some form of flood control legislation was going to emerge from Congress, Jadwin decided to make it as palatable as possible by writing the legislation himself. His proposal, known as the "Jadwin Plan," was embraced by Coolidge as it required substantial funding from the states and relied heavily on levees, which were the preferred form of flood control to the USACE. Compared to other plans that were being considered, Jadwin's proposal required far less construction and was thus far cheaper than the competition. Congress in general was very critical of Jadwin's proposal, especially the sections concerning funding. The states affected by the flooding in 1927 had been economically devastated and did not have the ability to pay for flood control that was obviously desperately needed. Congress was subsequently able to rid the legislation of that requirement, thereby setting the precedent that it was the responsibility of the federal government to fund flood control endeavors on the nation's navigable waters.

Having succeeded in removing the funding requirement, Congress used the remainder of Jadwin's proposal as the framework for the Flood Control Act of 1928. They did this despite warnings from outside experts that Jadwin's minimalist approach to flood protection would not provide the protection to the people living in the Mississippi River floodplain that he claimed it would deliver. Unfortunately, this was proven true in 1937 when the Mississippi River suffered an even more devastating flood than the one that occurred a decade earlier.

FURTHER READING

Barry, John M. 1997. *Rising Tide: The Great Mississippi Flood of 1927 and How It Changed America*. New York: Simon & Schuster.

Daniel, Pete. 1996. *Deep'n as It Come: The 1927 Mississippi River Flood*. Fayetteville: University of Arkansas Press.

Welky, David. 2011. *The Thousand-Year Flood: The Ohio-Mississippi Disaster of 1937*. Chicago: University of Chicago Press.

"General Comprehensive Plan for Flood Control and Other Purposes in the Missouri River Basin"

- *Document:* Flood Control Act of 1944, excerpt
- *Date:* December 22, 1944
- *Where:* Washington, DC
- *Significance:* The act included the Pick-Sloan Plan, which authorized the USACE and the Bureau of Reclamation (BOR) to make significant alterations to the Missouri River.

DOCUMENT

Sec. 9 [Comprehensive Development of Missouri River Basin.]—(a) The general comprehensive plans set forth in House Document 475 and Senate Document 191, Seventy-eighth Congress, second session, as revised and coordinated by Senate Document 247, Seventy-eight Congress, second session, are hereby approved and the initial stages recommended are hereby authorized and shall be prosecuted by the War Department and Department of the Interior as speedily as may be consistent with budgetary requirements.

(b) The general comprehensive plan for flood control and other purposes in the Missouri River Basin approved by the Act of June 28, 1938, as modified by subsequent Acts, is hereby expanded to include the works referred to in paragraph (a) to be undertaken by the War Department; and said expanded plan shall be prosecuted under the direction of the Secretary of War and supervision of the Chief of Engineers.

(c) Subject to the basin-wide findings and recommendations regarding the benefits, the allocations of costs and the repayment of water users, made in said House and Senate documents, the reclamation and power developments to by undertaken by the Secretary of the Interior under said plans shall be governed by the Federal Reclamation Laws (Act of June 17, 1902, 32 Stat. 388, and Acts amendatory thereof or supplementary thereto), except that irrigation of Indian trust and tribal lands, and repayment therefor, shall be in accordance with the laws relating to Indian lands.

(d) In addition to previous authorizations there is hereby authorized to be appropriated the sum of $200,000,000 for the partial accomplishment of the works to be undertaken under said expanded plans by the Corps of Engineers.

(e) The sum of $200,000,000 is hereby authorized to be appropriated for the partial accomplishment of the works to be undertaken under said plans by the Secretary of the Interior. (58 Stat. 891).

SOURCE: U.S. Department of the Interior, Bureau of Reclamation. *Flood Control Act of 1944.* http://www.usbr.gov/power/legislation/fldcntra.pdf (accessed November 2, 2014).

ANALYSIS

On December 2, 1944, President Franklin D. Roosevelt signed the Flood Control Act of 1944. Section 9 of that document was the Pick-Sloan Plan, which authorized significant alterations to the Missouri River. The Act marked a disappointment for Roosevelt, who preferred the creation of a Missouri Valley Authority, using the Tennessee Valley Authority as a model. His vision stirred both the USACE and the BOR, normally competitors, to work together on modernizing the Missouri River, as neither wanted to see the creation of another competing federal agency involved in the construction and management of the nation's water infrastructure.

Although the redesign of the Missouri River had been considered in Congress for several decades, it took severe flooding on the waterway in 1943 to force the body into decisive action. They had two competing proposals before them. One was written by Colonel Lewis A. Pick on behalf of the USACE. His plan centered around dam construction on the Missouri River and many of its tributaries to control floodwaters. The other proposal was authored by W. G. Sloan, an engineer for the BOR. His plan revolved around irrigation and the generation of hydroelectricity. Once Congress decided to allow both USACE and BOR to work together on the Missouri River, they took portions of both of the competing proposals, dubbing the compromise legislation the Pick-Sloan Plan.

The Pick-Sloan Plan resulted in the construction of five dams by the USACE on the Missouri River: Big Bend Dam, Fort Randall Dam, Garrison Dam, and Oahe Dam. The Fort Peck Dam, already constructed, was assimilated into the plan as the USACE's sixth dam on the river. The Canyon Ferry Dam, also on the main stem of the Missouri River, was constructed by the BOR. In addition, between the two agencies, another 22 dams were constructed on the Missouri River's tributaries. In addition to the dams, more than 40 hydroelectric power plants were constructed within the Missouri River Basin. The plan also allowed for the construction of a six-foot navigation channel between Sioux City, Iowa, and St. Louis, Missouri, by the USACE.

The Pick-Sloan Plan proved devastating to Native American groups who resided in the vicinity of the Missouri River and its major tributaries as many of the reservoirs created by the dams inundated large portions of reservations. Garrison Dam, for example, buried more than 155,000 acres of land owned by the Mandan-Hidatsa-Arikara Nation, including some of their most productive agricultural lands. Ironically, the lake that caused such ruin was named after Sacajawea, the Shoshone woman who guided Lewis and Clark on their expedition.

Although the Pick-Sloan Plan proved successful in controlling much of the flooding on the Missouri River, it never produced the amount of water for irrigation that was envisioned by the BOR. This was especially true during drought years, as water shortages led competing interests going to court to ensure that their water needs were met. One of the major failings of the plan was that Congress believed that the irrigation projects could be paid for using revenues generated by the sale of hydroelectricity. When it became apparent that the funding scheme would not work, Congress passed legislation requiring that all unbuilt irrigation projects that were part of the Pick-Sloan Plan go through the authorization process in Congress for a second time. This allowed Congress to weigh the benefits versus the costs of individual projects to ensure that the project was worthy of the monies that were required for construction.

FURTHER READING

Ferrell, John R. 1993. *Big Dam Era: A Legislative and Institutional History of the Pick-Sloan Missouri Basin Program.* Omaha, NE: Missouri River Division, U.S. Army Corps of Engineers.

Lawson, Michael L. 1982. *Dammed Indians: The Pick-Sloan Plan and the Missouri River Sioux, 1944-1980.* Norman: University of Oklahoma Press.

Lawson, Michael L. 2009. *Dammed Indians Revisited: The Continuing History of the Pick-Sloan Plan and the Missouri River Sioux.* Pierre: South Dakota Historical Society.

Thorson, Jared E. 1994. *River of Promise, River of Peril: The Politics of Managing the Missouri River.* Lawrence: University Press of Kansas.

VanDevelder, Paul. 2010. *Coyote Warrior: One Man, Three Tribes, and the Trial that Forged a Nation.* 2nd ed. Lincoln: University of Nebraska Press.

"The Authorization for Any Flood Control Project Herein Adopted Requiring Local Cooperation Shall Expire Five Years from the Date on Which Local Interests Are Notified in Writing by the Department of the Army"

- *Document:* Flood Control Act of 1962, excerpts
- *Date:* October 23, 1962
- *Where:* Washington, DC
- *Significance:* The act included a provision that required local interests to give their approval for a construction project within a five-year period of having been notified in writing by the USACE of their plans to build. Also included was a requirement that all dams authorized for construction by the Act have the potential capability of producing hydroelectric power.

DOCUMENT

TITLE II – FLOOD CONTROL

Sec. 201. Section 3 of the Act approved June 22, 1936 (Public Law Numbered 738, Seventy-fourth Congress), as amended by section 2 of the Act approved June 28, 1938 (Public Law Numbered 761, Seventy-fifth Congress), shall apply to all works authorized in this title except that for any channel improvement or channel rectification project, provisions (a), (b), and (c) of section 3 of said Act of June 22, 1936, shall apply thereto, and except as otherwise provided by law; *Provided,* That the authorization for any flood control project herein adopted requiring local cooperation shall expire five years from the date on which local interests are notified in writing by the Department of the Army of the requirements of local co-operation, unless said interests shall within said time furnish assurances satisfactory to the Secretary of the Army that the required cooperation will be furnished.

. . .

Sec. 203. The following works of improvement for the benefit of navigation and the control of destructive floodwaters and other purposes are hereby adopted and authorized to be prosecuted under the direction of the Secretary of the Army and the supervision of the Chief of Engineers in accordance with the plans in the respective reports hereinafter designated and subject to the conditions set forth therein: *Provided*, That the necessary plans, specifications, and preliminary work may be prosecuted on any project authorized in this title with funds from appropriations hereafter made for flood control so as to be ready for rapid inauguration of a construction program: *Provided further*, That the projects authorized herein shall be initiated as expeditiously and prosecuted as vigorously as may be consistent with budgetary requirements: *And provided further*, That penstocks and other similar facilities adapted to possible future use in the development of hydroelectric power shall be installed in any dam authorized in the Act for construction by the Department of the Army when approved by the Secretary of the Army on the recommendation of the Chief of Engineers and the Federal Power Commission.

SOURCE: U.S. Army Corps of Engineers. n.d. Public Law 87-874. http://planning .usace.army.mil/toolbox/library/PL/RHA1962.pdf (accessed November 3, 2014).

ANALYSIS

Like all other iterations of the Flood Control Act, the 1962 legislation included water infrastructure construction projects for locales throughout the country. There were two provisions in the 1962 legislation that marked changes in federal priorities. First was the shortening of the time period that locales had to make a definitive commitment to a particular project. Under the guidelines introduced in 1962, communities had five years from the time that they received a written notification from the USACE that construction was imminent to produce their contribution to the project or cancelation would follow. Depending on a respective community's responsibilities, their contributions might include easements or other forms of in-kind gifts to help offset construction costs. This requirement had two purposes. First, requiring a contribution from a community forced them to demonstrate how important the project was to them. If they were unwilling to help pay for something that they supposedly needed, it signaled that their real need was not as dire as portrayed. Another reason for forcing a community to commit to a project was purely political. The USACE wanted to shorten the time from authorization to construction to lessen the time that environmental groups had to file lawsuits to block construction projects. This proved prescient as environmental groups throughout the 1960s and into the 1970s effectively used the federal courts to block numerous projects by both the USACE and the BOR that promised to commit serious damage to the environment.

It was also significant that Congress included language in the legislation requiring all dams constructed under the auspices of the Flood Control Act of 1962 to be capable of producing hydroelectric power. This demonstrated Congress's desire that all dams be multipurpose, which represented a better return on their investment than a dam used only for flood control. Under the legislation, some older dams, like California's New Melones Dam, were retrofitted to make them suitable for the generation of hydroelectric power.

FURTHER READING

Albert, Richard C. 1987. *Damming the Delaware: The Rise and Fall of the Tocks Island Dam.* University Park: Pennsylvania State University Press.

7

DAMS AND LEVEES

"To Reduce the Risks to Life and Property from Dam Failure in the United States"

- *Document:* National Dam Safety Program Act of 1996, excerpts
- *Date:* October 12, 1996
- *Where:* Washington, DC
- *Significance:* The act was designed to identify dams that were in danger of failing so that their weakness(es) could be addressed.

DOCUMENT

SEC. 215. NATIONAL DAM SAFETY PROGRAM.

(a) PURPOSE.—The purpose of this section is to reduce the risks to life and property from dam failure in the United States through the establishment and maintenance of an effective national dam safety program to bring together the expertise and resources of the Federal and non-Federal communities in achieving national dam safety hazard reduction. It is not the intent of this section to preempt any other Federal or State authorities nor is it the intent of this section to mandate State participation in the grant assistance program to be established under this section.

(b) EFFECT ON OTHER DAM SAFETY PROGRAMS.—Nothing in this section (including the amendments made by this section) shall preempt or otherwise affect any dam safety program of a Federal agency other than the Federal Emergency Management Agency, including any program that regulates, permits, or licenses any activity affecting a dam.

(c) DAM SAFETY PROGRAM.—The Act entitled "An Act to authorize the Secretary of the Army to undertake a national program of inspection of dams", approved August 8, 1972 (33 U.S.C 467 et seq.; Public Law 92–367), is amended—

(1) by striking the 1st section and inserting the following:

"SECTION 1. SHORT TITLE.

"This Act may be cited as the 'National Dam Safety Program Act'.";

. . .

"SEC. 2. DEFINITIONS.

"In this Act, the following definitions apply:

"(1) BOARD.—The term 'Board' means a National Dam Safety Review Board established under section 8(h).

"(2) DAM.—The term 'dam'—

"(A) means any artificial barrier that has the ability to impound water, wastewater, or any liquid-borne material, for the purpose of storage or control of water, that—

"(i) is 25 feet or more in height from—

"(I) the natural bed of the stream channel or watercourse measured at the downstream toe of the barrier; or

"(II) if the barrier is not across a stream channel or watercourse, from the lowest elevation of the outside limit of the barrier; to the maximum water storage elevation; or

"(ii) has an impounding capacity for maximum storage elevation of 50 acre-feet or more; but "(B) does not include—

"(i) a levee; or

"(ii) a barrier described in subparagraph (A) that—

"(I) is 6 feet or less in height regardless of storage capacity; or

"(II) has a storage capacity at the maximum water storage elevation that is 15 acre-feet or less regardless of height; unless the barrier, because of the location of the barrier or another physical characteristic of the barrier, is likely to pose a significant threat to human life or property if the barrier fails (as determined by the Director).

"(3) DIRECTOR.—The term 'Director' means the Director of FEMA.

"(4) FEDERAL AGENCY.—The term 'Federal agency' means a Federal agency that designs, finances, constructs, owns, operates, maintains, or regulates the construction, operation, or maintenance of a dam.

"(5) FEDERAL GUIDELINES FOR DAM SAFETY.—The term 'Federal Guidelines for Dam Safety' means the FEMA publication, numbered 93 and dated June 1979, that defines management practices for dam safety at all Federal agencies.

"(6) FEMA.—The term 'FEMA' means the Federal Emergency Management Agency.

"(7) HAZARD REDUCTION.—The term 'hazard reduction' means the reduction in the potential consequences to life and property of dam failure.

"(8) ICODS.—The term 'ICODS' means the Interagency Committee on Dam Safety established by section 7.

"(9) PROGRAM.—The term 'Program' means the national dam safety program established under section 8.

"(10) STATE.—The term 'State' means each of the several States of the United States, the District of Columbia, the Commonwealth of Puerto Rico, the Virgin Islands, Guam, American Samoa, the Commonwealth of the Northern Mariana Islands, and any other territory or possession of the United States.

"(11) STATE DAM SAFETY AGENCY.—The term 'State dam safety agency' means a State agency that has regulatory authority over the safety of non-Federal dams.

"(12) STATE DAM SAFETY PROGRAM.—The term 'State dam safety program' means a State dam safety program approved and assisted under section 8(f).

"(13) UNITED STATES.—The term 'United States', when used in a geographical sense, means all of the States."; (5) in section 3 (as redesignated by paragraph (3) of this subsection)—

(A) by striking "SEC. 3. As" and inserting the following:

"SEC. 3. INSPECTION OF DAMS.

. . .

"(b) STATE PARTICIPATION.—On request of a State dam safety agency, with respect to any dam the failure of which would affect the State, the head of a Federal agency shall—

"(1) provide information to the State dam safety agency on the construction, operation, or maintenance of the dam; or

"(2) allow any official of the State dam safety agency to participate in the Federal inspection of the dam.";

(6) in section 4 (as redesignated by paragraph (3) of this subsection) by striking "SEC. 4. As" and inserting the following:

"SEC. 4. INVESTIGATION REPORTS TO GOVERNORS.

. . .

"SEC. 5. DETERMINATION OF DANGER TO HUMAN LIFE AND PROPERTY.

. . .

"SEC. 6. NATIONAL DAM INVENTORY.

"The Secretary of the Army, acting through the Chief of Engineers, may maintain and periodically publish updated information on the inventory of dams in the United States.

"SEC. 7. INTERAGENCY COMMITTEE ON DAM SAFETY.

"(a) ESTABLISHMENT.—There is established an Interagency Committee on Dam Safety—

"(1) comprised of a representative of each of the Department of Agriculture, the Department of Defense, the Department of Energy, the Department of the Interior, the Department of Labor, FEMA, the Federal Energy Regulatory Commission, the Nuclear Regulatory Commission, the Tennessee Valley Authority, and the United States Section of the International Boundary Commission; and

"(2) chaired by the Director.

"(b) DUTIES.—ICODS shall encourage the establishment and maintenance of effective Federal and State programs, policies, and guidelines intended to enhance dam safety for the protection of human life and property through—

"(1) coordination and information exchange among Federal agencies and State dam safety agencies; and

"(2) coordination and information exchange among Federal agencies concerning implementation of the Federal Guidelines for Dam Safety.

"SEC. 8. NATIONAL DAM SAFETY PROGRAM.

"(a) IN GENERAL.—The Director, in consultation with ICODS and State dam safety agencies, and the Board shall establish and maintain, in accordance with this section, a coordinated national dam safety program. The Program shall—

"(1) be administered by FEMA to achieve the objectives set forth in subsection (c);

"(2) involve, to the extent appropriate, each Federal agency; and

"(3) include—

"(A) each of the components described in subsection (d);

"(B) the implementation plan described in subsection (e); and

"(C) assistance for State dam safety programs described in subsection (f).

"(b) DUTIES.—The Director shall—

"(1) not later than 270 days after the date of the enactment of this paragraph, develop the implementation plan described in subsection (e);

"(2) not later than 300 days after the date of the enactment of this paragraph, submit to the appropriate authorizing committees of Congress the implementation plan described in subsection (e); and

"(3) by regulation, not later than 360 days after the date of the enactment of this paragraph—

"(A) develop and implement the Program;

"(B) establish goals, priorities, and target dates for implementation of the Program; and

"(C) to the extent feasible, provide a method for cooperation and coordination with, and assistance to, interested governmental entities in all States.

"(c) OBJECTIVES.—The objectives of the Program are to—

"(1) ensure that new and existing dams are safe through the development of technologically and economically feasible programs and procedures for national dam safety hazard reduction;

"(2) encourage acceptable engineering policies and procedures to be used for dam site investigation, design, construction, operation and maintenance, and emergency preparedness;

"(3) encourage the establishment and implementation of effective dam safety programs in each State based on State standards;

"(4) develop and encourage public awareness projects to increase public acceptance and support of State dam safety programs;

"(5) develop technical assistance materials for Federal and non-Federal dam safety programs; and

"(6) develop mechanisms with which to provide Federal technical assistance for dam safety to the non-Federal sector.

"(d) COMPONENTS.—

"(1) IN GENERAL.—The Program shall consist of—

"(A) a Federal element and a non-Federal element; and

"(B) leadership activity, technical assistance activity, and public awareness activity.

"(2) ELEMENTS.—

"(A) FEDERAL.—The Federal element shall incorporate the activities and practices carried out by Federal agencies under section 7 to implement the Federal Guidelines for Dam Safety.

"(B) NON-FEDERAL.—The non-Federal element shall consist of—

"(i) the activities and practices carried out by States, local governments, and the private sector to safely build, regulate, operate, and maintain dams; and

"(ii) Federal activities that foster State efforts to develop and implement effective programs for the safety of dams.

"(3) FUNCTIONAL ACTIVITIES.—

"(A) LEADERSHIP.—The leadership activity shall be the responsibility of FEMA and shall be exercised by chairing ICODS to coordinate Federal efforts in cooperation with State dam safety officials.

"(B) TECHNICAL ASSISTANCE.—The technical assistance activity shall consist of the transfer of knowledge and technical information among the Federal and non-Federal elements described in paragraph (2).

"(C) PUBLIC AWARENESS.—The public awareness activity shall provide for the education of the public, including State and local officials, in the hazards of dam failure, methods of reducing the adverse consequences of dam failure, and related matters.

"(e) IMPLEMENTATION PLAN.—The Director shall—

"(1) develop an implementation plan for the Program that shall set, through fiscal year 2002, year-by-year targets that demonstrate improvements in dam safety; and

"(2) recommend appropriate roles for Federal agencies and for State and local units of government, individuals, and private organizations in carrying out the implementation plan.

"(f) ASSISTANCE FOR STATE DAM SAFETY PROGRAMS.—

"(1) IN GENERAL.—To encourage the establishment and maintenance of effective State programs intended to ensure dam safety, to protect human life and property, and to improve State dam safety programs, the Director shall provide assistance with amounts made available under section 12 to assist States in establishing and maintaining dam safety programs—

"(A) in accordance with the criteria specified in paragraph (2); and

"(B) in accordance with more advanced requirements and standards established by the Board and the Director with the assistance of established criteria such as the Model State Dam Safety Program published by FEMA, numbered 123 and dated April 1987, and amendments to the Model State Dam Safety Program.

"(2) CRITERIA AND BUDGETING REQUIREMENT.—For a State to be eligible for primary assistance under this subsection, a State dam safety program must be working toward meeting the following criteria and budgeting requirement, and for a State to be eligible for advanced assistance under this subsection, a State dam safety program must meet the following criteria and budgeting requirement and be working toward meeting the advanced requirements and standards established under paragraph (1)(B):

"(A) CRITERIA.—For a State to be eligible for assistance under this subsection, a State dam safety program must be authorized by State legislation to include substantially, at a minimum—

"(i) the authority to review and approve plans and specifications to construct, enlarge, modify, remove, and abandon dams;

"(ii) the authority to perform periodic inspections during dam construction to ensure compliance with approved plans and specifications;

"(iii) a requirement that, on completion of dam construction, State approval must be given before operation of the dam;

"(iv)(I) the authority to require or perform the inspection, at least once every 5 years, of all dams and reservoirs that would pose a significant threat to human life and property in case of failure to determine the continued safety of the dams and reservoirs; and

"(II) a procedure for more detailed and frequent safety inspections;

"(v) a requirement that all inspections be performed under the supervision of a State-registered professional engineer with related experience in dam design and construction;

"(vi) the authority to issue notices, when appropriate, to require owners of dams to perform necessary maintenance or remedial work, revise operating procedures, or take other actions, including breaching dams when necessary;

"(vii) regulations for carrying out the legislation of the State described in this subparagraph;

"(viii) provision for necessary funds—

"(I) to ensure timely repairs or other changes to, or removal of, a dam in order to protect human life and property; and

"(II) if the owner of the dam does not take action described in subclause (I), to take appropriate action as expeditiously as practicable;

"(ix) a system of emergency procedures to be used if a dam fails or if the failure of a dam is imminent; and

"(x) an identification of—

"(I) each dam the failure of which could be reasonably expected to endanger human life;

"(II) the maximum area that could be flooded if the dam failed; and

"(III) necessary public facilities that would be affected by the flooding.

. . .

ANALYSIS

The National Dam Safety Program Act was Title 12 of the Water Resources Development Act of 1996. It was intended to protect people and their property from losses caused by the failure of dams. The Act charged the Federal Emergency Management Agency (FEMA) with developing a strategic plan that would provide general guidelines to be followed by parties inspecting and repairing the many dams around the country. FEMA was also responsible for overseeing all federal funds dispersed to the states to improve dam safety within their respective borders.

To identify which of nation's 78,000 dams posed the highest risks, the United States Army Corps of Engineers (USACE) was tasked with expanding the already existing National Inventory of Dams (NID), which had been created by the National Dam Inspection Act of 1972. Although the goal of the USACE is to eventually include all of the dams in the country in their database, it presently lists dams that fall into one of the four categories: dams whose failures will kill at least one person; dams whose failures would probably kill people but would either certainly destroy significant amounts of property or severely damage local ecosystems; dams that are 25-feet high or higher and impound at least 15 acre-feet of water; or are at least 6 feet high and impound at least 50 acre-feet of water.

At the federal level, dam safety improvements were the responsibility of the agency that maintained the respective dams. This resulted in significant work for both the USACE and the Bureau of Reclamation. Since the Federal Energy Regulatory Commission had oversight responsibility for dams that generated hydroelectric power but were not owned by the federal government, it was provided monies to help shore up the dams that fell under its purview.

Since a vast majority of the dams in the United States were not owned by the federal government, most of the responsibility for the inspection, maintenance, and repair of dams fell on state authorities. While some states seized the money provided through the National Dam Safety Program and improved a number of dams that were deteriorating and strengthened local standards for dam safety established by federal authorities discussed earlier, others states proved less enthusiastic. A common refrain was that the increased costs to businesses resulting from higher safety standards would hurt the local economy. The disparity between states in both levels of regulation enacted and the amount of money spent shoring up dams has resulted in some states still having an abundance of weakened and deteriorating dams that pose an increasing threat to those individuals living downriver.

FURTHER READING

Le Moigne, Guy, Shawki Barghouti, and Herve Plusquellec, eds. 1990. *Dam Safety and the Environment*. Washington, DC: World Bank.

Poff, N. Leroy, and David D. Hart. 2002. "How Dams Vary and Why It Matters for the Emerging Science of Dam Removal: An Ecological Classification of Dams Is Needed to Characterize How the Tremendous Difference in Size, Operational Mode, Age, and Number of Dams in a River Basin Influences the Potential for Restoring Regulated Rivers Via Dam Removal." *BioScience* 52, no. 8: 659–668.

U.S. Department of Homeland Security, Federal Emergency Management Agency. n.d. *The National Dam Safety Program: 25 Years of Excellence*. http://www.damsafety.org/media/Documents/PDF/ndsp_25_years.pdf.

"The Preparation for and Response to Hurricane Katrina Should Disturb All Americans"

- *Document:* A Failure of Initiative: Final Report of the Select Bipartisan Committee to Investigate the Preparation for and Response to Hurricane Katrina, Conclusion
- *Date:* February 15, 2006
- *Where:* The report in general studied the impact of Hurricane Katrina on Alabama, Louisiana, and Mississippi. Conditions in New Orleans, Louisiana drew specific criticisms.
- *Significance:* Hurricane Katrina struck the Gulf Coast on August 29, 2005. It resulted in the deaths of more than 1,300 people in the states of Alabama, Louisiana, and Mississippi. New Orleans, Louisiana, suffered severe flooding as the levee system built to protect the city failed. The impact of the storm was magnified by poor decisions made by politicians at all levels from the time before the hurricane struck to days after the immensity of the calamity was revealed.

DOCUMENT

CONCLUSION

The preparation for and response to Hurricane Katrina should disturb all Americans. While the Select Committee believes all people involved, at all levels of government, were trying their best to save lives and ease suffering, their best just wasn't good enough.

In this report we have tried to tell the story of the inadequate preparation and response. We cover a lot of territory—from evacuations to medical care, communications to contracting. We hope our findings will prompt the changes needed to make all levels of government better prepared and better able to respond the next time.

The resolution that created the Select Committee charged us with compiling findings, not recommendations. But in reality that's a distinction without a difference. Moving from our findings to legislative, organizational, and policy changes need not be a long or difficult journey.

We are left scratching our heads at the range of inefficiency and ineffectiveness that characterized government behavior right before and after this storm. But passivity did the most damage. The failure of initiative cost lives, prolonged suffering, and left all Americans justifiably concerned our government is no better prepared to protect its people than it was before 9/11, even if we are.

How can we set up a system to protect against passivity? Why do we repeatedly seem out of synch during disasters? Why do we continually seem to be one disaster behind?

We have not found every fact nor contemplated all successes and failures. What we have done over four months is intensely focus on a three-week period, uncovering a multitude of problems. We have learned more than enough to instruct those who will now have to craft and execute changes for the future.

We leave it to readers to determine whether we have done a fair and thorough job, and whether we identified and supported findings in a way that will foster change. Some predicted we would place disproportionate blame on one person or another, or that we would give some others a pass. We hope it is clear we have done neither. We have not sought to assign individual blame, though it is clear in our report that some were not up to the challenge that was Katrina. Rather, we have tried to tell the story of government's preparation for and response to a massive storm, and identify lessons learned.

Our interaction with the White House illustrates this point. Some insist the White House's failure to provide, for example, e-mails to and from the White House Chief

DID YOU KNOW?

Teton Dam Failure

The U.S. Bureau of Reclamation (BOR) built the Teton Dam in Idaho's Teton River Canyon to control flooding on the Teton River, a tributary of the Snake River. While the reservoir behind the dam was filling for the first time, the dam ruptured. Beginning on June 5, 1976, floodwaters raged for three days down the Teton and Snake Rivers. The flood was finally contained 90-miles away by the American Falls Reservoir. The dam's failure resulted in more than $1 billion in damages and cost 11 people their lives.

Construction of the Teton Dam was authorized by Congress in 1964, but the $80 million budgeted for the project was inadequate to meet all the preconstruction requirements and build the dam. Ground was about to be broken in 1971 when a coalition of environmental groups filed suit against the BOR alleging that the project violated the National Environmental Policy Act. One of the accusations levied was that the site selected for the dam was unsafe because the region was seismically active, thus local geological features were not stable. The lawsuit ultimately failed to halt construction.

After construction commenced in February 1972, it was noted that the rocks at the dam site were porous, due to numerous cracks and fissures. BOR engineers addressed the problem by using large amounts of grout to create a waterproof "curtain." A year later, officials at the United States Geological Survey questioned the geological stability of the dam site but their concerns were ignored. The 305-foot dam was completed on November 26, 1975, although work on parts of the structure, such as spillways, continued until 1976.

Since it was unknown whether the dam was leakproof, the BOR was only going to allow the reservoir to fill at a rate of one foot a day. The fill rate would have allowed for the repair of any leaks that appeared. The limit was lifted after the region suffered from heavy snowfall the winter of 1975–1976, which allowed the reservoir to fill at a rate up to four feet a day. This resulted in the dam filling in half the time scheduled. Such rapid filling put immense pressure on the dam, which began springing leaks on June 3, 1956. Two days later, the dam's failure released 80 billion gallons of water downriver. In the aftermath of the disaster, two independent groups blamed the failure on the overreliance of grout to make the dam watertight.

The Teton Dam disaster proved a cautionary tale on the need to carefully consider a site's limitations before commencing dam construction. In order to ameliorate the chances of another dam failure, the BOR established within its bureaucracy a Division of Dam Safety. It also established a program that they dubbed the Safety Evaluation of Existing Dams. The disaster also spurred action within the United States Congress, which enacted the Reclamation Safety of Dams Act of 1978.

FURTHER READING

McDonald, Dylan J. 2006. *The Teton Dam Disaster.* Charleston: Arcadia.
U.S. Department of the Interior Teton Dam Review Group. *Failure of Teton Dam: A Report of Findings.* Washington, DC: U.S. Government Printing Office, 1977.

of Staff means we have insufficient information to determine why government failed. That view exalts political curiosity over the practical realities of a serious investigation.

While our dealings with the White House proved frustrating and difficult, we ended up with more than enough information to determine what went wrong there, to form a picture of a White House that, like many entities, was overcome by the fog of war. There is a big difference between having enough information to find institutional fault, which we do, and having information to assign individual blame, which, in the case of the White House, in large part we do not.

It's the former that's important if the goal is to be better prepared the next time. This was not about some individual's failure of initiative. It was about organizational and societal failures of initiative. There was more than enough failure to go around:

- Tardy and ineffective execution of the National Response Plan.
- An under-trained and under-staffed Federal Emergency Management Agency.
- A Catastrophic Incident Annex that was never invoked, and doubt that it would have done the job anyway.
- A perplexing inability to learn from Hurricane Pam and other exercises.
- Levees not built to withstand the most severe hurricanes.
- An incomplete evacuation that led to deaths and tremendous suffering.
- A complete breakdown in communications that paralyzed command and control and made situational awareness murky at best.
- The failure of state and local officials to maintain law and order.
- Haphazard and incomplete emergency shelter and housing plans.
- An overwhelmed FEMA logistics and contracting system that could not support the effective provision of urgently needed supplies.

The Select Committee encountered shortcomings and challenges even among those response elements that went relatively well and saved many lives. The military performed an invaluable role once forces were deployed, but encountered coordination problems with FEMA, the National Guard, and state officials. State-to-state emergency aid compacts were critical in restoring law and order and accelerating relief supplies, but too many people remain unfamiliar with the process. Contributions from charitable groups were enormously helpful, but they too were overwhelmed by the size of the storm.

Many of our findings are mixed in nature. Evacuations of general populations, for example, went relatively well in all three states. But declarations of mandatory evacuations in metropolitan New Orleans came late or not at all, and that, coupled with the decision to shelter but not evacuate the remaining population prolonged suffering. We saw heroic examples of medical care and patient needs being met under dire circumstances. But too often the deployment of medical personnel was reactive, not proactive.

The Select Committee acknowledges it was often torn between sympathy and incredulity, compassion and criticism. On the one hand, we understood Katrina was so big and so devastating that death and chaos were inevitable. We understood that top federal, state, and local officials overlooked some steps and some needs in the hours and days after landfall because they were focused on saving lives. But on the other hand, a dispassionate review made it clear that even an extraordinary lack of situational awareness could not excuse many of the shortcomings and organizational inaction evident in the documents and communications the Select Committee reviewed.

Leadership requires decisions to be made even when based on flawed and incomplete information. Too often during the immediate response to Katrina, sparse or conflicting information was used as an excuse for inaction rather than an imperative to step in and fill an obvious vacuum. Information passed through the maze of departmental operations centers and ironically named "coordinating" committees, losing timeliness and relevance as it was massaged and interpreted for internal audiences.

As a result, leaders became detached from the changing minute-to-minute realities of Katrina. Information translated into pre-cast bureaucratic jargon put more than geographic distance between Washington and the Gulf coast. Summaries and situation reports describing the gross totals of relief supplies directed to affected areas did not say when or how or to whom those desperately needed supplies would be delivered. And apparently no one asked.

Communications aren't a problem when you're only talking to yourself.

The Select Committee believes too many leaders failed to lead. Top aides failed as well, primarily in misprioritizing their bosses' attention and action. Critical time was wasted on issues of no importance to disaster response, such as winning the blame game, waging a public relations battle, or debating the advantages of wardrobe choices.

We have spared our readers a rehashing of unflattering e-mails involving Michael Brown and Governor Blanco and others, as they have been given more than enough attention by the media. We will pause only briefly here to urge future responders to make people, not politics, their priority.

We further urge public officials confronting the next Katrina to remember disaster response must be based on knowledge, not rumors. Government at all levels lost credibility due to inaccurate or unsubstantiated public statements made by officials regarding law and order, levee breaches, and overall response efforts.

The media must share some of the blame here. The Select Committee agrees the media can and should help serve as the public's "first informer" after disasters. In the 21st century, Americans depend on timely and accurate reporting, especially during times of crisis. But it's clear accurate reporting was among Katrina's many victims. If anyone rioted, it was the media. Many stories of rape, murder, and general lawlessness were at best unsubstantiated, at worst simply false. And that's too bad, because this storm needed no exaggeration.

As discussed in our report, widely-distributed uncorroborated rumors caused resources to be deployed, and important time and energy wasted, chasing down the imaginary. Already traumatized people in the Superdome and elsewhere, listening to their transistor radios, were further panicked.

"The sensational accounts delayed rescue and evacuation efforts already hampered by poor planning and a lack of coordination among local, state, and federal agencies. People rushing to the Gulf coast to fly rescue helicopters or to distribute food, water and other aid steeled themselves for battle. In communities near and far, the seeds were planted that the victims of Katrina should be kept away, or at least handled with extreme caution," the *Washington Post* reported on October 5.

Lt. Gen. H Steven Blum told the Select Committee on October 27, "We focused assets and resources based on situational awareness provided to us by the media, frankly. And the media failed in their responsibility to get it right. . . . we sent forces and capabilities to places that didn't need to go there in numbers that were far in excess of what was required, because they kept running the same B roll over and over . . . and the impression to us that were watching it was that the condition did not change. But the conditions were continually changing."

E-mails obtained by the Select Committee reinforce the conclusion that top military officials were relying on news reports for information—information used to plan and deploy resources.

The Select Committee does not mean to suggest the media is solely responsible for responders' lack of situational awareness, or the destruction of communications infrastructure that thrust television into the role of first informer for the military as well as the general public. Nor is the media solely responsible for reporting comments from sources they believed to be credible—especially top officials.

The Select Committee does, however, believe such circumstances make accurate reporting, especially in the period immediately after the storm, all the more important. Skepticism and fact-checking are easier when the sea is calm, but more vital when it is not.

As with so many other failures related to Katrina, what's most vexing is that emergency managers should have known such problems would arise among the chaos. Dr. Kathleen Tierney, head of the University of Colorado-Boulder Natural Hazards Center, told Select Committee staff that misleading or completely false media reports should have been among the most foreseeable elements of Katrina. "It's a well-documented element of disaster response," she said. "What you do has to be based on knowledge, not rumor, and you're going to be faced with a lot of rumors."

Benigno Aguirre, sociology professor at the University of Delaware Disaster Research Center, told the *Philadelphia Inquirer*, "It's discouraging for those who spend their lives studying disaster behavior that journalists so often get it wrong."

Former FEMA Director Michael Brown told the Select Committee one of his biggest failures was failing to properly utilize the media as first informer. "I failed initially to set up a series of regular briefings to the media about what FEMA was doing throughout the Gulf coast region," Brown said at the Select Committee's September 27 hearing. "Instead, I became tied to the news shows, going on the news shows early in the morning and late at night, and that was just a mistake. We should have been feeding that information to the press . . . in the manner and time that we wanted to, instead of letting the press drive us."

Finally, a word about public communications. Both the message and the messengers were ineffective before and after Katrina. Messages to the public were uncoordinated and often confusing, leaving important questions unanswered. Federal, state, and local officials did not have a unified strategy for communicating with the public.

Risk communication is a well-researched field of study. There are accepted core principles for successfully communicating risks to the public. Information about threats should be consistent, accurate, clear, and provided repeatedly through multiple methods. It should be timely. It should be specific about the potential threat. It needs to get to people regardless of their level of access to information.

The Select Committee heard loud and clear from Gulf coast residents that the dangers of the coming hurricane could have been presented in a more effective manner, an issue which also carried racial and socioeconomic implications. If people don't hear a message from someone they trust, they will be skeptical.

Doreen Keeler, a New Orleans resident who evacuated before Mayor Nagin called for a mandatory evacuation, told the Select Committee local officials should have called for mandatory evacuations earlier, noting how difficult it was to convince the elderly residents of New Orleans to leave. "If a mandatory evacuation would have been called earlier," she said, "it would have been easier to move seniors out of the area and many lives would have been saved. It took me almost 24 hours to get my in-laws to leave. Others tell the same story. The severity of the storm was not stressed by elected officials."

The relevant "elected officials," we are sure, would contest that. In fact they did, in testimony before the Select Committee. But it's the public perception of what was stressed that's important here. The failure of initiative was also a failure of empathy, a myopia to the need to reach more people on their own terms.

Four and half years after 9/11, Americans deserve more than the state of nature after disaster strikes. With this report we have tried to identify where and why chaos ensued, so that even a storm the size of Katrina can be met with more order, more urgency, more coordination, and more initiative.

SOURCE: Select Bipartisan Committee to Investigate the Preparation for and Response to Hurricane Katrina. 2006. *A Failure of Initiative: Final Report of the Select Bipartisan Committee to Investigate the Preparation for and Response to Hurricane Katrina.* http://www.gpo.gov/fdsys/pkg/CRPT-109hrpt377/pdf/CRPT-109hrpt377.pdf (accessed August 15, 2014).

ANALYSIS

The states of Alabama, Louisiana, and Mississippi were struck by Hurricane Katrina, a Category 3 storm, on August 29, 2005. Louisiana was particularly susceptible to hurricane damage because its coastal wetlands had been disappearing for decades. The storm caused New Orleans' flood-control system to be compromised as a number of levees failed, which resulted in waters from Lake Pontchartrain to flood significant portions of the city. The catastrophe proved a major embarrassment to government officials at the local, state, and federal levels as many of the city's poor and destitute were not evacuated prior to the flooding. It was not until September 3 that many of those individuals were rescued from locales such as the Louisiana Superdome.

The levee failures were blamed on shoddy construction methods employed by the United States Army Corps of Engineers (USACE). The sites they selected to construct the levees were comprised of soils that were too soft to support concrete levees when stressed by floodwaters. The resulting problems were compounded by the construction of pilings that were too short. The failure of their engineering efforts in New Orleans led the USACE to reexamine other water structures that they had built that relied on similar assumptions that had been proven wrong in New Orleans. Dams around the country that were previously deemed safe were suddenly being strengthened. For example, the USACE spent millions improving the Wolf Creek Dam in Kentucky, whose failure promised to ultimately flood Nashville, Tennessee.

In the aftermath of the disaster, the United States Army Corps of Engineers began repairing and upgrading New Orleans' flood-control system. Critics of the effort noted that the planned upgrades were not sufficient for the city to withstand a direct hit from another Category 3 hurricane, let alone one with the strength of a Category 4 or 5. Years after Hurricane Katrina struck, significant portions of New Orleans still have not recovered from the catastrophe.

FURTHER READING

Brinkley, Douglas. 2006. *The Great Deluge: Hurricane Katrina, New Orleans, and the Mississippi Gulf Coast.* New York: HarperCollins.

Horne, Jed. 2006. *Breach of Faith: Hurricane Katrina and the Near Death of a Great American City.* New York: Random House.

Van Heerden, Ivor, and Mike Bryan. 2006. *The Storm: What Went Wrong and Why During Hurricane Katrina; the Inside Story from One Louisiana Scientist.* New York: Viking.

Verchick, Robert, R. M. 2010. *Facing Catastrophe: Environmental Action for a post-Katrina World.* Cambridge: Harvard University Press.

Part V

ENVIRONMENTAL ISSUES

8

WATER POLLUTION

"It Is Not Lawful to Deposit Refuse into the Navigable Water of the United States"

- *Document:* Refuse Act of 1899
- *Date:* March 3, 1899
- *Where:* Washington, DC
- *Significance:* The act banned the dumping of refuse into the nation's navigable rivers unless one had obtained a permit to do so from the U.S. Army Corps of Engineers. In areas with harbors, the only exception was refuse in liquid form that originated on streets or sewers.

DOCUMENT

SEC. 13. That it shall not be lawful to throw, discharge, or deposit, or cause, suffer, or procure to be thrown, discharged, or deposited either from or out of any ship, barge, or other floating craft of any kind, or from the shore, wharf, manufacturing establishment, or mill of any kind, and refuse matter of any kind or description whatever other than that flowing from streets and sewers and passing therefrom in a liquid state, into any navigable water of the United States, or into any tributary of any navigable water from which the same shall float or be washed into such navigable water; and it shall not be lawful to deposit, or cause, suffer, or procure to be deposited material of any kind in any place on the bank of any navigable water, or on the bank of any tributary of any navigable water, where the same shall be liable to be washed into such navigable water, either by ordinary or high tides, or by storms or floods, or otherwise, whereby navigation shall or may be impeded or obstructed: *Provided*, That nothing herein contained shall extend to, apply to, or prohibit the operations in connection with the improvement of navigable waters or construction of public works, considered necessary and proper by the United States officers supervising such improvement or public work: *And provided further,* That the Secretary of War, whenever in the judgment of the Chief of Engineers anchorage and navigation will not be injured thereby, may permit the deposit of any material above mentioned in navigable waters, within limits to be defined and under conditions to be prescribed by him, provided application is made to him prior to depositing such material; and whenever any permit is so granted the conditions thereof shall be strictly complied with, and any violation thereof shall be unlawful.

SOURCE: United States Congress. 2000. *Sections 9 to 20 of the Act of March 3, 1899.* http://www.epw.senate.gov/rivers.pdf (accessed August 29, 2014).

ANALYSIS

The Refuse Act, also known as Section 13 of the Rivers and Harbors Appropriation Act of 1899, banned the dumping of all refuse with the exception of liquid waste from streets and sewers into the nation's navigable waters unless the entity doing the depositing had obtained a permit from the U.S. Army Corps of Engineers. In waterways where harbors were not present, the act contained another exception that allowed mining companies to deposit debris in waterways as long as the refuse did not interfere with shipping. The special consideration given to mining companies was not surprising since the hydraulic mining of precious metals, especially silver and gold, was a significant economic engine at the end of the nineteenth century. This exception ran contrary to the purpose of the Refuse Act in general as, by its very nature, hydraulic mining created refuse that flowed into navigable waters.

Although at first glance the Refuse Act appeared to make the protection of the nation's waterways from pollution the priority, its primary purpose was to provide the federal government a tool that it could use to financially punish individuals or companies that interfered with commerce by impeding shipping. The act allowed for the assessment of fines ranging from $500 to $2,500 per violation. The federal government needed the ability to issue fines to address issues that were plaguing shipping, especially those that were not easily seen. One major problem affecting shipping was the presence of underwater obstructions that boats were crashing into. These accidents were not only killing people but were creating even more obstructions as ships sunk. With the Refuse Act in place, the federal government had the ability to punish the entities that were responsible for the presence of the obstructions.

Although the federal government was empowered by the Refuse Act of 1899, it was reticent to use that authority. The U.S. Army Corps of Engineers ultimately issued few permits because the vast majority of the citizenry refused to make application. They really did not need the permits, as the federal government failed to enforce the act's edicts. Interest in the Refuse Act of 1899 began to emerge within the Environmental Movement in the 1960s. Environmentalists saw the legislation as a means to clean up the nation's waterways, especially considering that the vast majority of the industrial plants in the country were depositing their wastes into the nation's rivers. This activity was one of the reasons that the Cuyahoga River in Ohio had proven flammable on several occasions. Despite the pleas from environmentalists, the Nixon Administration initially refused to utilize the power provided by the Refuse Act. The administration reconsidered its position in 1970 when it discovered that the only way that it could punish 11 companies for dumping mercury into the nation's waters was to use the act. President Richard Nixon subsequently issued a presidential order on December 23, 1970, that ordered the U.S. Army Corps of Engineers to reinstitute the issuance of permits as originally required by the 1899 legislation.

FURTHER READING

Degler, Stanley E. 1971. *Federal Pollution Control Problems: Water, Air, and Solid Wastes.* Washington, DC: Bureau of National Affairs.

Eames, Diane D. 1970. "The Refuse Act of 1899: Its Scope and Role in Control of Water Pollution." *California Law Review* 58, no. 6: 1444–1473.

Mushal, Raymond W. 2009. "Up From the Sewers: A Perspective on the Evolution of the Federal Environmental Crimes Program." *Utah Law Review* 2009, no. 4: 1103–1127.

"To Recognize, Preserve, and Protect the Primary Responsibilities and Rights of the States in Controlling Water Pollution"

- *Document:* Water Pollution Control Act of 1948, excerpt
- *Date:* June 30, 1948
- *Where:* Washington, DC
- *Significance:* The act represented an effort by Congress to regulate the pollution of surface waters around the country. To achieve its goals, Congress delegated the primary responsibility for addressing pollution problems to the respective states.

DOCUMENT

An Act

To provide for water pollution control activities in the Public Health Service of the Federal Security Agency and in the Federal Works Agency, and for other purposes.

Be it enacted by the Senate and House of Representatives of the United States of America in Congress assembled, That in connection with the exercise of jurisdiction over the waterways of the nation and in consequence of the benefits resulting to the public health and welfare by the abatement of stream pollution, it is hereby declared to be the policy of Congress to recognize, preserve, and protect the primary responsibilities and rights of the States in controlling water pollution, to support and aid technical research to devise and perfect methods of treatment of industrial wastes which are not susceptible to known effective methods of treatment, and to provide Federal technical services to State and interstate agencies and to industries, and financial aid to State and interstate agencies and to municipalities, in the formulation and execution of their stream pollution abatement programs. To this end, the Surgeon General of the Public Health Service (under the supervision and direction of the Federal Security Administrator) and the Federal Works Administrator shall have the responsibilities and authority relating to water pollution control vested in them respectively by this Act.

Sec. 2 (a) The Surgeon General shall, after careful investigation, and in cooperation with other Federal Agencies, with State water pollution agencies and interstate agencies, and with the municipalities and industries involved, prepare or adopt comprehensive programs for eliminating or reducing the pollution of interstate waters and tributaries thereof and improving the sanitary condition of surface and underground waters. In the development of such comprehensive programs due regard shall be given to the improvements which are necessary to conserve such waters for public water supplies, propagation of fish and aquatic life, recreational purposes, and agricultural, industrial, and other legitimate uses. For the purpose of this subsection the Surgeon General is authorized to make joint investigations with any such agencies of the condition of any waters in any State or States, and of the discharges of any sewage, industrial wastes, or substance which may deleteriously affect such waters.

(b) The Surgeon General shall encourage cooperative activities by the States for the prevention and abatement of water pollution; encourage the enactment of uniform State laws relating to water pollution; encourage compacts between States for the prevention and abatement of water pollution; collect and disseminate information relating to water pollution and the prevention and abatement thereof; support and aid technical research to devise and perfect methods of treatment of industrial wastes which are not susceptible to known effective methods of treatment; make available to State and interstate agencies, municipalities, industries, and individuals the results of surveys, studies, investigations, research, and experiments relating to water pollution and the prevention and abatement thereof conducted by the Surgeon General and by authorized cooperating agencies; and furnish such assistance to State agencies as may be authorized by law.

(c) The consent of the Congress is hereby given to two or more States to negotiate and enter into agreements or compacts, not in conflict with any law or treaty of the United States, for (1) cooperative effort and mutual assistance for the prevention and abatement of water pollution and the enforcement of their respective laws relating thereto, and (2) the establishment of such agencies, joint or otherwise, as they may deem desirable for making effective such agreements and compacts. No such agreement or compact shall be binding or obligatory upon any State a party thereto unless and until it has been approved by the Congress.

(d) (1) The pollution of interstate waters in or adjacent to any State or States (whether the matter causing or contributing to such pollution is discharged directly into such waters or reaches such waters after discharge into a tributary of such waters), which endangers the health or welfare of persons in a State other than that in which the discharge originates, is hereby declared to be a public nuisance and subject to abatement as herein provided.

(2) Whenever the Surgeon General, on the basis of reports, surveys, and studies, finds that any pollution declared to be a public nuisance by paragraph (1) of this subsection is occurring, he shall give formal notification thereof to the person or persons discharging any matter causing or contributing to such pollution and shall advise the water pollution agency or interstate agency of the State or States where such discharge or discharges originate of such notification. This notification may outline recommended remedial measures which are reasonable and equitable in that case and shall specify a reasonable time to secure abatement of the pollution. If action calculated to secure abatement of the pollution within the time specified is not commenced, this failure shall again be brought to the attention of the person or persons discharging the matter and of the water pollution agency or interstate agency of the State or States where such discharge or discharges originate. The notification to such agency may be accompanied by a recommendation that it initiate a suit to abate the pollution in a court of proper jurisdiction.

(3) If, within a reasonable time after the second notification by the Surgeon General, the person or persons discharging the matter fail to initiate action to abate the pollution or the State water pollution agency or interstate agency fails to initiate a suit to secure abatement, the Federal Security Administrator is authorized to call a public hearing, to be held in or near one or more of the places where the discharge or discharges causing or contributing to such pollution originate, before a board of five or more persons appointed by the Administrator, who may be officers or employees of the Federal Security Agency or of the water pollution agency or interstate agency of the State or States where such discharge or discharges originate (except that at least one of the members of the board shall be a representative of the water pollution agency of the State or States where such discharge or discharges originate and at least one shall be a representative of the Department of Commerce, and not less than a majority of the board shall be persons other than officers or employees of the Federal Security Agency). On the basis of the evidence presented at such hearing the board shall make its recommendations to the Federal Security Administrator concerning the measures, if any, which it finds to be reasonable and equitable to secure abatement of such pollution.

(4) After affording the person or persons discharging the matter causing or contributing to the pollution reasonable opportunity to comply with the recommendation of the board, the Federal Security Administrator may, with the consent of the water pollution agency (or of any officer or agency authorized to give such consent) of the State or States in which the matter causing or contributing to the pollution is discharged, request the Attorney General to bring a suit on behalf of the United States to secure abatement of the pollution.

(5) Before or after any suit authorized by paragraph (4) is commenced, any person who is alleged to be discharging matter contributing to the pollution, abatement of which is sought, may, with the consent of the water pollution agency (or of any officer or agency authorized to give such consent)) of the State in which such matter is discharged, be joined as a defendant. The court shall have power to enforce its judgment against any such defendant.

(6) In any suit brought pursuant to paragraph (4) in which two or more persons in different judicial districts are originally joined as defendants, the suit may be

commenced in the judicial district in which any discharge caused by any of the defendants occurs.

(7) The court shall receive in evidence in any such suit a transcript of the proceedings before the board and a copy of the board's recommendation; and may receive such further evidence as the court in its discretion deems proper. The court, giving due consideration to the practicability and to the physical and economic feasibility of securing abatement of any pollution proved, shall have jurisdiction to enter such judgment, and orders enforcing such judgment, as the public interest and the equities of the case may require. The jurisdiction of the Surgeon General, or any other agency which has jurisdiction pursuant to the provisions of this Act, shall not extend to any region or areas nor shall it affect the rights or jurisdiction of any public body where there are in effect provisions for sewage disposal pursuant to agreement between the United States of America and any such public body by stipulation entered in the Supreme Court of the United States. While any such stipulation or modification thereof is in force and effect, no proceedings of any kind may be maintained by virtue of this Act against any such public body or any public agency, corporation, or individual within its jurisdiction. Neither this provision nor any provision of the Act shall be construed to give to the Surgeon General or any other person or agency the right to intervene in the said proceedings wherein such stipulation was entered.

(8) As used in this subsection the term "person" includes an individual, corporation, partnership, association, a State, municipality, and a political subdivision of a State.

Sec. 3. The Surgeon General may, upon request of any State water pollution agency or interstate agency, conduct investigations and research and make surveys concerning any specific problem of water pollution confronting any State, interstate agency, community, municipality, or industrial plant, with a view to recommending a solution of such problem.

Sec. 4. The Surgeon General shall prepare and publish, from time to time, reports of such surveys, studies, investigations, research, and experiments made under the authority of this Act as he may consider desirable, together with appropriate recommendations with regard to the control of water pollution.

. . .

SOURCE: U.S. Congress. n.d. *Water Pollution Control Act of 1948*. https://www.wilderness.net/NWPS/documents/publiclaws/PDF/80-845.pdf (accessed November 4, 2014).

ANALYSIS

Since the beginning of the twentieth century, individual congressmen had attempted to pass bills through both the House of Representatives and the Senate to stop pollutants from entering the nation's waterways but were never successful.

The consequence from the inaction was that rivers and streams became much more polluted, largely due to industrial waste and urbanization. By the late 1940s, the situation had become so dire that some of the tributaries to the Great Lakes had become flammable. To ameliorate the problem, Congress passed the Water Pollution Control Act (WPCA) of 1948. It became the first federal law to comprehensively address the impact of pollution on the nation's surface waters.

Although strong legislation was obviously needed, the WPCA was significantly weakened as it made its way through the legislative process. The law that emerged from the process did not give federal authorities the power to regulate pollutants or establish minimum water quality standards. Instead, federal employees were relegated to serving as advisors and researchers for corporate interests, individuals, municipalities, state or interstate agencies, and state governments. It was left to the individual states to regulate pollutants within their borders. If the states did not aggressively target polluters, the federal government could only identify the problems and the guilty parties but not prosecute them. The only time that federal officials were allowed to directly intervene with polluters was when the pollution from one state was affecting people in a neighboring state. Under that circumstance, the federal government could act if it could get the permission of the state where there pollution was being introduced into a waterway.

Due to the inherent weaknesses of the WPCA, application of the law varied widely between the states. Some were able to significantly improve the water quality while others chose to ignore the law. Predictably, the state of the nation's waterways only grew worse. This was best exemplified by the Cuyahoga River, a tributary to Lake Erie, which caught fire on multiple occasions. In 1972, the WPCA was amended by the Clean Water Act.

FURTHER READING

Andrews, Richard N. L. 2006. *Managing the Environment, Managing Ourselves: A History of American Environmental Policy.* New Haven, CT: Yale University Press.

Dzurik, Andrew A., and David A. Theriaque. 2002. *Water Resources Planning.* Lanham, MD: Rowman & Littlefield.

Stoddard, Andrew, et al. 2002. *Municipal Wastewater Treatment: Evaluating Improvements in National Water Quality.* New York: John Wiley and Sons.

"To Promote a More Adequate National Program of Water Research"

- *Document:* Water Resources Research Act of 1964, excerpts
- *Date:* July 17, 1964
- *Where:* Washington, DC
- *Significance:* The act established a water resources research institute at each of the nation's land-grant universities.

DOCUMENT

An Act

To establish water resources research centers, to promote a more adequate national program of water research, and for other purposes.

Be it enacted by the Senate and House of Representatives of the United States in Congress assembled, That (a) this Act may be cited as the "Water Resources Research Act of 1964."

(b) In order to assist in assuring the Nation at all times of a supply of water sufficient in quantity and quality to meet the requirements of its expanding population, it is the purpose of Congress, by this Act, to stimulate, sponsor, provide for, and supplement present programs for the conduct of research, investigations, experiments, and the training of scientists in the fields of water and of resources which affect water.

TITLE I—STATE WATER RESOURCES RESEARCH INSTITUTES

Sec. 100. (a) There are authorized to be appropriated to the Secretary of the Interior for the fiscal year 1965 and each subsequent year thereafter sums adequate to provide $75,000 to each of the several States in the first year, $87,500 in each of the second and third years, and $100,000 each year thereafter to assist each participating State in establishing and carrying on the work of a competent and qualified water resources research institute, center, or equivalent agency (hereinafter referred to as "institute") at one college or university in that state, which college or university shall be a college or university established in accordance with the Act approved July 2, 1862 (12 Stat. 503), entitled "An Act donating public lands to the several States and territories which may provide colleges for the benefit of agriculture and mechanic arts" or some other institution designated by Act of the legislature of the State concerned: *Provided*, That (1) if there is more than one such college or university in a State, established in accordance with said Act of July 2, 1862, funds under this Act shall, in the absence of a designation to the contrary by act of the legislature of the State, be paid to the one such college or university designated by the Governor of the State to receive the same subject to the Secretary's determination that such college or university has, or may reasonably be expected to have, the capability of doing effective under this Act; (2) two or more States may cooperate in the designation of a single interstate or regional institute, in which event the sums assignable to all of the cooperating States shall be paid to such institute; and (3) a designated college or university may, as authorized by appropriate State authority, arrange with other colleges and universities within the State to participate in the work of the institute.

(b) It shall be the duty of each such institute to plan and conduct and/or arrange for a component or components of the college or university with which it is affiliated to conduct competent research, investigations, and experiments of either a basic or practical nature, or both, in relation to water resources and to provide for the training of scientists through such research, investigations, and experiments. Such research, investigations, experiments, and training may include, without being limited to, aspects of the hydrologic cycle; supply and demand for water; conservation and best use of available supplies of water; methods of increasing such supplies; and economic , legal, social, engineering, recreational, biological, geographic, ecological, and other aspects of water problems, having due regard to the varying conditions and needs of the respective States, to water research projects being conducted by agencies of the Federal and State Governments, the agricultural experiment stations, and others, and to avoidance of any undue displacement of scientists and engineers elsewhere engaged in water resources research.

. . .

TITLE II—ADDITIONAL WATER RESOURCES RESEARCH PROGRAMS

Sec. 200. There is authorized to be appropriated to the Secretary of the Interior $1,000,000 in fiscal year 1965 and $1,000,000 in each of the nine fiscal years thereafter from which he may make grants, contracts, matching, or other arrangements with educational institutions (other than those establishing institutes under Title I of this Act), private foundations or other institutions; with private firms and individuals; and with local, State and Federal Government agencies, to undertake research into any aspects of water problems related to the mission of the Department of the Interior, which may be deemed desirable and are not otherwise being studied. The Secretary shall submit each such proposed grant, contract, or other arrangement to the President of the Senate and the Speaker of the House of

Representatives, and no appropriation shall be made to finance the same until 60 calendar days (which 60 days, however, shall not include days on which either the House of Representatives or the Senate is not in session because of an adjournment of more than three calendar days) after such submission and then only if, within said 60 days, neither the Committee on Interior and Insular Affairs of the House of Representatives nor the Committee on Interior and Insular Affairs of the Senate disapproves the same.

. . .

SOURCE: U.S. Congress. *Public Law 88-379.* http://www.gpo.gov/fdsys/pkg/STATUTE-78/pdf/STATUTE-78-Pg329.pdf (accessed November 3, 2014).

ANALYSIS

The Water Resources Research Act (WRRA) of 1964 was designed to stimulate research on water issues facing the United States at academic institutions around the country. Toward that end, the WRRA proposed the creation of water resources research and technology institutes or centers at each of the nation's land-grant institutions. The respective institutes were charged with conducting research into water issues impacting the nation, training scientists and researchers for work in fields related to water resources, and disseminating research for use by professionals in the field and the general populace. The research conducted at the institutes is overseen by the U.S. Geological Survey, operating under the auspices of the secretary of the interior. There are presently 54 institutes in operation. Each of the 50 states has one, along with the District of Columbia, Guam, Puerto Rico, and the United States Virgin Islands.

During the early 1970s, the Congressional Research Service (CRS) began evaluating the various institutes to determine whether they had proven a good use of public money. Although underfunded, the CRS determined that the institutes had proven to be a valuable resource for water planners and politicians at all levels of government. Congress responded by increasing the funding for the institutes over the course of the 1970s into the early 1980s. The entire program was broadened and reauthorized through the Water Resources Research Act of 1984.

FURTHER READING

Milazzo, Paul Charles. 2006. *Unlikely Environmentalists: Congress and Clean Water, 1945–1972.* Lawrence: University Press of Kansas.
National Research Council, Committee on Assessment of Water Resources Research. 2004. *Confronting the Nation's Water Problems: The Role of Research.* Washington, DC: National Academies Press.

"For the Optimum Development of the Nation's Natural Resources"

- *Document:* Water Resources Planning Act of 1965, excerpts
- *Date:* July 22, 1965
- *Where:* Washington, DC
- *Significance:* The act was intended to create a framework where federal, state, and local officials and agencies could plan in concert how to address the water issues plaguing the country.

DOCUMENT

An Act

To provide for the optimum development of the Nation's natural resources through the coordinated planning of water and related land resources, through the establishment of a water resources council and river basin commissions, and by providing financial assistance to the States in order to increase State participation in such planning.

Be it enacted by the Senate and House of Representatives of the United States of America in Congress assembled,

SHORT TITLE

Section 1. This Act may be cited as the "Water Resources Planning Act."

STATEMENT OF POLICY

Sec. 2. In order to meet the rapidly expanding demands for water throughout the Nation, it is hereby declared to be the policy of the Congress to encourage the conservation, development, and utilization of water and related land resources of the

United States on a comprehensive and coordinated basis by the Federal Government, States, localities, and private enterprise with the cooperation of all affected Federal agencies, States, local governments, individuals, corporations, business enterprises, and others concerned.

. . .

TITLE I—WATER RESOURCES COUNCIL

Sec. 101. There is hereby established a Water Resources Council (hereinafter referred to as the "Council") which shall be composed of the Secretary of the Interior, the Secretary of Agriculture, the Secretary of the Army, the Secretary of Health, Education, and Welfare, and the Chairman of the Federal Power Commission. The Chairman of the Council shall request the heads of other Federal Agencies to participate with the Council when matters affecting their responsibilities are considered by the Council. The Chairman of the Council shall be designated by the President.

Sec. 102. The Council shall—

(a) Maintain a continuing study and prepare an assessment biennially, or at such less frequent intervals as the Council may determine, or the adequacy of supplies of water necessary to meet the water requirements in each water resource region in the United States and the national interest therein; and

(b) Maintain a continuing study of the relation of regional or river basin plans and programs to the requirements of larger regions of the Nation and of the adequacy of administrative and statutory means for the coordination of the water and related land resources policies and programs of several Federal agencies; it shall appraise the adequacy of existing and proposed policies and programs to meet such requirements; and it shall make recommendations to the President with respect to Federal policies and programs.

. . .

TITLE II—RIVER BASIN COMMISSIONS

Creation of Commissions

Sec. 201. (a) The President is authorized to declare the establishment of a river basin water and related land resources commission upon request therefore by the Council, or request addressed to the Council by a State within which all or part of the basin or basins concerned are located, if the request by the Council or by a State (1) defines the area, river basin, or group of related river basins for which a commission is requested, (2) is made in writing by the Governor or in such manner as State law may provide, or by the Council, and (3) is concurred in by the Council and by not less than one-half of the States within which portions of the basin or basins concerned are located and, in the event the Upper Colorado River Basin is involved, by at least three of the four States of Colorado, New Mexico, Utah, and Wyoming or, in the event the Columbia River Basin is involved, by at least three of the four States of Idaho, Montana, Oregon, and Washington. Such concurrences must be in writing.

(b) Each such commission for an area, river basin, or group of river basins shall, to the extent consistent with section 3 of this Act—

(1) serve as the principal agency for the coordination of Federal, State, interstate, local and nongovernmental plans for the development of water and related land resources in its area, river basin, or group of river basins;

(2) prepare and keep up to date, to the extent practicable, a comprehensive, coordinated, joint plan for Federal, State, interstate, local and nongovernmental development of water and related resources: *Provided,* That the plan shall include an evaluation of all reasonable alternative means of achieving optimum development of water and related land resources of the basin or basins, and it may be prepared in stages, including recommendations with respect to individual projects;

(3) recommend long-range schedules of priorities for the collection and analysis of basic data and for investigation, planning, and construction of such projects; and

(4) foster and undertake such studies of water and related land resources problems in its area, river basin, or group of river basins as are necessary in the preparation of the plan described in clause (2) of this subsection.

. . .

SOURCE: U.S. Congress. *Public Law 89-80.* http://www.gpo.gov/fdsys/pkg/STATUTE-79/pdf/STATUTE-79-Pg224-2.pdf (accessed November 3, 2014).

ANALYSIS

The Water Resources Planning Act (WRPA) of 1965 was intended to coordinate planning between federal, state, and local officials and agencies so that the country could make "optimum" use of its water and land resources. In particular, there were two issues that the federal government wanted to address through the planning process: determine how best to utilize the waters in the West while also not negatively impacting the region's economic growth and a reduction of the pollution in the nation's surface waters. To encourage and oversee the planning efforts, the WRPA created the Water Resources Council (WRC).

The WRC initially consisted of the secretary of agriculture, secretary of commerce, secretary of energy, secretary of housing and urban development, secretary of the interior, and the secretary of transportation. Representation from the Environmental Protection Agency was added in 1970. The WRPC received a significant amount of criticism in 1973 when it issued its *Principles and Standards for Planning Water and Related Land Sources.* Critics alleged that the document favored environmental concerns over economic development. In 1983, President Reagan had the WRC issue revised guidelines, which were published as *Economic and Environmental Principles and Guidelines for Water and Related Land Resources Implementation Studies.* With that task accomplished, Reagan abolished the WRC.

In Title II, the WRPA also provided funding for the creation of up to 50 river basin commissions, one for each state. This was a significant step forward as it represented the realization that the issues affecting a waterway extended beyond its shores. To adequately address problems like water pollution within a stream or river, the entire river basin had to be considered. At the same time, providing each state a river basin commission meant that their authority ended at the state line. Later legislation would address this problem, giving interstate basin authorities the ability to consider the health of the entire river basin, not just a segment.

FURTHER READING

Brooks, Richard Oliver, Ross Jones, and Ross A. Virginia. 2002. *Law and Ecology: The Rise of the Ecosystem Regime*. Burlington, VT: Ashgate.

Newson, Malcolm. 2009. *Land, Water, and Development: Sustainable Management of River Basin Systems*. 3rd ed. New York: Routledge.

Water Resources Council. 1973. *Principles and Standards for Planning Water and Related Land Resources*. Washington, DC: U.S. Government Printing Office.

Water Resources Council. 1983. *Economic and Environmental Principles and Guidelines for Water and Related Land Resources Implementation Studies*. Washington, DC: U.S. Water Council, Department of the Interior.

"To Amend the Federal Water Pollution Control Act in Order to Improve and Make More Effective"

- *Document:* Clean Water Restoration Act of 1966, excerpts
- *Date:* November 3, 1966
- *Where:* Washington, DC
- *Significance:* The act strengthened regulations and penalties contained within both the Oil Pollution Act of 1924 and the Water Pollution Control Act of 1948.

DOCUMENT

An Act

To amend the Federal Water Pollution Control Act in order to improve and make more effective certain programs pursuant to such Act.

Be it enacted by the Senate and House of Representatives of the United States in Congress assembled, That this Act may be cited as the "Clean Water Restoration Act of 1966."

TITLE I

SEC. 101. Section 3 of the Federal Water Pollution Control Act, as amended, is amended by adding at the end thereof the following:

"(c)(1) The Secretary shall, at the request of the Governor of a State, or a majority of the governors when more than one State is involved, make a grant to pay not to exceed 50 per centum of the administrative expenses of a planning agency for a period not to exceed 3 years, if such agency provides for adequate representation of appropriate State, interstate, local, or (when appropriate) international, interests in the basin or portion thereof involved and is capable of developing an effective, comprehensive water quality control and abatement plan for a basin.

"(2) Each planning agency receiving a grant under this subsection shall develop a comprehensive pollution control and abatement plan for the basin which—

"(A) is consistent with any applicable water quality standards established pursuant to current law within the basin;

"(B) recommends such treatment works and sewer systems as will provide the most effective and economical means of collection, storage, treatment, and purification of wastes and recommends means to encourage both municipal and industrial use of such works and systems; and

"(C) recommends maintenance and improvement of water quality standards within the basin or portion thereof and recommends methods of adequately financing those facilities as may be necessary to implement the plan.

"(3) For the purposes of this subsection, the term 'basin' includes, but is not limited to, rivers and their tributaries, streams, coastal waters, sounds, estuaries, bays, lakes, and portions thereof, as well as lands drained thereby."

TITLE II

SEC. 201. (a) Section 6 of the Federal Water Pollution Control Act is amended to read as follows:

"Grants for Research and Development

"Sec. 6 (a) The Secretary is authorized to make grants to any State, municipality, or intermunicipal or interstate agency for the purpose of—

"(1) assisting in the development of any project which will demonstrate a new or improved method of controlling the discharge into any waters of untreated or inadequately treated sewage or other wastes from sewers which carry storm water or both storm water and sewage and other wastes, or

"(2) assisting in the development of any project which will demonstrate advanced waste treatment and water purification methods (including the temporary use of new or improved chemical additives which provide substantial immediate improvement to existing treatment processes) or new and improved methods of joint treatment systems for municipal and industrial wastes, and for the purpose of reports, plans, and specifications in connection therewith.

"(b) The Secretary is authorized to make grants to persons for research and demonstration projects for prevention of pollution of waters by industry including, but not limited to, treatment of industrial waste.

"(c) Federal grants under subsection (a) of this section shall be subject to the following limitations:

"(1) No grant shall be made for any project pursuant to this section unless such project shall have been approved by the appropriate State water pollution control agency or agencies and by the Secretary;

"(2) No grant shall be made for any project in an amount exceeding 75 per centum of the estimated reasonable cost thereof as determined by the Secretary; and

"(3) No grant shall be made for any project under this subsection unless the Secretary determines that such project will serve as a useful demonstration for the purpose set forth in clause (1) or (2) of subsection (a).

. . .

"(g) (1) The Secretary, shall, in cooperation with the Secretary of the Army, the Secretary of Agriculture, the Water Resources Council, and with other appropriate Federal, State, Interstate, or local public bodies and private organizations, institutions, and individuals, conduct and promote, and encourage contributions to, a comprehensive study of the effects of pollution, including sedimentation, in the estuaries and estuarine zones of the United States on fish and wildlife, on sport and commercial fishing, on recreation, on water supply and water power, and on other beneficial purposes. Such study shall also consider the effect of demographic trends, the exploitation of mineral resources and fossil fuels, land and industrial development, navigation, flood and erosion control, and other uses of estuaries and estuarine zones upon the pollution of the waters therein.

"(2) In conducting the above study, the Secretary shall assemble, coordinate, and organize all existing pertinent information on the Nation's estuaries and estuarine zones; carry out a program of investigations and surveys to supplement existing information in representative estuaries and estuarine zones; and identify the problems and areas where further research and study are required.

"(3) The Secretary shall submit to the Congress a final report of the study authorized by this subsection not later than three years after the date of enactment of this subsection. . . .

SEC. 206 Section 10(d) of the Federal Water Pollution Control Act is amended by redesignating paragraphs (2) and (3) as paragraphs (3) and (4), respectively, and by inserting immediately after paragraph (1) the following new paragraph:

"(2) Whenever the Secretary, upon receipt of reports, surveys, or studies from any duly constituted international agency, has reason to believe that any pollution referred to in subsection (a) of this section which endangers the health or welfare of persons in a foreign country is occurring, and the Secretary of State requests him to abate such pollution, he shall give formal notification thereof to the State water pollution control agency of the State in which such discharge or discharges originate and to the interstate water pollution control agency, if any, and shall call promptly a conference of such agency or agencies, if he believes that such pollution is occurring in sufficient quantity to warrant such action. The Secretary, through the Secretary of State, shall invite the foreign country, which may be adversely affected by the pollution to attend and participate in the conference, and the representative of such country shall, for the purpose of the conference and any further proceeding resulting from such conference, have all the rights of a State water pollution control agency. This paragraph shall apply only to a foreign country which the Secretary determines has given the United States essentially the same rights with respect to the prevention and control of water pollution occurring in that country as is given that country by this paragraph. Nothing in this paragraph shall be construed to modify, amend, repeal, or otherwise affect the provisions of the 1909 Boundary Waters Treaty between Canada and the United States or the Water Utilization Treaty of 1944 between Mexico and the

United States (59 Stat. 1219), relative to the control and abatement of water pollution in waters covered by those treaties."

. . .

SEC. 211. (a) The Oil Pollution Act, 1924 (43 Stat. 604; 33 U.S.C. 431 et seq.) is amended to read as follows: "That this Act may be cited as the 'Oil Pollution Act of 1924'.

"Sec. 2. When used in this Act, unless the context otherwise requires—

"(1) 'oil' means oil of any kind or in any form, including fuel oil, sludge, and oil refuse;

"(2) 'person' means an individual, company, partnership, corporation, or association; any owner, operator, master, officer, or employee of a vessel; and any officer, agent or employee of the United States;

"(3) 'discharge' means any grossly negligent, or willful spilling, leaking, pumping, pouring, emitting, or emptying of oil;

"(4) 'navigable waters of the United States' means all portions of the sea within the territorial jurisdiction of the United States, and all inland waters navigable in fact; and

"(5) 'Secretary' means the Secretary of the Interior.

"Sec. 3. (a) Except in case of emergency imperiling life or property, or unavoidable accident, collision, or stranding, and except as otherwise permitted by regulations prescribed by the Secretary as hereinafter authorized, it is unlawful for any person to discharge or permit the discharge from any boat or vessel of oil by any method, means, or manner into or upon the navigable waters of the United States, and adjoining shorelines of the United States.

. . .

"Sec. 4. (a) Any person who violates section 3(a) of this Act shall, upon conviction thereof, be punished by a fine not exceeding $2,500 or by imprisonment not exceeding one year, or by both such fine and imprisonment for each offense.

"(b) Any boat or vessel other than a boat or vessel owned by the United States from which oil is discharged in violation of section 3(a) of this Act shall be liable for a penalty of not more than $10,000. Clearance of a boat or vessel liable for this penalty from a port of the United States may be withheld until the penalty is paid. The penalty shall constitute a lien on such boat or vessel which may be recovered in proceedings by libel in rem in the district court of the United States for any district within which such boat or vessel may be.

SEC. 5. The Commandant of the Coast Guard may, subject to the provisions of section 4450 of the Revised Statutes, as amended (46 U.S.C. 239), suspend or revoke a license issued to the master or other licensed officer of any boat or vessel found violating the provisions of section 3 of this Act.

. . .

SOURCE: U.S. Congress. *Clean Water Restoration Act of 1966.* http://www.gpo.gov/fdsys/pkg/STATUTE-80/pdf/STATUTE-80-Pg1246.pdf (accessed November 9, 2014).

ANALYSIS

The Clean Water Restoration Act (CWRA) of 1966 was intended to address some of the weaknesses that had become evident in the Water Pollution Control Act of 1948. One of the obvious changes that was made in the legislation was that the secretary of the interior was granted the authority to oversee much of the federal government's activities concerning the protection of the nation's surface waters.

In Title II, Section 201, Section 6 (g), the secretary of the interior was tasked with conducting a comprehensive study on the effects of pollution on the nation's estuaries and estuarine zones. The study explored the potential impacts of the degradation of estuaries on fish and wildlife, water quality and supply, commercial and recreational fishing, and other uses. Once completed, the report was used to inform congressmen involved in writing environmental laws on further protections required for estuaries and estuarine zones.

A change to Section 201 of Title II was also notable as it provided for foreign countries suffering from the effects of pollution originating in the United States to have their problem addressed through action by the secretary of state. The aggrieved country even received voting authority in conferences convened to address the pollution problem within their borders. At face value, it appeared that the United States was being generous to its neighbors, but a country could only take advantage of the offer if they extended the same considerations to the United States on pollution originating in their country.

Concluding the CWRA were amendments to the Oil Pollution Act of 1924. The key change to the original legislation was the expansion of the definition of navigable waters of the United States, to include "all portions of the sea within the territorial jurisdiction of the United States, and all inland waters navigable in fact." The amendments also raised the fines for both individuals and the owner(s) of a boat or vessel that polluted the nation's waters with oil. While the penalties appeared significant at the time, they proved woefully inadequate for spills on the scale committed by the *Exxon Valdez* in March 1989.

FURTHER READING

Andreen, William L. 2003. "The Evolution of Water Pollution Control in the United States—State, Local, and Federal Efforts, 1789–1972: Part II. *Stanford Environmental Law Journal* 22: 215–294.

Milazzo, Paul Charles. 2006. *Unlikely Environmentalists: Congress and Clean Water, 1945–1972*. Lawrence: University Press of Kansas.

"To Restore and Maintain the Chemical, Physical, and Biological Integrity of the Nation's Waters"

- *Document:* Clean Water Act of 1972, with 1977 Amendments, excerpt
- *Date:* The Clean Water Act was enacted on October 18, 1972. The 1977 Amendment was signed on December 27, 1977.
- *Where:* Washington, DC
- *Significance:* The act was a landmark piece of legislation that called for the improvement in the quality of water in the nation's waterways.

DOCUMENT

SUBCHAPTER I—RESEARCH AND RELATED PROGRAMS

Sec. 1251. Congressional declaration of goals and policy

(a) Restoration and maintenance of chemical, physical and biological integrity of Nation's waters; national goals for achievement of objective. The objective of this chapter is to restore and maintain the chemical, physical, and biological integrity of the Nation's waters. In order to achieve this objective it is hereby declared that, consistent with the provisions of this chapter—

(1) it is the national goal that the discharge of pollutants into the navigable waters be eliminated by 1985;

(2) it is the national goal that wherever attainable, an interim goal of water quality which provides for the protection and propagation of fish, shellfish, and wildlife and provides for recreation in and on the water be achieved by July 1, 1983;

(3) it is the national policy that the discharge of toxic pollutants in toxic amounts be prohibited;

(4) it is the national policy that Federal financial assistance be provided to construct publicly owned waste treatment works;

(5) it is the national policy that area wide waste treatment management planning processes be developed and implemented to assure adequate control of sources of pollutants in each State;

(6) it is the national policy that a major research and demonstration effort be made to develop technology necessary to eliminate the discharge of pollutants into the navigable waters, waters of the contiguous zone, and the oceans; and

(7) it is the national policy that programs for the control of nonpoint sources of pollution be developed and implemented in an expeditious manner so as to enable the goals of this chapter to be met through the control of both point and nonpoint sources of pollution.

(b) Congressional recognition, preservation, and protection of primary responsibilities and rights of States. It is the policy of the Congress to recognize, preserve, and protect the primary responsibilities and rights of States to prevent, reduce, and eliminate pollution, to plan the development and use (including restoration, preservation, and enhancement) of land and water resources, and to consult with the Administrator in the exercise of his authority under this chapter. It is the policy of Congress that the States manage the construction grant program under this chapter and implement the permit programs under sections 1342 and 1344 of this title. It is further the policy of the Congress to support and aid research relating to the prevention, reduction, and elimination of pollution and to provide Federal technical services and financial aid to State and interstate agencies and municipalities in connection with the prevention, reduction, and elimination of pollution.

(c) Congressional policy toward Presidential activities with foreign countries. It is further the policy of Congress that the President, acting through the Secretary of State and such national and international organizations as he determines appropriate, shall take such action as may be necessary to insure that to the fullest extent possible all foreign countries shall take meaningful action for the prevention, reduction, and elimination of pollution in their waters and in international waters and for the achievement of goals regarding the elimination of discharge of pollutants and the improvement of water quality to at least the same extent as the United States does under its laws.

(d) Administrator of Environmental Protection Agency to administer chapter. Except as otherwise expressly provided in this chapter, the Administrator of the Environmental Protection Agency (hereinafter in this chapter called "Administrator") shall administer this chapter.

(e) Public participation in development, revision, and enforcement of any regulation, etc. Public participation in the development, revision, and enforcement of any regulation, standard, effluent limitation, plan, or program established by the Administrator or any State under this chapter shall be provided for, encouraged, and assisted by the Administrator and the States. The Administrator, in cooperation with the States, shall develop and publish regulations specifying minimum guidelines for public participation in such processes.

(f) Procedures utilized for implementing chapter. It is the national policy that to the maximum extent possible the procedures utilized for implementing this chapter shall encourage the drastic minimization of paperwork and interagency decision procedures, and the best use of available manpower and funds, so as to prevent needless duplication and unnecessary delays at all levels of government.

(g) Authority of States over water. It is the policy of Congress that the authority of each State to allocate quantities of water within its jurisdiction shall not be superseded, abrogated or otherwise impaired by this chapter. It is the further policy of Congress that nothing in this chapter shall be construed to supersede or abrogate rights to quantities of water which have been established by any State. Federal agencies shall co-operate with State and local agencies to develop comprehensive solutions to prevent, reduce and eliminate pollution in concert with programs for managing water resources.

Sec. 1252. Comprehensive programs for water pollution control

(a) Preparation and development. The Administrator shall, after careful investigation, and in cooperation with other Federal agencies, State water pollution control agencies, interstate agencies, and the municipalities and industries involved, prepare or develop comprehensive programs for preventing, reducing, or eliminating the pollution of the navigable waters and ground waters and improving the sanitary condition of surface and underground waters. In the development of such comprehensive programs due regard shall be given to the improvements which are necessary to conserve such waters for the protection and propagation of fish and aquatic life and wildlife, recreational purposes, and the withdrawal of such waters for public water supply, agricultural, industrial, and other purposes. For the purpose of this section, the Administrator is authorized to make joint investigations with any such agencies of the condition of any waters in any State or States, and of the discharges of any sewage, industrial wastes, or substance which may adversely affect such waters.

(b) Planning for reservoirs; storage for regulation of streamflow.

(1) In the survey or planning of any reservoir by the Corps of Engineers, Bureau of Reclamation, or other Federal agency, consideration shall be given to inclusion of storage for regulation of streamflow, except that any such storage and water releases shall not be provided as a substitute for adequate treatment or other methods of controlling waste at the source.

(2) The need for and the value of storage for regulation of streamflow (other than for water quality) including but not limited to navigation, salt water intrusion, recreation, esthetics, and fish and wildlife, shall be determined by the Corps of Engineers, Bureau of Reclamation, or other Federal agencies.

(3) The need for, the value of, and the impact of, storage for water quality control shall be determined by the Administrator, and his views on these matters shall be set forth in any report or presentation to Congress proposing authorization or construction of any reservoir including such storage.

(4) The value of such storage shall be taken into account in determining the economic value of the entire project of which it is a part, and costs shall be

allocated to the purpose of regulation of streamflow in a manner which will insure that all project purposes, share equitably in the benefit of multiple-purpose construction.

(5) Costs of regulation of streamflow features incorporated in any Federal reservoir or other impoundment under the provisions of this chapter shall be determined and the beneficiaries identified and if the benefits are widespread or national in scope, the costs of such features shall be nonreimbursable.

(6) No license granted by the Federal Energy regulatory for a hydroelectric power project shall include storage for regulation of streamflow for the purpose of water quality control unless the Administrator shall recommend its inclusion and such reservoir storage capacity shall not exceed such proportion of the total storage required for the water quality control plan as the drainage area of such reservoir bears to the drainage area of the river basin or basins involved in such water quality control plan.

(c) Basins; grants to State agencies.

(1) The Administrator shall, at the request of the Governor of a State, or a majority of the Governors when more than one State is involved, make a grant to pay not to exceed 50 per centum of the administrative expenses of a planning agency for a period not to exceed three years, which period shall begin after October 18, 1972, if such agency provides for adequate representation of appropriate State, interstate, local, or (when appropriate) international interests in the basin or portion thereof involved and is capable of developing an effective, comprehensive water quality control plan for a basin or portion thereof.

(2) Each planning agency receiving a grant under this subsection shall develop a comprehensive pollution control plan for the basin or portion thereof which—

(A) is consistent with any applicable water quality standards effluent and other limitations, and thermal discharge regulations established pursuant to current law within the basin;

(B) recommends such treatment works as will provide the most effective and economical means of collection, storage, treatment, and elimination of pollutants and recommends means to encourage both municipal and industrial use of such works;

(C) recommends maintenance and improvement of water quality within the basin or portion thereof and recommends methods of adequately financing those facilities as may be necessary to implement the plan; and

(D) as appropriate, is developed in cooperation with, and is consistent with any comprehensive plan prepared by the Water Resources Council, any areawide waste management plans developed pursuant to section 1288 of this title, and any State plan developed pursuant to section 1313(e) of this title.

(3) For the purposes of this subsection the term "basin" includes, but is not limited to, rivers and their tributaries, streams, coastal waters, sounds, estuaries, bays, lakes, and portions thereof as well as the lands drained thereby.

Sec. 1252a. Reservoir projects, water storage; modification; storage for other than for water quality, opinion of Federal agency, committee resolutions of approval;

provisions inapplicable to projects with certain prescribed water quality benefits in relation to total project benefits.

In the case of any reservoir project authorized for construction by the Corps of Engineers, Bureau of Reclamation, or other Federal agency when the Administrator of the Environmental Protection Agency determines pursuant to section 1252(b) of this title that any storage in such project for regulation of streamflow for water quality is not needed, or is needed in a different amount, such project may be modified accordingly by the head of the appropriate agency, and any storage no longer required for water quality may be utilized for other authorized purposes of the project when, in the opinion of the head of such agency, such use is justified. Any such modification of a project where the benefits attributable to water quality are 15 per centum or more but not greater than 25 per centum of the total project benefits shall take effect only upon the adoption of resolutions approving such modification by the appropriate committees of the Senate and House of Representatives. The provisions of the section shall not apply to any project where the benefits attributable to water quality exceed 25 per centum of the total project benefits.

Sec. 1253. Interstate cooperation and uniform laws

(a) The Administrator shall encourage cooperative activities by the States for the prevention, reduction, and elimination of pollution, encourage the enactment of improved and, so far as practicable, uniform State laws relating to the prevention, reduction, and elimination of pollution; and encourage compacts between States for the prevention and control of pollution.

(b) The consent of the Congress is hereby given to two or more States to negotiate and enter into agreements or compacts, not in conflict with any law or treaty of the United States, for (1) cooperative effort and mutual assistance for the prevention and control of pollution and the enforcement of their respective laws relating thereto, and (2) the establishment of such agencies, joint or otherwise, as they may deem desirable for making effective such agreements and compacts. No such agreement or compact shall be binding or obligatory upon any State a party thereto unless and until it has been approved by the Congress.

Sec. 1254. Research, investigations, training, and information

(a) Establishment of national programs; cooperation; investigations; water quality surveillance system; reports. The Administrator shall establish national programs for the prevention, reduction, and elimination of pollution and as part of such programs shall—

(1) in cooperation with other Federal, State, and local agencies, conduct and promote the coordination and acceleration of, research, investigations, experiments, training, demonstrations, surveys, and studies relating to the causes, effects, extent, prevention, reduction, and elimination of pollution;

(2) encourage, cooperate with, and render technical services to pollution control agencies and other appropriate public or private agencies, institutions, and organizations, and individuals, including the general public, in the conduct of activities referred to in paragraph (1) of this subsection;

(3) conduct, in cooperation with State water pollution control agencies and other interested agencies, organizations and persons, public investigations

concerning the pollution of any navigable waters, and report on the results of such investigations;

(4) establish advisory committees composed of recognized experts in various aspects of pollution and representatives of the public to assist in the examination and evaluation of research progress and proposals and to avoid duplication of research;

(5) in cooperation with the States, and their political subdivisions, and other Federal agencies establish, equip, and maintain a water quality surveillance system for the purpose of monitoring the quality of the navigable waters and ground waters and the contiguous zone and the oceans and the Administrator shall, to the extent practicable, conduct such surveillance by utilizing the resources of the National Aeronautics and Space Administration, the National Oceanic and Atmospheric Administration, the United States Geological Survey, and the Coast Guard, and shall report on such quality in the report required under subsection (a) of section 1375 of this title; and

(6) initiate and promote the coordination and acceleration of research designed to develop the most effective practicable tools and techniques for measuring the social and economic costs and benefits of activities which are subject to regulation under this chapter; and shall transmit a report on the results of such research to the Congress not later than January 1, 1974.

(b) Authorized activities of Administrator. In carrying out the provisions of subsection (a) of this section the Administrator is authorized to—

(1) collect and make available, through publications and other appropriate means, the results of and other information, including appropriate recommendations by him in connection therewith, pertaining to such research and other activities referred to in paragraph (1) of subsection (a) of this section;

(2) cooperate with other Federal departments and agencies, State water pollution control agencies, interstate agencies, other public and private agencies, institutions, organizations, industries involved, and individuals, in the preparation and conduct of such research and other activities referred to in paragraph (1) of subsection (a) of this section;

(3) make grants to State water pollution control agencies, interstate agencies, other public or nonprofit private agencies, institutions, organizations, and individuals, for purposes stated in paragraph (1) of subsection (a) of this section;

(4) contract with public or private agencies, institutions, organizations, and individuals, without regard to section 3324(a) and (b) of title 31 and section 5 of title 41, referred to in paragraph (1) of subsection (a) of this section;

(5) establish and maintain research fellowships at public or nonprofit private educational institutions or research organizations;

(6) collect and disseminate, in cooperation with other Federal departments and agencies, and with other public or private agencies, institutions, and organizations having related responsibilities, basic data on chemical, physical, and biological effects of varying water quality and other information pertaining to pollution and the prevention, reduction, and elimination thereof; and

(7) develop effective and practical processes, methods, and prototype devices for the prevention, reduction, and elimination of pollution.

(c) Research and studies on harmful effects of pollutants; cooperation with Secretary of Health and Human Services. In carrying out the provisions of subsection (a) of this section the Administrator shall conduct research on, and survey the results of other scientific studies on, the harmful effects on the health or welfare of persons caused by pollutants. In order to avoid duplication of effort, the Administrator shall, to the extent practicable, conduct such research in cooperation with and through the facilities of the Secretary of Health and Human Services.

(d) Sewage treatment; identification and measurement of effects of pollutants; augmented streamflow. In carrying out the provisions of this section the Administrator shall develop and demonstrate under varied conditions (including conducting such basic and applied research, studies, and experiments as may be necessary):

(1) Practicable means of treating municipal sewage, and other waterborne wastes to implement the requirements of section 1281 of this title;

(2) Improved methods and procedures to identify and measure the effects of pollutants, including those pollutants created by new technological developments; and

(3) Methods and procedures for evaluating the effects on water quality of augmented streamflows to control pollution not susceptible to other means of prevention, reduction, or elimination.

(e) Field laboratory and research facilities. The Administrator shall establish, equip, and maintain field laboratory and research facilities, including, but not limited to, one to be located in the northeastern area of the United States, one in the Middle Atlantic area, one in the southeastern area, one in the midwestern area, one in the southwestern area, one in the Pacific Northwest, and one in the State of Alaska, for the conduct of research, investigations, experiments, field demonstrations and studies, and training relating to the prevention, reduction and elimination of pollution. Insofar as practicable, each such facility shall be located near institutions of higher learning in which graduate training in such research might be carried out. In conjunction with the development of criteria under section 1343 of this title, the Administrator shall construct the facilities authorized for the National Marine Water Quality Laboratory established under this subsection.

(f) Great Lakes water quality research. The Administrator shall conduct research and technical development work, and make studies, with respect to the quality of the waters of the Great Lakes, including an analysis of the present and projected future water quality of the Great Lakes under varying conditions of waste treatment and disposal, an evaluation of the water quality needs of those to be served by such waters, an evaluation of municipal, industrial, and vessel waste treatment and disposal practices with respect to such waters, and a study of alternate means of solving pollution problems (including additional waste treatment measures) with respect to such waters.

(g) Treatment works pilot training programs; employment needs forecasting; training projects and grants; research fellowships; technical training; report to the President and transmittal to Congress.

(1) For the purpose of providing an adequate supply of trained personnel to operate and maintain existing and future treatment works and related activities, and for the purpose of enhancing substantially the proficiency of those engaged

in such activities, the Administrator shall finance pilot programs, in cooperation with State and interstate agencies, municipalities, educational institutions, and other organizations and individuals, of manpower development and training and retraining of persons in, on entering into, the field of operation and maintenance of treatment works and related activities. Such program and any funds expended for such a program shall supplement, not supplant, other manpower and training programs and funds available for the purposes of this paragraph. The Administrator is authorized, under such terms and conditions as he deems appropriate, to enter into agreements with one or more States, acting jointly or severally, or with other public or private agencies or institutions for the development and implementation of such a program.

(2) The Administrator is authorized to enter into agreements with public and private agencies and institutions, and individuals to develop and maintain an effective system for forecasting the supply of, and demand for, various professional and other occupational categories needed for the prevention, reduction, and elimination of pollution in each region, State, or area of the United States and, from time to time, to publish the results of such forecasts.

(3) In furtherance of the purposes of this chapter, the Administrator is authorized to—

(A) make grants to public or private agencies and institutions and to individuals for training projects, and provide for the conduct of training by contract with public or private agencies and institutions and with individuals without regard to section 3324(a) and (b) of title 31 and section 5 of title 41;

(B) establish and maintain research fellowships in the Environmental Protection Agency with such stipends and allowances, including traveling and subsistence expenses, as he may deem necessary to procure the assistance of the most promising research fellows; and

(C) provide, in addition to the program established under paragraph (1) of this subsection, training in technical matters relating to the causes, prevention, reduction, and elimination of pollution for personnel of public agencies and other persons with suitable qualifications.

(4) The Administrator shall submit, through the President, a report to the Congress not later than December 31, 1973, summarizing the actions taken under this subsection and the effectiveness of such actions, and setting forth the number of persons trained, the occupational categories for which training was provided, the effectiveness of other Federal, State, and local training programs in this field, together with estimates of future needs, recommendations on improving training programs, and such other information and recommendations, including legislative recommendations, as he deems appropriate.

(h) Lake pollution. The Administrator is authorized to enter into contracts with, or make grants to, public or private agencies and organizations and individuals for (A) the purpose of developing and demonstrating new or improved methods for the prevention, removal, reduction, and elimination of pollution in lakes, including the undesirable effects of nutrients and vegetation, and (B) the construction of publicly owned research facilities for such purpose.

(i) Oil pollution control studies. The Administrator, in cooperation with the Secretary of the Department in which the Coast Guard is operating, shall—

(1) engage in such research, studies, experiments, and demonstrations as he deems appropriate, relative to the removal of oil from any waters and to the prevention, control, and elimination of oil and hazardous substances pollution;

(2) publish from time to time the results of such activities; and

(3) from time to time, develop and publish in the Federal Register specifications and other technical information on the various chemical compounds used in the control of oil and hazardous substances spills. In carrying out this subsection, the Administrator may enter into contracts with, or make grants to, public or private agencies and organizations and individuals.

(j) Solid waste disposal equipment for vessels. The Secretary of the department in which the Coast Guard is operating shall engage in such research, studies, experiments, and demonstrations as he deems appropriate relative to equipment which is to be installed on board a vessel and is designed to receive, retain, treat, or discharge human body wastes and the wastes from toilets and other receptacles intended to receive or retain body wastes with particular emphasis on equipment to be installed on small recreational vessels. The Secretary of the department in which the Coast Guard is operating shall report to Congress the results of such research, studies, experiments, and demonstrations prior to the effective date of any regulations established under section 1322 of this title. In carrying out this subsection the Secretary of the department in which the Coast Guard is operating may enter into contracts with, or make grants to, public or private organizations and individuals.

(k) Land acquisition. In carrying out the provisions of this section relating to the conduct by the Administrator of demonstration projects and the development of field laboratories and research facilities, the Administrator may acquire land and interests therein by purchase, with appropriated or donated funds, by donation, or by exchange for acquired or public lands under his jurisdiction which he classifies as suitable for disposition. The values of the properties so exchanged either shall be approximately equal, or if they are not approximately equal, the values shall be equalized by the payment of cash to the grantor or to the Administrator as the circumstances require.

(l) Collection and dissemination of scientific knowledge on effects and control of pesticides in water.

(1) The Administrator shall, after consultation with appropriate local, State, and Federal agencies, public and private organizations, and interested individuals, as soon as practicable but not later than January 1, 1973, develop and issue to the States for the purpose of carrying out this chapter the latest scientific knowledge available in indicating the kind and extent of effects on health and welfare which may be expected from the presence of pesticides in the water in varying quantities. He shall revise and add to such information whenever necessary to reflect developing scientific knowledge.

(2) The President shall, in consultation with appropriate local, State, and Federal agencies, public and private organizations, and interested individuals, conduct studies and investigations of methods to control the release of pesticides into the environment which study shall include examination of the persistency of

pesticides in the water environment and alternatives thereto. The President shall submit reports, from time to time, on such investigations to Congress together with his recommendations for any necessary legislation.

(m) Waste oil disposal study.

(1) The Administrator shall, in an effort to prevent degradation of the environment from the disposal of waste oil, conduct a study of (A) the generation of used engine, machine, cooling, and similar waste oil, including quantities generated, the nature and quality of such oil, present collecting methods and disposal practices, and alternate uses of such oil; (B) the long-term, chronic biological effects of the disposal of such waste oil; and (C) the potential market for such oils, including the economic and legal factors relating to the sale of products made from such oils, the level of subsidy, if any, needed to encourage the purchase by public and private nonprofit agencies of products from such oil, and the practicability of Federal procurement, on a priority basis, of products made from such oil. In conducting such study, the Administrator shall consult with affected industries and other persons.

(2) The Administrator shall report the preliminary results of such study to Congress within six months after October 18, 1972, and shall submit a final report to Congress within 18 months after such date.

(n) Comprehensive studies of effects of pollution on estuaries and estuarine zones; reports.

(1) The Administrator shall, in cooperation with the Secretary of the Army, the Secretary of Agriculture, the Water Resources Council, and with other appropriate Federal, State, interstate, or local public bodies and private organizations, institutions, and individuals, conduct and promote, and encourage contributions to, continuing comprehensive studies of the effects of pollution, including sedimentation, in the estuaries and estuarine zones of the United States on fish and wildlife, on sport and commercial fishing, on recreation, on water supply and water power, and on other beneficial purposes. Such studies shall also consider the effect of demographic trends, the exploitation of mineral resources and fossil fuels, land and industrial development, navigation, flood and erosion control, and other uses of estuaries and estuarine zones upon the pollution of the waters therein.

(2) In conducting such studies, the Administrator shall assemble, coordinate, and organize all existing pertinent information on the Nation's estuaries and estuarine zones; carry out a program of investigations and surveys to supplement existing information in representative estuaries and estuarine zones; and identify the problems and areas where further research and study are required.

(3) The Administrator shall submit to Congress, from time to time, reports of the studies authorized by this subsection but at least one such report during any six-year period. Copies of each such report shall be made available to all interested parties, public and private.

(4) For the purpose of this subsection, the term "estuarine zones" means an environmental system consisting of an estuary and those transitional areas which are consistently influenced or affected by water from an estuary such as, but not limited to, salt marshes, coastal and intertidal areas, bays, harbors, lagoons,

inshore waters, and channels, and the term "estuary" means all or part of the mouth of a river or stream or other body of water having unimpaired natural connection with open sea and within which the sea water is measurably diluted with fresh water derived from land drainage.

(o) Methods of reducing total flow of sewage and unnecessary water consumption; reports.

(1) The Administrator shall conduct research and investigations on devices, systems, incentives, pricing policy, and other methods of reducing the total flow of sewage, including, but not limited to, unnecessary water consumption in order to reduce the requirements for, and the costs of, sewage and waste treatment services. Such research and investigations shall be directed to develop devices, systems, policies, and methods capable of achieving the maximum reduction of unnecessary water consumption.

(2) The Administrator shall report the preliminary results of such studies and investigations to the Congress within one year after October 18, 1972, and annually thereafter in the report required under subsection (a) of section 1375 of this title. Such report shall include recommendations for any legislation that may be required to provide for the adoption and use of devices, systems, policies, or other methods of reducing water consumption and reducing the total flow of sewage. Such report shall include an estimate of the benefits to be derived from adoption and use of such devices, systems, policies, or other methods and also shall reflect estimates of any increase in private, public, or other cost that would be occasioned thereby.

(p) Agricultural pollution. In carrying out the provisions of subsection (a) of this section the Administrator shall, in cooperation with the Secretary of Agriculture, other Federal agencies, and the States, carry out a comprehensive study and research program to determine new and improved methods and the better application of existing methods of preventing, reducing, and eliminating pollution from agriculture, including the legal, economic, and other implications of the use of such methods.

(q) Sewage in rural areas; national clearinghouse for alternative treatment information; clearinghouse on small flows.

(1) The Administrator shall conduct a comprehensive program of research and investigation and pilot project implementation into new and improved methods of preventing, reducing, storing, collecting, treating, or otherwise eliminating pollution from sewage in rural and other areas where collection of sewage in conventional, communitywide sewage collection systems is impractical, uneconomical, or otherwise infeasible, or where soil conditions or other factors preclude the use of septic tank and drainage field systems.

(2) The Administrator shall conduct a comprehensive program of research and investigation and pilot project implementation into new and improved methods for the collection and treatment of sewage and other liquid wastes combined with the treatment and disposal of solid wastes.

(3) The Administrator shall establish, either within the Environmental Protection Agency, or through contract with an appropriate public or private nonprofit organization, a national clearinghouse which shall (A) receive reports and

information resulting from research, demonstrations, and other projects funded under this chapter related to paragraph (1) of this subsection and to subsection (e)(2) of section 1255 of this title; (B) coordinate and disseminate such reports and information for use by Federal and State agencies, municipalities, institutions, and persons in developing new and improved methods pursuant to this subsection; and (C) provide for the collection and dissemination of reports and information relevant to this subsection from other Federal and State agencies, institutions, universities, and persons.

(4) Small flows clearinghouse. Notwithstanding section 1285(d) of this title, from amounts that are set aside for a fiscal year under section 1285(i) of this title and are not obligated by the end of the 24-month period of availability for such amounts under section 1285(d) of this title, the Administrator shall make available $1,000,000 or such unobligated amount, whichever is less, to support a national clearinghouse within the Environmental Protection Agency to collect and disseminate information on small flows of sewage and innovative or alternative wastewater treatment processes and techniques, consistent with paragraph (3). This paragraph shall apply with respect to amounts set aside under section 1285(i) of this title for which the 24-month period of availability referred to in the preceding sentence ends on or after September 30, 1986.

(r) Research grants to colleges and universities. The Administrator is authorized to make grants to colleges and universities to conduct basic research into the structure and function of freshwater aquatic ecosystems, and to improve understanding of the ecological characteristics necessary to the maintenance of the chemical, physical, and biological integrity of freshwater aquatic ecosystems.

(s) River Study Centers. The Administrator is authorized to make grants to one or more institutions of higher education (regionally located and to be designated as "River Study Centers") for the purpose of conducting and reporting on interdisciplinary studies on the nature of river systems, including hydrology, biology, ecology, economics, the relationship between river uses and land uses, and the effects of development within river basins on river systems and on the value of water resources and water related activities. No such grant in any fiscal year shall exceed $1,000,000.

(t) Thermal discharges. The Administrator shall, in cooperation with State and Federal agencies and public and private organizations, conduct continuing comprehensive studies of the effects and methods of control of thermal discharges. In evaluating alternative methods of control the studies shall consider (1) such data as are available on the latest available technology, economic feasibility including cost-effectiveness analysis, and (2) the total impact on the environment, considering not only water quality but also air quality, land use, and effective utilization and conservation of freshwater and other natural resources. Such studies shall consider methods of minimizing adverse effects and maximizing beneficial effects of thermal discharges. The results of these studies shall be reported by the Administrator as soon as practicable, but not later than 270 days after October 18, 1972, and shall be made available to the public and the States, and considered as they become available by the Administrator in carrying out section 1326 of this title and by the States in proposing thermal water quality standards.

SOURCE: Clean Water Act of 1977. U.S. Code 33 § 1251.

ANALYSIS

Officially known as the Federal Water Pollution Control Act Amendments of 1972, the Clean Water Act was actually a significantly amended version of the 1948 Federal Water Pollution Control Act. The purpose of the 1972 act was to restore the water quality of the nation's waterways. In the early 1970s, most of the waterways in the country were suffering from the impacts of pollution, much of it created by industrial plants. An oft-cited example from that era was the Cuyahoga River in Cleveland, Ohio, which caught on fire on several occasions. Through the Clean Water Act, Congress launched an ambitious effort to not only clean up the nation's streams and rivers, but also ensure that once improved, they were maintained in that state.

Among the legislation's many achievements was the creation of the National Pollution Discharge Elimination Permit system. Through the permitting process, the federal government was able to control the amount and types of pollutants being introduced by industries into waterways. The permitting system empowered the government to set standards as to what could be dumped into the nation's waters and what could not. The authority for overseeing the permit program was given to the Environmental Protection Agency (EPA), which at the time was a relatively new agency.

Congress also desired that industries adopt the newest technologies available to limit the industrial waste that they introduced into the environment. Toward that end, they raised the minimum pollution control standards to force industries to utilize the desired technologies. Although companies protested the regulations that forced their hands to spend funds on expensive technologies, the law did not allow for any other options.

One of the goals of Congress was to make the enforcement of the Clean Water Act a joint venture between the federal government and the respective states. Federal authorities created the minimum standards but allowed states to create their own programs, including enforcement, as long as approved by the EPA. In hindsight, this proved a mistake in some cases. It was anticipated that states might create stricter standards than those mandated by the federal government. In most states, the federal standards were adopted. Unfortunately, in many of those states, enforcement was lax. Local authorities were loath to heavily regulate local industries because those companies were often the largest employers in the area and thus central to the local economy. It thus became more important to protect the interests of the respective companies and corporations than it was to improve local environs.

In 1977, Congress amended the Federal Water Pollution Control Act Amendments of 1972. Among the changes was the name, officially becoming the Clean Water Act. It also expanded the power of the EPA, giving it more tools to address industrial pollution. The permitting process was also expanded in 1977, with people being required to obtain permits if they were directly dumping waste into a waterway. The legislation worked efficiently until President Ronald Reagan took office in 1981. Since his administration was more business-friendly than those of his predecessors, EPA officials during his terms were less forceful in applying the Clean Water Act's standards than what its originators envisioned. Succeeding Republican administrations likewise favored business interests over those of environmentalists.

Although the Clean Water Act of 1972 and the 1977 amendment resulted in much cleaner waterways, the legislation has nonetheless bred a significant number of critics. Many point to the fact that the Clean Water Act largely ignored significant sources of pollution, such as agricultural operations and urban sewers. Although the sources of these types of pollution were difficult to ascertain, by not attempting to regulate them at all, significant pollution was allowed to continue unabated. The impact on the nation's surface waters by agricultural substances, notably phosphorous, has been substantial, as evidenced by the algal blooms that are occurring quite frequently in the Great Lakes and thus threatening the drinking water supplies used by large numbers of municipalities.

FURTHER READING

Adler, Robert W., Jessica C. Landman, and Diane M. Cameron. 1993. *The Clean Water Act 20 Years Later*. Washington, DC: Island Press.

Ashford, Nicholas A., and Charles C. Caldart. 2008. *Environmental Law, Policy, and Economics: Reclaiming the Environmental Agenda*. Cambridge, MA: MIT Press.

Copeland, Claudia. 2012. *Clean Water Act: A Summary of the Law*. Washington, DC: Congressional Research Service.

Hoornbeek, John A. 2011. *Water Pollution Policies and the American States: Runaway Bureaucracies or Congressional Control?* Albany: State University of New York Press.

Milazzo, Paul Charles. 2006. *Unlikely Environmentalists: Congress and Clean Water, 1945–1972*. Lawrence: University Press of Kansas.

"National Drinking Water Standards"

- *Document:* Safe Drinking Water Act of 1974, as Amended Through 2002, excerpts
- *Date:* The Safe Drinking Water Act of 1974 was signed on December 16, 1974. The 1986 amendments were signed on June 20, 1986. The 1996 amendments were signed on August 6, 1996. The 2002 amendments were enacted on December 31, 2002.
- *Where:* Washington, DC
- *Significance:* The act required the Environmental Protection Agency to set regulations concerning the maximum amount of contaminants that could be present in drinking water and still be considered safe. It also set regulations to protect groundwater from contamination. Enforcement of the regulations was assigned to the states.

DOCUMENT

TITLE XIV OF THE PUBLIC HEALTH SERVICE ACT (THE SAFE DRINKING WATER ACT)

. . .

PART B—PUBLIC WATER SYSTEMS
COVERAGE

SEC. 1411. Subject to sections 1415 and 1416, national primary drinking water regulations under this part shall apply to each public water system in each State; except that such regulations shall not apply to a public water system—

(1) which consists only of distribution and storage facilities (and does not have any collection and treatment facilities);

(2) which obtains all of its water from, but is not owned or operated by, a public water system to which such regulations apply;

(3) which does not sell water to any person; and

(4) which is not a carrier which conveys passengers in interstate commerce.

SEC. 1412. (a)(1) Effective on the enactment of the Safe Drinking Water Act Amendments of 1986, each national interim or revised primary drinking water regulation promulgated under this section before such enactment shall be deemed to be a national primary drinking water regulation under subsection (b). No such regulation shall be required to comply with the standards set forth in subsection (b)(4) unless such regulation is amended to establish a different maximum contaminant level after the enactment of such amendments.

(2) After the enactment of the Safe Drinking Water Act Amendments of 1986 each recommended maximum contaminant level published before the enactment of such amendments shall be treated as a maximum contaminant level goal.

(3) Whenever a national primary drinking water regulation is proposed under subsection (b) for any contaminant, the maximum contaminant level goal for such contaminant shall be proposed simultaneously. Whenever a national primary drinking water regulation is promulgated under subsection (b) for any contaminant, the maximum contaminant level goal for such contaminant shall be published simultaneously.

(4) Paragraph (3) shall not apply to any recommended maximum contaminant level published before the enactment of the Safe Drinking Water Act Amendments of 1986.

(b) STANDARDS.—

(1) IDENTIFICATION OF CONTAMINANTS FOR LISTING.—

(A) GENERAL AUTHORITY.—The Administrator shall, in accordance with the procedures established by this subsection, publish a maximum contaminant level goal and promulgate a national primary drinking water regulation for a contaminant (other than a contaminant referred to in paragraph (2) for which a national primary drinking water regulation has been promulgated as of the date of enactment of the Safe Drinking Water Act Amendments of 1996) if the Administrator determines that—

(i) the contaminant may have an adverse effect on the health of persons;

(ii) the contaminant is known to occur or there is a substantial likelihood that the contaminant will occur in public water systems with a frequency and at levels of public health concern; and

(iii) in the sole judgment of the Administrator, regulation of such contaminant presents a meaningful opportunity for health risk reduction for persons served by public water systems.

(B) REGULATION OF UNREGULATED CONTAMINANTS.—

(i) LISTING OF CONTAMINANTS FOR CONSIDERATION.—

(I) Not later than 18 months after the date of enactment of the Safe Drinking Water Act Amendments of 1996 and every 5 years thereafter, the Administrator, after consultation with the scientific community,

DID YOU KNOW?

Do Not Use the Water in Toledo, Ohio

At 2 a.m. on August 2, 2014, approximately 400,000 people in Toledo, Ohio, and surrounding communities were told not to use the water from their taps because it was contaminated with a toxic bacteria known as microcystin. In humans, microcystin can cause diarrhea, fever, nausea, rash, vomiting, and even long-term liver problems. The toxin was produced in a blue-green algal bloom that had emerged in Lake Erie, the source of drinking water for the city. Even boiling the water was not an option since all that was accomplished was the concentration of the toxin. Residents thus had to persist on either bottled water or water transported by the National Guard until August 5 when the water was once again safe to drink.

Unfortunately, the water problem in Toledo was a symptom of a long-term issue that appears to be getting worse. In 1972, Canada and the United States signed the Great Lakes Water Quality Agreement (GLWQA). One of the problems the two countries agreed to address was the amount of phosphorous being introduced into Lake Erie. Amendments to the GLWQA in 1978 and 1987 contained provisions to further restrict the introduction of phosphorous to the lake but the phosphorous levels in Lake Erie remained high. The phosphorous, much of it coming from fertilizers used on industrial farms, feed the algal blooms that develop on the lake. Although the blooms have been emerging periodically for decades, they are becoming almost an annual occurrence due to climate change. Although one of the largest lakes in the world, Lake Erie is relatively shallow, especially when compared to the other Great Lakes. The waters thus warm quicker than lakes that are deeper. Due to the global warming and the abundant presence of phosphorous, algal blooms on Lake Erie are developing much more often and are growing to immense sizes. When one considers that more than 11 million people in both Canada and the United States depend on Lake Erie as the source of their drinking water, a long-term solution to the problems that plague the lake need to be implemented or it is inevitable that other people in the Lake Erie Basin will find that their drinking water is periodically unsafe.

FURTHER READING

Kilbert, Kenneth, Tiffany Tisler, and M. Zack Hohl. 2012. "Legal Tools for Reducing Harmful Algal Blooms in Lake Erie." *University of Toledo Law Review* 44, no. 1: 69–122.

McGucken, William. 2000. *Lake Erie Rehabilitated: Controlling Cultural Eutrophication, 1960s–1990s.* Akron, OH: University of Akron Press.

including the Science Advisory Board, after notice and opportunity for public comment, and after considering the occurrence data base established under section 1445(g), shall publish a list of contaminants which, at the time of publication, are not subject to any proposed or promulgated national primary drinking water regulation, which are known or anticipated to occur in public water systems, and which may require regulation under this title.

(II) The unregulated contaminants considered under subclause (I) shall include, but not be limited to, substances referred to in section 101(14) of the Comprehensive Environmental Response, Compensation, and Liability Act of 1980, and substances registered as pesticides under the Federal Insecticide, Fungicide, and Rodenticide Act.

. . .

PART C—PROTECTION OF UNDERGROUND SOURCES OF DRINKING WATER REGULATIONS FOR STATE PROGRAMS

SEC. 1421. (a)(1) The Administrator shall publish proposed regulations for State underground injection control programs within 180 days after the date of enactment of this title. Within 180 days after publication of such proposed regulations, he shall promulgate such regulations with such modifications as he deems appropriate. Any regulation under this subsection may be amended from time to time.

(2) Any regulation under this section shall be proposed and promulgated in accordance with section 553 of title 5, United States Code (relating to rule-making), except that the Administrator shall provide opportunity for public hearing prior to promulgation of such regulations. In proposing and promulgating regulations under this section, the Administrator shall consult with the Secretary, the National Drinking Water Advisory Council, and other appropriate Federal entities and with interested State entities.

(b)(1) Regulations under subsection (a) for State underground injection programs shall contain minimum requirements for effective programs to prevent underground injection which endangers drinking water sources within the meaning of subsection (d)(2). Such regulations shall require that a State program, in order to be approved under section 1422—

(A) shall prohibit, effective on the date on which the applicable underground injection control program takes effect, any underground injection in such State which is not authorized by a permit issued by the State (except that the regulations may permit a State to authorize underground injection by rule);

(B) shall require (i) in the case of a program which provides for authorization of underground injection by permit, that the applicant for the permit to inject must satisfy the State that the underground injection will not endanger drinking water sources, and (ii) in the case of a program which provides for such an authorization by rule, that no rule may be promulgated which authorizes any underground injection which endangers drinking water sources;

(C) shall include inspection, monitoring, recordkeeping, and reporting requirements; and

(D) shall apply (i) as prescribed by section 1447(b) 1, to underground injections by Federal agencies, and (ii) to underground injections by any other person whether or not occurring on property owned or leased by the United States.

(2) Regulations of the Administrator under this section for State underground injection control programs may not prescribe requirements which interfere with or impede—

(A) the underground injection of brine or other fluids which are brought to the surface in connection with oil or natural gas production or natural gas storage operations, or

(B) any underground injection for the secondary or tertiary recovery of oil or natural gas, unless such requirements are essential to assure that underground sources of drinking water will not be endangered by such injection.

(3)(A) The regulations of the Administrator under this section shall permit or provide for consideration of varying geologic, hydrological, or historical conditions in different States and in different areas within a State.

(B)(i) In prescribing regulations under this section the Administrator shall, to the extent feasible, avoid promulgation of requirements which would unnecessarily disrupt State underground injection control programs which are in effect and being enforced in a substantial number of States.

(ii) For the purpose of this subparagraph, a regulation prescribed by the Administrator under this section shall be deemed to disrupt a State underground injection control program only if it would be infeasible to comply with both such regulation and the State underground injection control program.

(iii) For the purpose of this subparagraph, a regulation prescribed by the Administrator under this section shall be deemed unnecessary only if, without such regulation, underground sources of drinking water will not be endangered by any underground injection.

(C) Nothing in this section shall be construed to alter or affect the duty to assure that underground sources of drinking water will not be endangered by any underground injection.

(c)(1) The Administrator may, upon application of the Governor of a State which authorizes underground injection by means of permits, authorize such State to issue (without regard to subsection (b)(1)(B)(i)) temporary permits for underground injection which may be effective until the expiration of four years after the date of enactment of this title, if—

(A) the Administrator finds that the State has demonstrated that it is unable and could not reasonably have been able to process all permit applications within the time available;

(B) the Administrator determines the adverse effect on the environment of such temporary permits is not unwarranted;

(C) such temporary permits will be issued only with respect to injection wells in operation on the date on which such State's permit program approved under this part first takes effect and for which there was inadequate time to process its permit application; and

(D) the Administrator determines the temporary permits require the use of adequate safeguards established by rules adopted by him.

(2) The Administrator may, upon application of the Governor of a State which authorizes underground injection by means of permits, authorize such State to issue (without regard to subsection (b)(1)(B)(i)), but after reasonable notice and hearing, one or more temporary permits each of which is applicable to a particular injection well and to the underground injection of a particular fluid and which may be effective until the expiration of four years after the date of enactment of this title, if the State finds, on the record of such hearing—

(A) that technology (or other means) to permit safe injection of the fluid in accordance with the applicable underground injection control program is not generally available (taking costs into consideration);

(B) that injection of the fluid would be less harmful to health than the use of other available means of disposing of waste or producing the desired product; and

(C) that available technology or other means have been employed (and will be employed) to reduce the volume and toxicity of the fluid and to minimize the potentially adverse effect of the injection on the public health.

(d) For purposes of this part:

(1) The term "underground injection" means the subsurface emplacement of fluids by well injection. Such term does not include the underground injection of natural gas for purposes of storage.

(2) Underground injection endangers drinking water sources if such injection may result in the presence in underground water which supplies or can reasonably be expected to supply any public water system of any contaminant, and if the presence of such contaminant may result in such system's not complying with any national primary drinking water regulation or may otherwise adversely affect the health of persons.

. . .

INTERIM REGULATION OF UNDERGROUND INJECTIONS

SEC. 1424. (a)(1) Any person may petition the Administrator to have an area of a State (or States) designated as an area in which no new underground injection well may be operated during the period beginning on the date of the designation and ending on the date on which the applicable underground injection control program covering such area takes effect unless a permit for the operation of such well has been issued by the Administrator under subsection (b). The Administrator may so designate an area within a State if he finds that the area has one aquifer which is the sole or principal drinking water source for the area and which, if contaminated, would create a significant hazard to public health.

(2) Upon receipt of a petition under paragraph (1) of this subsection, the Administrator shall publish it in the Federal Register and shall provide an opportunity to interested persons to submit written data, views, or arguments thereon. Not later than the 30th day following the date of the publication of a petition under this paragraph in the Federal Register, the Administrator shall either make the designation for which the petition is submitted or deny the petition.

(b)(1) During the period beginning on the date an area is designated under subsection (a) and ending on the date the applicable underground injection control program covering such area takes effect, no new underground injection well may be operated in such area unless the Administrator has issued a permit for such operation.

(2) Any person may petition the Administrator for the issuance of a permit for the operation of such a well in such an area. A petition submitted under this paragraph shall be submitted in such manner and contain such information as the Administrator may require by regulation. Upon receipt of such a petition, the Administrator shall publish it in the Federal Register. The Administrator shall give notice of any proceeding on a petition and shall provide opportunity for agency hearing. The Administrator shall act upon such petition on the record of any hearing held pursuant to the preceding sentence respecting such petition. Within 120 days of the publication in the Federal Register of a petition submitted under this paragraph, the Administrator shall either issue the permit for which the petition was submitted or shall deny its issuance.

(3) The Administrator may issue a permit for the operation of a new underground injection well in an area designated under subsection (a) only if he finds that the operation of such well will not cause contamination of the aquifer of such area so as to create a significant hazard to public health. The Administrator may condition the issuance of such a permit upon the use of such control measures in connection with the operation of such well, for which the permit is to be issued, as he deems necessary to assure that the operation of the well will not contaminate the aquifer of the designated area in which the well is located so as to create a significant hazard to public health.

(c) Any person who operates a new underground injection well in violation of subsection (b), (1) shall be subject to a civil penalty of not more than $5,000 for each day in which such violation occurs, or (2) if such violation is willful, such person may, in lieu of the civil penalty authorized by clause (1), be fined not more than $10,000 for each day in which such violation occurs. If the Administrator has reason to believe that any person is violating or will violate subsection (b), he may petition the United States district court to issue a temporary restraining order or injunction (including a mandatory injunction) to enforce such subsection.

(d) For purposes of this section, the term "new underground injection well" means an underground injection well whose operation was not approved by appropriate State and Federal agencies before the date of the enactment of this title.

(e) If the Administrator determines, on his own initiative or upon petition, that an area has an aquifer which is the sole or principal drinking water source for the area and which, if contaminated, would create a significant hazard to public health, he shall publish notice of that determination in the Federal Register. After the publication of any such notice, no commitment for Federal financial assistance (through a grant, contract, loan guarantee, or otherwise) may be entered into for any project which the Administrator determines may contaminate such aquifer through a recharge zone so as to create a significant hazard to public health, but a commitment for Federal financial assistance may, if authorized under another provision of law, be entered into to plan or design the project to assure that it will not so contaminate the aquifer.

. . .

SOURCE: U.S. Congress. n.d. Title XIV of the Public Health Service Act Safety of Public Water Systems (Safe Drinking Water Act). http://www.epw.senate.gov/sdwa.pdf (accessed October 13, 2014).

ANALYSIS

The Safe Drinking Water Act (SDWA) of 1974 was signed by President Gerald Ford on December 16, 1974. It became the primary law regulating drinking water around the country. It was envisioned as a joint effort between the federal government and the respective states. The Environmental Protection Agency (EPA) was charged with establishing the Maximum Contaminant Levels (MCLS) that drinking water could contain and still be considered safe for human consumption. The initial legislation specifically identified 21 contaminants to be monitored. It was left to the states to enforce the regulations within their borders.

The SDWA was viewed by many as companion legislation to the Clean Water Act (CWA) of 1972. While the CWA addressed pollution in navigable surface waters, the SDWA focused on contaminants within drinking water. This was viewed as a national issue due in part to a study by federal officials conducted on drinking water in Louisiana that had as its original source the Mississippi River. The supposedly safe drinking water contained more than 36 chemicals that were considered harmful to human health. The respective chemicals had entered the Mississippi's waters from many sources, such as factories and farms. To reduce the levels of these chemicals in the drinking water, the SDWA encouraged the use of technological innovations such as filtration systems.

One major component of the SDWA could be found in Part C of the legislation, which focused on groundwater. In general, the goal was to ensure that few contaminants polluted aquifers. In the early 1970s, it was perceived that the greatest threat to aquifers was the use of injection wells. Section 1424 thus contained specific limitations on their use. Unfortunately, the legislation also made it possible for someone to obtain a permit to utilize injection wells as long as groundwater sources were not threatened. In practical terms, the continued allowance of the use of injection wells meant that groundwater around the country was infused with the very contaminants the legislation was supposedly protecting against.

Since 1974, the SDWA has been amended multiple times. One of the notable additions to the legislation in 1996 was the creation of the State Drinking Water Revolving Loan Fund, which helped municipalities with limited funds to improve their local water systems. The amendments passed in 2002 reflected the influence of the terrorist attacks on September 11, 2001. To protect the nation's water systems from terrorist attack, any water system serving more than 3,300 people was required to draft emergency response plans. The common thread between the original SDWA and its amendments has been the growth in the number of contaminants being regulated by the EPA. Today, the SDWA monitors approximately 90 contaminants found in drinking water.

FURTHER READING

Andrews, Richard. 1999. *Managing the Environment, Managing Ourselves: A History of American Environmental Policy.* New Haven, CT: Yale University Press.

Jacangelo, Joseph G., Daniel J. Askenaizer, and Kellog Schwab. 2006. "Research Needs in Drinking Water: A Basis in Regulations in the United States." *Journal of Water & Health* 4: Supplement 1–9.

Roberson, J. Alan, and P. E. Roberson. 2011. "What's Next After 40 Years of Drinking Water Regulations." *Environmental Science & Technology* 45, no. 1: 154–160.

"There Is a Need to Regulate Surface Mining Operations"

- *Document:* Surface Mining Control and Reclamation Act of 1977, excerpt
- *Date:* August 3, 1977
- *Where:* Washington, DC
- *Significance:* The act was crafted to regulate surface mining, also known as strip mining. Its regulations included the establishment of water quality standards for waterways in the vicinity of mining activities.

DOCUMENT

TITLE I—STATEMENT OF FINDINGS AND POLICY FINDINGS

SEC. 101. The Congress finds and declares that—

(a) extraction of coal and other minerals from the earth can be accomplished by various methods of mining, including surface mining;

(b) coal mining operations presently contribute significantly to the Nation's energy requirements; surface coal mining constitutes one method of extraction of the resource; the overwhelming percentage of the Nation's coal reserves can only be extracted by underground mining methods, and it is, therefore, essential to the national interest to insure the existence of an expanding and economically healthy underground coal mining industry;

(c) many surface mining operations result in disturbances of surface areas that burden and adversely affect commerce and the public welfare by destroying or diminishing the utility of land for commercial, industrial, residential, recreational, agricultural, and forestry purposes, by causing erosion and landslides, by contributing to floods, by polluting the water, by destroying fish and wildlife habitats, by impairing natural beauty, by damaging the property of citizens, by creating hazards dangerous to life and property by degrading the quality of life in local communities, and by counteracting governmental programs and efforts to conserve soil, water, and other natural resources;

(d) the expansion of coal mining to meet the Nation's energy needs makes even more urgent the establishment of appropriate standards to minimize damage to the environment and to productivity of the soil and to protect the health and safety of the public.

(e) surface mining and reclamation technology are now developed so that effective and reasonable regulation of surface coal mining operations by the States and by the Federal Government in accordance with the requirements of this Act is an appropriate and necessary means to minimize so far as practicable the adverse social, economic, and environmental effects of such mining operations;

(f) because of the diversity in terrain, climate, biologic, chemical, and other physical conditions in areas subject to mining operations, the primary governmental responsibility for developing, authorizing, issuing, and enforcing regulations for surface mining and reclamation operations subject to this Act should rest with the States:

(g) surface mining and reclamation standards are essential in order to insure that competition in interstate commerce among sellers of coal produced in different States will not be used to undermine the ability of the several States to improve and maintain adequate standards on coal mining operations within their borders;

(h) there are a substantial number of acres of land throughout major regions of the United States disturbed by surface and underground coal on which little or no reclamation was conducted, and the impacts from these unreclaimed lands impose social and economic costs on residents in nearby and adjoining areas as well as continuing to impair environmental quality;

(i) while there is a need to regulate surface mining operations for minerals other than coal, more data and analyses are needed to serve as a basis for effective and reasonable regulation of such operations;

(j) surface and underground coal mining operations affect interstate commerce, contribute to the economic well-being, security, and general welfare of the Nation and should be conducted in an environmentally sound manner; and

(k) the cooperative effort established by this Act is necessary to prevent or mitigate adverse environmental effects of present and future surface coal mining operations.

PURPOSES

SEC. 102. It is the purpose of this Act to—

(a) establish a nationwide program to protect society and the environment from the adverse effects of surface coal mining operations;

(b) assure that the rights of surface landowners and other persons with a legal interest in the land or appurtenances thereto are fully protected from such operations;

(c) assure that surface mining operations are not conducted where reclamation as required by this Act is not feasible;

(d) assure that surface coal mining operations are so conducted as to protect the environment;

(e) assure that adequate procedures are undertaken to reclaim surface areas as contemporaneously as possible with the surface coal mining operations;

(f) assure that the coal supply essential to the Nation's energy requirements, and to its economic and social well-being is provided and strike a balance between protection of the environment and agricultural productivity and the Nation's need for coal as an essential source of energy;

(g) assist the States in developing and implementing a program to achieve the purposes of this Act;

(h) promote the reclamation of mined areas left without adequate reclamation prior to the enactment of this Act and which continue, in their unreclaimed condition, to substantially degrade the quality of the environment, prevent or damage the beneficial use of land or water resources, or endanger the health or safety of the public;

(i) assure that appropriate procedures are provided for the public participation in the development, revision, and enforcement of regulations, standards, reclamation plans, or programs established by the Secretary or any State under this Act;

(j) provide a means for development of the data and analyses necessary to establish effective and reasonable regulation of surface mining operations for other minerals;

(k) encourage the full utilization of coal resources through the development and application of underground extraction technologies;

(1) stimulate, sponsor, provide for and/or supplement present programs for the conduct of research investigations, experiments, and demonstrations, in the exploration, extraction, processing, development, and production of minerals and the training of mineral engineers and scientists in the field of mining, minerals resources, and technology, and the establishment of an appropriate research and training center in various States; and

(m) wherever necessary, exercise the full reach of Federal constitutional powers to insure the protection of the public interest through effective control of surface coal mining operations.

. . .

SOURCE: 95th Congress. n.d. *Public Law 95-87—August 3, 1977.* http://www.gpo.gov/fdsys/pkg/STATUTE-91/pdf/STATUTE-91-Pg445.pdf (accessed August 27, 2014).

ANALYSIS

Historically, most mining occurred underground. That began to change in the middle of the twentieth century as technology made it much more profitable to extract substances such as coal through surface mining. This was due to the development of diesel-powered earth moving equipment and much more powerful explosives. Suddenly mining companies were able to quickly remove tons of earth and rock to access the substance they were mining, rather than having to wait for human miners using primitive equipment to extract the substance at a much smaller scale. This new type of mining obviously had far more environmental impacts than traditional deep mining. The explosives being used were so strong that they sometimes cracked the foundations of people's homes. All of the soil and rock that was removed was often either dumped into locales that had already been stripped or into valleys. Waterways were being polluted, often by acid mine drainage resulting from abandoned mines or emanating from the materials dumped as a result of surface mining, which made the water unsafe for human consumption. Recognizing the threat posed by surface mining, some congressmen began working toward regulating the respective mining industries. Their efforts, with the assistance of environmental activists, appeared to bear fruit in the mid-1970s when they were able to get legislation regulating surfacing mining passed in Congress. The legislation did not become law due to President Gerald Ford's veto. It was not until President Jimmy Carter had taken office that the Surface Mining Control and Reclamation Act (SMCRA) of 1977 was enacted.

The legislation created the Office of Surface Mining and Enforcement (OSME) within the Department of the Interior to implement the SMCRA. The OSME was charged with regulating the surface mining within the country. That included determining which lands could be mined and which could not. It was also tasked with overseeing the reclamation of lands that were mined to their original state. One of their most important responsibilities was the collection of a tonnage tax that collected revenue that was subsequently used to reclaim abandoned mines. This was especially necessary as acid mine drainage from those types of mines were befouling waters nationwide. Although the SMCRA was primarily focused on surface mining, it did include provisions that applied to underground mines that were negatively impacting surface areas.

To get the SMCRA through Congress, proponents were essentially required to give immense power to the states to regulate industry compliance with the SMCRA within their borders. As long as a state passed more stringent standards than that included in the SMCRA, they could implement their own program. Most states that had mining interests within their borders complied by enacting higher standards. Unfortunately, just because the standards existed did not mean that they were going to be enforced. In states like Kentucky and West Virginia, where the support of the coal industry is just about essential to win a state-wide or federal political position, this meant that coal mining companies could act with impunity with little fear of retribution.

Another problem with the SMCRA was that it did not account for improvement in mining technologies. Earth moving equipment was developed that enabled mining companies to strip mine at a scale that was incomprehensible in 1977. A new type of strip mining known as mountaintop removal came into vogue. In Appalachia, mountains that had stood for millions of years were being completely leveled in less than a year to extract coal. The waste from this type of mining was filling entire valleys very quickly. When local activists demanded that the coal companies begin reclaiming the valleys they were destroying, as well as the remnants of the mountains, they got an exemption to the SMCRA that allowed them to begin reclamation efforts after they had completed their surface mining in the area. This has resulted in a substantial amount of land going unreclaimed, and as the metals and other contaminants in the fills oxidizes, acid mine drainage seeps into whatever waters are nearby.

FURTHER READING

Biggers, Jeff. 2010. *Reckoning at Eagle Creek: The Secret Legacy of Coal in the Heartland*. New York: Nation Books.

Clinton, Robert L. 1989. "Federal Court Involvement in the Application of Surface Mining Law." *Policy Studies Review* 9, no. 1: 88–97.

Eller, Ronald D. 2008. *Uneven Ground: Appalachia Since 1945*. Lexington: University Press of Kentucky.

Harris, Richard. 1989. "Federal-State Relations in the Implementation of Surface Mining Policy." *Policy Studies Review* 9, no. 1: 69–78.

Vestal, Theodore M. 1989. "The Surface Mining Control and Reclamation Act of 1977 in Oklahoma: State and Federal Cohabitation." *Policy Studies Review* 9, no. 1: 143–151.

"To Provide for Liability, Compensation, Cleanup, and Emergency Response for Hazardous Substances Released into the Environment"

- *Document:* Comprehensive Environmental Response, Compensation, and Liability Act of 1980 (Superfund), as Amended Through P.L. 107–377, December 31, 2002, excerpts
- *Date:* The 1980 legislation was passed on December 11, 1980. Its 2002 amendments became law on December 31, 2002.
- *Where:* Washington, DC
- *Significance:* The act was designed to clean up sites containing contaminants or hazardous waste that threatened the environment. One of its features was the creation of the Hazardous Substances Response Trust Fund, better known as the "Superfund."

DOCUMENT

COMPREHENSIVE ENVIRONMENTAL RESPONSE, COMPENSATION, AND LIABILITY ACT OF 1980 (SUPERFUND).

AN ACT To provide for liability, compensation, cleanup, and emergency response for hazardous substances released into the environment and the cleanup of inactive hazardous waste disposal sites.

Be it enacted by the Senate and House of Representatives of the United States of America in Congress assembled, That this Act may be cited as the "Comprehensive, Environmental Response, Compensation, and Liability Act of 1980".

TITLE I—HAZARDOUS SUBSTANCES RELEASES, LIABILITY,
COMPENSATION

. . .

USES OF FUND

SEC. 111. (a) IN GENERAL.—For the purposes specified in this section there is
authorized to be appropriated from the Hazardous Substance Superfund established
under subchapter A of chapter 98 of the Internal Revenue Code of 1986 not more
than $8,500,000,000 for the 5-year period beginning on the date of enactment of
the Superfund Amendments and Reauthorization Acts of 1986, and not more than
$5,100,000,000 for the period commencing October 1, 1991, and ending Septem-
ber 30, 1994, and such sums shall remain available until expended. The preceding
sentence constitutes a specific authorization for the funds appropriated under title
II of Public Law 99-160 (relating to payment to the Hazardous Substances Trust
Fund). The President shall use the money in the Fund for the following purposes:

(1) Payment of governmental response costs incurred pursuant to section 104 of this title, including costs incurred pursuant to the Intervention
on the High Seas Act.

(2) Payment of any claim for necessary response costs incurred by any
other person as a result of carrying out the national contingency plan established under section 311(c) of the Clean Water Act and amended by section
105 of this title: *Provided, however,* That such costs must be approved under
said plan and certified by the responsible Federal official.

(3) Payment of any claim authorized by subsection (b) of this section
and finally decided pursuant to section 112 of this title, including those costs
set out in subsection 112(c)(3) of this title.

(4) Payment of costs specified under subsection (c) of this section.

(5) GRANTS FOR TECHNICAL ASSISTANCE.—The cost of
grants under section 117(e) (relating to public participation grants for technical assistance).

(6) . . .

The President shall not pay for any administrative costs or expenses out of the Fund
unless such costs and expenses are reasonably necessary for and incidental to the
implementation of this title.

(b)(1) IN GENERAL.—Claims asserted and compensable but unsatisfied under
provisions of section 311 of the Clean Water Act, which are modified by section
304 of this Act may be asserted against the Fund under this title for injury to, or
destruction or loss of, natural resources, including cost for damage assessment: *Provided, however,* That any such claim may be asserted only by the President, as trustee,
for natural resources over which the United States has sovereign rights, or natural
resources within the territory or the fishery conservation zone of the United States
to the extent they are managed or protected by the United States, or by any State
for natural resources within the boundary of that State belonging to, managed by,
controlled by, or appertaining to the State, or by any Indian tribe or by the United
States acting on behalf of any Indian tribe for natural resources belonging to, managed by, controlled by, or appertaining to such tribe, or held in trust for the benefit

of such tribe, or belonging to a member of such tribe if such resources are subject to a trust restriction on alienation.

. . .

SEC 118. HIGH PRIORITY FOR DRINKING WATER SUPPLIES.

For purposes of taking action under section 104 or 106 and listing facilities on the National Priorities List, the President shall give a high priority to facilities where the release of hazardous substances or pollutants or contaminants has resulted in the closing of drinking water wells or has contaminated a principal drinking water supply.

[42 U.S.C. 9618]

. . .

SOURCE: U.S. Senate. n.d. *Comprehensive Environmental Response, Compensation, and Liability Act of 1980 (Superfund)*. http://www.epw.senate.gov/cercla.pdf (accessed November 3, 2014).

ANALYSIS

The Comprehensive Environmental Response, Compensation, and Liability Act (CERCLA) of 1980 was passed to clean up portions of the United States that had been tainted by toxic waste or other contaminants that threatened the environment. A key part of the act was the creation of the Hazardous Substances Response Trust Fund, better known as the Superfund, which was intended to provide the funding necessary for clean-up efforts. The Superfund, administered by the Environmental Protection Agency (EPA), received its revenues from a tax levied on the chemical and petroleum industries. Over the first five years of the Superfund's existence, the taxes raised $1.6 billion. That sum proved paltry, as it only allowed the EPA to clean-up six of the approximately 1,800 hazardous sites that had been identified as eligible for Superfund monies. The underfunding of the Superfund was due to the national political climate at the time that CERCLA was enacted. Democrats in Congress were eager to get the legislation passed and on the president's desk before Ronald Reagan took office so they drafted a version of CERCLA that would be able to quickly pass Congress. The very traits that made it innocuous to Republicans and thus passable also limited its functionality.

Since CERCLA was only authorized for a five year period, Congress had to pass an extension. The Superfund and Reauthorization Act of 1986 addressed some of the original CERCLA's shortcomings, including its funding deficiencies. The federal government added $9 billion to the trust fund, which was renamed the Hazardous Substances Superfund. The tax base for the Superfund was broadened by levying taxes to include corporations related to, but outside of, the chemical and petroleum industries.

The scope of the Hazardous Substances Superfund was expanded through the Oil Pollution Act of 1990 to include oil spill clean-up, which was a direct response to the Exxon Valdez accident. Despite seeing the Superfund as a viable means of cleaning up threats to the environment, Congress tended to be leery of CERCLA as a whole. Throughout the 1990s and into the 2000s, Congress only passed annual authorizations to keep CERCLA functioning. It was not until 2002 that Congress once again reauthorized and expanded CERCLA to meet the needs of the twenty-first century.

FURTHER READING

Anderson, Terry Lee, ed. 2000. *Political Environmentalism: Going Behind the Green Curtain.* Stanford, CA: Hoover Institution Press.

Barnett, Harold C. 1994. *Toxic Debts and the Superfund Dilemma.* Chapel Hill: University of North Carolina Press.

Hird, John A. 1994. *Superfund: The Political Economy of Environmental Risk.* Baltimore: Johns Hopkins University Press.

Nakamura, Robert T., and Thomas W. Church. 2003. *Taming Regulation: Superfund and the Challenge of Regulatory Reform.* Washington, DC: Brookings Institution Press.

Switzer, Carole Stern, and Peter Gray. 2008. *CERCLA: Comprehensive Environmental Response, Compensation, and Liability Act (Superfund).* 2nd ed. Chicago: American Bar Association, Section of Environment, Energy, and Resources.

"Cost Sharing"

- *Document:* Water Resources Development Act of 1986, excerpts
- *Date:* November 17, 1986
- *Where:* Washington, DC
- *Significance:* The act fundamentally changed how water projects were funded by instituting cost-sharing programs that required local and state entities to help pay for the infrastructure that they desired.

DOCUMENT

An Act

To provide for the conservation and development of water and related resources and the improvement and rehabilitation of the Nation's water resources infrastructure.

Be it enacted by the Senate and House of Representatives of the United States of America in Congress assembled,

SECTION 1. SHORT TITLE AND TABLE OF CONTENTS.

(a) Short Title.—This Act may be cited as the "Water Resources Development Act of 1986".

(b) Table of Contents.—

. . .

TITLE I—COST SHARING

SEC. 101. HARBORS.

(a) Construction.—

(1) Payments during construction.—The non-Federal interests for a navigation project for a harbor or inland harbor, or any separable element thereof, on which a contract for physical construction has not been awarded before the date of enactment of this Act shall pay, during the period of construction of the project, the following costs associated with general navigation features:

(A) 10 percent of the cost of construction of the portion of the project which has a depth not in excess of 20 feet; plus

(B) 25 percent of the cost of construction of the portion of the project which has a depth in excess of 20 feet but not in excess of 45 feet; plus

(C) 50 percent of the cost of construction of the portion of the project which has a depth in excess of 45 feet.

(2) Additional 10 percent payment over 30 years.—The non-Federal interests for a project to which paragraph (1) applies shall pay an additional 10 percent of the cost of the general navigation features of the project in cash over a period not to exceed 30 years, at an interest rate determined pursuant to section 106. The value of lands, easements, rights-of-way, relocations, and dredged material disposal areas provided under paragraph (3) shall be credited toward the payment required under this paragraph.

(3) Lands, easements, and rights-of-way.—The non-Federal interests for a project to which paragraph (1) applies shall provide the lands, easements, rights-of-way, relocations (other than utility relocations under paragraph (4)), and dredged material disposal areas necessary for the project.

(4) Utility relocations.—The non-Federal interests for a project to which paragraph (1) applies shall perform or assure the performance of all relocations of utilities necessary to carry out the project, except that in the case of a project for a deep-draft harbor and in the case of a project constructed by non-Federal interests under section 204, one-half of the cost of each such relocation shall be borne by the owner of the facility being relocated and one-half of the cost of each such relocation shall be borne by the non-Federal interests.

(b) Operation and Maintenance.—The Federal share of the cost of operation and maintenance of each navigation project for a harbor or inland harbor constructed pursuant to this Act shall be 100 percent, except that in the case of a deep-draft harbor, the non-Federal interests shall be responsible for an amount equal to 50 percent of the excess of the cost of the operation and maintenance of such project over the cost which the Secretary determines would be incurred for operation and maintenance of such project if such project had a depth of 45 feet.

(c) Erosion or Shoaling Attributable to Federal Navigation Works.—Costs of constructing projects or measures for the prevention or mitigation of erosion or shoaling damages attributable to Federal navigation works shall be shared in the same proportion as the cost sharing provisions applicable to the project causing such erosion or shoaling. The non-Federal interests for the project causing the erosion or shoaling shall agree to operate and maintain such measures.

(d) Non-Federal Payments During Construction.—The amount of any non-Federal share of the cost of any navigation project for a harbor or inland harbor shall be paid to the Secretary. Amounts required to be paid during construction shall be paid on an annual basis during the period of construction, beginning not later than one year after construction is initiated.

(e) Agreement.—Before initiation of construction of a project to which this section applies, the Secretary and the non-Federal interests shall enter into a cooperative agreement according to the provisions of section 221 of the Flood Control Act of 1970. The non-Federal interests shall agree to—

(1) provide to the Federal Government lands, easements, and rights-of-way, and to provide dredged material disposal areas and perform the necessary relocations required for construction, operation, and maintenance of such project;

(2) hold and save the United States free from damages due to the construction or operation and maintenance of the project, except for damages due to the fault or negligence of the United States or its contractors;

(3) provide to the Federal Government the non-Federal share of all other costs of construction of such project; and

(4) in the case of a deep-draft harbor, be responsible for the non-Federal share of operation and maintenance required by subsection (b) of this section.

. . .

SEC. 904. MATTERS TO BE ADDRESSED IN PLANNING.

Enhancing national economic development (including benefits to particular regions of the Nation not involving the transfer of economic activity to such regions from other regions), the quality of the total environment, the well-being of the people of the United States, the prevention of loss of life, and the preservation of cultural and historical values shall be addressed in the formulation and evaluation of water resources projects to be carried out by the Secretary, and the associated benefits and costs, both quantifiable and unquantifiable, shall be displayed in the benefits and costs of such projects.

SEC. 905. FEASIBILITY REPORTS.

(a) In the case of any water resources project-related study authorized to be undertaken by the Secretary, the Secretary shall prepare a feasibility report, subject to section 105 of this Act. Such feasibility report shall describe, with reasonable certainty, the economic, environmental, and Social benefits and detriments of the recommended plan and alternative plans considered by the Secretary and the engineering features (including hydrologic and geologic information), the public acceptability, and the purposes, scope, and scale of the recommended plan. The feasibility report shall also include the views of other Federal agencies and non-Federal agencies with regard to the recommended plan, a description of a nonstructural alternative to the recommended plan when such plan does not have significant nonstructural features, and a description of the Federal and non-Federal participation in such plan, and shall demonstrate that States, other non-Federal interests, and Federal agencies have been consulted in the development of the recommended plan. This subsection shall not apply to (1) any study with respect to which a report has been submitted to Congress before the date of enactment of this Act, (2) any study for a project, which project is authorized for construction by this Act and is not subject to section 903(b), (3) any study for a project which is authorized under any of the following sections: section 205 of the Flood Control Act of 1948 (33 U.S.C. 701s), section 2 of the Flood Control Act of August 28, 1946 (33 U.S.C. 701r), section 107 of the River and Harbor Act of 1960 (33 U.S.C. 577), section 3 of the Act entitled "An Act authorizing Federal participation in the cost of protecting the shores of publicly owned property", approved August 13, 1946 (33 U.S.C. 426g), and section 111 of the River and Harbor Act of 1968 (33 U.S.C. 426i), and (4) general studies not intended to lead to recommendation of a specific water resources project.

(b) Before initiating any feasibility study under subsection (a) of this section after the date of enactment of this Act, the Secretary shall first perform, at Federal expense, a reconnaissance study of the water resources problem in order to identify potential solutions to such problem in sufficient detail to enable the Secretary to determine whether or not planning to develop a project should proceed to the preparation of a feasibility report. Such reconnaissance study shall include a preliminary analysis of the Federal interest, costs, benefits, and environmental impacts of such project, and an estimate of the costs of preparing the feasibility report. The duration of a reconnaissance study shall normally be no more than twelve months, but in all cases is to be limited to eighteen months.

(c) For purposes of studies undertaken pursuant to this section, the Secretary is authorized to consider benefits which may accrue to Indian tribes as a result of a project resulting from such a study.

(d) The Secretary shall undertake such measures as are necessary to ensure that standard and uniform procedures and practices are followed by each district office (and each division office for any area in which there is no district office) of the United States Army Corps of Engineers in the preparation of feasibility reports on water resources projects.

SEC. 906. FISH AND WILDLIFE MITIGATION.

(a)(1) In the case of any water resources project which is authorized to be constructed by the Secretary before, on, or after the date of enactment of this Act, construction of which has not commenced as of the date of enactment of this Act, and which necessitates the mitigation of fish and wildlife losses, including the acquisition of lands or interests in lands to mitigate losses to fish and wildlife, as a result of such project, such mitigation, including acquisition of the lands or interests—

(A) shall be undertaken or acquired before any construction of the project (other than such acquisition) commences, or

(B) shall be undertaken or acquired concurrently with lands and interests in lands for project purposes (other than mitigation of fish and wildlife losses), whichever the Secretary determines is appropriate, except that any physical construction required for the purposes of mitigation may be undertaken concurrently with the physical construction of such project.

(2) For the purposes of this subsection, any project authorized before the date of enactment of this Act on which more than 50 percent of the land needed for the project, exclusive of mitigation lands, has been acquired shall be deemed to have commenced construction under this subsection.

(b)(1) After consultation with appropriate Federal and non-Federal agencies, the Secretary is authorized to mitigate damages to fish and wildlife resulting from any water resources project under his jurisdiction, whether completed, under construction, or to be constructed. Such mitigation may include the acquisition of lands, or interests therein, except that—

(A) acquisition under this paragraph shall not be by condemnation in the case of projects completed as of the date of enactment of this Act or on which at least 10 percent of the physical construction on the project has been completed as of the date of enactment of this Act; and (B) acquisition of water, or interests therein, under this paragraph, shall not be by condemnation. The Secretary, shall, under the terms of this paragraph, obligate no more than $30,000,000 in any fiscal year. With respect to any water resources project, the authority under this subsection shall not apply to measures that cost more than $7,500,000 or 10 percent of the cost of the project, whichever is greater.

(2) Whenever, after his review, the Secretary determines that such mitigation features under this subsection are likely to require condemnation under subparagraph (A) or (B) of paragraph (1) of this subsection, the Secretary shall transmit to Congress a report on such proposed modification, together with his recommendations.

(c) Costs incurred after the date of enactment of this Act for implementation and operation, maintenance, and rehabilitation to mitigate damages to fish and wildlife shall be allocated among authorized project purposes in accordance with applicable cost allocation procedures, and shall be subject to cost sharing or reimbursement to the same extent as such other project costs are shared or reimbursed, except that when such costs are covered by contracts entered into prior to the date of enactment of this Act, such costs shall not be recovered without the consent of the non-Federal interests or until such contracts are complied with or renegotiated.

(d) After the date of enactment of this Act, the Secretary shall not submit any proposal for the authorization of any water resources project to the Congress unless such report contains (1) a recommendation with a specific plan to mitigate fish and wildlife losses created by such project, or (2) a determination by the Secretary that such project will have negligible adverse impact on fish and wildlife. Specific mitigation plans shall ensure that impacts to bottomland hardwood forests are mitigated in-kind, to the extent possible. In carrying out this subsection, the Secretary shall consult with appropriate Federal and non-Federal agencies.

(e) In those cases when the Secretary, as part of any report to Congress, recommends activities to enhance fish and wildlife resources, the first costs of such enhancement shall be a Federal cost when—

(1) such enhancement provides benefits that are determined to be national, including benefits to species that are identified by the National Marine Fisheries Service as of national economic importance, species that are subject to treaties or international convention to which the United States is a party, and anadromous fish;

(2) such enhancement is designed to benefit species that have been listed as threatened or endangered by the Secretary of the Interior under the terms of the Endangered Species Act, as amended (16 U.S.C. 1531, et seq.), or

(3) such activities are located on lands managed as a national wildlife refuge. When benefits of enhancement do not qualify under the preceding sentence, 25 percent of such first costs of enhancement shall be provided by non-Federal interests under a schedule of reimbursement determined by the Secretary. The non-Federal share of operation, maintenance, and rehabilitation of activities to enhance fish and wildlife resources shall be 25 percent.

(f) Fish and wildlife enhancement measures carried out as part of the project for Atchafalaya Floodway System, Louisiana, authorized by Public Law 99-88, and the project for Mississippi Delta Region, Louisiana, authorized by the Flood Control Act of 1965, shall be considered to provide benefits that are national for purposes of this section.

(g) The provisions of subsections (a), (b), and (d) shall be deemed to supplement the responsibility and authority of the Secretary pursuant to the Fish and Wildlife Coordination Act, and nothing in this section is intended to affect that Act.

SEC. 907. BENEFITS AND COSTS ATTRIBUTABLE TO ENVIRONMEN-
TAL MEASURES.

In the evaluation by the Secretary of benefits and costs of a water resources project, the benefits attributable to measures included in a project for the purpose of environmental quality, including improvement of the environment and fish and wildlife enhancement, shall be deemed to be at least equal to the costs of such measures.

. . .

SEC. 924. OFFICE OF ENVIRONMENTAL POLICY.

The Secretary shall establish in the Directorate of Civil Works of the Office of the Chief of Engineers an Office of Environmental Policy. Such Office shall be responsible for the formulation, coordination, and implementation of all matters concerning environmental quality and policy as they relate to the water resources program of the United States Army Corps of Engineers. Such Office shall, among other things, develop, and monitor compliance with, guidelines for the consideration of environmental quality in formulation and planning of water resources projects carried out by the Secretary, the preparation and coordination of environmental impact statements for such projects, and the coordination with Federal, State, and local agencies of environmental aspects of such projects and regulatory responsibilities of the Secretary.

SEC. 925. COMPILATION OF LAWS; ANNUAL REPORTS.

(a) Within one year after the date of enactment of this Act, the laws of the United States relating to the improvement of rivers and harbors, flood control, beach erosion, and other water resources development enacted after November 8, 1966, and before January 1, 1987, shall be compiled under the direction of the Secretary and the Chief of Engineers and printed for the use of the Department of the Army, the Congress, and the general public. The Secretary shall reprint the volumes containing such laws enacted before November 8, 1966. In addition, the Secretary shall include an index in each volume so compiled or reprinted. The Secretary shall transmit copies of each such volume to Congress.

(b) The Secretary shall prepare and submit the annual report required by section 8 of the Act of August 11, 1888, in two volumes. Volume I shall consist of a summary and highlights of Corps of Engineers' activities, authorities, and accomplishments. Volume II shall consist of detailed information and field reports on Corps of Engineers' activities. The Secretary shall publish an index with each annual report.

(c) The Secretary shall prepare biennially for public information a report for each State containing a description of each water resources project under the jurisdiction of the Secretary in such State and the status of each such project. Each report shall include an index. The report for each State shall be prepared in a separate volume. The reports under this subsection shall be published at the same time and the first such reports shall be published not later than one year after the date of the enactment of this Act.

. . .

SEC. 1109. PROHIBITION ON GREAT LAKES DIVERSIONS.

(a) The Congress finds and declares that—

(1) the Great Lakes are a most important natural resource to the eight Great Lakes States and two Canadian provinces, providing water supply for domestic and industrial use, clean energy through hydropower production, an efficient transportation mode for moving products into and out of the Great Lakes region, and recreational uses for millions of United States and Canadian citizens;

(2) the Great Lakes need to be carefully managed and protected to meet current and future needs within the Great Lakes basin and Canadian provinces;

(3) any new diversions of Great Lakes water for use outside of the Great Lakes basin will have significant economic and environmental impacts, adversely affecting the use of this resource by the Great Lakes States and Canadian provinces; and

(4) four of the Great Lakes are international waters and are defined as boundary waters in the Boundary Waters Treaty of 1909 between the United States and Canada, and as such any new diversion of Great Lakes water in the United States would

affect the relations of the Government of the United States with the Government of Canada.

(b) It is therefore declared to be the purpose and policy of the Congress in this section—

(1) to take immediate action to protect the limited quantity of water available from the Great Lakes system for use by the Great Lakes States and in accordance with the Boundary Waters Treaty of 1909;

(2) to prohibit any diversion of Great Lakes water by any State, Federal agency, or private entity for use outside the Great Lakes basin unless such diversion is approved by the Governor of each of the Great Lakes States; and

(3) to prohibit any Federal agency from undertaking any studies that would involve the transfer of Great Lakes water for any purpose for use outside the Great Lakes basin.

(c) As used in this section, the term "Great Lakes State" means each of the States of Illinois, Indiana, Michigan, Minnesota, Ohio, Pennsylvania, New York, and Wisconsin.

(d) No water shall be diverted from any portion of the Great Lakes within the United States, or from any tributary within the United States of any of the Great Lakes, for use outside the Great Lakes basin unless such diversion is approved by the Governor of each of the Great Lake States.

(e) No Federal agency may undertake any study, or expend any Federal funds to contract for any study, of the feasibility of diverting water from any portion of the Great Lakes within the United States, or from any tributary within the United States of any of the Great Lakes, for use outside the Great Lakes basin, unless such study or expenditure is approved by the Governor of each of the Great Lakes States. The prohibition of the preceding sentence shall not apply to any study or data collection effort performed by the Corps of Engineers or other Federal agency under the direction of the International Joint Commission in accordance with the Boundary Waters Treaty of 1909.

(f) This section shall not apply to any diversion of water from any of the Great Lakes which is authorized on the date of the enactment of this Act.

SOURCE: U.S. Congress. n.d. *Water Resources Development Act of 1986.* http://www.fws.gov /habitatconservation/omnibus/WRDA1986.pdf (accessed October 12, 2014).

ANALYSIS

The Water Resources Development Act of 1986 (WRDA) was the first legislation in sixteen years that authorized the U.S. Army Corps of Engineers (USACE) to construct projects in legislative districts around the country. The members of Congress enthusiastically embraced the legislation, which authorized pre-construction planning or construction of approximately 270 projects. The legislation also included modifications for another 70 projects that were already underway.

Embedded in the hundreds of pages of legislation were a number of environmental regulations that would ordinarily have had a difficult time passing through Congress, but went largely unnoticed as the members of Congress loaded up the omnibus bill with water infrastructure projects greatly desired by their constituents. An example was the establishment within the Directorate of Civil Works of the Office of the Chief of Engineers of an Office of Environmental Policy (OEP). The OEP was intended to ensure that the USACE followed all environmental guidelines and laws.

The major change that the WRDA made to federal water policy in the United States was the institution of cost-sharing programs. The federal government had traditionally funded all of the projects undertaken by the USACE. But due to budget shortages, Congress began requiring the states and agencies to help pay for the projects that directly benefited them. This change had two effects. First, at the federal level, it allowed Congress to fund more projects. At the local level, it proved a deterrent to construction because some locales simply did not have the funds available to pay what the federal government viewed as their fair share.

Another major part of the WRDA was Section 1109, which concerned the transfer of waters from the Great Lakes. It had the effect of making the Great Lakes Charter (GLC) of 1985 a legally binding agreement. The GLC was an agreement between the governors of Illinois, Indiana, Michigan, Minnesota, New York, Ohio, Pennsylvania, and Wisconsin, and the premiers of Ontario and Quebec to protect the Great Lakes by preventing waters from the respective lakes to be transferred outside of the Great Lakes Basin. Within the United States, the agreement was nonbinding because states did not have the constitutional authority to negotiate international agreements. The passage of the WRDA solved that problem by making most of the GLC legal through Section 1109. The federal legislation proved even more stringent than the original GLC agreement as it also made it nearly impossible to make water transfers within the Great Lakes Basin, even if the transfer did not cross an international boundary.

The WRDA has proven to have been a landmark piece of legislation due to the cost-sharing programs. One of the consequences of requiring states and agencies to help share in the expenses has been an increase in local input on the decisions made during the pre-planning and construction processes. The act also streamlined what projects were constructed and which were not, since unnecessary water projects were no longer advanced just because they created jobs. This was due to the need for parties to justify to their respective constituencies that the value of the project exceeded their real costs.

FURTHER READING

Glass, Charles F., Jr. 2003. "Enforcing Great Lakes Water Export Restrictions Under the Water Resources Development Act of 1986." *Columbia Law Review* 103, no. 6: 1503–1537.

Riley, Ann L. 1989. "Overcoming Federal Water Policies." *Environment* 39, no. 10: 12–31.

"To Provide for the Renewal of the Quality of the Nation's Waters"

- *Document:* Water Quality Act of 1987, excerpts
- *Date:* February 4, 1987
- *Where:* Washington, DC
- *Significance:* The Water Quality Act of 1987 was the second set of amendments to the Clean Water Act of 1972. One of its primary focuses was the regulation of stormwater runoff.

DOCUMENT

An Act

To amend the Federal Water Pollution Control Act to provide for the renewal of the quality of the Nation's waters, and for other purposes.

Be it enacted by the Senate and House of Representatives of the United States in Congress assembled,

Section 1. SHORT TITLE; TABLE OF CONTENTS; AMENDMENTS TO FEDERAL WATER POLLUTION CONTROL ACT; DEFINITION OF ADMINISTRATOR.

(a) SHORT TITLE.—This Act may be cited as the "Water Quality Act of 1987".
(b) TABLE OF CONTENTS.—

TITLE I—AMENDMENTS TO TITLE 1

(c) AMENDMENT OF FEDERAL WATER POLLUTION CONTROL ACT.—

Except as otherwise expressly provided, whenever in this Act an amendment or repeal is expressed in terms of an amendment to, or repeal of, a section or other provision, the reference shall be considered to be made to a section or other provision of the Federal Water Pollution Control Act.

(d) DEFINITION.—For purposes of this Act, the term "Administrator" means the Administrator of the Environmental Protection Agency.

SEC. 2. LIMITATION ON PAYMENTS

No payments may be made under this Act except to the extent provided in advance in appropriation Acts.

. . .

TITLE IV—PERMITS AND LICENSES
SEC. 401. STORMWATER RUNOFF FROM OIL, GAS, AND MINING OPERATIONS.

(a) LIMITATION ON PERMIT REQUIREMENT.—Section 402(l) is amended by inserting "(1) AGRICULTURAL RETURN FLOWS.—" before "The Administrator" and by adding at the end thereof the following: "(2) STORMWATER RUNOFF FROM OIL, GAS, AND MINING OPERATIONS.—The Administrator shall not require a permit under this section, nor shall the Administrator directly or indirectly require any State to require a permit for discharges of stormwater runoff from mining operations or oil and gas exploration, production, processing, or treatment operations or transmission facilities, composed entirely of flows which are not from conveyances or systems of conveyances (including but not limited to pipes, conduits, ditches, and channels) used for collecting and conveying precipitation runoff and which are not contaminated by contact with, or do not come into contact with, any overburden, raw material, intermediate products, finished product, byproduct, or waste products located on the site of such operations."

(b) CONFORMING AMENDMENTS.—Section 402(l) is further amended—

(1) by inserting "LIMITATION OF PERMIT REQUIREMENT.—" After "(l)" and by indenting paragraph (1) of such section, as designated by subsection (a) of this section, and aligning such paragraph with paragraph (2) of such section, as added by such subsection (a).

. . .

SEC. 405. MUNICIPAL AND INDUSTRIAL STORMWATER DISCHARGES.

Section 402 is amended by adding at the end thereof the following new subsection:

"(p) MUNICIPAL AND INDUSTRIAL STORMWATER DISCHARGES.—

"(1) GENERAL RULE.—Prior to October 1, 1992, the Administrator or the State (in the case of a permit program approved under section 402 of this Act) shall not require a permit under this section for discharges composed entirely of stormwater.

"(2) EXCEPTIONS.—Paragraph (1) shall not apply with respect to the following stormwater discharges:

"(A) discharge with respect to which a permit has been issued under this section before the date of the enactment of this subsection.

"(B) discharge associated with industrial activity.

"(C) A discharge from a municipal separate storm sewer system serving a population of 250,000 or more.

"(D) A discharge from municipal separate storm sewer system serving a population of 100,000 or more but less than 250,000.

"(E) A discharge for which the Administrator or the State, as the case may be, determines that the stormwater discharge contributes to a violation of a water quality standard or is a significant contributor of pollutants to waters of the United States.

"(3) PERMIT REQUIREMENTS.—

"(A) INDUSTRIAL DISCHARGES.—Permits for discharges associated with industrial activity shall meet all applicable provisions of this section and section 301.

"(B) MUNICIPAL DISCHARGE.—Permits for discharges from municipal storm sewers—

"(i) may be issued on a system- or jurisdiction-wide basis;

"(ii) shall include a requirement to effectively prohibit nonstormwater discharges into the storm sewers; and

"(iii) shall require controls to reduce the discharge of pollutants to the maximum extent practicable, including management practices, control techniques and system, design and engineering methods, and such other provisions as the Administrator or the State determines appropriate for the control of such pollutants.

"(4) PERMIT APPLICATION REQUIREMENTS.—

"(A) INDUSTRIAL AND LARGE MUNICIPALITY DISCHARGES.—Not later than 2 years after the date of the enactment of this subsection, the Administrator shall establish regulations setting for the permit application requirements for stormwater discharges described in paragraph (2)(B) and (2)(C). Applications for permits for such discharges shall be filed no later than 3 years after such date enactment. Not later than 4 years after such date of enactment, the Administrator or the State, as the case may be, shall issue or deny each such permit. Any such permit shall provide for compliance as expeditiously as practicable, but in no event later than 3 years after the date of issuance of such permit.

"(B) OTHER MUNICIPAL DISCHARGES. – Not later than 4 years after the date of the enactment of the subsection, the Administrator shall establish regulations setting forth the permit application requirements for stormwater discharges described in paragraph (2)(D). Applications for permits for such discharges shall be filed no later than 5 years after such date of enactment. Not later than 6 years after such date of enactment, the Administrator or the State, as the case may be, shall issue or deny any permit. Any such permit shall provide for compliance as expeditiously as practicable, but in no event later than 3 years after the date of issuance of such permit.

"(5) STUDIES.—The Administrator, in consultation with the States, shall conduct a study for the purposes of—

"(A) identifying those stormwater discharges or classes of stormwater discharges for which permits are not required pursuant to paragraphs (1) and (2) of this subsection;

"(B) determining to the maximum extent practicable, the nature and extent of pollutants in such discharges; and

"(C) establishing procedures and methods to control stormwater discharges to the extent necessary to mitigate impacts on water quality.

Not later than October 1, 1988, the Administrator shall submit to Congress a report on the results of the study described in subparagraphs (A) and (B). Not later than October 1, 1989, the Administrator shall submit to Congress a report on the results of the study described in subparagraph (C).

"(6) REGULATIONS.—Not later than October 1, 1992, the Administrator, in consultation with State and local officials, shall issue regulations (based on the results of the studies conducted under paragraph (5)) which designate stormwater discharges, other than those discharges described in paragraph (2), to be regulated to protect water quality and shall establish a comprehensive program to regulate such designated sources. The program shall, at the minimum, (A) establish priorities, (B) establish requirements for State stormwater management programs, and (C) establish expeditious deadlines. The program may include performance standards, guidelines, guidance, and management practices and treatment requirements, as appropriate."

. . .

TITLE V—MISCELLANEOUS PROVISIONS

. . .

SEC. 503. AGRICULTURAL STORMWATER DISCHARGES.

Section 502(14) (relating to the definition of point source) is amended by inserting after "does not include" the following: "agricultural stormwater discharges and".

SOURCE: U.S. Congress. *Public Law 89-80.* http://www.gpo.gov/fdsys/pkg/STATUTE-101/pdf/STATUTE-101-Pg7.pdf (accessed November 5, 2014).

ANALYSIS

To ensure that the Clean Water Act could pass through Congress, its authors omitted regulations concerning stormwater. To have included them would have drawn the ire of congressmen representing urban areas. The same political equation was present when the first amendment to the Clean Water Act, namely the Clean Water Act of 1977, was being considered in Congress. By 1987, many studies were conducted that demonstrated that stormwater from industries and urban areas were significant contributors to water pollution. The studies provided the impetus for making the regulation of stormwater a major priority in the Water Quality Act (WQA) of 1987.

In Sections 401 and 405 of the WQA's Title IV, the WQA essentially required industrial operations and cities to create separate systems for stormwater and industrial waste or municipal waste so that stormwater entering surface waters were as clean of pollutants as possible. If industrial interests or cities could not ensure that their stormwater was clean, they had to obtain permits through the National

Pollutant Discharge Elimination System, which was intended to assist them in reducing their introduction of pollutants into the nation's surface waters. It is clear that Congress was only interested in industrial and municipal waste at the time, as they exempted agricultural operations in Section 503.

The WQA faced absolutely no challenges in Congress as it passed the House of Representatives by a vote of 408 to 0 and the Senate 96 to 0. When the legislation reached the desk of President Ronald Reagan, he chose to issue a veto. He claimed that the legislation was too expensive for the country to afford, as it promised the issuance of approximately $18 billion in grants and loans over eight years. The bill was reintroduced in both houses of Congress in January 1987 and the veto was easily overridden.

FURTHER READING

Ferguson, Bruce K. 1998. *Introduction to Stormwater: Concept, Purpose, Design*. New York: Wiley.

Korpics, J. Joseph. 1988. "Regulation of Storm Water Point Source Discharges." *Journal of the Water Pollution Control Federation* 61, no. 5: 50–56.

"Isolated Ponds Are Not 'Waters of the United States'"

- **Document:** *Rapanos et ux., et al. v. United States*, excerpt from syllabus
- **Date:** June 19, 2006
- **Where:** Washington, DC
- **Significance:** The Rapanos decision narrowed the definition of "navigable waters," thereby making it more difficult for agencies like the U.S. Army Corps of Engineers and the Environmental Protection Agency to apply the Clean Water Act.

DOCUMENT

Syllabus

RAPANOS ET UX., ET AL. v. UNITED STATES

CERTIORARI TO THE UNITED STATES COURT OF APPEALS FOR THE SIXTH CIRCUIT

No. 04–1034. Argued February 21, 2006—Decided June 19, 2006*

As relevant here, the Clean Water Act (CWA or Act) makes it unlawful to discharge dredged or fill material into "navigable waters" without a permit, 33 U. S. C. §§1311(a), 1342(a), and defines "navigable waters" as "the waters of the United States, including the territorial seas," §1362(7). The Army Corps of Engineers (Corps), which issues permits for the discharge of dredged or fill material into navigable waters, interprets "the waters of the United States" expansively to include not only traditional navigable waters, 33 CFR §328.3(a)(1),but also other defined waters, §328.3(a)(2), (3); "[t]ributaries" of such waters, §328.3(a)(5); and wetlands "adjacent" to such waters and tributaries, §328.3(a)(7). "[A]djacent" wetlands include those "bordering, contiguous [to], or neighboring" waters of the United States even when they are "separated from [such] waters ... by man-made dikes ... and the like." §328.3(c). These cases involve four Michigan wetlands lying near ditches or man-made drains that eventually empty into traditional navigable waters. In No. 04–1034, the United States brought civil enforcement proceedings against the Rapanos petitioners, who had backfilled three of the areas without a permit. The District Court found federal jurisdiction over the wetlands because they were adjacent to "waters of the United States" and held petitioners liable for CWA violations. Affirming, the Sixth Circuit found federal jurisdiction based on the sites' hydrologic connections to the nearby ditches or drains, or to more remote navigable waters. In No. 04–1384, the Carabell petitioners were denied a permit to deposit fill in a wetland that was separated from a drainage ditch by an impermeable berm. The Carabells sued, but the District Court found federal jurisdiction over the site. Affirming, the Sixth Circuit held that the wetland was adjacent to navigable waters.

Held: The judgments are vacated, and the cases are remanded. No. 04–1034, 376 F. 3d 629, and No. 04–1384, 391 F. 3d 704, vacated and remanded. JUSTICE SCALIA, joined by THE CHIEF JUSTICE, JUSTICE THOMAS, and JUSTICE ALITO, concluded:

1. The phrase "the waters of the United States" includes only those relatively permanent, standing or continuously flowing bodies of water "forming geographic features" that are described in ordinary parlance as "streams," "oceans, rivers, [and] lakes," Webster's New International Dictionary 2882 (2d ed.), and does not include channels through which water flows intermittently or ephemerally, or channels that periodically provide drainage for rainfall. The Corps' expansive interpretation of that phrase is thus not "based on a permissible construction of the statute." *Chevron U. S. A. Inc. v. Natural Resources Defense Council, Inc.,* 467 U. S. 837, 843. Pp. 12–21.

(a) While the meaning of "navigable waters" in the CWA is broader than the traditional definition found in The Daniel Ball, 10 Wall. 557, see Solid Waste Agency of Northern Cook Cty. v. Army Corps of Engineers, 531 U. S. 159, 167 (SWANCC); United States v. Riverside Bayview Homes, Inc., 474 U. S. 121, 133, the CWA authorizes federal jurisdiction only over "waters." The use of the definite article "the" and the plural number "waters" show plainly that §1362(7) does not refer to water in general, but more narrowly to water "[a]s found in streams," "oceans, rivers, [and] lakes," Webster's New International Dictionary 2882 (2d ed.). Those terms all connote relatively permanent bodies of water, as opposed to ordinarily dry channels through which water occasionally or intermittently flows. Pp. 12–15.

(b) The Act's use of the traditional phrase "navigable waters" further confirms that the CWA confers jurisdiction only over relatively permanent bodies of water. Traditionally, such "waters" included only discrete bodies of water, and the term still carries some of its original substance, SWANCC, supra, at 172. This Court's subsequent interpretation of "the waters of the United States" in the CWA likewise confirms this limitation. See, e.g., Riverside

Bayview, supra, at 131. And the CWA itself categorizes the channels and conduits that typically carry intermittent flows of water separately from "navigable waters," including them in the definition of "'point sources,'" U. S. C. §1362(14). Moreover, only the foregoing definition of "waters" is consistent with CWA's stated policy "to recognize, preserve, 3 Cite as: 547 U. S. _____ (2006) and protect the primary responsibilities and rights of the States . . . to plan the development and use . . . of land and water resources. . . ." §1251(b). In addition, "the waters of the United States" hardly qualifies as the clear and manifest statement from Congress needed to authorize intrusion into such an area of traditional state authority as land-use regulation; and to authorize federal action that stretches the limits of Congress's commerce power. See SWANCC, supra, at 173. Pp. 15–21.

1. A wetland may not be considered "adjacent to" remote "waters of the United States" based on a mere hydrologic connection. Riverside Bayview rested on an inherent ambiguity in defining where the "water" ends and its abutting ("adjacent") wetlands begin, permitting the Corps to rely on ecological considerations only to resolve that ambiguity in favor of treating all abutting wetlands as waters. Isolated ponds are not "waters of the United States" in their own right, see SWANCC, supra, at 167, 171, and present no boundary-drawing problem justifying the invocation of such ecological factors. Thus, only those wetlands with a continuous surface connection to bodies that are "waters of the United States" in their own right, so that there is no clear demarcation between the two, are "adjacent" to such waters and covered by the Act. Establishing coverage of the Rapanos and Carabell sites requires finding that the adjacent channel contains a relatively permanent "wate[r] of the United States," and that each wetland has a continuous surface connection to that water, making it difficult to determine where the water ends and the wetland begins. Pp. 21–24.
2. Because the Sixth Circuit applied an incorrect standard to determine whether the wetlands at issue are covered "waters," and because of the paucity of the record, the cases are remanded for further proceedings. P. 39.

JUSTICE KENNEDY concluded that the Sixth Circuit correctly recognized that a water or wetland constitutes "navigable waters" under the Act if it possesses a "significant nexus" to waters that are navigable in fact or that could reasonably be so made, Solid Waste Agency of Northern Cook Cty. v. Army Corps of Engineers, 531 U. S. 159, 167, 172 (SWANCC), but did not consider all the factors necessary to determine that the lands in question had, or did not have, the requisite nexus. United States v. Riverside Bayview Homes, Inc., 474 U. S. 121, and SWANCC establish the framework for the inquiry here. The nexus required must be assessed in terms of the Act's goals and purposes. Congress enacted the law to "restore and maintain thechemical, physical, and biological integrity of the Nation's waters," U. S. C. §1251(a), and it pursued that objective by restricting dumping and filling in "waters of the United States," §§1311(a), 1362(12).

The rationale for the Act's wetlands regulation, as the Corps has recognized, is that wetlands can perform critical functions related to the integrity of other waters—such as pollutant trapping, flood control, and runoff storage. 33 C. F. R. §320.4(b) (2). Accordingly, wetlands possess the requisite nexus, and thus come within the statutory phrase "navigable waters," if the wetlands, alone or in combination with similarly situated lands in the region, significantly affect the chemical, physical, and biological integrity of other covered waters understood as navigable in the traditional sense. When, in contrast, their effects on water quality are speculative or insubstantial, they fall outside the zone fairly encompassed by the term "navigable waters." Because the Corps' theory of jurisdiction in these cases—adjacency to tributaries, however remote and insubstantial—goes beyond the Riverside Bayview holding, its assertion of jurisdiction cannot rest on that case. The breadth of the Corps' existing standard for tributaries—which seems to leave room for regulating drains, ditches, and streams remote from any navigable-in-fact water and carrying only minor water-volumes toward it—precludes that standard's adoption as the determinative measure of whether adjacent wetlands are likely to play an important role in the integrity of an aquatic system comprising navigable waters as traditionally understood. Absent more specific regulations, the Corps must establish a significant nexus on a case-by-case basis when seeking to regulate wetlands based on adjacency to nonnavigable tributaries, in order to avoid unreasonable applications of the Act. In the instant cases the record contains evidence pointing to a possible significant nexus, but neither the agency nor the reviewing courts considered the issue in these terms. Thus, the cases should be remanded for further proceedings. Pp. 1–30.

. . .

SOURCE: U.S. Supreme Court. 2006. *Rapanos et ux., et al. v. United States.* http://www.epa.gov/owow/wetlands/pdf/Rapanos_SupremeCourt.pdf (accessed August 24, 2014).

ANALYSIS

The background for the case involved the business activities of John Rapanos and some associates. They wanted to construct some homes and a shopping center in Michigan on some wetlands. They were informed by the Michigan Department of Environmental Quality that they could not fill in the wetlands without a permit due to the Clean Water Act. The Environmental Protection Agency also warned Rapanos and his partners that it is illegal to dump fill into wetlands without proper permission. Despite the warnings, Rapanos eschewed the permit process and filled in approximately 54 acres of land. Rapanos justified his actions by arguing that the wetlands in question were not connected to the "navigable waters" of the United

States thus the Clean Water Act did not apply. The federal government disagreed and began legal proceeding against him and his associates. In a number of federal court decisions, Rapanos was found guilty of violating the Clean Water Act because the wetlands in question were connected by man-made ditches to navigable waters.

When the United Supreme Court looked at the particulars of the case, they agreed in part with Rapanos. In a case settled by a 5–4 vote, the majority agreed that the wetlands in question were not part of the navigable waters of the United States because the man-made ditches that justified earlier rulings were often dry and thus not always connected to other sources of water. As an example of that point, Justice Scalia observed that "isolated ponds are not 'waters of the United States' in their own right." Through their ruling, the justices limited the definition of "navigable waters" that was utilized by a number of federal agencies. The practical impact of the decision was that respective federal agencies became reticent to enforce the Clean Water Act. This was due to the necessity of proving that a wetland or other isolated source of water had a "significant nexus" to the navigable waters of the country. One of the other problems arising from the decision was the definition of "significant nexus," as the court left that determination vague.

Although Rapanos was vindicated on his interpretation of what defined navigable water, he nonetheless lost the case because he had ignored the warnings to obtain a permit before filling in three separate wetlands. He settled with the U.S. government by agreeing to pay a $150,000 fine. He also had to construct a 100 acre wetland in Michigan's Arenac and Midland Counties to help replace the wetlands he destroyed.

Democratic Party members in Congress responded to the Rapanos decision by drafting legislation that would broaden the definition of "navigable waters" to the level that it was before the Rapanos decision but have been unsuccessful in their efforts. The most recent effort to broaden the definition was launched by the EPA and the U.S. Army Corps of Engineers in 2014. Through their "Proposed Rule: Definition of 'Waters of the United States' Under the Clean Water Act," they are trying to make the change administratively. It remains to be seen if their effort will prove successful.

FURTHER READING

Arnold, Gwen. 2013. "The Influence of Organizations and Institutions on Wetland Policy Stability: The Rapanos Case." *Policy Studies Journal* 41, no. 2: 343–364.

Brader, Cory Ruth. 2012. "Toward a Constitutional Chevron: Lessons from Rapanos." *University of Pennsylvania Law Review* 160, no. 5: 1479–1525.

Gardner, Royal C. 2011. *Lawyers, Swamps, and Money: U.S. Wetland Law, Policy, and Politics*. Washington, DC: Island Press.

Savage, David G. 2009. "*Rapanos v. United States*: Wading Into the Wetlands." In *A Good Quarrel: America's Top Legal Reporters Share Stories from Inside the Supreme Court*, ed. Timothy R. Johnson, and Jerry Goldman. Ann Arbor: University of Michigan Press.

"A Proposed Rule Defining the Scope of Waters Protected Under the Clean Water Act"

- **Document:** Proposed Rule: Definition of "Waters of the United States" Under the Clean Water Act, excerpts
- **Date:** April 21, 2014
- **Where:** Washington, DC
- **Significance:** By broadening the definition of "Waters of the United States," both the U.S. Army Corps of Engineers and the Environmental Protection Agency would significantly expand their jurisdictions.

DOCUMENT

II. Background

  A. Executive Summary

The U.S. Environmental Protection Agency (EPA) and the U.S. Army Corps of Engineers (Corps) publish for public comment a proposed rule defining the scope of waters protected under the Clean Water Act (CWA), in light of the U.S. Supreme Court cases in U.S. v. *Riverside Bayview Homes, Solid Waste Agency of Northern Cook County* v. U.S. *Army Corps of Engineers* (SWANCC), and *Rapanos* v. *United States* (*Rapanos*). The purposes of the proposed rule are to ensure protection of our nation's aquatic resources and make the process of identifying "waters of the United States" less complicated and more efficient. The rule achieves these goals by increasing CWA program transparency, predictability, and consistency. This rule will result in more effective and efficient CWA permit evaluations with increased certainty and less litigation. This rule provides increased clarity regarding the CWA regulatory definition of "waters of the United States" and associated definitions and concepts.

EPA's Office of Research and Development prepared a draft peer-reviewed synthesis of published peer-reviewed scientific literature discussing the nature of connectivity and effects of streams and wetlands on downstream waters (U.S. Environmental Protection Agency, *Connectivity of Streams and Wetlands to Downstream Waters: A Review and Synthesis of the Scientific Evidence,* (Washington, DC: U.S. Environmental Protection Agency, 2013)) ("Report"). The Report is under review by EPA's Science Advisory Board, and the rule will not be finalized until that review and the final Report are complete. This proposal is also supported by a body of peer-reviewed scientific literature on the connectivity of tributaries, wetlands, adjacent open waters, and other open waters to downstream waters and the important effects of these connections on the chemical, physical, and biological integrity of those downstream waters.

Appendix A of this preamble summarizes currently available scientific literature and the Report that are part of the administrative record for this proposal and explains how this scientific information supports the proposed rule. Additional data and information likely will become available during the rulemaking process, including that provided during the public comment process, and by additional research, studies, and investigations that take place before the rulemaking process is concluded. The agencies are specifically requesting information that would inform the decision on how best to address "other waters." At the conclusion of the rulemaking process, the agencies will review the entirety of the completed administrative record and determine at that time what, if any, adjustments are appropriate for the final rule.

"Waters of the United States," which include wetlands, rivers, streams, lakes, ponds and the territorial seas, provide many functions and services critical for our nation's economic and environmental health. In addition to providing habitat, rivers, lakes, ponds and wetlands cleanse our drinking water, ameliorate storm surges, provide invaluable storage capacity for some flood waters, and enhance our quality of life by providing myriad recreational opportunities, as well as important water supply and power generation benefits. A desire to protect these vital resources led Congress to pass the CWA in 1972 in order to restore and maintain the chemical, physical, and biological integrity of our nation's waters while recognizing, preserving, and protecting the primary responsibilities and rights of states to prevent, reduce, and eliminate pollution within their borders. Decades of experience implementing the CWA's programs and existing science provide strong support for the regulatory and policy underpinnings of the proposed rule. The proposed rule was developed with an enhanced understanding of the importance of all aspects of tributary, wetland, and lake and pond systems and the ecological functions and services they provide.

The proposed rule will reduce documentation requirements and the time currently required for making jurisdictional determinations. It will provide needed clarity for regulators, stakeholders and the regulated public for identifying waters as "waters of the United States," and reduce time and resource demanding case-specific analyses prior to determining jurisdiction and any need for permit or enforcement actions.

The modern Clean Water Act was established by the Federal Water Pollution Control Act Amendments of 1972, which was substantially amended in 1977 and 1987. (The 1972 amendments were to the Federal Water Pollution Control Act originally enacted in 1948.) As stated in section 101(a), the objective of the CWA is to restore and maintain the chemical, physical, and biological integrity of the Nation's waters. Prior to the CWA, the Rivers and Harbors Appropriations Act of 1899 protected navigation and protected some waters from discharges of pollution.

The 1899 Act continues in force and applies primarily to the "navigable waters of the United States." The 1948 Federal Water Pollution Control Act called for programs eliminating or reducing the pollution of interstate waters and tributaries thereof, and improving the sanitary condition of surface and underground waters. The jurisdictional scope of the CWA is "navigable waters," defined in section 502(7) of the statute as "waters of the United States, including the territorial seas." Both the legislative history and the caselaw confirm that "waters of the United States" in the CWA are not limited to the traditional navigable waters. It is the CWA definition that is the subject of this proposed rule.

The term "navigable waters" is used in a number of provisions of the CWA, including the section 402 National Pollutant Discharge Elimination System (NPDES) permit program, the section 404 permit program, the section 311 oil spill prevention and response program, the water quality standards and total maximum daily load programs under section 303, and the section 401 state water quality certification process. However, while there is only one CWA definition of "waters of the United States," there may be other statutory factors that define the reach of a particular CWA program or provision.

The CWA leaves it to EPA and the Corps to define the term "waters of the United States." Existing regulations (last codified in 1986) define "waters of the United States" as traditional navigable waters, interstate waters, all other waters that could affect interstate or foreign commerce, impoundments of waters of the United States, tributaries, the territorial seas, and adjacent wetlands. . . .

The U.S. Supreme Court addressed the scope of "waters of the United States" protected by the CWA in *United States* v. *Riverside Bayview Homes*, 474 U.S. 121 (1985), which involved wetlands adjacent to a traditional navigable water in Michigan. In a unanimous opinion, the Court deferred to the Corps' judgment that adjacent wetlands are "inseparably bound up" with the waters to which they are adjacent, and upheld the inclusion of adjacent wetlands in the regulatory definition of "waters of the United States." The Court observed that the broad objective of the CWA to restore the integrity of the nation's waters "incorporated a broad, systemic view of the goal of maintaining and improving water quality. . . .Protection of aquatic ecosystems, Congress recognized, demanded broad federal authority to control pollution, for '[w]ater moves in hydrologic cycles and it is essential that discharge of pollutants be controlled at the source.' In keeping with these views, Congress chose to define the waters covered by the Act broadly." *Id.* at 133 (citing Senate Report 92-414).

The issue of CWA regulatory jurisdiction over "waters of the United States" was addressed again by the Supreme Court in *Solid Waste Agency of Northern Cook County v. U.S. Army Corps of Engineers*, 531 U.S. 159 (2001). In SWANCC, the Court (in a 5-4 opinion) held that the use of "isolated" nonnavigable intrastate ponds by migratory birds was not by itself a sufficient basis for the exercise of Federal regulatory authority under the CWA. The Court noted that in the *Riverside* case it had "found that Congress' concern for the protection of water quality and aquatic ecosystems indicated its intent to regulate wetlands 'inseparably bound up with the "waters" of the United States'" and that "[i]t was the significant nexus between the wetlands and 'navigable waters' that informed our reading of the CWA" in that case. *Id.* at 167.

Five years after *SWANCC*, the Court again addressed the CWA term "waters of the United States" in *Rapanos v. United States*, 547 U.S. 715 (2006). *Rapanos* involved two consolidated cases in which the CWA had been applied to wetlands adjacent to nonnavigable tributaries of traditional navigable waters. All Members of the Court agreed that the term "waters of the United States" encompasses some waters that are not navigable in the traditional sense. A four-Justice plurality in *Rapanos* interpreted the term "waters of the United States" as covering "relatively permanent, standing or continuously flowing bodies of water ..." *id.* at 739, that are connected to traditional navigable waters, *id.* at 742, as well as wetlands with a continuous surface connection to such relatively permanent water bodies, *id.* The *Rapanos* plurality noted that its reference to "relatively permanent" waters did "not necessarily exclude streams, rivers, or lakes that might dry up in extraordinary circumstances, such as drought," or "*seasonal* rivers, which contain continuous flow during some months of the year but no flow during dry months. ..." *Id.* at 732 n. 5 (emphasis in original).

Justice Kennedy's concurring opinion took a different approach than the plurality's. Justice Kennedy concluded that the term "waters of the United States" encompasses wetlands that "possess a 'significant nexus' to waters that are or were navigable in fact or that could reasonably be so made." *Id.* at 759 (Kennedy, J., concurring in the judgment) (quoting SWANCC, 531 U.S. at 167). He stated that wetlands possess the requisite significant nexus if the wetlands, "either alone or in combination with similarly situated [wet]lands in the region, significantly affect the chemical, physical, and biological integrity of other covered waters more readily understood as 'navigable.'" 547 U.S. at 780. Kennedy's opinion notes that such a relationship with navigable waters must be more than "speculative or insubstantial." *Id.* Because Justice Kennedy identified "significant nexus" as the touchstone for CWA jurisdiction, the agencies determined that it is reasonable and appropriate to apply the "significant nexus" standard for CWA jurisdiction that Justice Kennedy's opinion applied to adjacent wetlands to other categories of water bodies as well (such as to tributaries of traditional navigable waters or interstate waters, and to "other waters") to determine whether they are subject to CWA jurisdiction, either by rule or on a case-specific basis.

. . .

The proposed rule would revise the existing definition of "waters of the United States" consistent with the science and the above Supreme Court cases. The proposed rule retains much of the structure of the agencies' longstanding definition of "waters of the United States," and many of the existing provisions of that definition where revisions are not required in light of Supreme Court decisions or other bases for revision. As a result of the Supreme Court decisions in *SWANCC* and *Rapanos*, the scope of regulatory jurisdiction of the CWA in this proposed rule is narrower than that under the existing regulations.

The most substantial change is the proposed deletion of the existing regulatory provision that defines "waters of the United States" as all other waters such as intrastate lakes, rivers, streams (including intermittent streams), mudflats, sandflats, wetlands, sloughs, prairie potholes, wet meadows, playa lakes, or natural ponds, the use, degradation or destruction of which could affect interstate or foreign commerce including any such waters: Which are or could be used by interstate or foreign travelers for recreational or other purposes; from which fish or shellfish are or could be taken and sold in interstate or foreign commerce; or which are used or could be used for industrial purposes by industries in interstate commerce. . . . Under the proposed rule, these "other waters" (those which do not fit within the proposed categories of waters jurisdictional by rule) would only be jurisdictional upon a case-specific determination that they have a significant nexus as defined by the proposed rule. Waters in a watershed in which there is no connection to a traditional navigable water, interstate water or the territorial seas would not be "waters of the United States." In addition, the proposed rule would for the first time explicitly exclude some features and waters over which the agencies have not generally asserted jurisdiction and in so doing would eliminate the authority of the agencies to determine in case specific circumstances that some such waters are jurisdictional "waters of the United States."

The agencies propose a rule that is clear and understandable and that protects the nation's waters, consistent with the law and currently available scientific and technical expertise. Continuity with the existing regulations, where possible, will reduce confusion and will reduce transaction costs for the regulated community and the agencies. To that same end, the agencies also propose, where consistent with the law and their scientific and technical expertise, categories of waters that are and are not jurisdictional, as well as categories of waters and wetlands that require a case-specific significant nexus evaluation to determine whether they are "waters of the United States" and protected by the CWA. Finally, the agencies propose definitions for some of the terms used in the proposed regulation.

. . .

Under the proposed first section of the regulation, section (a), the agencies propose to define the "waters of the United States" for all sections (including sections 301, 311, 401, 402, 404) of the CWA to mean:

- All waters which are currently used, were used in the past, or may be susceptible to use in interstate or foreign commerce, including all waters which are subject to the ebb and flow of the tide;
- All interstate waters, including interstate wetlands;
- The territorial seas;
- All impoundments of a traditional navigable water, interstate water, the territorial seas or a tributary;

- All tributaries of a traditional navigable water, interstate water, the territorial seas or impoundment;
- All waters, including wetlands, adjacent to a traditional navigable water, interstate water, the territorial seas, impoundment or tributary; and
- On a case-specific basis, other waters, including wetlands, provided that those waters alone, or in combination with other similarly situated waters, including wetlands, located in the same region, have a significant nexus to a traditional navigable water, interstate water or the territorial seas.

As discussed in further detail below, the rule would not change the following provisions of the existing rule (although some provisions have been renumbered): Traditional navigable waters; interstate waters; the territorial seas; and impoundments of "waters of the United States." In paragraph (a)(5) of the proposed rule, the agencies propose that all tributaries as defined in the proposed rule are "waters of the United States." While tributaries are "waters of the United States" under the existing regulation, the rule would for the first time include a regulatory definition of "tributary."

With this proposed rule, the agencies conclude, based on existing science and the law, that a significant nexus exists between tributaries (as defined in the proposed rule) and the traditional navigable waters, interstate waters, and the territorial seas into which they flow; and between adjacent water bodies (as defined in the proposed rule) and traditional navigable waters, interstate waters, and the territorial seas, respectively. Consequently, this rule establishes as "waters of the United States," all tributaries (as defined in the proposal), of the traditional navigable waters, interstate waters, and the territorial seas, as well as all adjacent waters (including wetlands). This will eliminate the need to make a case-specific significant nexus determination for tributaries or for their adjacent waters because it has been determined that as a category, these waters have a significant nexus and thus are "waters of the United States."

In paragraph (a)(6) of the proposed rule, the rule would clarify that adjacent waters, rather than simply adjacent wetlands, are "waters of the United States." The rule would further clarify the meaning of "adjacent" by defining one of its elements, "neighboring." The related terms of "riparian area" and "floodplain" are also defined in the proposed rule.

. . .

The proposed section (b) excludes specified waters and features from the definition of "waters of the United States." Waters and features that are determined to be excluded under section (b) of the proposed rule will not be jurisdictional under any of the categories in the proposed rule under section (a), even if they would otherwise satisfy the regulatory definition. Those waters and features that would not be "waters of the United States" are:

- Waste treatment systems, including treatment ponds or lagoons, designed to meet the requirements of the Clean Water Act.
- Prior converted cropland. Notwithstanding the determination of an area's status as prior converted cropland by any other Federal agency, for the purposes of the Clean Water Act the final authority regarding Clean Water Act jurisdiction remains with EPA.

- Ditches that are excavated wholly in uplands, drain only uplands, and have less than perennial flow.
- Ditches that do not contribute flow, either directly or through another water, to a traditional navigable water, interstate water, the territorial seas or an impoundment of a jurisdictional water.
- The following features:
  - Artificially irrigated areas that would revert to upland should application of irrigation water to that area cease;
  - artificial lakes or ponds created by excavating and/or diking dry land and used exclusively for such purposes as stock watering, irrigation, settling basins, or rice growing;
  - artificial reflecting pools or swimming pools created by excavating and/or diking dry land;
  - small ornamental waters created by excavating and/or diking dry land for primarily aesthetic reasons;
  - water-filled depressions created incidental to construction activity;
  - groundwater, including groundwater drained through subsurface drainage systems; and
  - gullies and rills and non-wetland swales.

The rule does not affect longstanding exemptions in the CWA for farming, silviculture, ranching and other activities, does not change regulatory exclusions for waste treatment systems and prior converted cropland, and does not change the regulatory status of water transfers. Where waters would be determined jurisdictional under the proposed rule, applicable exemptions of the CWA would continue to preclude application of CWA permitting requirements.

. . .

SOURCE: Engineers Corps and the Environmental Protection Agency. 2014. *Proposed Rule: Definition of "Waters of the United States" Under the Clean Water Act.* https:// www.federalregister.gov/articles/2014/04/21/2014-07142/definition-of-waters-of-the-united-states-under-the-clean-water-act (accessed August 27, 2014).

ANALYSIS

The Clean Water Act of 1972 has proven over time to have been among the most influential pieces of environmental legislation ever passed by the U.S. Congress. Unfortunately, as has been pointed out repeatedly by legal scholars, some of the language used in the document was quite ambiguous. Rather than defining key terms, such as what constitutes a "wetland" or what exactly are "the waters of the United States," the members of Congress left it to government agencies, such as the Environmental Protection Agency (EPA) and United States Army Corps of Engineers (USACE), to do the defining. Not surprisingly, these agencies defined the terms quite broadly, thereby expanding their jurisdictional authority. Inevitably, this also led to court cases as others sought to stem what they viewed as an abuse of power by federal authorities.

A watershed moment in the history of the Clean Water Act of 1972 occurred in 2006, when the U.S. Supreme Court ruled on *Rapanos v. United States*. In the case, a developer wanted to build some houses and a shopping center on some wetlands in Michigan and was sued by the federal government because he did not have a permit to build on or adjacent to "navigable waters." Since the wetlands were deemed a navigable waterway, and thus part of the "waters of the United States," the wetlands fell under the auspices of the Clean Water Act. The problem was the definition of "waters of the United States" utilized by the EPA and other federal agencies. To navigate those wetlands, one would have needed to make use of man-made ditches or drains to reach another water source. Those ditches were sometimes dry, thus not always connected to other navigable waters. In short, under the reasoning of the EPA, a puddle could have qualified as a wetland as long as it could have conceivably traveled to a nearby waterway that was navigable, such as a stream or river. In a narrow decision, the Supreme Court justices ruled against the United States, thereby narrowing the definition of navigable waters of the United States. The test mandated by the justices in applying the Clean Water Act was whether government officials could prove a "significant nexus" between a particular body of water and another existed. This was widely seen as a blow to the enforcement of the Clean Water Act. Even if a significant nexus could be proven, compiling the evidence could prove both time-consuming and expensive.

In an effort to once again expand the authority of government agencies to apply the Clean Water Act widely and easily, the EPA and USACE have proposed unambiguous language that would define "waters of the United States" in as broad a fashion as possible. Under the proposed language, just about any collection of water in the country, no matter the size, could conceivably be determined to be a part of the waters of the United States because it could soak into the ground and become part of a groundwater system that might feed an aquifer or flow into a body of water. Whether the EPA and the USACE will be successful in their efforts remains to be seen as this effort is politically quite contentious. While the administration of President Barack Obama and many of its supporters in Congress advocate for this legislation, most Republican Party members in Washington, DC are equally passionate about stopping what they view as government attempts to harm businesses through overregulation. How this conflict evolves will signal whether the federal government is more interested in protecting short-term economic gains versus the long-term health of the environment.

FURTHER READING

Adler, Robert W. 2013. "The Decline and (Possible) Renewal of Aspiration in the Clean Water Act." *Washington Law Review* 88, no. 3: 759–812.

9

WATER HABITATS

"The Most Valuable Food Fishes of the Coast and the Lakes of the United States Are Rapidly Diminishing in Number"

- *Document:* Joint Resolution for the Protection and Preservation of the Food Fishes of the Coast of the United States
- *Date:* February 9, 1871
- *Where:* Washington, DC
- *Significance:* The resolution created the position of commissioner of fish and fisheries.

DOCUMENT

Joint Resolution for the Protection and Preservation of the Food Fishes of the Coast of the United States.

Whereas it is asserted that the most valuable food fishes of the coast and the lakes of the United States are rapidly diminishing in number, to the public injury, and so as materially to affect the interests of trade and commerce: Therefore,

Be it resolved by the Senate and House of Representatives of the United States of America in Congress assembled, That the President be, and he hereby is, authorized and required to appoint, by and with the advice and consent of the Senate, from among the civil officers or employees of the government, one person of proved scientific and practical acquaintance with the fishes of the coast, to be commissioner of fish and fisheries, to serve without additional salary.

SEC. 2. **And be it further resolved,** That it shall be the duty of said commissioner to prosecute investigations and inquiries on the subject, with the view of ascertaining whether any and what diminution in the number of the food fishes of the coast and the lakes of the United States has taken place; and, if so, to what causes the same is due; and also whether any and what protective, prohibitory, or precautionary measures should be adopted in the premises; and to report upon the same to Congress.

SEC. 3. **And be it further resolved,** That the heads of the executive departments be, and they are hereby, directed to cause to be rendered all necessary and practicable aid to the said commissioner in the prosecution of the investigations and inquiries aforesaid.

SEC. 4. **And be it further resolved,** That it shall be lawful for said commissioner to take, or cause to be taken, at all times, in the waters of the sea-coast of the United States, where the tide ebbs and flows, and also in the waters of the lakes, such fish or specimens thereof as may in his judgment, from time to time, be needful or proper for the conduct of his duties as aforesaid, any law, custom, or usage of any State to the contrary notwithstanding.

APPROVED, February 9, 1871.

SOURCE: National Oceanic & Atmospheric Administration. n.d. *Joint Resolution for the Protection and Preservation of the Food Fishes of the Coast of the United States.* http://www.history.noaa.gov/legacy/act3.html (accessed September 14, 2014).

ANALYSIS

The very existence of the *Joint Resolution for the Protection and Preservation of the Food Fishes of the Coast of the United States* is due to the pioneering work of Spencer Fullerton Baird. He was a renowned zoologist who in 1850 became assistant secretary and curator at the Smithsonian Institution. While working at the Smithsonian to build its ichthyology collections, he noted that fisheries were in rapid decline along the ocean coasts around the country. He thus began studies on topics such as the transportation of live fish, hatching of fish eggs, and methods of raising fish in ponds and lakes. In 1871, Baird shared his concerns about the state of the nation's coastal fisheries and possible ways to reverse their declines with members of Congress. His lobbying led to the drafting and passage of the *Joint Resolution for the Protection and Preservation of the Food Fishes of the Coast of the United States*, which created the post of commissioner of fish and fisheries. Not surprisingly, President Ulysses S. Grant tabbed Baird to fill the position. As commissioner of fish and fisheries, a post he held concurrently with his job as an administrator for the Smithsonian Institution, he was responsible for both developing and protecting the economic health of the nation's fisheries. Baird quickly used his clout to put the results of his studies to use, for example, harvesting, fertilizing, and shipping salmon eggs from the West Coast for transplantation on the Atlantic seaboard. The commission that Baird envisioned and got Congress to create became a forbearer of the U.S. Fish and Wildlife Service.

FURTHER READING

Allard, Dean C. 1978. *Spencer Fullerton Baird and the U.S. Fish Commission.* New York: Arno Press.

Cart, Theodore Whaley. 1988. "The Federal Fisheries Service, 1871–1940: Its Origins, Organization, and Accomplishments." *Marine Fisheries Review* 66, no. 4: 1–46.

Guinan, John A., and Ralph E. Curtis. 1971. *A Century of Conservation.* http://www.nefsc.noaa.gov/history/stories/century.html.

Rivinus, Edward F., and E. M. Youssef. 1992. *Spencer Baird of the Smithsonian.* Washington, DC: Smithsonian Institution Press.

"For the Purpose of Recognizing the Vital Contribution of Our Wildlife Resources to the Nation"

- *Document:* Fish and Wildlife Coordination Act of 1934, excerpts
- *Date:* March 10, 1934
- *Where:* Washington, DC
- *Significance:* Passed during the New Deal, the act was designed to protect fish and wildlife whose habitats were threatened by the federal government's construction of large water projects, most notably dams.

DOCUMENT

§ 661. Declaration of purpose; cooperation of agencies; surveys and investigations; donations

For the purpose of recognizing the vital contribution of our wildlife resources to the Nation, the increasing public interest and significance thereof due to expansion of our national economy and other factors, and to provide that wildlife conservation shall receive equal consideration and be coordinated with other features of water-resource development programs through the effectual and harmonious planning, development, maintenance, and coordination of wildlife conservation and rehabilitation for the purposes of sections 661 to 666c of this title in the United States, its Territories and possessions, the Secretary of the Interior is authorized (1) to provide assistance to, and cooperate with, Federal, State, and public or private agencies and organizations in the development, protection, rearing, and stocking of all species of wildlife, resources thereof, and their habitat, in controlling losses of the same from disease or other causes, in minimizing damages from overabundant species, in providing public shooting and fishing areas, including easements across public lands for access thereto, and in carrying out other measures necessary to effectuate the purposes of said sections; (2) to make surveys and investigations of the wildlife of the public domain, including lands and waters or interests therein acquired or controlled by any agency of the United States; and (3) to accept donations of land and contributions of funds in furtherance of the purposes of said sections.

§ 662. Impounding, diverting, or controlling of waters
(a) Consultations between agencies

Except as hereafter stated in subsection (h) of this section, whenever the waters of any stream or other body of water are proposed or authorized to be impounded, diverted, the channel deepened, or the stream or other body of water otherwise controlled or modified for any purpose whatever, including navigation and drainage, by any department or agency of the United States, or by any public or private agency under Federal permit or license, such department or agency first shall consult with the United States Fish and Wildlife Service, Department of the Interior, and with the head of the agency exercising administration over the wildlife resources of the particular State wherein the impoundment, diversion, or other control facility is to be constructed, with a view to the conservation of wildlife resources by preventing loss of and damage to such resources as well as providing for the development and improvement thereof in connection with such water-resource development.

(b) Reports and recommendations; consideration

In furtherance of such purposes, the reports and recommendations of the Secretary of the Interior on the wildlife aspects of such projects, and any report of the head of the State agency exercising administration over the wildlife resources of the State, based on surveys and investigations conducted by the United States Fish and Wildlife Service and such State agency for the purpose of determining the possible damage to wildlife resources and for the purpose of determining means and measures that should be adopted to prevent the loss of or damage to such wildlife resources, as well as to provide concurrently for the development and improvement of such resources, shall be made an integral part of any report prepared or submitted by any agency of the Federal Government responsible for engineering surveys and construction of such projects when such reports are presented to the Congress or to any agency or person having the authority or the power, by administrative action or otherwise, (1) to authorize the construction of water-resource development projects or (2) to approve a report on the modification or supplementation of plans for previously authorized projects, to which sections 661 to 666c of this title apply. Recommendations of the Secretary of the Interior shall be as specific as is practicable with respect to features recommended for wildlife conservation and development, lands to be utilized or acquired for such purposes, the results expected, and shall describe the damage to wildlife attributable to the project and the measures proposed for mitigating or compensating for these damages. The reporting officers in project reports of the Federal agencies shall give full consideration to the report and recommendations of the Secretary of the Interior and to any report of the State agency on the wildlife aspects of such projects, and the project plan shall include such justifiable means and measures for wildlife purposes as the reporting agency finds should be adopted to obtain maximum overall project benefits.

. . .

(f) Estimation of wildlife benefits or losses

In addition to other requirements, there shall be included in any report submitted to Congress supporting a recommendation for authorization of any new project for the control or use of water as described herein (including any new division of such project or new supplemental works on such project) an estimation of the wildlife benefits or losses to be derived therefrom including benefits to be derived from measures recommended specifically for the development and improvement of wildlife resources, the cost of providing wildlife benefits (including the cost of additional facilities to be installed or lands to be acquired specifically for that particular phase of wildlife conservation relating to the development and improvement of wildlife), the part of the cost of joint-use facilities allocated to wildlife, and the part of such costs, if any, to be reimbursed by non-Federal interests.

. . .

§ 663. Impoundment or diversion of waters

(a) Conservation, maintenance, and management of wildlife resources; development and improvement

Subject to the exceptions prescribed in section 662(h) of this title, whenever the waters of any stream or other body of water are impounded, diverted, the channel deepened, or the stream or other body of water otherwise controlled or modified for any purpose whatever, including navigation and drainage, by any department or agency of the United States, adequate provision, consistent with the primary purposes of such impoundment, diversion, or other control, shall be made for the use thereof, together with any areas of land, water, or interests therein, acquired or administered by a Federal agency in connection therewith, for the conservation, maintenance, and management of wildlife resources thereof, and its habitat thereon, including the development and improvement of such wildlife resources pursuant to the provisions of section 662 of this title.

(b) Use and availability of waters, land, or interests therein

The use of such waters, land, or interests therein for wildlife conservation purposes shall be in accordance with general plans approved jointly (1) by the head of the particular department or agency exercising primary administration in each instance, (2) by the Secretary of the Interior, and (3) by the head of the agency exercising the administration of the wildlife resources of the particular State wherein the waters and areas lie. Such waters and other interests shall be made available, without cost for administration, by such State agency, if the management of the properties relate to the conservation of wildlife other than migratory birds, or by the Secretary of the Interior, for administration in such manner as he may deem advisable, where the particular properties have value in carrying out the national migratory bird management program: Provided, That nothing in this section shall be construed as affecting the authority of the Secretary of Agriculture to cooperate with the States or in making lands available to the States with respect to the management of wildlife and wildlife habitat on lands administered by him.

(c) Acquisition of land, waters, and interests therein; report to Congress

When consistent with the purposes of sections 661 to 666c of this title and the reports and findings of the Secretary of the Interior prepared in accordance with section 662 of this title, land, waters, and interests therein may be acquired by Federal construction agencies for the wildlife conservation and development purposes of sections 661 to 666c of this title in connection with a project as reasonably needed to preserve and assure for the public benefit the wildlife potentials of the particular project area: Provided, That before properties are acquired for this purpose, the probable extent of such acquisition shall be set forth, along with other data necessary for project authorization, in a report submitted to the Congress, or in the case of a project previously authorized, no such properties shall be acquired unless specifically authorized by Congress, if specific authority for such acquisition is recommended by the construction agency.

. . .

(f) National forest lands

Any lands acquired pursuant to this section by any Federal agency within the exterior boundaries of a national forest shall, upon acquisition, be added to and become national forest lands, and shall be administered as a part of the forest within which they are situated, subject to all laws applicable to lands acquired under the provisions of the Act of March 1, 1911 (36 Stat. 961), unless such lands are acquired to carry out the National Migratory Bird Management Program.

. . .

§ 666c. Applicability to Tennessee Valley Authority

The provisions of sections 661 to 666c of this title shall not apply to the Tennessee Valley Authority.

SOURCE: U.S. Bureau of Reclamation. n.d. *Fish and Wildlife Coordination Act*. http://www.usbr.gov/power/legislation/fwca.pdf (accessed August 29, 2014).

ANALYSIS

Passed as part of the New Deal, the Fish and Wildlife Coordination Act (FWCA) of 1934 was intended to protect the habitats of fish and wildlife that were threatened by the federal government's construction of numerous water projects, including dams such as Grand Coulee Dam and Hoover Dam. In theory, it represented an acknowledgment by the federal government that the massive projects undertaken during the New Deal to put unemployed people to work posed significant threats to the environment, and thus it needed to create protections to ensure that the short-term projects did not permanently hurt fish and wildlife. In practice, the federal government put far more importance on the employment benefits of the projects than the potential threats to the environment. The most egregious example of their priorities concerned the Tennessee Valley Authority (TVA).

One of the most curious aspects of the act was that it exempted the TVA from its terms. The government agency had been created just the year before and marked the most ambitious regional economic development program ever undertaken by the federal government. It included the creation of nearly 50 dams and associated reservoirs. Through the TVA, the federal government totally remade significant portions of the Tennessee River Valley and thus had extreme impacts on hundreds of thousands of acres of land utilized by fish and wildlife. A notable exemplar of the impact occurred during the construction process of the Tellico Dam. The filling of the dam's reservoir promised to destroy the habitat of the snail darter, a type of perch that lived nowhere else. To protect the endangered fish, environmentalists turned to the courts of the United States. The U.S. Supreme Court ultimately resolved the debate through the landmark 1978 case *Tennessee Valley Authority v. Hill*. The fact that it took the involvement of the U.S. Supreme Court to save the snail darter demonstrated how shortsighted it was to release the TVA from the obligations of the FWCA.

FURTHER READING

Plater, Zygmunt J. B. 2013. *The Snail Darter and the Dam: How Pork-Barrel Politics Endangered a Little Fish and Killed a River*. New Haven, CT: Yale University Press.

Veiluva, Michael. 1980. "The Fish and Wildlife Coordination Act in Environmental Legislation." *Ecology Law Quarterly* 9, no. 1: 489–517.

Wheeler, William Bruce, and Michael J. McDonald. 1986. *TVA and the Tellico Dam, 1936–1979: A Bureaucratic Crisis in Post-Industrial America*. Knoxville: University of Tennessee Press.

"For the Benefit and Enjoyment of Present and Future Generations"

- *Document:* Wild and Scenic Rivers Act of 1968, excerpt
- *Date:* October 2, 1968
- *Where:* Washington, DC
- *Significance:* The act marked a major change in national water policy because it created a program to keep all or part of rivers with cultural, natural, or recreational benefits in their original free-flowing state.

DOCUMENT

Wild & Scenic Rivers Act

An Act

To provide for a National Wild and Scenic Rivers System, and for other purposes.

Be it enacted by the Senate and House of Representatives of the United States of America in Congress assembled, that

SECTION 1.

(a) This Act may be cited as the "Wild and Scenic Rivers Act."

(b) It is hereby declared to be the policy of the United States that certain selected rivers of the Nation which, with their immediate environments, possess outstandingly remarkable scenic, recreational, geologic, fish and wildlife, historic, cultural, or other similar values, shall be preserved in free-flowing condition, and that they and their immediate environments shall be protected for the benefit and enjoyment of present and future generations. The Congress declares that the established national policy of dam and other construction at appropriate sections of the rivers of the United States needs to be complemented by a policy that would preserve other selected rivers or sections thereof in their free-flowing condition to protect the water quality of such rivers and to fulfill other vital national conservation purposes.

(c) The purpose of this Act is to implement this policy by instituting a national wild and scenic rivers system, by designating the initial components of that system, and by prescribing the methods by which and standards according to which additional components may be added to the system from time to time.

SECTION 2.

(a) The national wild and scenic rivers system shall comprise rivers

(i) that are authorized for inclusion therein by Act of Congress, or

(ii) that are designated as wild, scenic or recreational rivers by or pursuant to an act of the legislature of the State or States through which they flow, that are to be permanently administered as wild, scenic or recreational rivers by an agency or political subdivision of the State or States concerned, that are found by the Secretary of the Interior, upon application of the Governor of the State or the Governors of the States concerned, or a person or persons thereunto duly appointed by him or them, to meet the criteria established in this Act and such criteria supplementary thereto as he may prescribe, and that are approved by him for inclusion in the system, including, upon application of the Governor of the State concerned, the Allagash Wilderness Waterway, Maine; that segment of the Wolf River, Wisconsin, which flows through Langlade County and that segment of the New River in North Carolina extending from its confluence with Dog Creek downstream approximately 26.5 miles to the Virginia State line.

Upon receipt of an application under clause (ii) of this subsection, the Secretary shall notify the Federal Energy Regulatory Commission and publish such application in the Federal Register. Each river designated under clause (ii) shall be administered by the State or political subdivision thereof without expense to the United States other than for administration and management of federally owned lands. For purposes of the preceding sentence, amounts made available to any State or political subdivision under the Land and Water Conservation [Fund] Act of 1965 or any other provision of law shall not be treated as an expense to the United States. Nothing in this subsection shall be construed to provide for the transfer to, or administration by, a State or local authority of any federally owned lands which are within the boundaries of any river included within the system under clause (ii).

(b) A wild, scenic or recreational river area eligible to be included in the system is a free-flowing stream and the related adjacent land area that possesses one or more of the values referred to in Section 1, subsection (b) of this Act. Every wild, scenic or recreational river in its free-flowing condition, or upon restoration to this condition, shall be considered eligible for inclusion in the national wild and scenic rivers system and, if included, shall be classified, designated, and administered as one of the following:

(1) Wild river areas—Those rivers or sections of rivers that are free of impoundments and generally inaccessible except by trail, with watersheds or shorelines essentially primitive and waters unpolluted. These represent vestiges of primitive America.

(2) Scenic river areas—Those rivers or sections of rivers that are free of impoundments, with shorelines or watersheds still largely primitive and shorelines largely undeveloped, but accessible in places by roads.

(3) Recreational river areas—Those rivers or sections of rivers that are readily accessible by road or railroad, that may have some development along their shorelines, and that may have undergone some impoundment or diversion in the past.

SOURCE: U.S. Congress. n.d. *Wild and Scenic Rivers Act.* http://www.ferc.gov/legal/fed-sta/ wsr-act.pdf (accessed August 29, 2014).

ANALYSIS

Since the founding of the United States, entrepreneurs and politicians have sought ways to utilize waterways for economic purposes. Early examples included the construction of the Erie Canal to connect Lake Erie and the Hudson River and the establishment of water-powered mills in Lowell, Massachusetts. Over the centuries, the scale of the projects increased to include the massive hydroelectric dams constructed in the twentieth century by the Bureau of Reclamation and the U.S. Army Corps of Engineers. By the 1950s, most of the nation's waterways had been put to use for hydroelectric power generation, irrigation, or other economic use. This troubled a number of conservationists, who began lobbying politicians to preserve what few rivers still flowed in their "wild" state. Their efforts began to bear fruit in 1965 with the creation of the federal Water Resources Council. The council was charged with balancing the benefits of water development with preservation needs. While the council's existence demonstrated progress, it was not powerful enough to protect rivers adequately from other federal organizations, most notably the U.S. Department of the Interior's Bureau of Reclamation and the U.S Corps of Engineers, who had benefited greatly from water infrastructure construction projects for decades. The desires of those federal agencies were not effectively curbed until the signing of the Wild and Scenic Rivers Act by President Lyndon Baines Johnson on October 2, 1968. The act marked a sea change in federal policy as it was acknowledged that, in some cases, rivers were more valuable to the country in their natural free-flowing state than they were if "improved."

The Wild and Scenic Rivers Act was designed to protect three types of rivers, which were designated "wild," "scenic," or "recreational." Wild rivers are defined as being located in remote areas that are generally inaccessible to people using motorized vehicles. These are rivers that have not been improved in any fashion and are generally free of development along their respective shorelines and watersheds. Scenic rivers, or parts of rivers designated as scenic, are rivers that flow freely but have suffered from some form of development on its shorelines or within their respective watersheds. One example of the development in their watersheds is the presence of roads that make them more accessible for the public to enjoy their scenic beauty. Recreational rivers tend to have a history of development, including impoundments or diversions of their waters. Many of these rivers have developed shorelines, and all are easily accessible by automobile. Despite the many alterations that they have suffered, all recreational rivers have features that are deemed worth protecting. Inclusion in the national wild and scenic rivers system protects the respective rivers from the construction of water projects that require licenses from the Federal Energy Regulatory Commission. The rivers are also protected from any sort of development that could potentially threaten the river's state in the future.

There are several ways that a river, or part thereof, can become a part of the national wild and scenic rivers system. Most of the rivers in the network were put there through legislation passed through the U.S. Congress. The secretary of the interior also has the authority to designate rivers but normally does so after receiving suggestions from the state where the waterway is located. If the state makes the recommendation to add a river, or part of one, it also assumes the responsibility for managing it into the future. If Congress adds the waterway to the system, then the river will most likely be managed by the Bureau of Land Management, National Park Service, U.S. Fish and Wildlife Service, or U.S. Forest Service.

In 1968, the wild and scenic rivers system consisted of 12 rivers. According to the national wild and scenic rivers system, as of September 2012, 203 rivers are part of the system. Together, they represent 12,602.1 miles of protected rivers. Of that amount, wild rivers comprise 6,167.7 miles, scenic rivers 2,722.1, and recreational rivers 3,712.3. Although at first glance the mileage appears impressive, it represents less than 0.5 percent of the nation's rivers.

FURTHER READING

Lowry, William R. 2003. *Dam Politics: Restoring America's Rivers.* Washington, DC: Georgetown University Press.

National Wild and Scenic Rivers System. 2007. "National Wild and Scenic Rivers System." http://www.rivers.gov.

Palmer, Tim. 2004. *Endangered Rivers and the Conservation Movement.* 2nd ed. Lanham, MD: Rowman & Littlefield.

"To Establish a National Policy for the Environment"

- *Document:* National Environmental Policy Act of 1969, as Amended, excerpt
- *Date:* January 1, 1970
- *Where:* Washington, DC
- *Significance:* The act made it the policy of the federal government to consider the potential environmental impacts of a project and how they might be remediated before receipt of final approval for construction.

DOCUMENT

The National Environmental Policy Act of 1969, as amended

An Act to establish a national policy for the environment, to provide for the establishment of a Council on Environmental Quality, and for other purposes.

Be it enacted by the Senate and House of Representatives of the United States of America in Congress assembled, That this Act may be cited as the "National Environmental Policy Act of 1969."

Purpose

Sec. 2 [42 USC § 4321]. The purposes of this Act are: To declare a national policy which will encourage productive and enjoyable harmony between man and his environment; to promote efforts which will prevent or eliminate damage to the environment and biosphere and stimulate the health and welfare of man; to enrich the understanding of the ecological systems and natural resources important to the Nation; and to establish a Council on Environmental Quality.

TITLE I

CONGRESSIONAL DECLARATION OF NATIONAL ENVIRONMENTAL POLICY

Sec. 101 [42 USC § 4331].

(a) The Congress, recognizing the profound impact of man's activity on the interrelations of all components of the natural environment, particularly the profound influences of population growth, high-density urbanization, industrial expansion, resource exploitation, and new and expanding technological advances and recognizing further the critical importance of restoring and maintaining environmental quality to the overall welfare and development of man, declares that it is the continuing policy of the Federal Government, in cooperation with State and local governments, and other concerned public and private organizations, to use all practicable means and measures, including financial and technical assistance, in a manner calculated to foster and promote the general welfare, to create and maintain conditions under which man and nature can exist in productive harmony, and fulfill the social, economic, and other requirements of present and future generations of Americans.

(b) In order to carry out the policy set forth in this Act, it is the continuing responsibility of the Federal Government to use all practicable means, consist with other essential considerations of national policy, to improve and coordinate Federal plans, functions, programs, and resources to the end that the Nation may—

1. fulfill the responsibilities of each generation as trustee of the environment for succeeding generations;

2. assure for all Americans safe, healthful, productive, and aesthetically and culturally pleasing surroundings;

3. attain the widest range of beneficial uses of the environment without degradation, risk to health or safety, or other undesirable and unintended consequences;

4. preserve important historic, cultural, and natural aspects of our national heritage, and maintain, wherever possible, an environment which supports diversity, and variety of individual choice;

5. achieve a balance between population and resource use which will permit high standards of living and a wide sharing of life's amenities; and

6. enhance the quality of renewable resources and approach the maximum attainable recycling of depletable resources.

(c) The Congress recognizes that each person should enjoy a healthful environment and that each person has a responsibility to contribute to the preservation and enhancement of the environment.

Sec. 102 [42 USC § 4332]. The Congress authorizes and directs that, to the fullest extent possible: (1) the policies, regulations, and public laws of the United States shall be interpreted and administered in accordance with the policies set forth in this Act, and (2) all agencies of the Federal Government shall—

(A) utilize a systematic, interdisciplinary approach which will insure the integrated use of the natural and social sciences and the environmental design arts in planning and in decision making which may have an impact on man's environment;

(B) identify and develop methods and procedures, in consultation with the Council on Environmental Quality established by title II of this Act, which will insure that presently unquantified environmental amenities and values may be given appropriate consideration in decision making along with economic and technical considerations;

(C) include in every recommendation or report on proposals for legislation and other major Federal actions significantly affecting the quality of the human environment, a detailed statement by the responsible official on—

(i) the environmental impact of the proposed action,

(ii) any adverse environmental effects which cannot be avoided should the proposal be implemented,

(iii) alternatives to the proposed action,

(iv) the relationship between local short-term uses of man's environment and the maintenance and enhancement of long-term productivity, and

(v) any irreversible and irretrievable commitments of resources which would be involved in the proposed action should it be implemented.

Prior to making any detailed statement, the responsible Federal official shall consult with and obtain the comments of any Federal agency which has jurisdiction by law or special expertise with respect to any environmental impact involved. Copies of such statement and the comments and views of the appropriate Federal, State, and local agencies, which are authorized to develop and enforce environmental standards, shall be made available to the President, the Council on Environmental Quality and to the public as provided by section 552 of title 5, United States Code, and shall accompany the proposal through the existing agency review processes;

(D) Any detailed statement required under subparagraph (C) after January 1, 1970, for any major Federal action funded under a program of grants to States shall not be deemed to be legally insufficient solely by reason of having been prepared by a State agency or official, if:

(i) the State agency or official has statewide jurisdiction and has the responsibility for such action,

(ii) the responsible Federal official furnishes guidance and participates in such preparation,

(iii) the responsible Federal official independently evaluates such statement prior to its approval and adoption, and

(iv) after January 1, 1976, the responsible Federal official provides early notification to, and solicits the views of, any other State or any Federal land management entity of any action or any alternative thereto which may have significant impacts upon such State or affected Federal land management entity and, if there is any disagreement on such impacts, prepares a written assessment of such impacts and views for incorporation into such detailed statement.

The procedures in this subparagraph shall not relieve the Federal official of his responsibilities for the scope, objectivity, and content of the entire statement or of any other responsibility under this Act; and further, this subparagraph does not affect the legal sufficiency of statements prepared by State agencies with less than statewide jurisdiction.

(E) study, develop, and describe appropriate alternatives to recommended courses of action in any proposal which involves unresolved conflicts concerning alternative uses of available resources;

(F) recognize the worldwide and long-range character of environmental problems and, where consistent with the foreign policy of the United States, lend appropriate support to initiatives, resolutions, and programs designed to maximize international cooperation in anticipating and preventing a decline in the quality of mankind's world environment;

(G) make available to States, counties, municipalities, institutions, and individuals, advice and information useful in restoring, maintaining, and enhancing the quality of the environment;

(H) initiate and utilize ecological information in the planning and development of resource-oriented projects; and

(I) assist the Council on Environmental Quality established by title II of this Act.

SOURCE: U.S. Congress. n.d. *The National Environmental Policy Act of 1969, as Amended.* http://energy.gov/sites/prod/files/nepapub/nepa_documents/RedDont/Req-NEPA.pdf (accessed August 29, 2014).

ANALYSIS

When President Richard M. Nixon signed the National Environmental Policy Act (NEPA) of 1969 , it marked the conclusion of more than a decade of wrangling over the federal government's role in protecting the environment. The legislative history can be traced to Senator James Murray's unsuccessful attempt in 1959 to get the Resources and Conservation Act passed. Over the years, other senators, including George McGovern, attempted to usher similar legislation through Congress to no avail. The failure of the various bills was not the result of partisan politics, as both the Eisenhower and Kennedy administrations actively lobbied against the various forms of the environmental legislation.

In 1969, the political climate changed as proponents of environmental legislation controlled not only Congress but the presidency. The Senate version of NEPA was introduced by Washington Senator Henry Jackson, who quickly shepherded it through the body. The effort to advance similar legislation in the House of Representatives was far more acrimonious. Although the House eventually passed a version of the bill originally introduced by Michigan's John Dingell, it was the Senate version that made up the majority of the conference committee's NEPA bill.

NEPA made it the policy of the federal government to consider the potential environmental impacts of any projects undertaken by a federal agency. If a threat to the environment was identified, environmental impact statements were required to determine how the impacts could be remediated. If harm to the environment was inevitable, the policy created the likelihood that the project in question would be abandoned. Through NEPA, the federal government clearly signaled that the protection and enhancement of the environment outweighed other concerns because humans needed a healthy ecosystem to thrive.

Title I of NEPA has two major components. First, it explains the need for prioritizing environmental concerns over projects that some deemed "progress." It also mandated the use of environmental impact statements to weigh the benefits of projects versus environmental harm. The environmental impact statements required the scientific studies to meet certain uniform standards, thus ensuring the legitimacy of the conclusions. These statements proved a serious obstacle for federal entities such as the Bureau of Reclamation and the U.S. Army Corps of Engineers, who had been accustomed for years to just build dams and related structures with no limitations on their work. Suddenly, every step of the construction process was being evaluated with respect to the needs of the environment. Conducting the studies and finding ways to address issues that emerged was not only time-consuming but also added immensely to the costs of construction. More importantly, if the environmental impact statements favored the needs of the environment, the project was canceled. This was extremely problematic to not only the federal agencies but also congressmen who had become accustomed to favoring large construction projects in their districts because they employed many people and thus aided the local economy. This reality meant that the well-intentioned legislation was soon being amended in Congress at the expense of environmental protection.

Title II of NEPA, which created the Council of Environmental Quality (CEQ), likewise became a target for opponents of environmental legislation. President Ronald Reagan unsuccessfully made repeated attempts to abolish the CEQ, arguing that it was a detriment to business growth. Likewise, President William Clinton tried to abolish the CEQ, although his motives for doing so were noble. He wanted to replace the council with a presidential advisor focused singularly on environmental issues.

Despite its critics, NEPA remains a vital tool for protecting the environment for the use of future generations. This is largely due to the continuing requirement to conduct environmental impact statements, which bring public scrutiny to environmental issues that would otherwise be ignored.

FURTHER READING

Caldwell, Lynton Keith. 1998. *The National Environmental Policy Act: An Agenda for the Future*. Bloomington: Indiana University Press.

Clark, Ray, and Larry W. Canter, eds. 1997. *Environmental Politics and NEPA: Past, Present, and Future*. Boca Raton, FL: St. Lucie Press.

Flippen, J. Brooks. 2000. *Nixon and the Environment*. Albuquerque: University of New Mexico Press.

Lindstrom, Matthew J. 2001. *The National Environmental Policy Act: Judicial Misconstruction, Legislative Indifference, & Executive Neglect*. College Station: Texas A&M University Press.

"Man Has Caused Changes in the Environment"

- *Document:* Environmental Quality Improvement Act of 1970, excerpt
- *Date:* April 3, 1970
- *Where:* Washington, DC
- *Significance:* The act was a companion piece of legislation to the National Environmental Policy Act of 1969.

DOCUMENT

THE ENVIRONMENTAL QUALITY IMPROVEMENT ACT OF 1970
SHORT TITLE

This title may be cited as the "Environmental Quality Improvement Act of 1970"

Sec. 4371. Congressional findings, declarations, and purposes

(a) The Congress finds—

(1) that man has caused changes in the environment;

(2) that many of these changes may affect the relationship between man and his environment; and

(3) that population increases and urban concentration contribute directly to pollution and the degradation of our environment.

(b)(1)The Congress declares that there is a national policy for the environment which provides for the enhancement of environmental quality. This policy is evidenced by statutes heretofore enacted relating to the prevention, abatement, and control of environmental pollution, water and land resources, transportation, and economic and regional development.

(2)The primary responsibility for implementing this policy rests with State and local government.

(3)The Federal Government encourages and supports implementation of this policy through appropriate regional organizations established under existing law.

(c)The purposes of this chapter are—

(1) to assure that each Federal department and agency conducting or supporting public works activities which affect the environment shall implement the policies established under existing law; and

(2) to authorize an Office of Environmental Quality, which, notwithstanding any other provision of law, shall provide the professional and administrative staff for the Council on Environmental Quality established by Public Law 91-190.

Sec. 4372. Office of Environmental Quality

(a) *Establishment; Director; Deputy Director*—There is established in the Executive Office of the President an office to be known as the Office of Environmental Quality (hereafter in this chapter referred to as the "Office"). The Chairman of the Council on Environmental Quality established by Public Law 91-190 shall be the Director of the Office. There shall be in the Office a Deputy Director who shall be appointed by the President, by and with the advice and consent of the Senate.

(b) *Compensation of Deputy Director*—The compensation of the Deputy Director shall be fixed by the President at a rate not in excess of the annual rate of compensation payable to the Deputy Director of the Office of Management and Budget.

(c) *Employment of personnel, experts, and consultants; compensation*—The Director is authorized to employ such officers and employees (including experts and consultants) as may be necessary to enable the Office to carry out its functions under this chapter and Public Law 91-190, except that he may employ no more than ten specialists and other experts without regard to the provisions of title 5, governing appointments in the competitive service, and pay such specialists and experts without regard to the provisions of chapter 51 and subchapter III of chapter 53 of such title relating to classification and General Schedule pay rates, but no such specialist or expert shall be paid at a rate in excess of the maximum rate for GS-18 of the General Schedule under section 5332 of title 5.

(d) *Duties and functions of Director*—In carrying out his functions the Director shall assist and advise the President on policies and programs of the Federal Government affecting environmental quality by—

(1) providing the professional and administrative staff and support for the Council on Environmental Quality established by Public Law 91-190.

(2) assisting the Federal agencies and departments in appraising the effectiveness of existing and proposed facilities, programs, policies, and activities of the Federal Government, and those specific major projects designated by the President which do not require

individual project authorization by Congress, which affect environmental quality;

(3) reviewing the adequacy of existing systems for monitoring and predicting environmental changes in order to achieve effective coverage and efficient use of research facilities and other resources;

(4) promoting the advancement of scientific knowledge of the effects of actions and technology on the environment and encourage the development of the means to prevent or reduce adverse effects that endanger the health and well-being of man;

(5) assisting in coordinating among the Federal departments and agencies those programs and activities which affect, protect, and improve environmental quality;

(6) assisting the Federal departments and agencies in the development and interrelationship of environmental quality criteria and standards established through the Federal Government;

(7) collecting, collating, analyzing, and interpreting data and information on environmental quality, ecological research, and evaluation.

(e) **Authority of Director to contract**—The Director is authorized to contract with public or private agencies, institutions, and organizations and with individuals without regard to section 3324(a) and (b) of title 31 and section 5 of title 41 in carrying out his functions

SOURCE: U.S. Congress. n.d. *The Environmental Quality Improvement Act of 1970.* http://energy.gov/sites/prod/files/nepapub/nepa_documents/RedDont/Req-Envt_Qual_Impr_Act.pdf (accessed August 29, 2014).

ANALYSIS

The Environmental Quality Improvement Act (EQIA) of 1970 was a companion piece of legislation to the National Environmental Policy Act (NEPA) of 1969. The EQIA provided the professional staffing, in the form of the Office of Environmental Quality (OEQ), for the Council on Environmental Quality (CEQ), which was created as part of NEPA. The chairman of the CEQ was charged with heading the OEQ. That was not the only change from the original job description for the position that was offered in NEPA. The scope of the person's advisory responsibilities to the president was detailed in the EQIA. The OEQ was made a part of the executive office of the president. This positioning was intended to assist in the CEQ's goal of coordinating the adherence to federal environmental policies by all federal entities.

President Richard Nixon had high hopes for the CEQ, as he intended for the office to support the work of the newly created Environmental Policy Agency. Under Nixon the CEQ was extremely influential, as it helped empower the federal agencies that Nixon created to address environmental issues. The CEQ also published an annual report that not only highlighted its work and that of related agencies but also identified problems needing to be addressed. The report was published until 1997, when opponents of environmental legislation were able to have it defunded through the Federal Reports Elimination and Sunset Act.

The influence of the CEQ has varied depending on who occupied the presidency. The CEQ was very influential under Presidents Nixon, Jimmy Carter, and Barack Obama. In administrations that favored rolling-back environmental legislation, such as Presidents Ronald Reagan, George H. W. Bush, and George W. Bush, the CEQ was largely ignored. Regardless of how much influence the CEQ has on the respective presidents, it continues to help chart the future of federal policies regarding the environment.

FURTHER READING

Flippen, J. Brooks. 2000. *Nixon and the Environment.* Albuquerque: University of New Mexico Press.

Lindstrom, Matthew J. 2001. *The National Environmental Policy Act: Judicial Misconstruction, Legislative Indifference, & Executive Neglect.* College Station: Texas A&M University Press.

The White House. n.d. "Council on Environmental Quality." http://www.whitehouse.gov/administration/eop/ceq.

"It Is the Policy of the United States to Regulate the Dumping of All Types of Materials into Ocean Waters"

- *Document:* Marine Protection, Research, and Sanctuaries Act of 1972, excerpts
- *Date:* October 23, 1972
- *Where:* Washington, DC
- *Significance:* The act was designed to reduce the dumping of garbage and other forms of waste into the ocean.

DOCUMENT

An Act

To regulate the transportation for dumping, and the dumping, of material into ocean waters, and for other purposes.

Be it enacted by the Senate and House of Representatives of the United States of America in Congress assembled That this Act may be cited as the "Marine Protection, Research, and Sanctuaries Act of 1972".

FINDING, POLICY, AND PURPOSE

SEC. 2. (a) Unregulated dumping of material into ocean waters endangers human health, welfare, and amenities, and the marine environment, ecological systems, and economic potentialities.

(b) The Congress declares that it is the policy of the United States to regulate the dumping of all types of materials into ocean waters and to prevent or strictly limit the dumping into ocean waters of any material which would adversely affect human health, welfare, or amenities, or the marine environment, ecological systems, or economic potentialities.

To this end, it is the purpose of this Act to regulate the transportation of material from the United States for dumping into ocean waters, and the dumping of material, transported from outside the United States, if the dumping occurs in ocean waters over which the United States has jurisdiction or over which it may exercise control, under accepted principles of international law, in order to protect its territory or territorial sea.

. . .

TITLE I—OCEAN DUMPING
PROHIBITED ACTS

SEC. 101. (a) No person shall transport from the United States any radiological, chemical, or biological warfare agent or any high-level radioactive waste, or except as may be authorized in a permit issued under this title, and subject to regulations issued under section 108 hereof by the Secretary of the Department in which the Coast Guard is operating, any other material for the purpose of dumping it into ocean waters.

(b) No person shall dump any radiological, chemical, or biological warfare agent or any high-level radioactive waste, or, except as may be authorized in a permit issued under this title, any other material, transported from any location outside the United States, (1) into the territorial sea of the United States, or (2) into a zone contiguous to the territorial sea of the United States, extending to a line twelve nautical miles seaward from the base line from which the breadth of the territorial sea is measured, to the extent that it may affect the territorial sea or the territory of the United States.

(c) No officer, employee, agent, department, agency, or instrumentality of the United States shall transport from any location outside the United States any radiological, chemical, or biological warfare agent or any high-level radioactive waste, or, except as may be authorized in a permit issued under this title, any other material for the purpose of dumping it into ocean waters.

. . .

TITLE II—COMPREHENSIVE RESEARCH ON OCEAN DUMPING

SEC. 201. The Secretary of Commerce, in coordination with the Secretary of the Department in which the Coast Guard is operating and with the Administrator shall, within six months of the enactment of this Act, initiate a comprehensive and continuing program of monitoring and research regarding the effects of the dumping of material into ocean waters or other coastal waters where the tide ebbs and flows or into the Great Lakes or their connecting waters and shall report from time to time, not less frequently than annually, his findings (including an evaluation of the short-term ecological effects and the social and economic factors involved) to the Congress.

SEC. 202. (a) The Secretary of Commerce, in consultation with other appropriate Federal departments, agencies, and instrumentalities shall, within six months of the enactment of this Act, initiate a comprehensive and continuing program of research with respect to the possible long-range effects of pollution, overfishing, and man-induced changes of ocean ecosystems. In carrying out such research, the Secretary of Commerce shall take into account such factors as existing and proposed international policies affecting oceanic problems, economic considerations involved in both the protection and the use of the oceans, possible alternatives to existing programs, and ways in which the health of the oceans may best be preserved for the benefit of succeeding generations of mankind.

. . .

TITLE III—MARINE SANCTUARIES

SEC. 301. Notwithstanding the provisions of subsection (h) of section 3 of this Act, the term "Secretary", when used in this title, means Secretary of Commerce.

SEC. 302. (a) The Secretary, after consultation with the Secretaries of State, Defense, the Interior, and Transportation, the Administrator, and the heads of other interested Federal agencies, and with the approval of the President, may designate as marine sanctuaries those areas of the ocean waters, as far seaward as the outer edge of the Continental Shelf, as defined in the Convention of the Continental Shelf (15 U.S.T. 74; TIAS 5578), of other coastal waters where the tide ebbs and flows, or of the Great Lakes and their connecting waters, which he determines necessary for the purpose of preserving or restoring such areas for their conservation, recreational, ecological, or esthetic values. The consultation shall include an opportunity to review and comment on a specific proposed designation.

(b) Prior to designating a marine sanctuary which includes waters lying within the territorial limits of any State or superjacent to the subsoil and seabed within the seaward boundary of a coastal State, as that boundary is defined in section 2 of title I of the Act of May 22, 1953 (67 Stat. 29), the Secretary shall consult with, and give due consideration to the views of, the responsible officials of the State involved. As to such waters, a designation under this section shall become effective sixty days after it is published, unless the Governor of any State involved shall, before the expiration of the sixty-day period, certify to the Secretary that the designation, or a specified portion thereof, is unacceptable to his State, in which case the designated sanctuary shall not include the area certified as unacceptable until such time as the Governor withdraws his certification of unacceptability.

(c) When a marine sanctuary is designated, pursuant to this section, which includes an area of ocean waters outside the territorial jurisdiction of the United States, the Secretary of State shall take such actions as may be appropriate to enter into negotiations with other Governments for the purpose of arriving at necessary agreements with those Governments, in order to protect such sanctuary and to promote the purposes for which it was established.

(d) The Secretary shall submit an annual report to the Congress, on or before November 1 of each year, setting forth a comprehensive review of his actions during the previous fiscal year undertaken pursuant to the authority of this section, together with appropriate recommendation for legislation considered necessary for the designation and protection of marine sanctuaries.

(e) Before a marine sanctuary is designated under this section, the Secretary shall hold public hearings in the coastal areas which would be most directly affected by such designation, for the purpose of receiving and giving proper consideration to the views of any interested party. Such hearings shall be held no earlier than thirty days after the publication of a public notice thereof.

(f) After a marine sanctuary has been designated under this section, the Secretary, after consultation with other interested Federal agencies, shall issue necessary and reasonable regulations to control any activities permitted within the designated marine sanctuary, and no permit, license, or other authorization issued pursuant to any other authority shall be valid unless the Secretary shall certify that the permitted activity is consistent with the purposes of this title and can be carried out within the regulations promulgated under this section.

(g) The regulations issued pursuant to subsection (f) shall be applied in accordance with recognized principles of international law, including treaties, conventions, and other agreements to which the United States is signatory. Unless the application of the regulations is in accordance with such principles or is otherwise authorized by an agreement between the United States and the foreign State of which the affected person is a citizen or, in the case of the crew of a foreign vessel, between the United States and flag State of the vessel, no regulation applicable to ocean waters outside the territorial jurisdiction of the United States shall be applied to a person not a citizen of the United States.

SOURCE: U.S. Congress. n.d. *Marine Protection, Research, and Sanctuaries Act of 1972.* http://www.gpo.gov/fdsys/pkg/STATUTE-86/pdf/STATUTE-86-Pg1052.pdf (accessed August 28, 2014).

ANALYSIS

On February 10, 1970, President Richard Nixon announced his 37-point plan to improve environmental quality, with a special emphasis being placed on both air and water quality. Exactly six months later, in his *Message to the Congress Transmitting the First Annual Report on the Council on Environmental Quality*, Nixon added specific requests to meet the goals of his plan. He specifically requested from Congress legislation to protect the oceans from dumping of waste. In an unrelated portion of the message, Nixon also noted the need to create an ocean sanctuary in California's Santa Barbara Channel, which had been recently befouled by an oil spill. Congress addressed both of Nixon's desires in the Marine Protection, Research, and Sanctuaries Act of 1972.

The passage of the act addressed a burgeoning conflict between New York and New Jersey. New York City was generating far more waste than it could bury in landfills. To address the problem, the city unsuccessfully attempted to bury its garbage in other locales. Without landfills as an option, New York considered incinerating its garbage. Although viable, it added to the city's air pollution. The city ultimately settled on dumping its waste in the ocean because it was cheaper. New Jersey was opposed to New York's designs and turned to the courts to protect its offshore waters. New Jersey's defense was based on the Refuse Act of 1899, which required that entities wanting to dump waste in the nation's navigable waters had to obtain a permit from the U.S. Army Corps of Engineers (USACE). It was a risky ploy on the part of New Jersey as the Refuse Act had largely been ignored for decades. The Marine Protection, Research, and Sanctuaries Act of 1972 made the whole issue moot as it transferred the authority to protect the nation's oceans from the USACE to the Environmental Protection Agency.

Unlike most pieces of congressional legislation, the Marine Protection, Research, and Sanctuaries Act was fairly straightforward. Title I essentially forbade the dumping of waste into the oceans without a permit. Title II called for research on how to improve ocean ecosystems damaged by the introduction of waste. It also called for studies on the impact that polluted coastlines posed to people living in those environs. Title III focused on the creation of marine sanctuaries, which were parts of the oceans or Great Lakes that were deemed to be of national significance.

The third title initially created a handful of marine sanctuaries, but the number grew significantly when it was reauthorized by Congress in 2002 as the National Marine Sanctuaries Act. The new legislation created the National Marine Sanctuaries System, which encompassed approximately 150,000 square miles of protected area. Although well intentioned, the massive expansion of protected marine territories proved quite controversial as grounds that were being used for commercial fisheries and other economic activities were suddenly unavailable. Those negatively impacted sought, and in some cases received, legislation to limit the scope of the protections offered to the sanctuaries.

FURTHER READING

Borrelli, Peter. 2009. *Stellwagen: The Making and Unmaking of a National Marine Sanctuary.* Lebanon, NH: University Press of New England.

Hallwood, Paul. 2014. *Economics of the Oceans: Rights, Rents, and Resources.* New York: Routledge.

Nixon, Richard M. 1994. "Message to the Congress Transmitting the First Annual Report of the Council on Environmental Quality." *The American Presidency Project.* http://www.presidency.ucsb.edu/ws/?pid=2618.

Ofiara, Douglas D., and Joseph J. Seneca. 2001. *Economic Losses from Marine Pollution: A Handbook for Assessment.* Washington, DC: Island Press.

"These Species of Fish, Wildlife, and Plants Are of Esthetic, Ecological, Educational, Historical, Recreational, and Scientific Value to the Nation and Its People"

- *Document:* Endangered Species Act of 1973, excerpt
- *Date:* December 28, 1973
- *Where:* Washington, DC
- *Significance:* The act was designed to protect flora and fauna, along with their habitats, which were threatened with potential extinction.

DOCUMENT

ENDANGERED SPECIES ACT OF 1973

An Act

To provide for the conservation of endangered and threatened species of fish, wildlife, and plants, and for other purposes.

Be it enacted by the Senate and House of Representatives of the United States of America in Congress assembled, That this Act may be cited as the "Endangered Species Act of 1973".

. . .

FINDINGS, PURPOSES, AND POLICY

SEC. 2. (a) FINDINGS.—The Congress finds and declares that—

(1) various species of fish, wildlife, and plants in the United States have been rendered extinct as a consequence of economic growth and development untempered by adequate concern and conservation;

(2) other species of fish, wildlife, and plants have been so depleted in numbers that they are in danger of or threatened with extinction;

(3) these species of fish, wildlife, and plants are of esthetic, ecological, educational, historical, recreational, and scientific value to the Nation and its people;

(4) the United States has pledged itself as a sovereign state in the international community to conserve to the extent practicable the various species of fish or wildlife and plants facing extinction, pursuant to—

(A) migratory bird treaties with Canada and Mexico;

(B) the Migratory and Endangered Bird Treaty with Japan;

(C) the Convention on Nature Protection and Wildlife Preservation in the Western Hemisphere;

(D) the International Convention for the Northwest Atlantic Fisheries;

(E) the International Convention for the High Seas Fisheries of the North Pacific Ocean;

(F) the Convention on International Trade in Endangered Species of Wild Fauna and Flora; and

(G) other international agreements; and

(5) encouraging the States and other interested parties, through Federal financial assistance and a system of incentives, to develop and maintain conservation programs which meet national and international standards is a key to meeting the Nation's international commitments and to better safeguarding, for the benefit of all citizens, the Nation's heritage in fish, wildlife, and plants.

(b) PURPOSES.—The purposes of this Act are to provide a means whereby the ecosystems upon which endangered species and threatened species depend may be conserved, to provide a program for the conservation of such endangered species and threatened species, and to take such steps as may be appropriate to achieve the purposes of the treaties and conventions set forth in subsection (a) of this section.

(c) POLICY.—(1) It is further declared to be the policy of Congress that all Federal departments and agencies shall seek to conserve endangered species and threatened species and shall utilize their authorities in furtherance of the purposes of this Act.

(2) It is further declared to be the policy of Congress that Federal agencies shall cooperate with State and local agencies to resolve water resource issues in concert with conservation of endangered species.

SOURCE: U.S. Senate Committee on Environment & Public Works. 2002. *Endangered Species Act of 1973*. http://www.epw.senate.gov/esa73.pdf (accessed August 23, 2014).

ANALYSIS

The Endangered Species Act (ESA) of 1973 gave the Department of the Interior the task of identifying and listing endangered plant and animals so that they and their habitats could be protected in hopes of reversing their declining numbers. The department was given broad powers to prevent the capturing, killing, or selling of flora or fauna that was on the endangered species list. Funding was also provided to purchase land to protect the ecosystems where an endangered species resided. Recognizing that partnerships were going to be necessary to adequately protect declining species, the legislation not only funded joint federal and state initiatives but also acknowledged the nation's duty to honor existing international agreements.

The act had its origins in 1964 when the Department of the Interior's U.S. Fish and Wildlife Service created the Committee on Rare and Endangered Wildlife Species to maintain a list of endangered species, which at the time was comprised only of animals and fish. Two years later, Congress passed the Endangered Species Preservation Act (ESPA) of 1966 to stop the trafficking of rare birds and animals. It quickly became apparent that even tougher legislation than the ESPA was required to address the burgeoning trade in exotic animals and birds, so Congress responded with the 1969 Endangered Species Conservation Act (ESCA). That act required the Department of the Interior to identify and list endangered species from around the world. Once a species was on the list, it was illegal to import it into the United States. The act also made the sale of endangered species within the United States illegal. The ESCA was superseded with the passage of the ESA. The ESA marked a significant change from its predecessors as, up to then, all of the legislation concerned the transport and sale of specific species. The ESA not only protected species but expanded to the preservation of their habitats.

The application of the ESA had led to constant controversy since it was enacted. Almost immediately, it made the construction of dams more expensive and difficult. As the ESA requires wildlife studies to be completed, it lengthens the construction time of projects. If the structure adversely affects an endangered species, then alterations are required to protect not only the species but also its habitat. The project is generally cancelled if the habitat cannot be completely protected. Environmentalist seized upon this last point to block many projects planned by either the Bureau of Reclamation or the U.S. Army Corps of Engineers.

The key test for the ESA was the battle over the construction of the Tellico Dam in Tennessee. Construction of the dam on the Little Tennessee River by the Tennessee Valley Authority was approved in 1963 and construction soon followed. As the dam was nearing completion, it was discovered that the habitat of the snail darter (Percina tanasi), an endangered species, was going to be adversely impacted by the dam's completion. A lawsuit was filed using the ESA to prevent the completion of the Tellico Dam. An injunction was granted as the case made its way to the U.S. Supreme Court. In a 6-3 ruling in the landmark case *Tennessee Valley Authority v. Hill*, the justices determined that Congress had made it explicitly clear in the ESA that it was the policy of the federal government that endangered species were not to be harmed. In the case of the snail darter, it would not only be harmed but rendered extinct. The justices did not completely seal the dam's fate as they did note that Congress had the power to make exceptions to the ESA. Senator Howard Baker of Tennessee was able to convince his colleagues in Congress to make an exception to the ESA for the completion of the Tellico Dam. Fortunately, the federal government was able to successfully establish a snail darter population on Tennessee's Hiwassee River before the Tellico Dam was completed in 1979.

FURTHER READING

Alagona, Peter S. 2013. *After the Grizzly: Endangered Species and the Politics of Place in California*. Berkeley: University of California Press.

Czech, Brian, and Paul R. Krausman. 2001. *The Endangered Species Act: History, Conservation, Biology, and Public Policy*. Baltimore: Johns Hopkins University Press.

Freeman, David M. 2010. *Implementing the Endangered Species Act on the Platte Basin Water Commons*. Boulder: University Press of Colorado.

Goble, David D., J. Michael Scott, and Frank W. Davis, eds. 2006. *The Endangered Species Act at Thirty*. 2 vols. Washington, DC: Island Press.

Plater, Zygmunt J. B. 2013. *The Snail Darter and the Dam: How Pork-Barrel Politics Endangered a Little Fish and Killed a River*. New Haven, CT: Yale University Press.

Roman, Joe. 2011. *Listed: Dispatches from America's Endangered Species Act*. Cambridge, MA: Harvard University Press.

"There Is a Growing Demand on the Soil, Water, and Related Resources of the Nation to Meet Present and Future Needs"

- *Document:* Soil and Water Resources Conservation Act of 1977, excerpts
- *Date:* November 18, 1977
- *Where:* Washington, DC
- *Significance:* The act charged the secretary of agriculture with the creation of program to evaluate and protect the nation's soil and water resources. Among the tasks prescribed were watershed protection, flood control, and the manner that subsurface waters were utilized.

DOCUMENT

An Act

To provide for furthering the conservation, protection, and enhancement of the Nation's soil, water, and related resources for sustained use, and for other purposes.

Be it enacted by the Senate and House of Representatives of the United States of America in Congress assembled, That this Act may be cited as the "Soil and Water Resources Conservation Act of 1977".

FINDINGS

SEC. 2. The Congress finds that:

(1) There is a growing demand on the soil, water, and related resources of the Nation to meet present and future needs.

(2) The Congress, in its concern for sustained use of the resource base, created the Soil Conservation Service of the United States Department of Agriculture which possesses information, technical expertise, and a delivery system for providing assistance to land users with respect to conservation and use of soils; plants; woodlands; watershed protection and flood prevention; the conservation, development, utilization, and disposal of water; animal husbandry; fish and wildlife management; recreation; community development; and related resource uses.

(3) Resource appraisal is basic to effective soil and water conservation. Since individual and governmental decisions concerning soil and water resources often transcend administrative boundaries and affect other programs and decisions, a coordinated appraisal and program framework are essential.

. . .

DECLARATIONS OF POLICY AND PURPOSE: PROMOTION THEREOF

SEC. 4. (a) In order to further the conservation of soil, water, and related resources, it is declared to be the policy of the United States and purpose of this Act that the conduct of programs administered by the Secretary of Agriculture for the conservation of such resources shall be responsive to the long-term needs of the Nation, as determined under the provisions of this Act.

(b) Recognizing that the arrangements under which the Federal Government cooperates with State soil and water conservation agencies and other appropriate State natural resource agencies such as those concerned with forestry and fish and wildlife and, through conservation districts, with other local units of government and land users, have effectively aided in the protection and improvement of the Nation's basic resources, including the restoration and maintenance of resources damaged by improper use, it is declared to be the policy of the United States that these arrangements and similar cooperative arrangements should be utilized to the fullest extent practicable to achieve the purpose of this Act consistent with the roles and responsibilities of the non-Federal agencies, landowners and land users.

(c) The Secretary shall promote the attainment of the policies and purposes expressed in this Act by—

(1) appraising on a continuing basis the soil, water, and related resources of the Nation;

(2) developing and updating periodically a program for furthering the conservation, protection, and enhancement of the soil, water, and related resources of the Nation consistent with the roles and program responsibilities of other Federal agencies and State and local governments; and

(3) providing to Congress and the public, through reports, the information developed pursuant to paragraphs (1) and (2) of this subsection, and by providing Congress with an annual evaluation report as provided in section 7.

SOURCE: 95th Congress. 1977. *Soil and Water Resources Conservation Act of 1977*. http://www.gpo.gov/fdsys/pkg/STATUTE-91/pdf/STATUTE-91-Pg1407.pdf (accessed August 28, 2014).

ANALYSIS

Through the Soil and Water Resources Conservation Act of 1977, Congress required the secretary of agriculture to utilize the expertise of his subordinates in the U.S. Department of Agriculture (USDA) to monitor the nation's soil and water resources and develop a program to protect and enhance both. The focus on the relationship between soil and water was a major step forward for Congress as its legislation had previously treated them as completely different issues, thus they had never been considered in concert. This was surprising considering that it had long been known, for example, that fertilizers utilized on farm lands eventually polluted streams, rivers, and groundwater. This showed an obvious connection between the soil on the land and the waters that flowed nearby. The secretary was provided a broad purview that included both federally owned lands and private property. This was necessary because Congress correctly surmised that factors negatively affecting the quality of both soil and water transcended borders, thus solutions had to follow suit. The data accumulated through the work of the USDA was then transmitted to Congress in the form of a comprehensive survey on a regular schedule to inform subsequent legislation.

"To Prevent and Control Infestations of the Coastal Inland Waters of the United States"

- *Document:* Nonindigenous Aquatic Nuisance Prevention and Control Act of 1990, as Amended Through P.L. 106–580, December 29, 2000, excerpt
- *Date:* December 29, 2000
- *Where:* Washington, DC
- *Significance:* The act was designed to prevent infestations of nonindigenous species in the nation's inland waters. In areas where invasive species were already established, the act included measures to address the growth of the alien populations.

DOCUMENT

NONINDIGENOUS AQUATIC NUISANCE PREVENTION AND CONTROL ACT OF 1990
[As Amended Through P.L. 106–580, Dec. 29, 2000]

An Act

To prevent and control infestations of the coastal inland waters of the United States by the zebra mussel and other nonindigenous aquatic nuisance species, to reauthorize the National Sea Grant College Program, and for other purposes.

Be it enacted by the Senate and House of Representatives of the United States of America in Congress assembled,

TITLE I—AQUATIC NUISANCE PREVENTION AND CONTROL
Subtitle A—General Provisions

SECTION 1001. SHORT TITLE.

This title may be cited as the "Nonindigenous Aquatic Nuisance Prevention and Control Act of 1990".

. . .

SEC. 1002. FINDINGS AND PURPOSES.

(a) FINDINGS.—The Congress finds that—

(1) the discharge of untreated water in the ballast tanks of vessels and through other means results in unintentional introductions of nonindigenous species to fresh, brackish, and saltwater environments;

(2) when environmental conditions are favorable, nonindigenous species become established, may compete with or prey upon native species of plants, fish, and wildlife, may carry diseases or parasites that affect native species, and may disrupt the aquatic environment and economy of affected nearshore areas;

(3) the zebra mussel was unintentionally introduced into the Great Lakes and has infested—

(A) waters south of the Great Lakes, into a good portion of the Mississippi River drainage;

(B) waters west of the Great Lakes, into the Arkansas River in Oklahoma; and

(C) waters east of the Great Lakes, into the Hudson River and Lake Champlain;

(4) the potential economic disruption to communities affected by the zebra mussel due to its colonization of water pipes, boat hulls and other hard surfaces has been estimated at $5,000,000,000 by the year 2000, and the potential disruption to the diversity and abundance of native fish and other species by the zebra mussel and ruffe, round goby, and other nonindigenous species could be severe;

(5) the zebra mussel was discovered on Lake Champlain during 1993 and the opportunity exists to act quickly to establish zebra mussel controls before Lake Champlain is further infested and management costs escalate;

(6) in 1992, the zebra mussel was discovered at the northernmost reaches of the Chesapeake Bay watershed;

(7) the zebra mussel poses an imminent risk of invasion in the main waters of the Chesapeake Bay;

(8) since the Chesapeake Bay is the largest recipient of foreign ballast water on the East Coast, there is a risk of further invasions of other nonindigenous species;

(9) the zebra mussel is only one example of thousands of nonindigenous species that have become established in waters of the United States and may be causing economic and ecological degradation with respect to the natural resources of waters of the United States;

(10) since their introduction in the early 1980's in ballast water discharges, ruffe—

(A) have caused severe declines in populations of other species of fish in Duluth Harbor (in Minnesota and Wisconsin);

(B) have spread to Lake Huron; and

(C) are likely to spread quickly to most other waters in North America if action is not taken promptly to control their spread;

(11) examples of nonindigenous species that, as of the date of enactment of the National Invasive Species Act of 1996, infest coastal waters of the United States and that have the potential for causing adverse economic and ecological effects include—

(A) the mitten crab (Eriocher sinensis) that has become established on the Pacific Coast;

(B) the green crab (Carcinus maenas) that has become established in the coastal waters of the Atlantic Ocean;

(C) the brown mussel (Perna perna) that has become established along the Gulf of Mexico; and

(D) certain shellfish pathogens;

(12) many aquatic nuisance vegetation species, such as Eurasian watermilfoil, hydrilla, water hyacinth, and water chestnut, have been introduced to waters of the United States from other parts of the world causing or having a potential to cause adverse environmental, ecological, and economic effects;

(13) if preventive management measures are not taken nationwide to prevent and control unintentionally introduced nonindigenous aquatic species in a timely manner, further introductions and infestations of species that are as destructive as, or more destructive than, the zebra mussel or the ruffe infestations may occur;

(14) once introduced into waters of the United States, aquatic nuisance species are unintentionally transported and introduced into inland lakes and rivers by recreational boaters, commercial barge traffic, and a variety of other pathways; and

(15) resolving the problems associated with aquatic nuisance species will require the participation and cooperation of the Federal Government and State governments, and investment in the development of prevention technologies.

(b) PURPOSES.—The purposes of this Act are—

(1) to prevent unintentional introduction and dispersal of nonindigenous species into waters of the United States through ballast water management and other requirements;

(2) to coordinate federally conducted, funded or authorized research, prevention control, information dissemination and other activities regarding the zebra mussel and other aquatic nuisance species;

(3) to develop and carry out environmentally sound control methods to prevent, monitor and control unintentional introductions of nonindigenous species from pathways other than ballast water exchange;

(4) to understand and minimize economic and ecological impacts of nonindigenous aquatic nuisance species that become established, including the zebra mussel; and

(5) to establish a program of research and technology development and assistance to States in the management and removal of zebra mussels.

SOURCE: Aquatic Nuisance Species Task Force. n.d. *Nonindigenous Aquatic Nuisance Prevention and Control Act of 1990.* http://www.anstaskforce.gov/Documents/nanpca90.pdf (accessed August 27, 2014).

ANALYSIS

Since the early nineteenth century, all levels of government have worked to connect waterways to spur economic activity. One of the unintended consequences of tying so many navigable bodies of water together is that it facilitates the movement of nonnative, or invasive, species. This was illustrated by the construction of the St. Lawrence Seaway by the United States and Canada, which once completed allowed for both the zebra mussel and the ruffe fish to be introduced to the Great Lakes from ballast waters dumped by ships. The mussels spread quickly and clogged many of the intakes that allowed communities to extract drinking water from the respective lakes. The introduction of the ruffe led to the decline of many native fish species as the ruffe tended to dine on their eggs. Both the zebra mussels and the ruffe subsequently spread to other water systems through various man-made canals. Their spread led to the passage of the Nonindigenous Aquatic Nuisance Prevention and Control Act (NANPCA) of 1990.

The NANPCA was primarily focused on the Great Lakes, as it restricted the dumping of ballast waters from ocean-going ships into the Great Lakes or the St. Lawrence Seaway. The legislation also encouraged research to address the damage to the ecosystems being caused by the invasive species that had already been introduced into the waterways. The NANPCA was amended on October 26, 1996, with the passage of the National Invasive Species Act of 1996. The new legislation moved beyond the Great Lakes to address the problem of invasive species in other parts of the country, such as the Chesapeake Bay, the Gulf of Mexico, and San Francisco Bay.

FURTHER READING

Galil, Bella S., Paul F. Clark, and James T. Carlton, eds. 2011. *In the Wrong Place: Alien Marine Crustaceans: Distribution, Biology, and Impacts.* New York: Springer.

Mooney, Harold A., ed. 2005. *Invasive Alien Species: A New Synthesis.* Washington, DC: Island Press.

Mooney, Harold A., and Richard J. Hobbs. 2000. *Invasive Species in a Changing World.* Washington, DC: Island Press.

U.S. Department of Agriculture, National Agricultural Library. 2014. "National Invasive Species Information Center: Aquatic Species." http://www.invasivespeciesinfo.gov/aquatics/main.shtml.

"A National Estuary Habitat Restoration Strategy"

- **Document:** Estuary Restoration Act of 2000, excerpts
- **Date:** January 24, 2000
- **Where:** Washington, DC
- **Significance:** The act provided technical expertise and funding for state or local groups engaged in estuary restoration projects.

DOCUMENT

An Act

To encourage the restoration of estuary habitat through more efficient project financing and enhanced coordination of Federal and non-Federal restoration programs, and for other purposes.

Be it enacted by the Senate and House of Representatives of the United States of America in Congress assembled,

SECTION 1. SHORT TITLE; TABLE OF CONTENTS.

(a) SHORT TITLE.—This Act may be cited as the "Estuaries and Clean Waters Act of 2000".

. . .

TITLE I—ESTUARY RESTORATION

SEC. 101. SHORT TITLE.

This title may be cited as the "Estuary Restoration Act of 2000".

SEC. 102. PURPOSES.

The purposes of this title are—

(1) to promote the restoration of estuary habitat;

(2) to develop a national estuary habitat restoration strategy for creating and maintaining effective estuary habitat restoration partnerships among public agencies at all levels of government and to establish new partnerships between the public and private sectors;

(3) to provide Federal assistance for estuary habitat restoration projects and to promote efficient financing of such projects; and

(4) to develop and enhance monitoring and research capabilities through the use of the environmental technology innovation program associated with the National Estuarine Research Reserve System established by section 315 of the Coastal Zone Management Act of 1972 (16 U.S.C. 1461) to ensure that estuary habitat restoration efforts are based on sound scientific understanding and innovative technologies.

. . .

SEC. 104. ESTUARY HABITAT RESTORATION PROGRAM.

(a) ESTABLISHMENT.—There is established an estuary habitat restoration program under which the Secretary may carry out estuary habitat restoration projects and provide technical assistance in accordance with the requirements of this title.

(b) ORIGIN OF PROJECTS.—A proposed estuary habitat restoration project shall originate from a non-Federal interest consistent with State or local laws.

(c) SELECTION OF PROJECTS.—

(1) IN GENERAL.—The Secretary shall select estuary habitat restoration projects from a list of project proposals submitted by the Estuary Habitat Restoration Council under section 105(b).

(2) REQUIRED ELEMENTS.—Each estuary habitat restoration project selected by the Secretary must—

(A) address restoration needs identified in an estuary habitat restoration plan;

(B) be consistent with the estuary habitat restoration strategy developed under section 106;

(C) include a monitoring plan that is consistent with standards for monitoring developed under section 107 to ensure that short-term and long-term restoration goals are achieved; and

(D) include satisfactory assurance from the non-Federal interests proposing the project that the non-Federal interests will have adequate personnel, funding, and authority to carry out items of local cooperation and properly maintain the project.

(3) FACTORS FOR SELECTION OF PROJECTS.—In selecting an estuary habitat restoration project, the Secretary shall consider the following factors:

(A) Whether the project is part of an approved Federal estuary management or habitat restoration plan.

(B) The technical feasibility of the project.

(C) The scientific merit of the project.

(D) Whether the project will encourage increased coordination and cooperation among Federal, State, and local government agencies.

(E) Whether the project fosters public-private partnerships and uses Federal resources to encourage increased private sector involvement, including consideration of the amount of private funds or in-kind contributions for an estuary habitat restoration activity.

(F) Whether the project is cost-effective.

(G) Whether the State in which the non-Federal interest is proposing the project has a dedicated source of funding to acquire or restore estuary habitat, natural areas, and open spaces for the benefit of estuary habitat restoration or protection.

(H) Other factors that the Secretary determines to be reasonable and necessary for consideration.

(4) PRIORITY.—In selecting estuary habitat restoration projects to be carried out under this title, the Secretary shall give priority consideration to a project if, in addition to meriting selection based on the factors under paragraph (3)—

(A) the project occurs within a watershed in which there is a program being carried out that addresses sources of pollution and other activities that otherwise would reimpair the restored habitat; or

(B) the project includes pilot testing of or a demonstration of an innovative technology having the potential for improved cost-effectiveness in estuary habitat restoration.

SOURCE: 106th Congress of the United States. n.d. *Estuaries and Clean Waters Act of 2000*. http://www.era.noaa.gov/pdfs/act_s835.pdf (accessed August 28, 2014).

ANALYSIS

The Estuary Restoration Act (ERA) of 2000 was Title 1 of the Clean Water and Clean Bays Act of 2000. The ERA called for the establishment of a national estuary habitat restoration strategy by November 1, 2001. It also set a goal of the restoration of more than 1 million acres of estuaries to be improved over a 10-year period. To reach the goal, funding was set aside for states and local groups who were actively engaged in the restoration of estuaries. The projects that received funding were selected by a federal council, which included representation from the U.S. Army Corps of Engineers, Environmental Protection Agency, Department of Agriculture, Department of Commerce, and Department of the Interior.

FURTHER READING

Day, John W., Jr., et al. 2013. *Estuarine Ecology*. 2nd ed. New York: Wiley-Blackwell.

Palaima, Arnas, ed. 2012. *Ecology, Conservation, and Restoration of Tidal Marshes: The San Francisco Estuary*. Berkeley: University of California Press.

Waldman, John. 2013. *Heartbeats in the Muck: The History, Sea Life, and Environment of New York Harbor*. Rev. ed. New York: Empire State Editions.

"To Develop an Effective and Fiscally Sustainable Asian Carp Control Program"

- *Document:* FY 2013 Asian Carp Control Strategy Framework, Executive Summary
- *Date:* July 2013
- *Where:* The Mississippi River, the Chicago Area Waterway System, and the Great Lakes
- *Significance:* Various species of Asian carp are threatening to invade the Great Lakes from the Mississippi River via the Chicago Area Waterway System.

DOCUMENT

EXECUTIVE SUMMARY

Asian carp, particularly bighead, silver, and black carp, pose a significant threat to the waters that they invade. One of the most severe aquatic invasive species (AIS) threats facing the Great Lakes today is movement of Asian carp species through the Chicago Area Waterway System (CAWS) and possibly other pathways that can connect the Great Lakes to the outside Mississippi River Basin.

The Obama Administration is implementing an unprecedented and comprehensive set of actions to prevent introduction and establishment of Asian carp populations in the Great Lakes. These actions are being carried out by the Asian Carp Regional Coordinating Committee (ACRCC), with support from federal, state, provincial, and local agencies, and from private stakeholders and citizens. The ACRCC implements actions for protecting and maintaining the integrity and safety of the Great Lakes ecosystem from an Asian carp invasion via all viable pathways. The ACRCC management strategy and current and future actions are reported annually in the Asian Carp Control Strategy Framework (Framework) (accessible at asiancarp.us). The best science available is applied to develop this Framework.

Actions that comprise the Framework's strategy are based upon the three typical stages of species invasion. Each Framework action item is categorized within one of the following stages of invasion and one of the management actions below that it would impact the most:

- Prevention and development of prevention technologies
- Monitoring and development of monitoring technologies
- Development of control technology and impact mitigation
- Other supporting actions (education, outreach, and regulatory support).

The ACRCC seeks development of an effective and fiscally sustainable Asian carp prevention and control program throughout the Great Lakes Basin. The near-term goal is to prevent entry of Asian carp to the Great Lakes, which will give the ACRCC time to complete the research and development necessary to meet the long-term goal of eradication/management through physical, chemical, and biological controls. Because Asian carp are already well established throughout the Mississippi River Basin, this program will be essential to decrease spread of Asian carp and prevent introduction of Asian carp into new waterways and inland lakes.

On-the-ground actions include studying and implementing options or controls that could prevent spread of Asian carp between the Mississippi River and Great Lakes Basins—possibly including hydrological separation to permanently solve the potential Asian carp problem at connection points along the CAWS, as well as to address other AIS. Engineering controls, biological controls, and responses to prevent further population expansion throughout the two basins are also under development and are undergoing field testing to deal with possible Asian carp introductions to the Great Lakes via other vectors such as human transport or unintentional releases.

The ACRCC has specified the following actions within the 2013 Framework:

- Provide a sound strategy for addressing the threat of an Asian carp invasion into the Great Lakes such that the Framework continues to provide direction to participating agencies and to provide modes of actions to reduce threats and identify areas of possible future mitigation of Asian carp population expansion.
- Identify an array of alternatives through the Great Lakes and Mississippi River Interbasin Study (GLMRIS) to prevent spread of aquatic nuisance species between the Great Lakes and Mississippi River basins.
- Identify efforts that supplement direct management action, such as education and outreach, or increased regulatory structure.
- Develop an effective and fiscally sustainable Asian carp control program throughout the Great Lakes Basin.
- Increase program sustainability through Framework action items such as robust control and removal efforts, and novel technology to detect and/or remove existing populations; and improve accuracy of known extent of Asian carp populations (including Dual-Frequency Identification Sonar

[DIDSON], hydro-acoustic, and other remote sensing technologies). Other mitigating action items contribute to the program base and can be implemented if an emergency arises—including rotenone stockpiling, net development, and advanced fishing strategies. Further development of biological control agents will help to eradicate novel populations where they arise or to deplete existing stocks.

- Identify ongoing or potential collaboration among ACRCC entities, and specify partner roles.
- Document, track, and communicate actions of ACRCC partners in applying full authorities, capabilities, and resources to prevent introduction and establishment of Asian carp in the Great Lakes.
- Further engage with governmental, industrial, environmental, and other stakeholders.
- Initiate development of a strategy for transferring technology, decision support tools, and/or information to resource managers.
- Apply technologies and lessons learned to areas below the electric dispersal barriers and to concurrent national Asian carp efforts, where applicable.
- Build upon developed collaborative roles in the Great Lakes Basin to fully prepare for other basin-wide efforts as these arise.

This Framework is a product of the best science available. Widespread agreement exists among scientists and stakeholders that prevention measures are critical to avoid the potential economic, environmental, and social costs associated with Asian carp establishment in the Great Lakes.

In addition to the efforts described in this document as part of ACRCC strategy, the Great Lakes states and the province of Ontario continue to undertake additional efforts against Asian carp and other invasive species. Through a cost-share grant program, the U.S. Fish and Wildlife Service (USFWS) has provided assistance to states for creating and implementing an Aquatic Nuisance Species (ANS) taskforce and state-supported AIS management plans and activities. Since 2009, the Great Lakes states have invested over $26.7 million in assessment, prevention, and control of AIS —of which almost $900,000 has been committed to Asian carp control efforts. The following are previous or current efforts by the Great Lakes states and Ontario as part of their AIS prevention, management, and control programs:

- New response and rapid assessment plans developed by Great Lakes states
- State-led response actions and other control efforts
- AIS education and outreach, including increased signage to inform the public about various AIS
- Inspections and enforcement of laws regarding AIS
- AIS barrier studies and design
- AIS monitoring and surveillance.

This Framework is a living document and is a continuation of previous iterations of the Asian Carp Framework. It is designed to be inclusive, allowing government agencies and outside stakeholders to engage in developing and implementing all plausible control actions. In this Framework, potential hurdles for control and prevention are recognized, and a collaborative community is established through which a compelling plan of action can be continued for the CAWS. Preventing introduction of a self-sustaining Asian carp population into the Great Lakes requires an understanding of ecological, economic, and hydrological complexities—leading to the conclusion that a comprehensive approach (which cannot rely on only a single strategy) is necessary to prevent additional spread of Asian carp into areas currently uninvaded.

The ACRCC, with support from U.S. and Canadian federal, state, provincial, and local agencies and other private stakeholders and citizens, is working to create a sustainable Asian carp control program to prevent introduction of Asian carp into the Great Lakes via all viable pathways. This Framework lays out the strategies and proposed action items necessary to achieve that goal.

SOURCE: Asian Carp Regional Coordinating Committee. 2013. *Asian Carp Control Strategy Framework, July 2013.* http://www.asiancarp.us/documents/2013Framework.pdf (accessed August 17, 2014).

ANALYSIS

The passage of the Nonindigenous Aquatic Nuisance Prevention and Control Act of 1990 signaled that the federal government had become extremely concerned about the introduction of invasive species into the Great Lakes, because the arrival of organisms such as the zebra mussel and Eurasian ruffe fish had caused so much ecological and economic damage. When those nonnative species spread to other waterways through man-made canals, environmentalists, scientists, and politicians quickly realized that the same process in reverse could result in invasive species moving from rivers, like the Mississippi, to the Great Lakes.

To address ecological damage to the Great Lakes, which collectively are one of the largest sources of freshwater in the world and correspondingly home to one of the most productive fisheries, a major federal initiative titled "The Great Lakes Restoration Initiative" was launched. As part of that initiative, threats to the Great Lakes were identified so that they too could be addressed. One of the primary threats that emerged was the potential introduction of five Asian carp species that had already moved from the Mississippi River to the Illinois River, namely the bighead, black, common, grass, and silver carp. Most of the respective carp species were introduced in the United States in the 1960s and 1970s. Some of the fish grow to approximately 40 pounds and are voracious eaters. Their size allows them to outcompete native fish for food sources. They subsist on plankton, consuming as much as 20 percent of their body weight over the course of a day. Their consumption of such a significant amount of plankton starves out smaller fish. As females can lay hundreds of thousands of eggs each time they spawn, their numbers expanded exponentially. They have no natural predators to control their populations. Even fishermen avoid them because their bony bodies make them an undesirable game fish. Due to all these factors, it is believed that their arrival in the Great Lakes would subsequently result in the population decline of many of the fish species native to the respective lakes.

Although population sampling in the Illinois River suggests that none of the Asian carp species has passed that far north, many environmental groups, state and federal government bodies, and scientists believe that they are far closer to the Great Lakes than officially acknowledged. Some scientists have argued that DNA evidence suggests that at least carp species has already arrived in Lake Michigan. The U.S. Army Corps of Engineers constructed three underwater electrical barriers designed to keep the carp from the Chicago Area Waterway System, which is the pathway that the carp must travel to reach Lake Michigan from the Illinois River. Believing that more must be done to protect the Great Lakes, the attorney generals from Michigan, Minnesota, Ohio, Pennsylvania, and Wisconsin sued Illinois in 2011 to try to get the state to create yet another barrier for the fish by closing the locks on the Chicago Area Waterway System. The sealing of the Chicago Area Waterway System's locks is a temporary solution to a long-term problem. A potential solution that is being examined by the U.S. Corps of Engineers is the permanent closing of the canal, which would disconnect the Great Lakes from the Mississippi River and all of its tributaries at a potential cost of $18 billion.

FURTHER READING

Riley, John L. 2013. *The Once and Future Great Lakes Country: An Ecological History*. Montreal, QC: McGill-Queen's University Press.

U.S. Army Corps of Engineers. 2014. *The GLMRIS Report: Great Lakes and Mississippi River Interbasin Study*. http://glmris.anl.gov/documents/docs/glmrisreport/GLMRIS_Report.pdf (accessed August 31, 2014).

Part VI

NEW THREATS TO WATER SUPPLY AND SAFETY

10

OIL SPILLS

"New Requirements for Contingency Planning by Both Government and Industry"

- *Document:* Oil Pollution Act of 1990, Overview
- *Date:* August 18, 1990
- *Where:* Washington, DC
- *Significance:* The act expands the authority of the Environmental Protection Agency to respond to oil spills.

DOCUMENT

OIL POLLUTION ACT OVERVIEW

Overview

The Oil Pollution Act (OPA) was signed into law in August 1990, largely in response to rising public concern following the *Exxon Valdez* incident. The OPA improved the nation's ability to prevent and respond to oil spills by establishing provisions that expand the federal government's ability, and provide the money and resources necessary, to respond to oil spills. The OPA also created the national Oil Spill Liability Trust Fund, which is available to provide up to one billion dollars per spill incident.

In addition, the OPA provided new requirements for contingency planning both by government and industry. The National Oil and Hazardous Substances Pollution Contingency Plan (NCP) has been expanded in a three-tiered approach: the Federal government is required to direct all public and private response efforts for certain types of spill events; Area Committees—composed of federal, state, and local government officials—must develop detailed, location-specific Area Contingency

Plans; and owners or operators of vessels and certain facilities that pose a serious threat to the environment must prepare their own Facility Response Plans.

Finally, the OPA increased penalties for regulatory noncompliance, broadened the response and enforcement authorities of the Federal government, and preserved State authority to establish law governing oil spill prevention and response.

Key Provisions of the Oil Pollution Act

§1002(a) Provides that the responsible party for a vessel or facility from which oil is discharged, or which poses a substantial threat of a discharge, is liable for: (1) certain specified damages resulting from the discharged oil; and (2) removal costs incurred in a manner consistent with the National Contingency Plan (NCP).

§1002(c) Exceptions to the Clean Water Act (CWA) liability provisions include: (1) discharges of oil authorized by a permit under Federal, State, or local law; (2) discharges of oil from a public vessel; or (3) discharges of oil from onshore facilities covered by the liability provisions of the Trans-Alaska Pipeline Authorization Act.

§1002(d) Provides that if a responsible party can establish that the removal costs and damages resulting from an incident were caused solely by an act or omission by a third party, the third party will be held liable for such costs and damages.

§1004 The liability for tank vessels larger than 3,000 gross tons is increased to $1,200 per gross ton or $10 million, whichever is greater. Responsible parties at onshore facilities and deepwater ports are liable for up to $350 million per spill; holders of leases or permits for offshore facilities, except deepwater ports, are liable for up to $75 million per spill, plus removal costs. The Federal government has the authority to adjust, by regulation, the $350 million liability limit established for onshore facilities.

§1016 Offshore facilities are required to maintain evidence of financial responsibility of $150 million and vessels and deepwater ports must provide evidence of financial responsibility up to the maximum applicable liability amount. Claims for removal costs and damages may be asserted directly against the guarantor providing evidence of financial responsibility.

§1018(a) The Clean Water Act does not preempt State Law. States may impose additional liability (including unlimited liability), funding mechanisms, requirements for removal actions, and fines and penalties for responsible parties.

§1019 States have the authority to enforce, on the navigable waters of the State, OPA requirements for evidence of financial responsibility. States are also given access to Federal funds (up to $250,000 per incident) for immediate removal, mitigation, or prevention of a discharge, and may be reimbursed by the Trust fund for removal and monitoring costs incurred during oil spill response and cleanup efforts that are consistent with the National Contingency Plan (NCP).

§4202 Strengthens planning and prevention activities by: (1) providing for the establishment of spill contingency plans for all areas of the U.S. (2) mandating the development of response plans for individual tank vessels and certain facilities for responding to a worst case discharge or a substantial threat of such a discharge;

and (3) providing requirements for spill removal equipment and periodic inspections.

§4301(a) and (c) The fine for failing to notify the appropriate Federal agency of a discharge is increased from a maximum of $10,000 to a maximum of $250,000 for an individual or $500,000 for an organization. The maximum prison term is also increased from one year to five years. The penalties for violations have a maximum of $250,000 and 15 years in prison.

§4301(b) Civil penalties are authorized at $25,000 for each day of violation or $1,000 per barrel of oil discharged. Failure to comply with a Federal removal order can result in civil penalties of up to $25,000 for each day of violation.

§9001(a) Amends the Internal Revenue Act of 1986 to consolidate funds established under other statutes and to increase permitted levels of expenditures. Penalties and funds established under several laws are consolidated, and the Trust Fund borrowing limit is increased from $500 million to $1 billion.

SOURCE: Environmental Protection Agency. n.d. *Oil Pollution Act Overview*. http:// www.epa.gov/osweroe1/content/lawsregs/opaover.htm#info (accessed August 18, 2014).

ANALYSIS

The Oil Pollution Act (OPA) of 1990 had its origins during the night of March 23–24, 1989, when the single-hulled *Exxon Valdez* struck Bligh Reef in Alaska's Prince William Sound. The accident led the ship to release approximately 11 million gallons of oil, which befouled more than 1,500 miles of shoreline. As the Environmental Protection Agency (EPA) and other federal entities began work to investigate the accident and address the damage that resulted, the limitations of their authority soon became evident. Outrage over the inability of the federal government to prevent the catastrophic damage that resulted led many citizens to complain to Congress. In a truly bipartisan effort, Congress responded with the drafting and passage of the act.

The influence of the *Exxon Valdez* accident was apparent with two of the mandates included in the OPA. First, ships carrying oil were required to have a double hull. If the *Exxon Valdez* had been outfitted with a double hull, the oil spill would still have occurred, but the amount of oil expelled would have been reduced by more than half. Much of the blame for the accident was placed on the captain of the tanker who was drunk when the accident occurred. To reduce the chance of that happening again, the OPA required that anyone holding a mariner's license was subject to testing for alcohol or drugs.

Other provisions of the OPA concerned the prevention of oil spills. Every ship transporting oil on the U.S. territorial waters was required to have a contingency plan for an oil spill that had been approved in advance by the U.S. Coast Guard. Ships and their parent companies also had to have prepositioned equipment available in the event of an oil spill to contain it within 12 hours. To ensure compliance with the legislation, Congress substantially increased the financial penalties that could be levied for an oil spill. As the OPA was heavily influenced by the disaster in Prince William Sound and its aftermath, the legislators who wrote it did not adequately anticipate other types of oil spills, such as the Deepwater Horizon blowout of April 20, 2010. While the penalties were daunting for spills that occurred on vessels or onshore facilities, it proved completely inadequate for a spill on the scale of the Deepwater Horizon, which gushed oil for approximately five months into the Gulf of Mexico.

FURTHER READING

Batik, Kevin. 2002. "OPA's Reach: The Geographic Scope of 'Navigable Waters' Under the Oil Pollution Act of 1990." *Review of Litigation* 21, no. 2: 419–453.

Davis, Andrew B. 2011. "Pure Economic Loss Claims Under the Oil Pollution Act: Combining Policy and Congressional Intent." *Columbia Journal of Law & Social Problems* 45, no. 5: 1–44.

Sump, David H. 2011. "The Oil Pollution Act of 1990: A Glance in the Rearview Mirror." *Tulane Law Review* 85, no. 4: 1101–1119.

U.S. Congress, House Committee on Merchant Marine and Fisheries. 1993. *Compilation of Selected Coast Guard and Marine Transportation Laws with the Oil Pollution Act of 1990*. Washington, DC: U.S. Government Printing Office.

Wiens, John A., ed. 2013. *Oil in the Environment: Legacies and Lessons of the Exxon Valdez Oil Spill*. New York: Cambridge University Press.

"Three Questions of Maritime Law"

- **Document:** *Exxon Shipping Co., et al., Petitioners, v. Grant Baker et al.*, 128 S. Ct. 2605, excerpts from Majority Opinion
- **Date:** June 25, 2008
- **Where:** Washington, DC
- **Significance:** The Exxon Shipping Company was able to get the punitive damages originally awarded to private citizens harmed by the *Exxon Valdez* oil spill significantly reduced.

DOCUMENT

Justice SOUTER delivered the opinion of the Court.

There are three questions of maritime law before us: whether a ship owner may be liable for punitive damages without acquiescence in the actions causing harm, whether punitive damages have been barred implicitly by federal statutory law making no provision for them, and whether the award of $2.5 billion in this case is greater than maritime law should allow in the circumstances. We are equally divided on the owner's derivative liability, and hold that the federal statutory law does not bar a punitive award on top of damages for economic loss, but that the award here should be limited to an amount equal to compensatory damages.

I

On March 24, 1989, the supertanker *Exxon Valdez* grounded on Bligh Reef off the Alaskan coast, fracturing its hull and spilling millions of gallons of crude oil into Prince William Sound. The owner, petitioner Exxon Shipping Co. (now SeaRiver Maritime, Inc.), and its owner, petitioner Exxon Mobil Corp. (collectively, Exxon), have settled state and federal claims for environmental damage, with payments exceeding $1 billion, and this action by respondent Baker and others, including commercial fishermen and native Alaskans, was brought for economic losses to individuals dependent on Prince William Sound for their livelihoods.

A

The tanker was over 900 feet long and was used by Exxon to carry crude oil from the end of the Trans-Alaska Pipeline in Valdez, Alaska, to the lower 48 States. On the night of the spill it was carrying 53 million gallons of crude oil, or over a million barrels. Its captain was one Joseph Hazelwood, who had completed a 28-day alcohol treatment program while employed by Exxon, as his superiors knew, but dropped out of a prescribed follow-up program and stopped going to Alcoholics Anonymous meetings. According to the District Court, "[t]here was evidence presented to the jury that after Hazelwood was released from [residential treatment], he drank in bars, parking lots, apartments, airports, airplanes, restaurants, hotels, at various ports, and aboard Exxon tankers." *In re Exxon Valdez*, No. A89-0095-CV, Order No. 265 (D.Alaska, Jan. 27, 1995), p. 5, App. F to Pet. for Cert. 255a-256a (hereinafter Order 265). The jury also heard contested testimony that Hazelwood drank with Exxon officials and that members of the Exxon management knew of his relapse. See *ibid*. Although Exxon had a clear policy prohibiting employees from serving onboard within four hours of consuming alcohol, see *In re Exxon Valdez*, 270 F.3d 1215, 1238 (C.A.9 2001), Exxon presented no evidence that it monitored Hazelwood after his return to duty or considered giving him a shoreside assignment, see Order 265, p. 5, *supra*, at 256a. Witnesses testified that before the *Valdez* left port on the night of the disaster, Hazelwood downed at least five double vodkas in the waterfront bars of Valdez, an intake of about 15 ounces of 80-proof alcohol, enough "that a non-alcoholic would have passed out." 270 F.3d, at 1236.

The ship sailed at 9:12 p.m. on March 23, 1989, guided by a state-licensed pilot for the first leg out, through the Valdez Narrows. At 11:20 p.m., Hazelwood took active control and, owing to poor conditions in the outbound shipping lane, radioed the Coast Guard for permission to move east across the inbound lane to a less icy path. Under the conditions, this was a standard move, which the last outbound tanker had also taken, and the Coast Guard cleared the *Valdez* to cross the inbound lane. The tanker accordingly steered east toward clearer waters, but the move put it in the path of an underwater reef off Bligh Island, thus requiring a turn back west into the shipping lane around Busby Light, north of the reef.

Two minutes before the required turn, however, Hazelwood left the bridge and went down to his cabin in order, he said, to do paperwork. This decision was inexplicable. There was expert testimony that, even if their presence is not strictly necessary, captains simply do not quit the bridge during maneuvers like this, and no paperwork could have justified it. And in fact the evidence was that Hazelwood's presence was required, both because there should have been two officers on the bridge at all times and his departure left only one, and because he was the only person on the entire ship licensed to navigate this part of Prince William Sound. To make matters worse, before going below Hazelwood put the tanker on autopilot, speeding it up, making the turn trickier, and any mistake harder to correct.

As Hazelwood left, he instructed the remaining officer, third mate Joseph Cousins, to move the tanker back into the shipping lane once it came abeam of Busby Light. Cousins, unlicensed to navigate in those waters, was left alone with helmsman Robert Kagan, a nonofficer. For reasons that remain a mystery, they failed to make the turn at Busby Light, and a later emergency maneuver attempted by Cousins came too late. The tanker ran aground on Bligh Reef, tearing the hull open and spilling 11 million gallons of crude oil into Prince William Sound.

After Hazelwood returned to the bridge and reported the grounding to the Coast Guard, he tried but failed to rock the *Valdez* off the reef, a maneuver which could have spilled more oil and caused the ship to founder. The Coast Guard's nearly immediate response included a blood test of Hazelwood (the validity of which Exxon disputes) showing a blood-alcohol level of .061 eleven hours after the spill. Supp.App. 307sa. Experts testified that to have this much alcohol in his bloodstream so long after the accident, Hazelwood at the time of the spill must have had a blood-alcohol level of around .241, Order 265, p. 5, *supra*, at 256a, three times the legal limit for driving in most States.

In the aftermath of the disaster, Exxon spent around $2.1 billion in cleanup efforts. The United States charged the company with criminal violations of the Clean Water Act, 33 U.S.C. §§ 1311(a) and 1319(c)(1); the Refuse Act of 1899, 33 U.S.C. §§ 407 and 411; the Migratory Bird Treaty Act, 16 U.S.C. §§ 703 and 707(a); the Ports and Waterways Safety Act, 33 U.S.C. § 1232(b)(1); and the Dangerous Cargo Act, 46 U.S.C. § 3718(b). Exxon pleaded guilty to violations of the Clean Water Act, the Refuse Act, and the Migratory Bird Treaty Act and agreed to pay a $150 million fine, later reduced to $25 million plus restitution of $100 million. A civil action by the United States and the State of Alaska for environmental harms ended with a consent decree for Exxon to pay at least $900 million toward restoring natural resources, and it paid another $303 million in voluntary settlements with fishermen, property owners, and other private parties.

B

The remaining civil cases were consolidated into this one against Exxon, Hazelwood, and others. The District Court for the District of Alaska divided the plaintiffs seeking compensatory damages into three classes: commercial fishermen, Native Alaskans, and landowners. At Exxon's behest, the court also certified a mandatory class of all plaintiffs seeking punitive damages, whose number topped 32,000. Respondents here, to whom we will refer as Baker for convenience, are members of that class.

For the purposes of the case, Exxon stipulated to its negligence in the *Valdez* disaster and its ensuing liability for compensatory damages. The court designed the trial accordingly: Phase I considered Exxon and Hazelwood's recklessness and thus their potential for punitive liability; Phase II set compensatory damages for commercial fishermen and Native Alaskans; and Phase III determined the amount of punitive damages for which Hazelwood and Exxon were each liable. (A contemplated Phase IV, setting compensation for still other plaintiffs, was obviated by settlement.)

In Phase I, the jury heard extensive testimony about Hazelwood's alcoholism and his conduct on the night of the spill, as well as conflicting testimony about Exxon officials' knowledge of Hazelwood's backslide. At the close of Phase I, the Court instructed the jury in part that

"[a] corporation is responsible for the reckless acts of those employees who are employed in a managerial capacity while acting in the scope of their employment. The reckless act or omission of a managerial officer or employee of a corporation, in the course and scope of the performance of his duties, is held in law to be the reckless act or omission of the corporation." App. K to Pet. for Cert. 301a.

The Court went on that "[a]n employee of a corporation is employed in a managerial capacity if the employee supervises other employees and has responsibility for, and authority over, a particular aspect of the corporation's business." *Ibid.* Exxon did not dispute that Hazelwood was a managerial employee under this definition, see App. G, *id.*, at 264a, n. 8, and the jury found both Hazelwood and Exxon reckless and thus potentially liable for punitive damages, App. L, *id.*, at 303a.

In Phase II the jury awarded $287 million in compensatory damages to the commercial fishermen. After the Court deducted released claims, settlements, and other payments, the balance outstanding was $19,590,257. Meanwhile, most of the Native Alaskan class had settled their compensatory claims for $20 million, and those who opted out of that settlement ultimately settled for a total of around $2.6 million.

In Phase III, the jury heard about Exxon's management's acts and omissions arguably relevant to the spill. See App. 1291-1320, 1353-1367. At the close of evidence, the court instructed the jurors on the purposes of punitive damages, emphasizing that they were designed not to provide compensatory relief but to punish and deter the defendants. See App. to Brief in Opposition 12a-14a. The court charged the jury to consider the reprehensibility of the defendants' conduct, their financial condition, the magnitude of the harm, and any mitigating facts. *Id.*, at 15a. The jury awarded $5,000 in punitive damages against Hazelwood and $5 billion against Exxon.

On appeal, the Court of Appeals for the Ninth Circuit upheld the Phase I jury instruction on corporate liability for acts of managerial agents under Circuit precedent. See *In re Exxon Valdez*, 270 F.3d, at 1236 (citing *Protectus Alpha Nav. Co. v. North Pacific Grain Growers, Inc.*, 767 F.2d 1379 (C.A.9 1985)). With respect to the size of the punitive damages award, however, the Circuit remanded twice for adjustments in light of this Court's due process cases before ultimately itself remitting the award to $2.5 billion. See 270 F.3d, at 1246-1247, 472 F.3d 600, 601, 625 (2006) (*per curiam*), and 490 F.3d 1066, 1068 (2007).

We granted certiorari to consider whether maritime law allows corporate liability for punitive damages on the basis of the acts of managerial agents, whether the Clean Water Act (CWA), 86 Stat. 816, 33 U.S.C. § 1251 *et seq.* (2000 ed. and Supp. V), forecloses the award of punitive damages in maritime spill cases, and whether the punitive damages awarded against Exxon in this case were excessive as a matter of maritime common law. 552 U.S., 128 S.Ct. 492, 169 L.Ed.2d 337 (2007). We now vacate and remand.

. . .

F

. . .

3

There is better evidence of an accepted limit of reasonable civil penalty, however, in several studies mentioned before, showing the median ratio of punitive to compensatory verdicts, reflecting what juries and judges have considered reasonable across many hundreds of punitive awards. See *supra*, at 2624-2625, and n. 14. We think it is fair to assume that the greater share of the verdicts studied in these comprehensive collections reflect reasonable judgments about the economic penalties appropriate in their particular cases.

These studies cover cases of the most as well as the least blameworthy conduct triggering punitive liability, from malice and avarice, down to recklessness, and even gross negligence in some jurisdictions. The data put the median ratio for the entire gamut of circumstances at less than 1:1, see *supra*, at 2624-2625, and n. 14, meaning that the compensatory award exceeds the punitive award in most cases. In a well-functioning system, we would expect that awards at the median or lower would roughly express jurors' sense of reasonable penalties in cases with no earmarks of exceptional blameworthiness within the punishable spectrum (cases like this one, without intentional or malicious conduct, and without behavior driven primarily by desire for gain, for example) and cases (again like this one) without the modest economic harm or odds of detection that have opened the door to higher awards. It also seems fair to suppose that most of the unpredictable outlier cases that call the fairness of the system into question are above the median; in theory a factfinder's deliberation could go awry to produce a very low ratio, but we have no basis to assume that such a case would be more than a sport, and the cases with serious constitutional issues coming to us have naturally been on the high side, see, *e.g.*, *State Farm*, 538 U.S., at 425, 123 S.Ct. 1513 (ratio of 145:1); *Gore*, 517 U.S., at 582, 116 S.Ct. 1589 (ratio of 500:1). On these assumptions, a median ratio of punitive to compensatory damages of about 0.65:1 probably marks the line near which cases like this one largely should be grouped. Accordingly, given the need to protect against the possibility (and the disruptive cost to the legal system) of awards that are unpredictable and unnecessary, either for deterrence or for measured retribution, we consider that a 1:1 ratio, which is above the median award, is a fair upper limit in such maritime cases.

The provision of the CWA respecting daily fines confirms our judgment that anything greater would be excessive here and in cases of this type. Congress set criminal penalties of up to $25,000 per day for negligent violations of pollution restrictions, and up to $50,000 per day for knowing ones. 33 U.S.C. §§ 1319(c)(1), (2). Discretion to double the penalty for knowing action compares to discretion to double the civil liability on conduct going beyond negligence and meriting punitive treatment.

And our explanation of the constitutional upper limit confirms that the 1:1 ratio is not too low. In *State Farm*, we said that a single-digit maximum is appropriate in all but the most exceptional of cases, and "[w]hen compensatory damages are substantial, then a lesser ratio, perhaps only equal to compensatory damages, can reach the outermost limit of the due process guarantee." 538 U.S., at 425, 123 S.Ct. 1513.

V

Applying this standard to the present case, we take for granted the District Court's calculation of the total relevant compensatory damages at $507.5 million. See *In re Exxon Valdez*, 236 F.Supp.2d 1043, 1063 (D.Alaska 2002). A punitive-to-compensatory ratio of 1:1 thus yields maximum punitive damages in that amount.

We therefore vacate the judgment and remand the case for the Court of Appeals to remit the punitive damages award accordingly.

It is so ordered.

SOURCE: *Exxon Shipping Co. v. Baker*, 554 U.S. 471 (2008).

ANALYSIS

During the night of March 23–24, 1991, the *Exxon Valdez* supertanker struck Bligh Reef in Prince William Sound in the Gulf of Alaska. The accident resulted in the third-largest oil spill in the history of the United States. Approximately 11 million gallons of crude oil was spilled, polluting more than 1,500 miles of shoreline. The spill decimated the local commercial fishing industry.

In the aftermath of the disaster, Exxon spent more than $2 billion to clean up the oil spill. The company was subsequently charged with violations of the Clean Water Act, the Refuse Act, and the Migratory Bird Treaty Act by the U.S. government. The company pleaded guilty and paid $125 million in fines. A subsequent civil suit brought by Alaska and the United States followed, which led Exxon to paying approximately $900 million to restore local ecosystems to their pre-spill state. To settle a significant number of private lawsuits, Exxon also agreed to pay another $303 million to fishermen, property owners, and other private parties.

Litigation from private interests continued to plague Exxon. In 1991, the company was ordered to pay approximately 32,000 plaintiffs $287 million in compensatory damages and $5 billion in punitive damages. Exxon appealed the decision and was able to get the punitive damages reduced by half. Believing that the penalty was still excessive, Exxon turned to the Supreme Court for relief. The company made its appeal on two points. First, the amount of compensatory damages should have been determined using maritime law rather than constitutional law. Second, it was not appropriate for them to be punished by excessive compensatory damages because the company had already been punished through the settlement it paid to the federal government for its violations of the Clean Water Act, the Refuse Act, and the Migratory Bird Treaty Act. In a 5-3 decision, the majority agreed with Exxon that the compensatory damages should have been determined under maritime law. This resulted in the figure for compensatory damages being reduced to $507.5 million.

FURTHER READING

Day, Angela. 2014. *Red Light to Starboard: Recalling the Exxon Valdez Disaster*. Pullman: Washington State University Press.

Lebedoff, David. 1997. *Cleaning Up: The Story Behind the Biggest Legal Bonanza of Our Time*. New York: Free Press.

Wiens, John A., ed. 2013. *Oil in the Environment: Legacies and Lessons of the Exxon Valdez Oil Spill*. New York: Cambridge University Press.

"Oiling a Rich Environment"

- *Document:* Deep Water: The Gulf Oil Disaster and the Future of Offshore Drilling: Report to the President, excerpt
- *Date:* The Deepwater Horizon blowout occurred on April 20, 2010. It leaked oil into the Gulf of Mexico until September 19, 2010. The National Commission on the BP Deepwater Horizon Oil Spill and Offshore Drilling report titled *Deep Water: The Gulf Oil Disaster and the Future of Offshore Drilling* was submitted to the president on January 2011.
- *Where:* The Gulf of Mexico
- *Significance:* The blowout of the Macondo well in the Gulf of Mexico led to the largest oil spill ever recorded.

DOCUMENT

"The worst environmental disaster America has ever faced."

Oiling a Rich Environment: Impacts and Assessment

When President Barack Obama addressed the nation from the Oval Office on June 15—nearly two months after the Macondo well began gushing crude oil and one month before engineers subdued it—he said:

Already, this oil spill is the worst environmental disaster America has ever faced. And unlike an earthquake or a hurricane, it's not a single event that does its damage in a matter of minutes or days. The millions of gallons of oil that have spilled into the Gulf of Mexico are more like an epidemic, one that we will be fighting for months and even years.

The Deepwater Horizon blowout produced the largest accidental marine oil spill in U.S. history, an acute human and environmental tragedy. Worse still, as discussed in Chapter 7, it occurred in the midst of environmental disasters related to land-based pollution and massive destruction of coastal wetlands—chronic crises that proceed insidiously and will require not months but decades of national effort to address and repair.

Laws guide resolution of damages from the spill itself. There is a suite of policies and programs aimed at improving discrete environmental issues within the Gulf and along its coast. The law also provides compensation for direct economic impacts. This chapter analyzes these immediate impacts, not only on the natural environment but also on the economy and on human health in the affected region. Unfortunately, the human-health effects are the least-recognized fallout from the spill, and those least-well addressed in existing law and policies.

The Impact on Nature

The Deepwater Horizon oil spill immediately threatened a rich, productive marine ecosystem. To mitigate both direct and indirect adverse environmental impacts, BP and the federal government took proactive measures in response to the unprecedented magnitude of the spill. Unfortunately, comprehensive data on conditions before the spill—the natural "status quo ante" from the shoreline to the deepwater Gulf—were generally lacking. Even now, information on the nature of the damage associated with the released oil is being realized in bits and pieces: reports of visibly oiled and dead wildlife, polluted marshes, and lifeless deepwater corals. Moreover, scientific knowledge of deepwater marine communities is limited, and it is there that a significant volume of oil was dispersed from the wellhead, naturally and chemically, into small droplets. Scientists simply do not yet know how to predict the ecological consequences and effects on key species that might result from oil exposure in the water column, both far below and near the surface. Much more oil might have made landfall, but currents and winds kept most of the oil offshore, and a large circulating eddy kept oil from riding the Loop Current toward the Florida Keys. Oil-eating microbes probably broke down a substantial volume of the spilled crude, and the warm temperatures aided degradation and evaporation—favorable conditions not present in colder offshore energy regions. (Oil-degrading microbes are still active in cold water, but less so than in warmer water.) However widespread (and in many cases severe) the natural resource damages are, those observed so far have fallen short of some of the worst expectations and reported conjectures during the early stages of the spill. So much remains unknown that will only become clearer after long-term monitoring of the marine ecosystem. Government scientists (funded by the responsible party) are undertaking a massive effort to assess the damages to the public's natural resources. Additionally, despite significant delays in funding and lack of timely access to the response zone, independent scientific research of coastal and marine impacts is proceeding as well.

A rich marine ecosystem. Particularly along the Louisiana coast, the Gulf of Mexico is no stranger to oil spills. But unlike past insults, this one spewed from the depths of the ocean, the bathypelagic zone (3,300–13,000 feet deep). Despite the cold, constant darkness and high pressure (over 150 atmospheres), scientists know that the region has abundant and diverse marine life. There are cold-water corals, fish, and worms that produce light like fireflies to compensate for the perpetual night. Bacteria, mussels, and tubeworms have adapted to life in an environment where oil, natural gas, and methane seep from cracks in the seafloor. Endangered sperm whales dive to this depth and beyond to feed on giant squid and other prey.

Higher up the water column, light and temperature gradually increase and the ascending sperm whales—and Macondo well oil—encounter sharks, hundreds of fish species, shrimp, jellyfish, sea turtles, and dolphins. As the sperm whales surface for air at the bright and balmy Gulf surface, they pass through multitudes of plankton, floating seaweed beds, and schools of fish. Some of these fish species spend their early lives in the coastal waters and estuaries; others travel along annual migration routes from the Atlantic Ocean to the Gulf. The floating seaweed beds (sargassum), fish larvae, and plankton drift with the surface currents and are driven by the wind—as is the oil rising from below. The critical sargassum habitats lure sea turtles, tuna, dolphins, and numerous game fish to feed on the snails, shrimp, crabs, and juvenile species that seek shelter and food in the seaweed.

Overhead are multitudes of seabirds—among them brown pelicans, northern gannets, and laughing gulls—that in turn feed in the ocean and coastal estuaries. Dozens of bird species fly the Mississippi migration route each year, a major attraction for bird watchers, who flock to coastal Louisiana and Texas to catch a glimpse of migrating and resident shorebirds and nesting seabirds. Some of these birds feed on estuarine shrimp, fish, and crabs; others depend on shellfish and other small organisms that populate the expansive mudflats. Larger wading birds stalk their prey in the shallow water of mangroves, marshes, and other habitats that shelter fish and frogs. Raptors, including ospreys, bald eagles, and peregrine falcons, also pluck their prey from any of these environments and carry it to their perches.

As the unprecedented volume of oil gushing from the Macondo blowout reached the surface, it had the potential to affect all of these marine and coastal organisms and to wash into the salt marshes, mudflats, mangroves, and sandy beaches—each in its way an essential habitat at one or more stages of many species' lifecycles. And these marine and coastal species are so interdependent that a significant effect on any one has the potential to disturb several existing populations in this complex food web.

Encountering oil. Organisms are exposed to oil through ingestion, filtration, inhalation, absorption, and fouling. Predators may ingest oil while eating other oiled organisms or mistaking oil globules for food. Filter feeders—including some fish, oysters, shrimp, krill, jellyfish, corals, sponges, and whale sharks—will ingest minute oil particles suspended in the water column. Surface-breathing mammals and reptiles surrounded by an oil slick may inhale oily water or its fumes. Birds are highly vulnerable to having their feathers oiled, reducing their ability to properly regulate body temperature. Moderate to heavy external oiling of animals can inhibit their ability to walk, fly, swim, and eat. Similarly, oiling of plants can impede their ability to transpire and conduct photosynthesis, and oiling of coastal sediments can smother the plants they anchor and the many organisms that live below.

Americans watched as the oil eventually came to rest along intermittent stretches of the Gulf coast. Before it arrived, scientists rushed to collect crucial baseline data on coastal and water-column conditions. Some of the oil propelled up from the well-head was dispersed by natural and chemical means (as described in Chapter 5), creating a deep-ocean plume of oil droplets and dissolved hydrocarbons. A portion of the oil that rose to the surface was also naturally and chemically dispersed in the shallow water column.

The oil that made landfall was fairly "weathered," consisting of emulsions of crude oil and depleted of its more volatile components. More than 650 miles of Gulf coastal habitats—been designated as moderately to heavily oiled. Louisiana's fragile delta habitats bore the brunt of the damage, with approximately 20 additional miles of Mississippi, Alabama, and Florida shorelines moderately to heavily oiled. Light oiling and tar balls extended east to Panama City, Florida. Except for occasional tar-balls, Deepwater Horizon oil never reached Texas or the tourism centers along the southwest Florida coast.

Assessing the mixture of oil and life at the water's edge. The most biologically productive area along a sandy beach occurs where seaweed and other organic materials wash up just above the high tide line in the "wrack zone." Here, shorebirds forage for insects and other small organisms. As oil moves onto a beach with the rising tide, it is deposited in the wrack zone. Removing oiled wrack is the most prudent means of removing the oil—but doing so removes the living community, too. As the response to the spill proceeded, the Audubon Society evaluated wrack density along shorelines; it found that the wrack density on beaches east of the Mississippi River, where cleanup activities occurred, was "nearly absent," indicating "diminished habitat quality."

Few beachgoers realize that millions of microscopic organisms live in the Gulf's soggy sands between high and low tide. By comparing samples taken before and after beaches were oiled, Holly Bik of the University of New Hampshire's Hubbard Center for Genome Studies, together with scientists at Auburn University and the University of Texas, hopes to determine the impact on this understudied community of sediment-dwelling microfauna.

Tidal mudflats, generally devoid of vegetation and exposed at low tide, are more sensitive to pollutants than beaches. The Louisiana delta and the estuarine bays of Mississippi and Alabama have large expanses of tidal mudflats, which support dense populations of burrowing species (vulnerable to smothering), foraging birds, crabs, and other organisms. As oil settles on the flats, crabs and other burrowing animals help mix the oil into the sediment layer (an ecological process called bioturbation), extending the potential damage below the surface.

Salt marsh and mangroves are both highly productive and sensitive habitats. Marsh grasses tolerate surface coating by weathered oil fairly well, but they will die if oil penetrates the saturated sediments and is absorbed by the root system. When that happens, the plants' root systems degrade, making the marsh much more susceptible to erosion and threatening the habitat on which a wide variety of animals depend. People and equipment deployed in response to the spill can themselves damage the marsh; for example, summer storms pushed boom (used to corral waterborne oil) deep into the marshes, from which it could only be removed by intrusive methods that caused additional harm to the marsh topography. Scientists working in oiled marshes observed new plant growth during the summer of 2010—a positive sign that oil had not penetrated into the rich, organic soils and inhibited root systems. Professor Eugene Turner of Louisiana State University's Coastal Ecology Institute plans to study the effects of oil on the local salt marshes for at least the next year. His preliminary observations, through the fall of 2010, indicate some stress resulting in loss of marsh along its edge, but the estimated loss "pales in comparison" to the annual loss associated with dredging and flood protection (described in Chapter 7).

The marine impacts. When water temperatures warm in the late spring, female oysters release millions of eggs into the water column. The timing of the Macondo oil spill may have been detrimental to oyster reproduction and the spawning of many other species. Submerged oil floating in the nearshore water column poses potential threats to diverse shellfish and fish species. Although the impacts are not yet known, the presence of oil in the nearshore environment has been documented. Oil that reached the Gulf's estuarine waters forced closures of and likely damaged substantial tracts of Louisiana oyster beds. Oyster mortality observed in the highly productive areas of Barataria Bay and Breton Sound, estuaries that flank the lower Mississippi River, appear to be due, in large part, to the flood of fresh water introduced through river diversions in what many believe was a futile attempt to keep oil from entering the estuarine areas.

Beyond their commercial import, oysters are a keystone species—an organism that exerts a shaping, disproportionate influence on its habitat and community. A single adult oyster can filter more than one gallon of water per hour, effectively removing impurities—including oil—from the water column. Oyster reefs established on an estuary's muddy bottom can increase the surface area fifty-fold, creating intricate habitats for crabs, small fish, and other animals, which in turn sustain larger species.

Harriet Perry, Director of the Center for Fisheries Research and Development at the University of Southern Mississippi, and scientists at Tulane University are studying the potential effects of oil on larvae of blue crabs, another keystone species. The slick from the Macondo oil spill ultimately covered about 40 percent of the offshore area used by larvae of the northern Gulf's estuarine-dependent species. The Gulf coast's blue crab population had already declined considerably during the past 8 to 10 years as a result of a regional drought. Perry and other scientists raced to take samples before the oil arrived and then after, hoping to be able to separate the oil-related impacts on wildlife from climate-related changes.

Many large fish species are dependent on the health of the estuarine and marine habitats and resources. The National Oceanic and Atmospheric Administration (NOAA) noted that species with "essential fish habitat" near the oil spill include scalloped hammerhead, shortfin mako, silky, whale, bigeye thresher, longfin mako, and oceanic whitetip sharks; and swordfish, white marlin, blue marlin, yellowfin tuna, bluefin tuna, longbill spearfish, and sailfish. Other important Gulf fish include red snapper, gag grouper, gray triggerfish, red drum, vermilion snapper, greater amberjack, black drum, cobia and dolphin (mahi-mahi); coastal migratory open-water species, such as king and Spanish mackerel; and open-water sharks.

Oil in the water column affects fish and other marine organisms through dermal contact, filtration, or ingestion. How much oil they accumulate depends on its concentration in food, water, and sediments they encounter, time and exposure, and the characteristics of each species—particularly the extent of their fatty tissue. Although oil is not very soluble in water, oil and lipids do mix very well, so high concentrations of petroleum can be found in the fat-rich tissues of the liver, brain, kidneys, and ovaries. Muscle generally has the lowest lipid concentrations, but fish with fatty flesh can accumulate more oil than leaner species. Oil constituents can be transferred through the food chain: heavier hydrocarbons can be passed from water to phytoplankton and then to zooplankton, or from sediments to polychaete worms and eventually to fish. Because animals that are several steps up the food chain, like small fish, have the capability to metabolize hydrocarbons fairly rapidly, their predators will actually not accumulate much from eating them. Accordingly, bioaccumulation of toxic oil components does occur in fish, but biomagnification, with increasingly higher concentrations in animals at each level, does not occur.

It would be impossible to sample and assess each of the thousands of marine fish and other species inhabiting the open-ocean water column. But scientists monitoring the spill along the shorelines and aboard research vessels have sampled plankton, shellfish, fish, water, sediment, and other environmental media to better understand the potential impacts on all terrestrial and marine organisms. Tens of thousands of samples have been collected. They will likely analyze the samples to determine concentrations of oil and dispersants, and combine that information with existing data on species populations and distributions to model the potential impact of contamination in the water column on different species. In addition, large fish—like bluefin tuna and whale sharks (the world's largest fish)—mammals, and turtles are being tagged with tracking devices so scientists can follow their movements in the hope of learning how they have been affected by the spill. By overlaying maps of the extent of the oil spill, derived from satellite images from the European Space Agency, with simulations of bluefin tuna spawning grounds and models of larval development, the Ocean Foundation estimated that the spill could have affected 20 percent of the 2010 season's population of bluefin tuna larvae, further placing at risk an already severely overfished species.

Birds, mammals, turtles. Oiled birds are often the most visually disturbing and widely disseminated images associated with a major oil spill—as in the landmark Santa Barbara accident of 1969. Through November 1, 2010, wildlife responders had collected 8,183 birds, 1,144 sea turtles, and 109 marine mammals affected by the spill—alive or dead, visibly oiled or not. Given the effects of hiding, scavenging, sinking, decomposition, and the sheer size of the search area, many more specimens were not intercepted. Therefore, scientists will assess the estimated total damage by applying a multiplier to the final observed number of casualties, and will likely issue separate estimates of sub-lethal effects and the impact of the spill on future populations.

In September 28 testimony before the Commission, Jane Lyder, Deputy Assistant Secretary of the Department of the Interior for Fish and Wildlife and Parks, said that "With more than 60 percent of the data verified, the three most affected [bird] species appear to be Brown Pelicans, Northern Gannets, and Laughing Gulls." She added that "The fall migration is underway. Songbirds and shorebirds began their migration to the Gulf coast in July. Waterfowl began arriving in late August and early September. We know there are significant impacts to marsh and coastal wetland habitats along sections of the Louisiana coast, particularly near Grand Isle, Louisiana. We are continuing to monitor what the full impact will be to migratory birds and other wildlife."

The potential impact on marine mammals and sea turtles is harder to assess. Tim Ragen, Executive Director of the federal Marine Mammal Commission, testifying before a House of Representatives subcommittee on June 10, 2010, could only conclude, "Unfortunately, the scientific foundation for evaluating the potential effects of the Deepwater Horizon spill on many marine mammals inhabiting the Gulf is weak."

According to NOAA, "Of the 28 species of marine mammals known to live in the Gulf of Mexico, all are protected, and six (sperm, sei, fin, blue, humpback and North Atlantic right whales) are listed as endangered under the Endangered Species Act." Also of note, "At least four species of threatened/endangered sea turtles (Kemp's ridley, green, leatherback, and loggerhead) are residents of the northern Gulf of Mexico and are represented by all life stages. A fifth species, the hawksbill turtle, can be found in the southern Gulf. The only nesting beaches in the world for Kemp's ridley turtles are in the western Gulf of Mexico." As of November 1, the Unified Area Command reported that nine marine mammals had been collected alive (and three were released). One hundred mammals were collected dead, though only four of those were visibly oiled. Most of the marine mammal mortalities were bottlenose dolphins. Also among the dead was one juvenile sperm whale; it was found floating more than 70 miles from the source of the spill, reportedly unoiled. More than 600 dead sea turtles were collected.

Deepwater plumes of dispersed oil. The highly visible damage to wildlife aside, public and scientific concern about the Deepwater Horizon spill—at unprecedented water depths—has for some time focused on the impacts of an invisible subsurface "plume," or more accurately "clouds" of minute oil droplets moving slowly over the seabed. As of November 2010, three independent, peer-reviewed studies confirmed the presence of a deepwater plume of highly dispersed oil droplets and dissolved gases at between 3,200 and 4,200 feet deep and extending for many miles, primarily to the southwest of the wellhead.

How will such substances affect the deepwater environment? One concern centered on decomposition and the resulting depletion of the oxygen supply on which aquatic species depend. Bacterial decomposition begins quickly for the light hydrocarbon gases, propane and ethane, but more slowly for the heavier hydrocarbons typically present in a liquid form and for the predominant gas, methane. The blooms of bacteria stimulated by lighter hydrocarbons prime the populations for degradation of other hydrocarbons. The degradation rates are sufficient to reduce the dissolved oxygen concentrations in the plume, but not to harmfully low levels associated with dead zones, where aquatic species cannot survive. Subsequent mixing with adjacent, uncontaminated waters by slow-flowing currents appears to have been sufficient to prevent any further depletion of dissolved oxygen in the aging plumes. These findings do not rule out potential impacts of deepwater oil and dispersant concentrations on individual species. Chemical analyses of water samples taken from the established deepwater plume in May 2010 suggest that hydrocarbon concentrations were high enough at the time to cause acute toxicity to exposed organisms, although concentrations declined over several miles from the well as the plume mixed with the surrounding water.

Federal scientists have estimated that about 15 percent of the oil escaping the wellhead was physically dispersed by the fluid turbulence around the flow of oil and gas. The deepwater plume would have formed even if chemical dispersants had not been injected at the wellhead. But the addition of 18,379 barrels of dispersants to the discharging oil and gas stream may have increased the volume of oil in the deepwater plumes to a degree comparable to that from physical dispersion alone. As of late 2010, there have been unconfirmed reports of oil deposited on the seafloor in the vicinity of the Macondo well. If confirmed by chemical analyses, this would not be particularly surprising because oil droplets can become entrained in denser particulate matter, including the flocks of organic matter (referred to by scientists as "marine snow") that characterize open-ocean waters, and settle on the ocean floor. There have also been recent reports of dead or dying deepwater corals living on rock outcrops that could have been impinged by the deep plumes.

Because the Deepwater Horizon spill was unprecedented in size, location, and duration, deepwater ecosystems were exposed to large volumes of oil for an extended period. It will take further investigation and more time to assess the impacts on these ecosystems, their extent and duration. Unfortunately, except for studies that have focused on rare and specialized communities associated with rocky outcrops or seeps, scientific understanding of the deepwater Gulf ecosystem has not advanced with the industrial development of deepwater drilling and production.

SOURCE: National Commission on the BP Deepwater Horizon Oil Spill and Offshore Drilling. 2011. *Deep Water: The Gulf Oil Disaster and the Future of Offshore Drilling.* http://www.gpo.gov/fdsys/pkg/GPO-OILCOMMISSION/pdf/GPO-OILCOMMISSION.pdf (accessed August 17, 2014).

ANALYSIS

The Deepwater Horizon rig was digging the Macondo Well when it blew out on April 20, 2010. The resulting explosion killed 11 people on the rig and opened a massive oil leak into the Gulf of Mexico, which was not completely contained until September 19, 2010. Millions of barrels of oil were dispersed during that period, resulting in severe damage to as much as 65,000 square miles of territory. In addition to incalculable damage to the environment, the spill resulted in severe economic harm to the fishing and tourism industries of the Gulf Coast states, most notably Florida, Alabama, Mississippi, and Louisiana. In an effort to contain the damage caused by the oil, officials spread more than 1.5 million gallons of Corexit oil dispersant to break up the oil emerging from the spill. Unfortunately, the dispersant caused even more environmental damage.

As the oil spill was the largest ever recorded by the petroleum industry, President Barack Obama appointed dignitaries to serve on the National Commission on the BP Deepwater Horizon Oil Spill and Offshore Drilling to investigate the accident. In their report, *Deep Water: The Gulf Oil Disaster and the Future of Offshore Drilling: Report to the President*, the commission cataloged the environmental damage that was caused over the course of the approximate five months that the well spewed oil. Also examined was the course of events that led to the blowout, which included identifying the decisions made by British Petroleum (BP) and its partners in the drilling endeavor, namely Transocean, which owned the oil rig, and Halliburton, which was responsible for the cement work on the well.

Predictably, the respective companies attempted to limit their liabilities due to numerous lawsuits that were filed by private, corporate, and governmental entities. To address some of the lawsuits, BP put $20 billion in a trust fund for damage claims. The company also paid $7.8 billion to settle a number of private claims. Agreements were also put in place between BP, Transocean, and Halliburton to settle liability issues that had emerged as they all dealt with legal issues. In November 2012, BP settled with the Department of Justice, which was perceived as the greatest financial threat to the corporation. In the agreement, BP pled guilty to charges of corporate manslaughter related to the 11 deaths on the oil rig, withholding information from the U.S. Congress, lying to law enforcement officials, and misdemeanor violations to the Clean Water Act and the Migratory Bird Treaty. As punishment, BP was required to pay $4.5 billion in fines. Although the penalties appeared heavy-handed, the inclusion of a misdemeanor violation of the Clean Water Act as a penalty was potentially a major victory for BP shareholders, and it appeared to protect them from extremely heavy fines required by the Clean Water Act should their actions have been considered "reckless." Many viewed the settlement as a major victory for the petroleum industry, as it was widely believed that the penalty they paid paled in comparison to the large revenues that were being enjoyed industry-wide. In short, the penalty was not large enough to serve as a deterrent to BP or its creditors.

On September 4, 2014, the landscape for BP and its partners changed as U.S. District Judge Carl Barbier determined in New Orleans, Louisiana, that BP had acted "recklessly" and with "willful misconduct" in making decisions that led to the blowout of the Macondo Well. His declaration exposed BP to potentially another $18 billion in fines related to violations of the Clean Water Act. Incensed by the ruling, BP's lawyers are appealing the decision to the Fifth Circuit Court of Appeals.

FURTHER READING

Committee on the Effects of the Deepwater Horizon Mississippi Canyon–252 Oil Spill on Ecosystem Services in the Gulf of Mexico; Ocean Studies Board; Division on Earth and Life Studies; National Resources Council. 2014. *An Ecosystem Services Approach* to *Assessing the Impacts of the Deepwater Horizon Oil Spill in the Gulf of Mexico.* Washington, DC: National Academies Press.

Fleming, Kenton. 2012. "What Happened at the Macondo Well: A Review of Offshore Drilling and the British Petroleum–Macondo Well Disaster of April, 2010." *Journal of Applied Global Research* 5, no. 15: 81–90.

Iaquinto, Christopher M. 2012. "A Silent Spring in Deep Water? Proposing Front-End Regulation of Dispersants After the Deepwater Horizon Disaster." *Boston College Environmental Affairs Law Review* 39, no. 2: 419–448.

Smith, Lawrence C., Jr., L. Murphy Smith, and Paul A. Ashcroft. 2011. "Analysis of Environmental and Economic Damages from British Petroleum's Deepwater Horizon Oil Spill." *Albany Law Review* 74, no. 1: 563–585.

Theriot, Jason P. 2014. *American Energy, Imperiled Coast: Oil and Gas Development in Louisiana's Wetlands.* Baton Rouge: Louisiana State University Press.

U.S. District Court for the Eastern District of Louisiana. 2014. *In Re: Oil Spill by the Oil Rig "Deepwater Horizon" in the Gulf of Mexico on April 20, 2010, This Document Applies To: No. 10-2771, In RE; The Complaint and Petition of Triton Asset Leasing GmbH, et al. and No. 10-4536, United States of America v. BP Exploration & Production, Inc., et al.* http://www.laed.uscourts.gov/OilSpill/Orders/9042014FindingsofFactand ConclusionsofLaw.pdf (accessed September 7, 2014).

11

CHEMICAL POLLUTION

"An Unreasonable Risk of Injury to Health or the Environment"

- *Document:* Toxic Substances Control Act of 1976, as Amended Through P.L. 107–377, December 31, 2002, excerpts
- *Date:* The original act was signed by President Gerald Ford on October 11, 1976. The 2002 amendment was enacted on December 31, 2002.
- *Where:* Washington, DC
- *Significance:* The act tasked the Environmental Protection Agency to study the health and environmental effects of chemicals that were already being used within the country and to also assess any new chemical compounds that were created after the legislation was enacted.

DOCUMENT

SEC. 2. FINDINGS, POLICY, AND INTENT.

(a) FINDINGS.—The Congress finds that—

(1) human beings and the environment are being exposed each year to a large number of chemical substances and mixtures.

(2) among the many chemical substances and mixtures which are constantly being developed and produced, there are some whose manufacture, processing, distribution in commerce, use, or disposal may present an unreasonable risk of injury to health or the environment; and

(3) the effective regulation of interstate commerce in such chemical substances and mixtures also necessitates the regulation of intrastate commerce in such chemical substances and mixtures.

(b) POLICY.—It is the policy of the United States that—

(1) adequate data should be developed with respect to the effect of chemical substances and mixtures on health and the environment and that the development of such data should be the responsibility of those who manufacture and those who process such chemical substances and mixtures;

(2) adequate authority should exist to regulate chemical substances and mixtures which present an unreasonable risk of injury to health or the environment, and to take action with respect to chemical substances and mixtures which are imminent hazards; and

(3) authority over chemical substances and mixtures should be exercised in such a manner as not to impede unduly or create unnecessary economic barriers to technological innovation while fulfilling the primary purpose of this Act to assure that such innovation and commerce in such chemical substances and mixtures do not present an unreasonable risk of injury to health or the environment.

(c) INTENT OF CONGRESS.—It is the intent of Congress that the Administrator shall carry out this Act in a reasonable and prudent manner, and that the Administrator shall consider the environmental, economic, and social impact of any action the Administrator takes or proposes to take under this Act.

. . .

SEC. 5. MANUFACTURING AND PROCESSING NOTICES.

. . .

(h) EXEMPTIONS.—(1) The Administrator may, upon application, exempt any person from any requirement of subsection (a) or (b) to permit such person to manufacture or process a chemical substance for test marketing purposes—

(A) upon a showing by such person satisfactory to the Administrator that the manufacture, processing, distribution in commerce, use, and disposal of such substance, and that any combination of such activities, for such purposes will not present any unreasonable risk of injury to health or the environment, and

(B) under such restrictions as the Administrator considers appropriate.

(2)(A) The Administrator may, upon application, exempt any person from the requirement of subsection (b)(2) to submit data for a chemical substance. If, upon receipt of an application under the preceding sentence, the Administrator determines that—

(i) the chemical substance with respect to which such application was submitted is equivalent to a chemical substance for which data has been submitted to the Administrator as required by subsection (b)(2), and

(ii) submission of data by the applicant on such substance would be duplicative of data which has been submitted to the Administrator in accordance with such subsection, the Administrator shall exempt the applicant from the requirement to submit such data on such substance. No exemption which is granted under this subparagraph with respect to the submission of data for a chemical substance may take effect before the beginning of the reimbursement period applicable to such data.

(B) If the Administrator exempts any person, under subparagraph (A), from submitting data required under subsection (b)(2) for a chemical substance because of the existence of previously submitted data and if such exemption is granted during the reimbursement period for such data, then (unless such person and the persons referred to in clauses (i) and (ii) agree on the amount and method of reimbursement) the Administrator shall order the person granted the exemption to provide fair and equitable reimbursement (in an amount determined under rules of the Administrator)—

(i) to the person who previously submitted the data on which the exemption was based, for a portion of the costs incurred by such person in complying with the requirement under subsection (b)(2) to submit such data, and

(ii) to any other person who has been required under this subparagraph to contribute with respect to such costs, for a portion of the amount such person was required to contribute.

In promulgating rules for the determination of fair and equitable reimbursement to the persons described in clauses (i) and (ii) for costs incurred with respect to a chemical substance, the Administrator shall, after consultation with the Attorney General and the Federal Trade Commission, consider all relevant factors, including the effect on the competitive position of the person required to provide reimbursement in relation to the persons to be reimbursed and the share of the market for such substance of the person required to provide reimbursement in relation to the share of such market of the persons to be reimbursed. For purposes of judicial review, an order under this subparagraph shall be considered final agency action.

(C) For purposes of this paragraph, the reimbursement period for any previously submitted data for a chemical substance is a period—

(i) beginning on the date of the termination of the prohibition, imposed under this section, on the manufacture or processing of such substance by the person who submitted such data to the Administrator, and

(ii) ending—

(I) five years after the date referred to in clause (i), or

(II) at the expiration of a period which begins on the date referred to in clause (i) and is equal to the period which the Administrator determines was necessary to develop such data, whichever is later.

(3) The requirements of subsections (a) and (b) do not apply with respect to the manufacturing or processing of any chemical substance which is manufactured or processed, or proposed to be manufactured or processed, only in small quantities (as defined by the Administrator by rule) solely for purposes of—

(A) scientific experimentation or analysis, or

(B) chemical research on, or analysis of such substance or another substance, including such research or analysis for the development of a product, if all persons engaged in such experimentation, research, or analysis for a manufacturer or processor are notified (in such form and manner as the Administrator may prescribe) of any risk to health which the manufacturer, processor, or the Administrator has reason to believe may be associated with such chemical substance.

(4) The Administrator may, upon application and by rule, exempt the manufacturer of any new chemical substance from all or part of the requirements of this section if the administrator determines that the manufacture, processing, distribution in commerce, use, or disposal of such chemical substance, or that any combination of such activities, will not present an unreasonable risk of injury to health or the

environment. A rule promulgated under this paragraph (and any substantive amendment to, or repeal of, such a rule) shall be promulgated in accordance with paragraphs (2) and (3) of section 6(c).

(5) The Administrator may, upon application, make the requirements of subsections (a) and (b) inapplicable with respect to the manufacturing or processing of any chemical substance (A) which exists temporarily as a result of a chemical reaction in the manufacturing or processing of a mixture or another chemical substance, and (B) to which there is no, and will not be, human or environmental exposure.

(6) Immediately upon receipt of an application under paragraph (1) or (5) the Administrator shall publish in the Federal Register notice of the receipt of such application. The Administrator shall give interested persons an opportunity to comment upon any such application and shall, within 45 days of its receipt, either approve or deny the application. The Administrator shall publish in the Federal Register notice of the approval or denial of such an application.

SOURCE: U.S. Congress. n.d. *Toxic Substances Control Act*. http://www.epw.senate.gov/tsca.pdf (accessed October 5, 2014).

ANALYSIS

The federal government's push to regulate toxic substances was initiated in 1971 by the president's Council on Environmental Quality (CEQ) with the issuance of a report focusing on the threat posed by metals and synthetic chemicals being introduced into the environment by a number of industries. The CEQ subsequently drafted legislation to research and regulate the chemicals, which they titled the Toxic Substances Control Act of 1971. Although the legislation was not enacted, it did spur discussions between the CEQ, Commerce Department, Congress, Environmental Protection Agency (EPA), and business interests on how to address the issue. From their negotiations, the Toxic Substances Control Act (TSCA) of 1971 emerged.

The TSCA required the EPA to test chemicals that were already in use to determine whether they were safe for the environment in general and humans in particular. If deemed unsafe, then the chemicals could no longer be utilized. The EPA was also to test any new chemicals that were developed to ensure their safety before being used for agricultural or industrial purposes. As noted in section 2 of the TSCA, the legislation was desperately needed because substantial evidence already existed that heavy metals and synthetic chemicals were harming the environment. Unfortunately, the TSCA was written in a manner that made enforcement of its provisions extremely difficult. The primary issue could be found in section 5h, which allowed for a significant number of exemptions to the rules. Basically, if a substance was either deemed safe or did not pose a significant risk to the environment, an exemption to the TSCA would be granted by the head of the EPA. Under the guidelines of the law, the entity that determined the safety of a chemical was the manufacturer. They certified that their synthetic creation was safe and that was the assumed truth unless the EPA could prove otherwise. With the number of chemicals in use by 1976, and those that were being created in laboratories, it was not feasible for the EPA to do all the testing necessary to prove that were not supposedly safe chemicals. The EPA essentially was forced to grandfather tens of thousands of chemicals in use at the time the act was drafted as they had already proven themselves "safe" over time. That was a curious decision considering that the act was justified by the presence of harmful metals and synthetic chemicals being introduced into the environment. One chemical deemed safe in 1976 and thus left unstudied was 4-methylcyclohexanemethanol, which in 2014 was leaked into the water supply of Charleston, West Virginia. In the midst of that disaster, it was discovered that health officials had no idea how the chemical would impact humans despite its use for more than 50 years. That was the very problem that the TSCA was supposed to fix in the first place.

The TSCA has been amended on several occasions but just to broaden its coverage to substances such as asbestos. Its massive loopholes have been left untouched. There has been some activity in Congress to update the legislation to address its many shortcomings. The most recent attempt was the proposed Safe Chemicals Act of 2013, but it languished in Congress without the necessary votes to pass. Its inability to pass is not a partisan issue, as many Democrats and Republicans fear that closing the TSCA's loopholes will severely impact the economies of their states as they would burden the industries that are their primary employers.

FURTHER READING

Collins, Craig. 2010. *Toxic Loopholes: Failures and Future Prospects for Environmental Law.* New York: Cambridge University Press.

DeRosa, Christopher. 2010. "The USEPA and the Toxic Substances Control Act (TSCA) of 1976: The Promise, the Reality, and the Reason(s) Why." *Human & Ecological Risk Assessment* 16, no. 6: 1227–1233.

U.S. Environmental Protection Agency. 2013. *Chemistry Assistance Manual for Premanufacture Notification Submitters: Appendix: The Toxics Substances Control Act: History and Implementation.* http://www.epa.gov/oppt/newschem/pubs/chem-pmn/appendix.pdf.

Vogel, Sarah A., and Jody A. Roberts. 2011. "Why the Toxic Substances Control Act Needs an Overhaul, and How to Strengthen Oversight of Chemicals in the Interim." *Health Affairs* 30, no. 5: 898–905.

"Known Toxicological Information"

- *Document:* Consent Agreement and Proposed Final Order to Resolve DuPont's Alleged Failure to Submit Substantial Risk Information Under the Toxic Substances Control Act (TSCA) and Failure to Submit Data Requested Under the Resource Conservation and Recovery Act (RCRA), excerpts
- *Date:* December 14, 2005
- *Where:* Washington, DC
- *Significance:* The Environmental Protection Agency leveled its largest fine up to that time to DuPont for violations of the Toxic Substances Control Act.

DOCUMENT

The Office of Enforcement and Compliance Assurance requests that the Environmental Appeals Board (Board) approve the accompanying Consent Agreement and proposed Final Order executed by E.I. du Pont de Nemours and Company (DuPont) and the Environmental Protection Agency (EPA) that settles this matter for $10.25 million in penalties plus an additional $6.25 million expenditure for Supplemental Environmental Projects (SEPs). This memorandum conforms to the Board's Consent Order Review Procedures dated January 5, 1993.

The Consent Agreement resolves violations of the Toxic Substances Control Act (TSCA), 15 U.S.C. §§ 2601 *et seq.*, and the Resource Conservation and Recovery Act (RCRA), 42 U.S.C. §§ 6901 *et seq.*, as alleged in two administrative complaints filed on July 8, 2004 (subsequently amended on October 13, 2004) and December 6, 2004, copies of which are included with this transmittal package as attachments A and B. The Consent Agreement also simultaneously commences and concludes four additional alleged violations of TSCA, as discussed below. All eight alleged violations are collectively referred to in this memorandum as EPA's Action.

The Consent Agreement complies with Section 22.18(b) of the Consolidated Rules of Practice Governing the Administrative Assessment of Civil Penalties and the Revocation/Termination or Suspension of Permits (Rules of Practice), 40 C.F.R. § 22.18(b). I have reviewed the Consent Agreement and determined that it is consistent with the statutes authorizing the Agency's action and that the civil penalty is appropriate.

1. Background

. . .

B. The Chemical at Issue

EPA's enforcement action against DuPont involves the synthetic chemical Amonium Perfluorooctanoate (APFO), also known as C-8 and sometimes called PFOA (Perfluorooctanoic Acid) because APFO disassociates to PFOA in water. PFOA is a perfluorinated detergent/surfactant which has been used by DuPont since 1951 in connection with Teflon®related products at its Washington Works facility outside Parkersburg, West Virginia. PFOA is produced synthetically and formed through the degradation or metabolism of other fluorochemical products, such as fluorinated telomers that are used in non-stick coatings on carpets, clothing, and food wrappers.

. . .

2. Summary of the Violations

3. Count 1 alleges that DuPont failed to comply with TSCA § 8(e) when it failed to submit to EPA the information from 1981 that demonstrated transplacental movement of PFOA in humans. This data was substantial risk information concerning PFOA.

4. Count 2 alleges that DuPont failed to comply with TSCA § 8(e) when it failed to submit to EPA the information concerning PFOA contamination of the drinking water inside people's homes. This data was substantial risk information concerning PFOA.

5. Count 3 alleges that DuPont violated RCRA § 3005(a) when DuPont failed to comply with the EPA request for "known toxicological information" by failing to submit the 1981 toxicity data concerning PFOA.

6. Count 4 alleges that DuPont failed to comply with TSCA § 8(e) when it failed to submit the information from 2004 concerning the elevated PFOA blood levels in twelve individuals living in the vicinity of the Washington Works facility. This data was substantial risk information concerning PFOA.

7. Count 5 alleges that DuPont failed to comply with TSCA § 8(e) when it failed to report data concerning blood test results of ten individuals living near the Washington Works facility with elevated levels of PFOA. This data was substantial risk information concerning PFOA.

8. Counts 6, 7 and 8 allege that DuPont failed to comply with TSCA § 8(e) on three occasions when it failed to report toxicity data about the three different rat inhalation studies performed on July 11, 1997 and August 29, 1997. Each of the three studies was substantial risk information concerning the aerosol form of a perfluorinated chemical.

SOURCE: U.S. Environmental Protection Agency. 2013. *Consent Agreement and Proposed Final Order to Resolve DuPont's Alleged Failure to Submit Substantial Risk Information Under the Toxic Substance Control Act (TSCA) and Failure to Submit Data Requested Under the Resource Conservation and Recovery Act (RCRA)*. http://www2.epa.gov/sites/production/files/2013-08/documents/eabmemodupontpfoasettlement121405.pdf (accessed August 23, 2014).

ANALYSIS

In 1984, DuPont became aware that some of the C8 produced at their Washington Works facility near Parkersburg, West Virginia, was leaking from containment ponds and making its way into local water supplies. C8, so-named because it contains an eight-carbon chain, is a perfluorooctanoic acid that was used to manufacture Teflon, Gore-Tex, and beauty supplies. According to the Toxic Substances Control Act (TSCA) of 1976, DuPont should have notified the Environmental Protection Agency (EPA) that the chemical had escaped into local water supplies and have informed the agency about its toxic properties. Instead the company asserted, as it had done since the early 1950s, that the substance was safe and thus exempt from the self-reporting requirement of the TSCA. Although publicly silent that the C8 was leaching into local ecosystems, DuPont did begin tracking the spread of C8 through local water systems. By the late 1980s, sampling by the company indicated that some of the levels of C8 in drinking water had become quite significant, so they began digging up the sludge in containment ponds and burying it in the Dry Run Landfill. Soon thereafter, cattle owned by the Tennant family in the vicinity of the landfill began dying. Unable to settle with DuPont over the loss of their cattle, the Tennants sued the company in 1999. Although they eventually settled with the company, the discovery process the Tennant family initiated through their lawyers alerted people in West Virginia and eastern Ohio that their drinking water was tainted with C8. This led to a class action suit that became known as *Leach v. E. I. DuPont de Nemours and Company*.

Alerted by a lawyer participating in the class action suit that DuPont had been violating the TSCA, the EPA initiated an investigation into the operations of the DuPont Washington Works plant. One of the first things determined by the agency's scientists was that the C8 was not only toxic but also widely distributed in the local countryside through landfills, groundwater, and surface waters. The toxicity had been privately confirmed by DuPont years earlier in a study performed on rats, but that information also had never been shared with the EPA as required by the TSCA. The failure to divulge information to the EPA was what put DuPont in violation of the TSCA. That legislation put the onus on the company to self-report violations. The EPA could only charge a company with a violation of the TSCA if it could prove that the company had intentionally hidden information that proved a substance dangerous to humans and the environment. This was nearly impossible for the EPA to do because the only way they could obtain the evidence to prove fault was to request companies to willfully share information that would prove they were violating the law. Thanks to the private litigation already underway, in this case, the EPA had the evidence it required. It thus levied the largest fine ever to a company found violating the TSCA. Unfortunately, this was one of the few times the agency was able to prove a company was in violation of a law in place since 1976.

FURTHER READING

Grossman, Elizabeth. 2009. *Chasing Molecules: Poisonous Products, Human Health, and the Promise of Green Chemistry*. Washington, DC: Island Press.

Hounshell, David A., and John Kenly Smith. 1988. *Science and Corporate Strategy: Du Pont R&D, 1902–1980*. New York: Cambridge University Press.

Lyons, Callie. 2007. *Stain-Resistant, Nonstick, Waterproof, and Lethal: The Hidden Dangers of C8*. Westport, CT: Praeger, 2007.

Woodhouse, Edward J. 1985. "External Influences on Productivity: EPA's Implementation of TSCA." *Policy Studies Review* 4, no. 3: 497–503.

"Groundwater Is the Primary Source of Water Used in the High Plains"

- *Document:* Water Quality in the High Plains Aquifer, Colorado, Kansas, Nebraska, New Mexico, Oklahoma, South Dakota, Texas, and Wyoming, 1999–2004, Overview of Major Findings and Implications
- *Date:* 2009
- *Where:* Reston, Virginia
- *Significance:* The High Plains Aquifer, also known as the Ogallala Aquifer, contains approximately 3 billion acre-feet of water, which underlies all or parts of eight states. In addition to being a source of drinking water, it supports a robust agricultural industry.

DOCUMENT

The National Water-Quality Assessment (NAWQA) assessment of water-quality conditions of the High Plains aquifer for the period 1999–2004 provides the first systematic and comprehensive regional assessment of water quality in this nationally important aquifer. NAWQA results show where, when, why, and how specific water-quality conditions occur in groundwater across the High Plains aquifer and yield science-based implications for assessing and managing the quality of this water resource. Understanding groundwater quality conditions and the natural and human factors that control water quality in this aquifer is important because of the implications to human health, the sustainability of rural agricultural economies, and the substantial costs associated with land and water management, conservation, and regulation.

Availability and Sustainability of Groundwater in the High Plains Aquifer are a Function of Water Quantity and Quality

Groundwater is the primary source of water used in the High Plains; thus, knowledge about groundwater availability and sustainability are essential for the informed management of this limited resource. Groundwater availability and sustainability are functions of many factors, one of which is water quality. Understanding groundwater quality is important because it directly affects how water can be used. Water quality generally has been overlooked in the High Plains because the primary focus has been on obtaining a sufficient water supply, and it has been broadly assumed that the aquifer contains high-quality water. For the most part, results from the NAWQA study support that assumption. See Chapters 4, 5, and 6 for more details.

IMPLICATIONS

- Groundwater quality, particularly regarding elevated nitrate or dissolved-solids concentrations, may be a limiting factor for some intended uses such as drinking- or irrigation-water supply at local and, in some instances, subregional scales.
- Groundwater quality, particularly regarding elevated nitrate concentrations in recently recharged groundwater, is changing over time and, because of the slow rates of water movement in the aquifer, could affect groundwater availability for decades and even millennia.

Conversion of Rangeland to Irrigated Cropland Affects Water Quality

NAWQA findings indicate that the nitrogen and pesticide applications on irrigated cropland result in substantially more nitrate and pesticides being transported to the water table at irrigated cropland settings than at rangeland settings. In some locations, however, the change in recharge chemistry following conversion of rangeland to cropland results from the mobilization by irrigation water of large natural nitrate and chloride deposits in the unsaturated zone (above the water table). See Chapter 4 for more details.

IMPLICATIONS

- Reducing the acreage of rangeland that is converted to irrigated cropland in areas that contain large natural subsurface nitrate and chloride deposits (currently not delineated across the entire High Plains aquifer) is likely to be an effective way to reduce the dissolution and transport of natural chemical constituents in recharge water and resulting adverse effects on water quality in the aquifer.
- Implementing efficient agricultural-chemical application and irrigation technologies in areas not currently implemented to reduce deep percolation of irrigation water and chemicals under cropland is likely to be an effective way to reduce the adverse effects on the quality of the recently recharged groundwater.

reluctant to reclassify it as hazardous, thus continuing to exempt it from regulation by the EPA.

FURTHER READING

Rauch, Alan. F. 2014. "Recovery at Kingston." *Power Engineering* 118, no. 2: 34–38.

Ruhl, Laura, et al. 2010. "Environmental Impacts of the Coal Ash Spill in Kingston, Tennessee: An 18-Month Survey." *Environmental Science & Technology* 44, no. 24: 9272–9278.

Chemical Transport to the Water Table Follows Fast and Slow Paths

NAWQA findings indicate that chemical transport to the water table occurs by fast and slow paths through the unsaturated zone. In most locations studied, estimated chemical transit times from land surface to the water table exceeded the period of agricultural activity and imply that agricultural chemicals should not yet be present at the water table. In fact, agricultural chemicals are commonly detected at the water table beneath irrigated cropland. This apparent discrepancy is explained by localized fast or preferential flow paths that enable water and chemicals to move quickly through the unsaturated zone to the water table. Fast paths are most likely to be present beneath topographic depressions in the land surface in which surface runoff from irrigation or precipitation collects. Slow paths are most likely to be present in areas of fine-grained sediments or beneath flat terrain where surface water does not collect. Along fast paths, water and chemicals from land surface may reach the water table in months to decades. Along slow paths, water and chemicals from land surface are likely to reach the water table in centuries to millennia. See Chapter 4 for more details.

IMPLICATIONS

- Reducing the amount of untreated agricultural and urban runoff to topographic depressions or other fast-path zones is likely to reduce the rapid transport of contaminants to the water table and be an effective management strategy toward minimizing groundwater contamination.

Important Differences Exist Between the Quality of Shallow Groundwater and Deep Groundwater

NAWQA findings indicate that changes in water quality have occurred over time that may affect the sustainability of the groundwater resource in the High Plains aquifer. Important spatial differences in the concentrations of dissolved solids, nitrate, pesticides, arsenic, and other constituents were observed between the quality of shallow and relatively young groundwater and the quality of deep and relatively old groundwater. Dissolved-solids concentrations in shallow groundwater generally increased from north to south in the High Plains aquifer and were significantly greater in the southern part (median of 800 milligrams per liter [mg/L]) than in the northern and central parts (medians of about 450 to 500 mg/L). Nitrate above local background concentrations (4 mg/L as nitrogen [Chapter 4]) in shallow groundwater was detected throughout the High Plains aquifer. Nitrate concentrations in shallow groundwater were greater than the background concentration in 90 percent of samples from the northern, 60 percent of samples from the central, and 55 percent of samples from the southern High Plains. Although widely detected, pesticide concentrations in shallow groundwater were less than USEPA drinking-water standards in all but 2 of 119 samples. Atrazine and its degradate deethylatrazine were the most commonly detected pesticide compounds. Concentrations of arsenic in shallow groundwater were significantly greater in samples from the southern High Plains than in samples from the northern High Plains. About 40 percent of the samples in the southern High Plains exceeded the USEPA arsenic drinking-water standard of 10 μg/L, whereas none exceeded the standard in the northern High Plains. See Chapter 4 for additional information about the quality of shallow groundwater that was mostly recharged during the past 50 years.

The quality of deeper groundwater that is used by many private, public-supply, and irrigation wells in the High Plains generally is of suitable quality for most uses, although some spatial differences in water quality are observed across the region. Based on USEPA drinking-water standards, the quality of deeper groundwater decreases from the northern High Plains to the southern High Plains where the water contains greater concentrations of dissolved solids, chloride, nitrate, fluoride, manganese, arsenic, and uranium. These elevated constituent concentrations in deeper groundwater from the southern High Plains are the result of natural processes, such as water/rock interactions, and human activities, such as the mixing of high-quality groundwater with lower-quality water from underlying hydrogeologic formations, induced by pumping of high-capacity wells. See Chapters 5 and 6 for more details.

IMPLICATIONS

- The quality of groundwater near the water table may not be currently suitable for human consumption in some locations of the aquifer because of elevated concentrations of salts, nitrate, and (or) pesticides. However, the quality of groundwater in deeper parts of the aquifer, with some exceptions, currently is generally suitable for human consumption.
- The quality of groundwater that is influenced by mixing with brackish surface water or water from underying [sic] hydrogeologic formations may not be suitable for irrigation or drinking-water supply in some locations of the aquifer because of the elevated concentrations of dissolved solids.

- Groundwater remediation is expensive, slow, and impractical across regional-scale aquifers. Therefore, management practices that prevent groundwater contamination are likely to be a more effective way to maintain the availability and sustainability of groundwater in the High Plains aquifer for the intended uses for human consumption and agricultural practices.

- Collecting long-term monitoring data is likely to be an effective way to detect gradual temporal trends and to provide early warning of water-quality problems (nitrate, for example) for which the aquifer may have limited natural-attenuation capacity.

Mixing of Groundwater by High-Capacity Wells with Long or Multiple Screens Adversely Affects Water Quality

NAWQA findings indicate that the quality of deeper groundwater from private, public-supply, and irrigation wells, which typically are completed using one long or multiple screens across much of the saturated thickness of the High Plains aquifer, is sometimes affected by mixing with poorer-quality water from the water table. The mixing is caused by leakage through long or multiple well screens and long-term pumping of high-capacity public-supply and irrigation wells. In other instances, pumping of high-capacity wells causes water in the aquifer to be affected by mixing with saline water from underlying bedrock aquifers or with water from streams that is of poorer quality based on USEPA drinking-water standards. See Chapter 5 for more details

IMPLICATIONS

- The following management strategies are likely to help reduce adverse effects on the quality of water in deep zones of the aquifer caused by mixing processes:
- reduce the screen length of public-supply and irrigation wells, and optimize the spatial and temporal distribution of pumping to minimize mixing and water-table drawdown;
- eliminate the practice of screening wells across confining layers in the aquifer; and
- practice screening wells below confining layers in the aquifer where contaminant sources at the land surface are a concern, and practice screening wells above confining layers in the aquifer where contaminant sources in underlying bedrock area concern.
- Proper construction of wells to limit the movement of low-quality groundwater above and (or) below a well screen will result in maintaining a higher-quality groundwater supply for a variety of uses.

The Aquifer Has Limited Ability to Naturally Attenuate Some Contaminants

NAWQA findings indicate that the High Plains aquifer is limited in its ability to naturally attenuate some contaminants, such as nitrate. Denitrification, the primary natural process for removing nitrate in groundwater, generally occurs very slowly in the aquifer and would require hundreds to thousands of years to lower nitrate concentrations by just 1 mg/L as nitrogen (N) in many locations. Additionally, because water residence times in the aquifer are long (several thousand years in some locations), simply flushing nitrate from the aquifer could take many years. These results highlight the importance of managing land use in the High Plains to minimize the amount of nitrate entering the aquifer. See Chapter 5 for more details.

IMPLICATIONS

- In the indefinite future, the aquifer will continue to be subject to the effects of mobilized agricultural chemicals on groundwater quality from ongoing irrigation, conversion of rangeland to cropland, or climate variability.
- The long transit times of nitrate through the unsaturated zone will undoubtedly delay future improvements in water quality from implementation of best management land-use practices.

The Quality of Most Water Produced by Private, Public-Supply, and Irrigation Wells is Suitable for the Intended Uses

NAWQA findings indicate that the quality of groundwater from deeper in the High Plains aquifer, where most private, public-supply, and irrigation wells are screened, is generally suitable for drinking and as irrigation water. Comparison of private well water quality to USEPA national primary and secondary drinking-water standards indicates that water from the Ogallala Formation in the northern and central High Plains had the best water quality, whereas water from the Ogallala Formation in the southern High Plains had the poorest quality. Most exceedances of primary and secondary drinking-water standards were those for dissolved solids, nitrate, arsenic, fluoride, iron, manganese, and nitrate. The most frequently detected pesticide compounds were atrazine and deethylatrazine, and the most frequently detected volatile organic compound was chloroform. None of the pesticide compounds or volatile organic compounds exceeded a primary drinking-water standard. See Chapter 6 for more details.

IMPLICATIONS

- If contaminated, the deep zones in the aquifer, in which production wells are screened, are not likely to be remediated quickly because of slow recharge rates, long water residence times in the aquifer, and slow rates of contaminant degradation.

SOURCE: Gurdak, Jason J., et al. 2009. *Water Quality in the High Plains Aquifer, Colorado, Kansas, Nebraska, New Mexico, Oklahoma, South Dakota, Texas, and Wyoming, 1999–2004.* http://pubs.usgs.gov/circ/1337/pdf/C1337.pdf (accessed August 19, 2014).

ANALYSIS

The High Plains Aquifer, also known as the Ogallala Aquifer, is approximately 175,000 miles in size and underlies portions of eight of the United States' states: Colorado, Kansas, Nebraska, New Mexico, Oklahoma, South Dakota, Texas, and Wyoming. It is estimated that it contains more than 3 billion acre-feet of water at depths ranging from 50 to 300 feet below the surface of the ground. The deepest parts of the aquifer are found in the northern portion of the aquifer, especially in Nebraska, with the amount of water decreasing southward. Much of the water found in the aquifer is fossil water that originated from glacial and snow melt from the Rocky Mountains between 10,000 and 25,000 years ago. The High Plains Aquifer is slowly recharged by waters that seep into its water-bearing rock formations, but the rate of recharge is not enough to compensate for the amount of water that is being extracted through more than 200,000 wells for the irrigation that makes the semiarid land of the region's plains and prairies suitable for agriculture. In some portions of the aquifer, water levels have dropped more than 150 feet. Water level decline has not been uniform throughout the aquifer, as portions of the aquifer have actually increased their water levels over time, but these areas are not used for agricultural purposes.

Although Native American peoples were the first to tap the waters of the High Plains Aquifer for agricultural purposes, they did not do so at a scale that threatened the aquifer's water levels. Large-scale use of the High Plains Aquifer did not occur until the railroad companies began building a transcontinental railroad through the region. They tapped the aquifer using windmill power to pump water from the ground. The railroads naturally encouraged settlement along its railroad lines, thus promoters began to spread the word of the available land fed by abundant rivers. Unfortunately, the reality was that the water available on the Great Plains was very limited. The High Plains Aquifer thus became the primary source of water for many agriculturalists in the region. It was initially believed that the aquifer held an inexhaustible source of water. Thus, farmers throughout the Great Plains began to pump water out of the aquifer to irrigate large expanses of land without any thought of good conservation practices. By the 1940s, hydrologists had noticed that water levels were dropping noticeably in some areas and began warning that the aquifer's waters were in fact finite. Unfortunately in the 1950s, more efficient pumping systems enabled farmers to extract even more water from the aquifer than they could previously. Technology combined with droughts that occurred during the decade to accelerate the depletion of the aquifer's resources. One positive outcome from this period was that groups began to form, such as the High Plains Underground Water Conservation District (HPUWCD), who dedicated themselves to the preservation of the High Plains Aquifer so that its waters would be available for future generations. Although improved conservation strategies have slowed the depletion of the aquifer's resources, the amount of water being pumped from the Ogallala for irrigation still exceeds the amount of surface water that is seeping through the ground to recharge it.

As people are aware that water levels in substantial portions of the aquifer are in decline, there are many ideas being put forth to protect the water source for the long term. Some are putting their hopes in more efficient use of the water and the implementation of improved conservation practices. Others are looking to all levels of government to pass laws designed to regulate how the water is utilized and by whom. Should the water levels continue to drop, the impact of the water loss will occur gradually. Springs will gradually disappear and the water found in streams and rivers will diminish. In all probability, this change will be accompanied by a decline in the populations of flora and fauna as they too will lose access to the waters necessary to sustain life. Eventually, the amount of land that can be irrigated will be reduced. Those lucky enough to have access to some water will be able to turn to some form of dryland farming. The question is whether there will be enough moisture on the ground to hold the soil down, as repeated drought cycles on the Great Plains, most notably in the 1920s, have shown the region is prone to dust storms that can just pick up the topsoil and carry it away for hundreds of miles. The worst-case scenario is that the lack of water in the region can result in the land once again becoming deserted as the plains become inhospitable to human habitation.

Although the High Plains Aquifer is facing long-term water availability issues, there are other threats within the aquifers waters that also bear watching. As shown in the portion of the document *Water Quality in the High Plains Aquifer, Colorado, Kansas, Nebraska, New Mexico, Oklahoma, South Dakota, Texas, and Wyoming, 1999–2004* that is presented, there is great concern about the chemicals that are appearing in the waters emerging from the aquifer. Many are coming from fertilizers that are being used on the respective farms. Although the present levels of the various chemicals are within what the federal government claims is safe, the report's authors warn that the concentrations of those very chemicals will inevitably rise as the aquifer continues to be drained by water pumps.

The High Plains Aquifer is also potentially threatened by the construction of the proposed Keystone XL pipeline. TransCanada, a Canadian oil and gas company, has proposed building an oil pipeline that would transfer tar sands oil from Alberta, Canada, to Port Arthur, Texas. As the pipeline crosses an international border, TransCanada petitioned the Obama administration in 2008 for a permit that has not yet been approved. It is a politically charged issue, as proponents of the pipeline claim it will create thousands of jobs within the United States and lessen the country's dependence on oil from the Middle East. Its opponents fear that the pipeline poses a severe threat to the High Plains Aquifer as an oil spill in Nebraska or South Dakota, which are both on the proposed route, could result in immeasurable harm to one of the United States' major water resources.

FURTHER READING

Glennon, Robert. 2002. *Water Follies: Groundwater Pumping and the Fate of America's Fresh Waters.* Washington, DC: Island Press.

Green, Donald E. 1973. *Land of the Underground Rain: Irrigation on the Texas High Plains, 1910–1970.* Austin: University of Texas Press.

Kromm, David E., and Stephen E. White, eds. 1992. *Groundwater Exploitation in the High Plains*. Lawrence: University Press of Kansas.

Lavin, Stephen J., Fred M. Shelley, and J. Clark Archer. 2011. *Atlas of the Great Plains*. Lincoln: University of Nebraska Press.

Opie, John. 2000. *Ogallala: Water for a Dry Land*. 2nd ed. Lincoln: University of Nebraska Press.

"A Short-Term Health Advisory for Drinking Water in and Around Charleston, West Virginia"

- *Document:* Summary Report of Short-term Screening Level Calculation and Analysis of Available Animal Studies for MCHM
- *Date:* January 20, 2014
- *Where:* The chemical spill occurred in the Elk River, near Charleston, West Virginia.
- *Significance:* Approximately 300,000 people in and around Charleston, West Virginia, were unable to use drinking water from local plumbing systems from January 9 to 13, 2014.

DOCUMENT

Summary Report of Short-term Screening Level Calculation and Analysis of Available Animal Studies for MCHM

This summary report explains how the Centers for Disease Control and Prevention (CDC) used generally accepted scientific methods to establish a short-term health advisory for drinking water in and around Charleston, West Virginia immediately after a chemical spill in the Elk River. The summary report also shows how CDC used animal studies—once they became available—to validate the initial short-term screening level of 1 part per million (ppm) calculated during the early stages of the emergency response.

Background

On January 9, 2014, approximately 7500 gallons of an industrial chemical, 4-Methylcyclohexanemethanol (MCHM – CAS# 34885-03-5), spilled into the Elk River just upstream from the Kanawha County municipal water intake in Charleston, West Virginia. This municipal water system serves nearly 300,000 people whose water was affected by the chemical spill. Due to the uncertainty over the chemical levels in the water supply, the Office of the Governor issued a "Do Not Use" order at 6:00 pm on January 9, 2014. Later that evening, the West Virginia Department of Health and Human Resources contacted CDC about the release and requested assistance to review water sampling data and provide a drinking water screening level for MCHM. In response to this urgent situation, a screening level of 1ppm was recommended. Based on the information available, a level of 1ppm or below is not likely to be associated with any adverse health effects.

Summary

The Centers for Disease Control and Prevention and the Agency for Toxic Substances and Disease Registry (CDC/ATSDR) used the most relevant available information to provide a scientifically supported recommendation for the protection of public health. Initial actions in the Charleston area were based upon limited available information and resulted in a decision to issue a short-term public health alert regarding all municipal water use in the Kanawha water distribution area.

The initial short-term screening level that CDC/ATSDR recommended for the Elk River spill followed common practices for the interpretation of toxicological information for public health purposes (see Methodology section below). Often such information is incomplete; this was the case for MCHM in this incident. CDC/ATSDR analyzed additional information, once it became available, to verify the initial short-term screening level and health advisory.

Data Review

On the evening of Thursday, January 9, 2014 emergency response staff from CDC/ATSDR, in cooperation with local and state health authorities, recommended an interim urgent short-term screening level based upon information available at the time. The short-term screening level was used to issue a warning to users of the local water district to avoid all contact with municipal water.

Since CDC/ATSDR recommended the emergency short-term screening level, state and federal officials have acquired several additional proprietary studies on the toxicology of MCHM. When these studies became available, the U.S. Department of Health & Human Services convened a Federal expert workgroup including scientists from the National Institute of Environmental Health Sciences and National Toxicology Program, the National Library of Medicine, the Environmental Protection Agency, and CDC/ATSDR to review the available animal studies and the methodology for the short-term screening level calculation. This workgroup concurred that the 1 ppm short-term screening level was appropriate.

The studies of pure MCHM and crude MCHM are summarized below. For a more detailed description of these studies, please see the National Library of Medicine's

Hazardous Substances Data Bank: http://toxnet.nlm.nih.gov/cgi-bin/sis/search/r?dbs +hsdb:@term+@DOCNO+8182.

1) Crude MCHM. Ames test for mutagenic potential. This test used multiple *Salmonella typhimurium* strains and one *E. coli* strain, with six doses, and with and without "S9 mix" to study the impact of possible metabolism of activity. No increase in revertants was noted. A repeat study confirmed these results.

2) Crude MCHM. Two-week daily dermal application. Male and female rats were dosed at 0, 100, 500, and 2000 mg/kg/day, 6 hours/day for 13 consecutive days. There was dermal irritation at all treatment levels and thus no No Observed Effect Level (NOEL) was identified. Because of the absence of significant histopathology and serum clinical chemistry changes, 2000 mg/kg was considered as the NOEL for systemic toxicity. One focus was to look at hematuria as a possible toxic effect seen in an earlier acute dermal study.

3) Crude MCHM acute single dose dermal. A single dose of 2000 mg/kg was applied to male and female rats, with a 14-day observation period. Dermal irritation was observed, and the dermal LD50 was greater than 2000 mg/kg.

4) Crude MCHM acute single dose oral. Male and female rats were dosed with 500, 1000, and 2000 mg/kg, followed by a 14-day observation period. The acute LD50 was calculated as 933 mg/kg for males and 707 mg/kg for females.

5) Pure MCHM 28 day daily oral. Rats received 0, 25, 100, and 400 mg/kg/day, 5 days a week, for 4 weeks. In this study, the administration of 400 mg/kg/day for 4 weeks was associated with erythropoietic, kidney, and liver effects, including increased liver weight, inflammation, and kidney tubular degeneration. The authors set a NOEL at 100 mg/kg/day. ***CDC used this study to establish the short-term health advisory for the MCHM spill in the Elk River.***

6) Crude MCHM acute single dose oral (repeat of earlier study). This is a study of a single oral dose to female rats (i.e., to look at hematuria as a possible toxic effect as seen in another study). The LD50 was calculated to be 500 mg/kg.

7) Pure MCHM acute battery:

a) Acute single dose oral toxicity. Male and female rats were dosed at 625, 1250, and 2500 mg/kg. The estimated LD50 was 1768 mg/kg in males and 884 mg/kg in females.

b) Acute single dose dermal exposure. Male and female rats were dosed at 2, 6, and 20 ml/kg. MCHM was irritating to skin at as low as the 2 ml/kg dose, but only in females at this dose.

c) Acute single exposure dermal irritation. Guinea pigs were dosed at 0.5 ml on the abdomen and covered with occlusive wrapping for 24 hours. They were observed for 48 hours after the wrap was removed. MCHM exposure led to strong skin irritation.

d) Acute toxicity, repeated application to skin. The backs of guinea pigs were exposed to 9 doses of 0.5 ml of MCHM "drop on" over 11 days. There was "... exacerbation of the irritant response with (multiple) application..."

e) Acute toxicity, evaluation of skin sensitizing potential. Male guinea pig footpads were exposed to 0.05 ml of a 1.0% solution MCHM in adjuvant (FCA) for induction. No sensitization was observed after a challenge application, and MCHM was concluded to have "a low potential to cause human sensitization."

f) Acute toxicity, eye irritation. One dose of 0.1 ml of MCHM was placed onto the eyes of rabbits, followed by washing or no washing. The washed eyes showed slight irritation, and the unwashed eyes showed moderate irritation. MCHM was concluded to be a "moderate irritant."

Together, these studies provide a much-improved (but still incomplete) understanding of MCHM's toxicology profile. In particular, one of the studies, the 4-week rat study (study 5 above), provides a NOEL in rats. This NOEL, established by the authors of the study, is 100 mg/kg/day. The 4-week NOEL represents a more scientifically sound study and point of departure for establishing a short-term health advisory for MCHM.

SOURCE: Centers for Disease Control and Prevention. 2014. *Summary Report of Short-Term Screening Level Calculation and Analysis of Available Animal Studies for MCHM.* http://www.bt.cdc.gov/chemical/MCHM/westvirginia2014/pdf/MCHM-Summary-Report.pdf (accessed August 24, 2014).

ANALYSIS

On January 9, 2014, some people in Charleston, West Virginia, reported that their drinking water smelled like licorice. Soon thereafter, Earl Ray Tomblin, governor of West Virginia, announced that the drinking water used by approximately 300,000 people in the vicinity of the state's capital was contaminated and thus unfit for use. The water was also unsafe for activities such as cooking, showering, or washing clothes. The resulting water ban lasted until January 18, when the final all-clear was issued. During the time that tap water was unavailable, the National Guard trucked in drinking water for use by the populace.

It was determined by the Environmental Protection Agency that the source of the contamination was a leaking tank located on a bank of the Elk River that contained 4-methylcyclohexanemethanol (MCHM), a coal-cleaning solvent. The spilled chemical was introduced into the local drinking water through the Kanawha County municipal water intake in the river. In total, 7,500 gallons of MCHM entered the Elk River, a tributary of the Kanawha River, which in turn is a tributary of the Ohio River. Several days after identifying the first chemical contained in their leaking tank, Freedom Industries Inc. admitted that the tank had also leaked a mixture of propylene glycol phenyl ether and dipropylene glycol phenyl ether into the water. In light of the impact of the disaster, Freedom Industries Inc. had to worry about not only fines coming from the Environmental Protection Agency for violations of the Clean Water Act and other applicable laws but also a significant amount of private litigation. Rather than seeing their finances decimated, the company filed for bankruptcy protection.

One of the most startling aspects of the disaster was that health officials did not know what kind of threat MCHM posed to the citizenry. Although the effect of the chemical had been briefly studied on rats, no research existed on human exposure. The reason was that the chemical had been exempted from the studies required by the Toxic Substance Control Act of 1976. The Centers for Disease Control and Prevention had to initiate some rudimentary studies on the West Virginia sample just to determine what basic symptoms they needed to be looking for when examining sick West Virginians. In the aftermath of the accident, U.S. congressmen began discussions on amending the Toxic Substance Control Act. Although a general consensus emerged that the regulations dating from 1976 required updating, no legislation toward that end has yet passed Congress.

FURTHER READING

Centers for Disease Control and Prevention. 2014. *2014 West Virginia Chemical Release.* http://www.bt.cdc.gov/chemical/MCHM/westvirginia2014/.

Manuel, John. 2014. "Crisis and Emergency Risk Communication: Lessons from the Elk River Spill." *Environmental Health Perspectives* 122, no. 8: A214–A219.

Osnos, Evan. 2014. "Letter from West Virginia: Chemical Valley." *The New Yorker* 90, no. 7. http://www.newyorker.com/magazine/letter-from-west-virginia.

Tullo, Alexander H. 2014. "Obscure Chemical Taints Water Supply." *Chemical & Engineering News* 92, no. 7: 10–15.

12

FRACKING

"The Injection of Hydraulic Fracturing Fluids into Coalbed Methane Wells Poses Little or No Threat to USDWs and Does Not Justify Additional Study at This Time"

- *Document:* Evaluation of Impacts to Underground Sources of Drinking Water by Hydraulic Fracturing of Coalbed Methane Reservoirs, Conclusions and Recommendations
- *Date:* June 2004
- *Where:* Washington, DC
- *Significance:* The Environmental Protection Agency's study determined how hydraulic fracturing, or fracking, was regulated by the federal government.

DOCUMENT

Based on the information collected and reviewed, EPA has concluded that the injection of hydraulic fracturing fluids into coalbed methane wells poses little or no threat to USDWs and does not justify additional study at this time. This decision is consistent with the process outlined in the April, 2001 Final Study Design, in which EPA indicated that it would determine whether further investigation was needed after analyzing the Phase I information. Specifically, EPA determined that it would not continue into Phase II of the study if the investigation found that no hazardous constituents were used in fracturing fluids, hydraulic fracturing did not increase the hydraulic connection between previously isolated formations, *and* reported incidents of water quality degradation were attributed to other, more plausible causes.

Although potentially hazardous chemicals may be introduced into Underground Sources of Drinking Waters (USDWs) when fracturing fluids are injected into coal seams that lie within USDWs, the risk posed to USDWs by introduction of these chemicals is reduced significantly by groundwater production and injected fluid recovery, combined with the mitigating effects of dilution and dispersion, adsorption, and potentially biodegradation. Additionally, EPA has reached an agreement with the major service companies to voluntarily eliminate diesel fuel from hydraulic fracturing fluids that are injected directly into USDWs for coalbed methane production.

Often, a high stress contrast between adjacent geologic strata results in a barrier to fracture propagation. This may occur in those coal zones where there is a geologic contact between a coalbed and a thick, higher-stress shale that is not highly fractured. Some studies that allow direct observation of fractures (i.e., mined-through studies) indicate many fractures that penetrate into, or sometimes through, formations overlying coalbeds can be attributed to the existence of pre-existing natural fractures. However, and as noted above, given the concentrations and flowback of injected fluids, and the mitigating effects of dilution and dispersion, fluid entrapment, and potentially biodegradation, EPA does not believe that possible hydraulic connections under these circumstances represent a significant potential threat to USDWs.

EPA also reviewed incidents of drinking water well contamination believed to be associated with hydraulic fracturing and found no confirmed cases that are linked to fracturing fluid injection into coalbed methane wells or subsequent underground movement of fracturing fluids. Although thousands of coalbed methane wells are fractured annually, EPA did not find confirmed evidence that drinking water wells have been contaminated by hydraulic fracturing fluid injection into coalbed methane wells.

SOURCE: Environmental Protection Agency. 2004. *Evaluation of Impacts to Underground Sources of Drinking Water by Hydraulic Fracturing of Coalbed Methane Reservoirs.* http://www.epa.gov/ogwdw/uic/pdfs/cbmstudy_attach_uic_ch07_conclusions.pdf (accessed August 18, 2014).

ANALYSIS

The Environmental Protection Agency's (EPA) landmark study titled *Evaluation of Impacts to Underground Sources of Drinking Water by Hydraulic Fracturing of Coalbed Methane Reservoirs* was embroiled in political controversy from the start. Although hydraulic fracturing had been done in small scale for decades, at the time the study was commissioned, its use was growing exponentially. Among the company's profiting greatly from its use was Halliburton, which had close ties to the Republican Party in general and the Bush family in particular. The ties were such that Richard "Dick" Cheney, secretary of defense to President George H. W. Bush and vice president to President George W. Bush, served in-between the two Bush administrations as Halliburton's chief executive officer. It has been alleged by many environmental groups that Vice-President Cheney's influence pervaded the EPA's conclusions.

The conclusion in the report that fracking did not pose a threat to the nation's drinking waters paved the way for President George W. Bush's administration to insert language into the Energy Policy Act of 2005, exempting natural gas drilling from provisions contained within the Safe Drinking Water Act of 1974. The practical effect of the exemption was that the EPA lost the ability to regulate hydraulic fracturing in any form. The EPA was also banned from forcing any state to regulate natural gas drilling within its borders. In essence, companies such as Halliburton were freed to pursue fracking without interference from federal regulators.

FURTHER READING

Gold, Russell. 2014. *The Boom: How Fracking Ignited the American Energy Revolution and Changed the World*. New York: Simon & Schuster.

Prud'homme, Alex. 2013. *Hydrofracking: What Everyone Needs to Know*. New York: Oxford University Press.

Shapiro, Jennifer, and Barbara Warner. 2013. "Fractured, Fragmented Federalism: A Study in Fracking Regulatory Policy." *Publius: The Journal of Federalism* 43, no. 3: 474–496.

Wilbur, Tom. 2012. *Under the Surface: Fracking Fortunes, and the Fate of the Marcellus Shale*. Ithaca, NY: Cornell University Press.

"Potential Impacts to Drinking Water Resources from Hydraulic Fracturing"

- *Document:* Study of the Potential Impacts of Hydraulic Fracturing on Drinking Water Resources: Progress Report, Executive Summary
- *Date:* December 2012
- *Where:* Washington, DC
- *Significance:* This study promises to either confirm that fracking does not pose a threat to ground water or provide the evidence that the nation's waters are in fact threatened by hydraulic fracturing operations.

DOCUMENT

Natural gas plays a key role in our nation's clean energy future. The United States has vast reserves of natural gas that are commercially viable as a result of advances in horizontal drilling and hydraulic fracturing technologies, which enable greater access to gas in rock formations deep underground. These advances have spurred a significant increase in the production of both natural gas and oil across the country.

Responsible development of America's oil and gas resources offers important economic, energy security, and environmental benefits. However, as the use of hydraulic fracturing has increased, so have concerns about its potential human health and environmental impacts, especially for drinking water. In response to public concern, the US House of Representatives requested that the US Environmental Protection Agency (EPA) conduct scientific research to examine the relationship between hydraulic fracturing and drinking water resources (USHR, 2009).

In 2011, the EPA began research under its *Plan to Study the Potential Impacts of Hydraulic Fracturing on Drinking Water Resources*. The purpose of the study is to assess the potential impacts of hydraulic fracturing on drinking water resources, if any, and to identify the driving factors that may affect the severity and frequency of such impacts. Scientists are focusing primarily on hydraulic fracturing of shale formations to extract natural gas, with some study of other oil- and gas-producing formations, including tight sands, and coalbeds. The EPA has designed the scope of the research around five stages of the hydraulic fracturing water cycle. Each stage of the cycle is associated with a primary research question:

- Water acquisition: What are the possible impacts of large volume water withdrawals from ground and surface waters on drinking water resources?
- Chemical mixing: What are the possible impacts of hydraulic fracturing fluid surface spills on or near well pads on drinking water resources?
- Well injection: What are the possible impacts of the injection and fracturing process on drinking water resources?
- Flowback and produced water: What are the possible impacts of flowback and produced water (collectively referred to as "hydraulic fracturing wastewater") surface spills on or near well pads on drinking water resources?
- Wastewater treatment and waste disposal: What are the possible impacts of inadequate treatment of hydraulic fracturing wastewater on drinking water resources?

This report describes 18 research projects underway to answer these research questions and presents the progress made as of September 2012 for each of the projects. Information presented as part of this report cannot be used to draw conclusions about potential impacts to drinking water resources from hydraulic fracturing. The research projects are organized according to five different types of research activities: analysis of existing data, scenario evaluations, laboratory studies, toxicity assessments, and case studies.

Analysis of Existing Data

Data from multiple sources have been obtained for review and analysis. Many of the data come directly from the oil and gas industry and states with high levels of oil and gas activity. Information on the chemicals and practices used in hydraulic fracturing has been collected from nine companies that hydraulically fractured a total of 24,925 wells between September 2009 and October 2010. Additional data on chemicals and water use for hydraulic fracturing are being pulled from over 12,000 well-specific chemical disclosures in FracFocus, a national hydraulic fracturing chemical registry operated by the Ground Water Protection Council and the Interstate Oil and Gas Compact Commission. Well construction and hydraulic fracturing records provided by well operators are being reviewed for 333 oil and gas wells across the United States; data within these records are being scrutinized to assess the effectiveness of current well construction practices at containing gases and liquids before, during, and after hydraulic fracturing.

Data on causes and volumes of spills of hydraulic fracturing fluids and wastewater are being collected and reviewed from state spill databases in Colorado, New Mexico, and Pennsylvania. Similar information is being collected from the National Response Center national database of oil and chemical spills.

In addition, the EPA is reviewing scientific literature relevant to the research questions posed in this study. A *Federal Register* notice was published on November 9, 2012, requesting relevant, peer-reviewed data and published reports, including information on advances in industry practices and technologies. This body of literature will be synthesized with results from the other research projects to create a report of results.

Scenario Evaluations

Computer models are being used to identify conditions that may lead to impacts on drinking water resources from hydraulic fracturing. The EPA has identified hypothetical, but realistic, scenarios pertaining to the water acquisition, well injection, and wastewater treatment and waste disposal stages of the water cycle. Potential impacts to drinking water sources from withdrawing large volumes of water in semi-arid and humid river basins—the Upper Colorado River Basin in the west and the Susquehanna River Basin in the east—are being compared and assessed.

Additionally, complex computer models are being used to explore the possibility of subsurface gas and fluid migration from deep shale formations to overlying aquifers in six different scenarios. These scenarios include poor well construction and hydraulic communication via fractures (natural and created) and nearby existing wells. As a first step, the subsurface migration simulations will examine realistic scenarios to assess the conditions necessary for hydraulic communication rather than the probability of migration occurring.

In a separate research project, concentrations of bromide and radium at public water supply intakes located downstream from wastewater treatment facilities discharging treated hydraulic fracturing wastewater are being estimated using surface water transport models.

Laboratory Studies

Laboratory studies are largely focused on identifying potential impacts of inadequately treating hydraulic fracturing wastewater and discharging it to rivers. Experiments are being designed to test how well common wastewater treatment processes remove selected contaminants from hydraulic fracturing wastewater, including radium and other metals. Other experiments are assessing whether or not hydraulic fracturing wastewater may contribute to the formation of disinfection byproducts during common drinking water treatment processes, with particular focus on the formation of brominated disinfection byproducts, which have significant health concerns at high exposure levels.

Samples of raw hydraulic fracturing wastewater, treated wastewater, and water from rivers receiving treated hydraulic fracturing wastewater have been collected for source apportionment studies. Results from laboratory analyses of these samples are being used to develop a method for determining if treated hydraulic fracturing wastewater is contributing to high chloride and bromide levels at downstream public water supplies.

Finally, existing analytical methods for selected chemicals are being tested, modified, and verified for use in this study and by others, as needed. Methods are being modified in cases where standard methods do not exist for the low-level detection of chemicals of interest or for use in the complex matrices associated with hydraulic fracturing wastewater. Analytical methods are currently being tested and modified for several classes of chemicals, including glycols, acrylamides, ethoxylatedalcohols, disinfection byproducts, radionuclides, and inorganic chemicals.

Toxicity Assessments

The EPA has identified chemicals reportedly used in hydraulic fracturing fluids from 2005 to 2011 and chemicals found in flowback and produced water. Appendix A contains tables with over 1,000 of these chemicals identified. Chemical, physical, and toxicological properties are being compiled for chemicals with known chemical structures. Existing models are being used to estimate properties in cases where information is lacking. At this time, the EPA has not made any judgment about the extent of exposure to these chemicals when used in hydraulic fracturing fluids or found in hydraulic fracturing wastewater, or their potential impacts on drinking water resources.

Case Studies

Two rounds of sampling at five case study locations in Colorado, North Dakota, Pennsylvania, and Texas have been completed. In total, water samples have been collected from over 70 domestic water wells, 15 monitoring wells, and 13 surface water sources, among others. This research will help to identify the source of any contamination that may have occurred. The EPA continues to work with industry partners to begin research activities at potential prospective case study locations, which involve sites where the research will begin before well construction. This will allow the EPA to collect baseline water quality data in the area. Water quality will be monitored for any changes throughout drilling, injection of fracturing fluids, flow-back, and production. Samples of flowback and produced water will be used for other parts of the study, such as assessing the efficacy of wastewater treatment processes at removing contaminants in hydraulic fracturing wastewater.

Invigorating the Research Study Through Consultation and Peer Review

The EPA is committed to conducting a study that uses the best available science, independent sources of information, and a transparent, peer-reviewed process that will ensure the validity and accuracy of the results. The agency is working in consultation with other federal agencies, state and interstate regulatory agencies, industry, non-governmental organizations, and others in the private and public sector. In addition to workshops held in 2011, stakeholders and technical experts are being engaged through technical roundtables and workshops, with the first set of roundtables held November 14–16, 2012. These activities will provide the EPA with ongoing access to a broad range of expertise and data, timely and constructive technical feedback, and updates on changes in industry practices and technologies relevant to the study. Technical roundtables and workshops will be followed by webinars for the general public and posting of summaries on the study's website. Increased stakeholder engagement will also allow the EPA to educate and inform the public of the study's goals, design, and progress.

To ensure scientifically defensible results, each research project is subjected to quality assurance and peer review activities. Specific quality assurance activities performed by the EPA make sure that the agency's environmental data are of sufficient quantity and quality to support the data's intended use. Research products, such as papers or reports, will be subjected to both internal and external peer review before publication, which make certain that the data are used appropriately. Published results from the research projects will be synthesized in a report of results that will inform the research questions associated with each stage of the hydraulic fracturing water cycle. The EPA has designated the report of results as a "Highly Influential Scientific Assessment," which will undergo peer review by the EPA's Science Advisory Board, an independent and external federal advisory committee that conducts peer reviews of significant EPA research products and activities. The EPA will seek input from individual members of an *ad hoc* expert panel convened under the auspices of the EPA Science Advisory Board. The EPA will consider feedback from the individual experts in the development of the report of results.

Ultimately, the results of this study are expected to inform the public and provide decision-makers at all levels with high-quality scientific knowledge that can be used in decision-making processes.

SOURCE: Environmental Protection Agency. 2012. *Study of the Potential Impacts of Hydraulic Fracturing on Drinking Water Resources: Progress Report.* http://www2.epa.gov/sites/production/files/documents/hf-progress-report-exec-summary20121214.pdf (accessed August 18, 2014).

ANALYSIS

The 2004 Environmental Protection Agency's (EPA) study, *Evaluation of Impacts to Underground Sources of Drinking Water by Hydraulic Fracturing of Coalbed Methane Reservoirs*, determined that hydraulic fracturing, also known as *fracking*, did not pose a threat to the nation's drinking water. On the basis of that conclusion, President George W. Bush's administration inserted language into the Energy Policy Act of 2005, which exempted natural gas drilling from provisions contained within the Safe Drinking Water Act of 1974. The exemption took away the EPA's ability to regulate hydraulic fracturing in any form. The EPA was also banned from forcing any state to regulate natural gas drilling within its borders. Many environmental groups alleged that the decision by the Bush administration was not informed by scientific fact but was instead motivated by political patronage. Despite their beliefs, they had no solid scientific evidence to support their opinion.

Gradually, circumstantial evidence began to emerge that fracking was impacting water sources. In 2008, the EPA commenced studying groundwater contamination on the Wind River Indian Reservation in Wyoming because some local wells contained methane. Although it could not be determined how the methane arrived in the wells, fracking was one of the few potential culprits in the region. During 2009, in both Pennsylvania and West Virginia, fracking by-products polluted local waterways, killing many fish.

With the EPA rendered impotent, Democrats in the U.S. House of Representatives brought the issue to the fore with the issuance of a report in April 2011 alleging that petroleum companies engaged in fracking used chemicals that contained at least 650 carcinogens, which are regulated by the Safe Drinking Water Act. Their claims were buttressed in December of the same year when the EPA released a three-year study on water contamination in Pavillion, Wyoming. The study alleged that there was a link between the contamination and a local natural gas operation. Despite the EPA's study, controversy continued to swirl as both supporters and opponents of fracking alleged that the available scientific evidence supported their positions. To develop more scientific evidence on the impact of fracking on water sources, the EPA launched 18 different projects that explored how different stages of the extraction of natural gas through hydraulic fracturing potentially impacted water sources. The executive summary of the *Study of the Potential Impacts of Hydraulic Fracturing on Drinking Water Resources: Progress Report* provides the research questions underlying the studies, along with updates on the respective studies. Also included is information about how the conclusions of the studies are going to be vetted, including peer review processes with outside experts, before being disseminated to the public. The EPA wants to ensure that when the results of the current study are completed, it has broad support from the scientific community to avoid the controversies that accompanied the release of the *Evaluation of Impacts to Underground Sources of Drinking Water by Hydraulic Fracturing of Coalbed Methane Reservoirs*, which is viewed more as a political document than a reputable scientific publication. Although the study is ongoing, leaked reports about its potential findings have generated a great deal of controversy as both supporters and opponents of hydraulic fracturing move to shape its conclusions to their benefit. Fracking proponents fear that if the EPA's study determines that gas extraction through hydraulic fracturing is polluting water sources, the agency will be empowered to once again regulate the petroleum companies that use fracking as an extraction method.

FURTHER READING

Gold, Russell. 2014. *The Boom: How Fracking Ignited the American Energy Revolution and Changed the World.* New York: Simon & Schuster.
113th Congress. 2013. *H.R. 2728—Protecting States' Rights to Promote American Energy Security Act.* http://beta.congress.gov/bill/113th-congress/house-bill/2728 (accessed August 18, 2014).
Prud'homme, Alex. 2013. *Hydrofracking: What Everyone Needs to Know.* New York: Oxford University Press.
Shapiro, Jennifer, and Barbara Warner. 2013. "Fractured, Fragmented Federalism: A Study in Fracking Regulatory Policy." *Publius: The Journal of Federalism* 43, no. 3: 474–496.
Wilbur, Tom. 2012. *Under the Surface: Fracking Fortunes, and the Fate of the Marcellus Shale.* Ithaca, NY: Cornell University Press.

"To Prohibit the Department of the Interior from Enforcing Any Federal Regulation, Guidance, or Permit Requirement Regarding Hydraulic Fracturing"

- *Document:* H.R. 2728—Protecting States' Rights to Promote American Energy Security Act
- *Date:* November 20, 2013
- *Where:* Washington, DC
- *Significance:* This proposed legislation from the U.S. House of Representatives was intended to deny the U.S. Department of the Interior's Bureau of Land Management the ability to regulate hydraulic fracturing on either federal or tribal lands.

DOCUMENT

Summary: H.R. 2728—113th Congress (2013–2014).

Title I: State Authority for Hydraulic Fracturing Regulation—Protecting States' Rights to Promote American Energy Security Act—(Sec. 102) Amends the Mineral Leasing Act to prohibit the Department of the Interior (Department) from enforcing any federal regulation, guidance, or permit requirement regarding hydraulic fracturing (including any component of that process), relating to oil, gas, or geothermal production activities on or under any land in any state that has regulations, guidance, or permit requirements for that activity.

Defines "hydraulic fracturing" as the process by which fracturing fluids (including a fracturing fluid system) are pumped into an underground geologic formation to generate fractures or cracks, thereby increasing rock permeability near the wellbore and improving production of natural gas or oil.

Requires the Department to recognize and defer to state regulations, permitting, and guidance for all activities regarding hydraulic fracturing relating to oil, gas, or geothermal production activities on federal land.

Requires each state to submit to the Bureau of Land Management (BLM) a copy of its regulations that: (1) apply to hydraulic fracturing operations on federal land, and (2) require disclosure of chemicals used in hydraulic fracturing operations on federal land.

Directs the Secretary of the Interior to make such state regulations available to the public.

(Sec. 103) Directs the Comptroller General (GAO) to examine the economic benefits of domestic shale oil and gas production resulting from hydraulic fracturing, including identification of: (1) state and federal revenue generated as a result of shale gas production, (2) jobs created as a result of shale oil and gas production, and (3) an estimate of potential energy prices without domestic shale oil and gas production.

(Sec. 104) Prohibits the Department from enforcing any federal regulation, guidance, or permit requirement governing the hydraulic fracturing process, or any of its components, relating to oil, gas, or geothermal production activities on land held either in trust or restricted status for the benefit of Indians except with the express consent of the beneficiary on whose behalf such land is held in trust or restricted status.

SOURCE: 113th Congress. 2013. *H.R. 2728—Protecting States' Rights to Promote American Energy Security Act.* http://beta.congress.gov/bill/113th-congress/house-bill/2728 (accessed August 18, 2014).

ANALYSIS

On May 4, 2012, Secretary of the Interior Ken Salazar proposed new rules governing hydraulic fracturing on federal and tribal lands. The regulations were desired because the existing rules were issued approximately 30 years earlier and did not reflect technological advances that had occurred during the intervening period. Salazar's proposal had three primary components: It required disclosure of all chemicals utilized during the fracking process once the extraction was complete; it required operators to ensure that the fluids generated during hydraulic fracturing were not contaminating groundwater; and the respective companies had a water management plan to address fluids that emerged to the ground's surface.

Using feedback generated from the initial proposal, the Department of the Interior's Bureau of Land Management issued a modified proposal on May 16, 2013, that not only included Salazar's original three components but also limited the methods that petroleum companies could utilize to demonstrate that local waters were not being contaminated. Petroleum industry interests opposed the new regulations, arguing that the federal government did not need to interfere with fracking on public or tribal lands because state governments were already successfully regulating the industry.

The Bureau of Land Management's proposal led the petroleum industry's supporters in the U.S. House of Representatives to propose the *Protecting States' Rights to Promote American Energy Security Act* on November 20, 2013. The language in the act was designed to deny the Bureau of Land Management the authority to regulate fracking in any manner in states where laws existed to regulate the extraction method. The legislation was not successful in passing through Congress, although proponents plan to continue efforts to pass similar legislation in the future. If the *Protecting States' Rights to Promote American Energy Security Act* had received the necessary support to reach President Barack Obama's desk, he had already vowed to veto the legislation.

FURTHER READING

Executive Office of the President, Office of Management and Budget. 2013. *Statement of Administration Policy: H.R. 2728—Protecting States' Rights to Promote American Energy Security Act.* http://www.whitehouse.gov/sites/default/files/omb/legislative/sap/113/saphr2728h_20131119.pdf (accessed August 18, 2014).

Gold, Russell. 2014. *The Boom: How Fracking Ignited the American Energy Revolution and Changed the World.* New York: Simon & Schuster.

Prud'homme, Alex. 2013. *Hydrofracking: What Everyone Needs to Know.* New York: Oxford University Press.

U.S. Department of the Interior, Bureau of Land Management. 2012. *Interior Releases Draft Rule Requiring Public Disclosure of Chemicals Used in Hydraulic Fracturing on Public and Indian Lands.* http://www.doi.gov/news/pressreleases/Interior-Releases-Draft-Rule-Requiring-Public-Disclosure-of-Chemicals-Used-in-Hydraulic-Fracturing-on-Public-and-Indian-Lands.cfm (accessed September 9, 2014).

13

THE IMPACT OF CLIMATE CHANGE ON WATER SUPPLY

"Clean and Safe Water to Protect the Nation's Public Health and Environment"

- *Document:* 2013 Highlights of Progress: Responses to Climate Change by the National Water Program, excerpt
- *Date:* April 24, 2014
- *Where:* Washington, DC
- *Significance:* The report provides an overview of the Environmental Protection Agency views on climate change and also details specific steps that the agency is undertaking to ensure the nation's water needs into the future.

DOCUMENT

NATIONAL PROGRAM HIGHLIGHTS
Vision Area 1:
Water Infrastructure
Vision: In the face of a changing climate, resilient and adaptable drinking water, wastewater and stormwater utilities (water sector) ensure clean and safe water to protect the nation's public health and environment by making smart investment decisions to improve the sustainability of their infrastructure and operations and the communities they serve, while reducing greenhouse gas emissions through greater energy efficiency.

1. Address Climate Change in Clean Water State Revolving Fund: In 2013, the Clean Water State Revolving Fund (CWSRF) program developed a comprehensive list of CWSRF-eligible projects to increase climate/weather-related resilience at water utilities to implement the Disaster Relief Appropriations Act of 2013.

Climate/weather-related eligibilities were also discussed at the fall Council for Infrastructure Financing Authorities conference, where the CWSRF program delivered a presentation to State and Regional counterparts regarding the CWSRF's ability to promote climate/weather-related resilience in the water sector.

The CWSRF program also revised its Annual Review Checklist to incorporate several questions on resilience to climate change and extreme weather and participated with the DWSRF in the development of a draft guide for small utilities that want to become more resilient to flooding.

2. Expand Climate Ready Water Utilities Program Outreach: Through the Climate Ready Water Utilities (CRWU) initiative, EPA has provided 15 workshops and webinars and reached over 2000 people. Key 2013 activities included:

➢ convening a working group to develop version 3.0 of the Climate Resilience Evaluation and Awareness Tool (CREAT) including utilities, academia, associations and other Federal partners;

➢ holding two-day emergency response workshops with demonstrations of tools and resources to aid utilities, review climate impacts, and discuss planning options with different sector stakeholders, such as local governments, first responders, and community leaders; and

➢ hosting webinars with the Water Utility Climate Alliance to help utilities plan for climate change and other threats.

Ten webinars were held in 2013 and there are plans for at least four more over 2014. Each webinar is recorded and archived on EPA's website at www.epa.gov/climatereadyutilities.

3. Publish Reports of Water Utility Extreme Weather Case Studies: EPA worked with partners to organize workshops in six communities with a focus on areas that have already experienced extreme events, including drought, flooding, wildfires, sea level rises, and heat waves. The communities where workshops were held included:

➢ Georgia: Upper Apalachicola- Chattahoochee-Flint River Basin;

➢ California: Russian River Watershed;

➢ Virginia: Tidewater Area;

➢ Washington DC: National Capital Area;

➢ Kansas/Missouri: Lower Missouri River Basin; and

➢ Texas: Central Region.

Fact sheets and reports on the lessons learned from these case studies were published throughout 2013. Fact sheets are available at: http://cpo.noaa.gov/ClimatePrograms/ClimateandSocietalInteractions/SARPProgram/ExtremeEventsCaseStudies.aspx. Partners included the National Oceanic and Atmospheric

Administration, Water Environment Research Foundation, Water Research Foundation, Concurrent Technologies Corporation, and Noblis.

4. Expand WaterSense to Commercial Kitchen Products: In September 2013, EPA finalized the first WaterSense specification for a commercial kitchen product. Pre-rinse spray valves—which remove excess food waste from dishes prior to dishwashing—are now eligible to earn the WaterSense label and help food service establishments save water, energy, and money. Pre-rinse spray valves can account for nearly one-third of the water used in a typical commercial kitchen. If every U.S. commercial food service establishment installed and used a WaterSense labeled pre-rinse spray valve, we could save more than 10 billion gallons of water, and more than $225 million in water and energy costs annually across the country. Because kitchens use hot water to rinse dishes, installing a WaterSense labeled pre–rinse spray valve can also reduce a commercial kitchen's annual natural gas use by more than 6,400 cubic feet per year.

5. Expand WaterSense Partners: In 2013, the number of WaterSense partners across the country continued to grow, increasing by close to 120 to a total of 1,474 partners, which includes water utilities, state and local governments, manufacturers, retailers, and builders

Vision Area 2:
Watersheds and Wetlands
Vision: Watersheds are protected, maintained and restored to ensure climate resilience and to preserve the social and economic benefits they provide; and the nation's wetlands are maintained and improved using integrated approaches that recognize their inherent value as well as their role in reducing the impacts of climate change.

6. Build State and Local Capacity to Protect Healthy Watersheds and Enhance Climate Change Resiliency: EPA's Healthy Watersheds Program (HWP) is working to build state and local capacity to identify and protect healthy watersheds using a systems approach that recognizes watersheds as dynamic, interconnected ecosystems. Natural, intact watersheds are better equipped to withstand, recover from, and adapt to natural and man-made disturbances, including climate change. Implementing strategies to maintain and protect healthy watersheds is key toward enhancing climate change resiliency. In 2013, HWP worked to build state and local capacity to identify and protect healthy watersheds at a variety of scales and locations:

> Identification and Protection of Kansas's Healthy Watersheds;
> California Integrated Assessment of Watershed Health;
> Aquatic Ecosystem Protection in Minnesota's Snake River Watershed;
> Establishing Temperature Regime Characteristics of High Quality Streams in Connecticut;
> Sustaining West Virginia's Natural Capital: A Framework for Green Infrastructure; and

➢ Green Infrastructure Practitioners Guide and Ulster County New York Case Study.

For more information on the Healthy Watershed Program see: www.epa.gov/healthywatersheds.

7. Sign Joint Memorandum of Understanding to Promote Healthy Watershed Protection: On February 22, 2013, EPA, The Nature Conservancy (TNC), and the Association of Clean Water Administrators (ACWA) jointly signed the Memorandum of Understanding (MOU) to promote EPA's Healthy Watersheds Program (HWP: www.epa.gov/healthywatersheds). This MOU formalizes a mutual collaboration between these groups as they strive to develop and implement healthy watersheds programs in states and with regional aquatic ecosystem programs. These programs include working with states and other partners to identify healthy watersheds state-wide and to implement healthy watershed protection plans, to integrate such protection into EPA programs and to increase awareness and understanding of the importance of protecting our remaining healthy watersheds. TNC, EPA, and ACWA recognize that healthy, intact watersheds can offset the potential impacts of climate change in a variety of ways including maintenance of baseflow during periods of drought, native vegetation that provides cooling during heat waves, carbon storage in native vegetation and soils, and enhanced stormwater infiltration capacity that mitigates downstream flooding.

The partners will promote data gathering/data sharing and evaluation of conservation and environmental outcomes resulting from the implementation of state and regional healthy watershed programs. See: http://water.epa.gov/polwaste/nps/watershed/hwi-mou.cfm.

8. Assess Climate Change in 20 Watersheds: The EPA Office of Research and Development released in 2013 a report that evaluated streamflow, nitrogen, phosphorus, and sediment in 20 different watersheds across the U.S. for the periods 1970-2000 and 2041-2070 to examine the effects of six different scenarios of climate change and urban/residential development. Additional scenarios were evaluated for five of the watersheds to examine implications of using different methodological choices for this and similar studies. The results indicate that different conditions by mid-21st century are possible for many watersheds, with larger differences likely where development is concentrated. The results also showed sensitivity to the methodological choices, such as use of different watershed models and approaches to downscaling results from global-scale models. (See EPA/600/R-12/058F). (http://www.epa.gov/ncea).

Vision Area 3:
Coastal and Ocean Waters
Vision: *Adverse effects of climate change and unintended adverse consequences of responses to climate change have been successfully prevented or reduced in the ocean and coastal environment. Federal, tribal, state, and local agencies, organizations, and*

institutions are working cooperatively; and information necessary to integrate climate change considerations into ocean and coastal management is produced, readily available, and used.

9. Publish for Peer Review *Being Prepared for Climate Change* workbook: A public draft of the Climate Ready Estuaries (CRE) Program workbook titled *Being Prepared for Climate Change* was sent out for peer review in September and posted on the CRE website in October 2013 for public comment. The workbook applies a risk management methodology for climate change adaptation and helps organizations prepare vulnerability assessments and action plans. The vulnerability assessment methodology of the *Being Prepared for Climate Change* workbook was shared with staff from NEPs, EPA Regions, EPA headquarters, and other federal partners. For more information see http://water.epa.gov/type/oceb/cre/news.cfm.

10. Hold Climate Change Vulnerability Workshop: On February 25, 2013, EPA held a climate change vulnerability assessment workshop with two main goals:

➢ to share the vulnerability assessment methodology of the *Being Prepared for Climate Change* workbook; and
➢ to hear from NEP staff (a main audience for the workbook) about what they want to know in order to prepare high-level, risk-based vulnerability assessments.

The workshop provided a step-by-step walk through of the vulnerability assessment steps in the CRE workbook. The San Juan Bay Estuary Program (SJBEP) also shared some of its experience working on a climate change vulnerability assessment. SJBEP was part of a 2012 Climate Ready Estuaries pilot project to use an early version of the workbook for their assessment.

11. Publish Study of Climate Change Impacts on Salmon Populations: EPA's Office of Research and Development used empirically based simulation modeling of 48 sockeye salmon populations to examine how reliably alternative monitoring designs and fish stock assessment methods can estimate the relative contribution of climate compared to non-climatic factors. The study covered a range of scenarios for ocean conditions, salmon productivity, and human-induced changes and found that distinguishing climate-related effects on salmon productivity from non-climate sources will be difficult, especially if climatic changes occur rapidly and concurrently with major anthropogenic disturbances. Better understanding of the mechanisms underlying the relationship between climate and salmon productivity may be essential to avoid undesirable management outcomes. *Fisheries Research* 147:10-23.

12. Publish Research on Sea Surface Temperatures in Pacific Northwest: A remotely-sensed dataset was used to focus on the nearshore environment of the North Pacific to identify and describe broad-scale sea surface temperature (SST) patterns. Satellite remotely-sensed mean, monthly SST data were used to create a 29-year nearshore (< 20 km offshore) time series of SST along the North Pacific coastline. The scalable nature of the methodology is useful to both broader-scale and more focused analyses, and puts an environmental factor of primary importance (SST) into the hands of researchers studying nearshore environments by providing web-based access to it. Reference: Payne, M. C., Reusser, D., Brown, C. A., and Lee II, H. (2012) "Ecoregional analysis of nearshore sea-surface temperature in the North Pacific." *PLoS ONE*, 7(1):12 pages.

Vision Area 4:
Water Quality
Vision: *The Nation's surface water, drinking water, and ground water quality are protected, and the risks of climate change to human health and the environment are diminished, through a variety of adaptation and mitigation strategies.*

13. Develop Climate Change Extension for the Stormwater Calculator: The Stormwater Calculator (SWC) is a desktop tool intended to help users at individual sites manage stormwater by reducing runoff through infiltration and retention (i.e., green infrastructure). The SWC was launched in 2013 and uses EPA's Stormwater Management Model (SWMM) as its computational engine. A climate change extension to the SWC was developed in 2013 and released in final form early in 2014. This extension allows users to apply different future climate change scenarios that modify the historical precipitation events and evaporation rates normally used by the calculator. This climate change extension will help site owners, developers, and planners design more robust stormwater management solutions in the face of uncertain future climatic conditions.

14. Develop Improved Monitoring of Water Temperature and Flow: EPA's Office of Research and Development released an external review draft report of technical "best practices" describing sensor deployment for and data collection of continuous temperature and flow at ungaged sites in wadeable streams. The draft report addresses questions related to equipment needs; configuration, placement, and installation of equipment; and data retrieval and processing. (See EPA/600/R-13/170). (http://cfpub.epa.gov/ncea/global/recordisplay.cfm?deid=261911).

15. Publish Study of Climate Impacts on Nitrogen in Water: EPA's Office of Research and Development investigated the effects of projected changes in land cover and climate (precipitation, temperature and atmospheric CO_2 concentrations) on simulated NO_3 and organic nitrogen discharge for two watersheds within the Neuse River Basin, NC for years 2010 to 2070. Results showed nitrogen discharges were most sensitive to changes in precipitation and temperature, with sensitivities to CO_2 and land cover only one-tenth as much. With nitrogen discharge showing high sensitivity to P+T change, this study suggests more emphasis should be placed on investigating impacts of climate change on nutrient transport compared to land cover change in the Neuse River Basin. (See "Relative Sensitivity of Simulated Nitrogen Discharge to Projected Changes in Climate and Land Cover for Two Watersheds in North Carolina, USA," presented at AGU Fall Meeting 2013, San Francisco, CA, December 09–13).

Vision Area 5:
Working with Tribes
Vision: Tribes are able to preserve, adapt, and maintain the viability of their culture, traditions, natural resources, and economies in the face of a changing climate.

16. Support EPA's Tribal-Focused Environmental Risk and Sustainability Tool (Tribal-FERST). The EPA Office of Water is working with the Office of Research and Development to develop and implement Tribal-FERST, which is a web-based geospatial decision support tool designed to serve as a research framework to provide tribes with easy access to the best available human health and ecological science.

Tribes and partners throughout the United States are providing input on the design and content of Tribal-FERST. The United South and Eastern Tribes (USET) is partnering with EPA to develop the Tribal-FERST guidance document and connect its water quality exchange database and data transfer network with Tribal-FERST. The Pleasant Point Passamaquoddy Tribe of Maine is currently piloting Tribal-FERST as part of its sustainable and healthy community effort. In addition, water programs in EPA's regional offices are working with Tribes to assist them in responding to a range of climate change related issues. These activities, described in greater detail in the next Part of this report, include:

➤ Region 2 is maintaining a dialog with the Tribal nations regarding **climate change adaptation and Traditional Ecological Knowledge (TEK). A climate change grant** to the Nations was extended through September 2013 to support vulnerability assessment of nation lands and planning climate adaptation strategies.

➤ Region 4 initiated collaboration with United South and Eastern Tribes, Inc., (USET), which serves 26 Tribes from Texas to Maine and is located in Nashville, TN. Region 4 is working with USET to **build their capacity to provide energy management assistance to Tribal water utilities.**

➤ Region 6 held a **climate change workshop in Albuquerque, NM for Tribal and Environmental Justice Communities** vulnerable to climate change impacts.

➤ Region 7 tribes are incorporating climate change science into their CWA 106 programs addressing **water quality monitoring.**

Vision Area 6:
Cross-cutting Program Support

17. Develop Office of Water Draft *Climate Change Adaptation Implementation Plan*: The Office of Water worked with EPA Regional Water Division staff to draft a *Climate Change Adaptation Implementation Plan.* The draft *Plan* was organized on the template adopted by EPA and is comparable to each of the 16 other national program office and Regional office climate change adaptation implementation plans. The Office of Water draft *Plan* was released for public comment in September 2013. A final *Plan* will be published in the fall of 2014. More information is available at: http://www.epa.gov/water/climatechange.

18. Co-Chair Climate Change Adaptation and Water Stakeholder Group: In 2013, the Office of Water staff served as co-chair of a newly established Climate Change Workgroup of the Advisory Committee on Water Information (ACWI). The Workgroup includes 40 representatives from federal agencies and stakeholder organizations and provides advice and comment to federal agencies on a range of climate change and water resources issues, including the progress in implementing the *National Action Plan: Priorities for Managing Freshwater Resources in a Changing Climate*. More information is available at www.acwi.org.

19. Contribute to Federal Interagency Climate Adaptation Projects: National Water Program staff also participated in a range of workgroups within EPA and among other federal agencies working to adapt to a changing climate including the:

- ➢ EPA Cross-Agency Climate Change Adaptation Workgroup;
- ➢ Interagency Council on Climate Resilience and Preparedness;
- ➢ Water Resources Workgroup of the Interagency Council on Climate Change Resilience and Preparedness;
- ➢ Interagency Joint Working Group implementing the final *Fish Wildlife and Plants Climate Adaptation Strategy*;
- ➢ *National Ocean Policy* Implementation Plan workgroup on climate change;
- ➢ Interagency Ocean Acidification Working Group; and
- ➢ Coral Reef Task Force.

The Office of Water also has an interagency agreement with NOAA in which climate adaptation is a joint focus.

SOURCE: U.S. Environmental Protection Agency. 2014. *2013 Highlights of Progress: Responses to Climate Change by the National Water Program*. http://water.epa.gov/scitech/climatechange/upload/Final-2013-NWP-Climate-Highlights-Report.pdf (accessed August 18, 2014).

ANALYSIS

The Environmental Protection Agency's Global Water Program publishes an annual report that includes six vision statements that guides its work related to global warming. Four of the statements relate directly to water. The other two relate to administrative functions, namely how to cooperatively work with native peoples and how to maximize the budget through cooperation. The report also details the projects that are completed in a given year and charts the direction for future research. Through this valuable document, readers can see the priorities emerging that will guide the future work of the EPA.

FURTHER READING

Christian-Smith, Juliet, and Peter H. Gleick. 2012. *A Twenty-First Century US Water Policy*. New York: Oxford University Press.

Environmental Protection Agency, Office of Water. 2014. *National Water Program Guidance Addendum: Fiscal Year 2015*. http://water.epa.gov/resource_performance/planning/upload/FY-2015-NWPG-4-22-2014-Narrative-with-covers.pdf (accessed September 17, 2014).

Ingram, B. Lynn, and Frances Malamud-Roam. 2013. *The West Without Water: What Past Floods, Droughts, and Other Climatic Clues Tell Us About Tomorrow*. Berkeley: University of California Press.

Nash, Stephen. 2014. *Virginia Climate Fever: How Global Warming Will Transform Our Cities, Shorelines, and Forests*. Charlottesville: University of Virginia Press.

"Climate Change Is Expected to Affect Water Demand"

- *Document:* Climate Change Impacts in the United States: Third National Climate Assessment, Finding 7 Water, excerpt
- *Date:* 2014
- *Where:* Washington, DC
- *Significance:* The National Climate Assessment is issued every four years by the U.S. Global Research Program to identify how climate change is presently impacting the country and what effects can be anticipated in the future.

DOCUMENT

Climate Change Impacts on the Water Cycle

Annual precipitation and river-flow increases are observed now in the Midwest and the Northeast regions. Very heavy precipitation events have increased nationally and are projected to increase in all regions. The length of dry spells is projected to increase in most areas, especially the southern and northwestern portions of the contiguous United States.

Short-term (seasonal or shorter) droughts are expected to intensify in most U.S. regions. Longer-term droughts are expected to intensify in large areas of the Southwest, southern Great Plains, and Southeast.

Flooding may intensify in many U.S. regions, even in areas where total precipitation is projected to decline.

DID YOU KNOW?

Groundwater Policy and the California Drought

As of late 2014, California was in the midst of one of its most severe and prolonged droughts in the history of the state. The drought created myriad problems, including the outbreak of many fires due to dry conditions and the significant shrinkage of many lakes, rivers, and streams. Among the steps that California governmental officials had implemented in response to the drought was the creation of the governor's Drought Task Force, the passage by the state legislature of a water bond issue that included $2.7 billion for both water restoration and the construction of water storage infrastructure, and the declaration of a water emergency, which restricted water use for certain functions.

California's agricultural sector was particularly impacted as many farmers found the waters they had become accustomed to using suddenly becoming unavailable. While some had no other alternative sources of water and thus could not farm, others turned to groundwater to augment their supply. In normal years, groundwater made up approximately 40 percent of the waters used for agricultural purposes. Due to the ongoing drought, some estimates suggested that the state's agricultural enterprises used more than 60 percent of the groundwater that was being utilized. Such rapid depletion of local aquifers was also requiring farmers and homeowners to continuously dig expensive and deeper wells to reach the water that they required. Obviously, that level of water use was not sustainable, so for the first time in the state's history, California enacted laws in 2014 to regulate and protect its supply of groundwater.

The groundwater legislation was passed by the state legislature late in their session in three separate bills: Assembly Bill 1739, Senate Bill 1168, and Senate Bill 1319. They became law with Governor Edmund G. Brown Jr.'s signature on September 16, 2014. Together, they required local water districts to create groundwater sustainability plans that took into account regional needs and resources. The respective plans were to be overseen by the state. Also required were the creation of measures that would allow groundwater sources, which had become depleted to recharge themselves and eventually become self-sustaining.

Although it is within California's purview to regulate groundwater in the same manner as it does surface waters, many are concerned that the initiative was not driven by normal legislative processes but instead by reactions to sudden climate change. The rapid drafting and passage

Climate change is expected to affect water demand, groundwater withdrawals, and aquifer recharge, reducing groundwater availability in some areas.

Sea level rise, storms and storm surges, and changes in surface and groundwater use patterns are expected to compromise the sustainability of coastal freshwater aquifers and wetlands.

Increasing air and water temperatures, more intense precipitation and runoff, and intensifying droughts can decrease river and lake water quality in many ways, including increases in sediment, nitrogen, and other pollutant loads

Climate Change Impacts on Water Resources Use and Management

Climate change affects water demand and the ways water is used within and across regions and economic sectors. The Southwest, Great Plains, and Southeast are particularly vulnerable to changes in water supply and demand.

Changes in precipitation and runoff, combined with changes in consumption and withdrawal, have reduced surface and groundwater supplies in many areas. These trends are expected to continue, increasing the likelihood of water shortages for many uses.

Increasing flooding risk affects human safety and health, property, infrastructure, economies, and ecology in many basins across the United States.

Adaptation and Institutional Responses

In most U.S. regions, water resources managers and planners will encounter new risks, vulnerabilities, and opportunities that may not be properly managed within existing practices.

Increasing resilience and enhancing adaptive capacity provide opportunities to strengthen water resources management and plan for climate change impacts. Many institutional, scientific, economic, and political barriers present challenges to implementing adaptive strategies.

SOURCE: U.S. Global Change Research Program. 2014. *Climate Change Impacts in the United States: Third National Climate Assessment.* http://nca2014.globalchange.gov/downloads (accessed August 18, 2014).

ANALYSIS

The United States Global Change Research Program (USGCRP) was charged by the U.S. Congress in the Global Change Research Act of 1990 to coordinate a broad scientific research program that would be used to study the impacts of global warming and what those changes portend for the future. The program was not created just for the use of constituencies within the United States, as one of its primary purposes was to help educate people around the world about how human activity was impacting global change. The hope was, and continues to be, that informed countries will act responsibly to help alleviate what is a global problem.

The work of the USGCRP is coordinated by an executive director who works with the following federal entities to coordinate climate change research: Department of Agriculture, Department of Commerce, Department of Defense, Department of Energy, Department of Health and Human Services, Department of the Interior, Department of State, Department of Transportation, Environmental Protection Agency, National Aeronautics and Space Administration, National Science Foundation, Smithsonian Institution, and U.S. Agency for International Development. As need arises, other federal departments and agencies are made available in the enabling legislation on an as needed basis. In

of such far-reaching legislation does not necessarily allow for sufficient consideration of the long-term consequences of such actions. In the short term, many agriculturalists believe the legislation will work to the detriment of many, as the state, through these bills, has the ability to prioritize the groundwater. By extension, this has the potential to severely limit the ability of farmers to acquire the water they need, even if they own the infrastructure to tap into available sources. Then again, short-term pain today is a necessity to ensure the availability of adequate groundwater for future generations of Californians.

FURTHER READING

CA.gov. 2014. *California Drought.* http://ca.gov/drought (accessed October 8, 2014).

Kuhne, Michael. 2014. *Drought Spurs Historic Laws to Limit California Groundwater Extraction.* http://www.accuweather.com/en/features/trend/drought_california_groundwater_law/35097894 (accessed October 8, 2014).

National Science Foundation. 2014. *Press Release 14-129 Cause of California Drought Linked to Climate Change.* http://www.nsf.gov/news/news_summ.jsp?cntn_id=132709&WT.mc_id=USNSF_51&WT.mc_ev=click (accessed October 8, 2014).

Office of Governor Edmund G. Brown Jr. 2014. *Governor Brown Signs Historic Groundwater Legislation.* http://gov.ca.gov/news.php?id=18701 (accessed October 8, 2014).

addition to federal resources, the USGCRP works with experts in higher education and other endeavors to ensure that they are utilizing as much of the available expertise on a particular subject that it available. These experts not only provide research expertise but also serve as peer reviewers. The work of both federal and private researchers is prevalent in the report excerpted portion of *Climate Change Impacts in the United States: Third National Climate Assessment.*

As climate change is an ongoing concern, the USGCRP regularly consults with government officials, at the state, federal, and international levels. It provides annual reports to both the president and Congress to help guide policies and legislation that impact the environmental health of the nation. Every four years, the USGCRP submits a comprehensive report, referred to as the "National Climate Assessment," to the president and Congress that details the present impacts of climate change and, using the data it has collected, forecasts the challenges that the United States will be facing 25 years into the future related to global warming.

FURTHER READING

Christian-Smith, Juliet, and Peter H. Gleick. 2012. *A Twenty-First Century US Water Policy.* New York: Oxford University Press.

Ingram, B. Lynn, and Frances Malamud-Roam. 2013. *The West Without Water: What Past Floods, Droughts, and Other Climatic Clues Tell Us About Tomorrow.* Berkeley: University of California Press.

Nash, Stephen. 2014. *Virginia Climate Fever: How Global Warming Will Transform Our Cities, Shorelines, and Forests.* Charlottesville: University of Virginia Press.

Schimel, David. 2013. *Climate and Ecosystems.* Princeton, NJ: Princeton University Press.

U.S. Global Change Research Program. "GlobalChange.gov." http://www.globalchange.gov.

CHRONOLOGY

1801   The first municipal waterworks system in the United States was completed in Philadelphia, Pennsylvania.

1825   The Erie Canal was completed in New York. Derisively known as *Clinton's Ditch*, it was a 363-mile-long canal that connected the Hudson River to Lake Erie.

1827   In *Tyler v. Wilkinson*, the Rhode Island Circuit Court determined that all landowners with riparian rights to a waterway had an equal right to the unimpeded flow of its waters. At the same time, the court created the "reasonable use doctrine," which gave upriver users the ability to make use of a "reasonable" amount of water without legally impeding the water traveling downriver.

1844   Through *Cary v. Daniels*, the Massachusetts Supreme Court set a precedent by suggesting that courts not settle cases involving water disputes strictly through riparian doctrine. Instead, courts should also consider factors such as whether the water was being used for industrial or agricultural purposes.

1850   The U.S. Congress passed the Swamp and Overflow Act of 1850. The act allowed states to alter wetlands for flood control or agricultural purposes.

1871   The U.S. Congress passed the *Joint Resolution for the Protection and Preservation of the Food Fishes of the Coast of the United States*. It created the position of commissioner of fish and fisheries.

1877   John Wesley Powell submitted *Reports of the Lands of the Arid Regions of the United States* to the U.S. Congress. Although he warned of the dangers of settling beyond the 100th meridian, his report was used to encourage migration to the West.

1882   The decision in the Colorado case *Coffin v. Left Hand Ditch Company* resulted in Colorado's complete abandonment of traditional riparian doctrine in favor of prior appropriation.

1886   *Lux v. Haggin* was a California Supreme Court case that tried to reconcile riparian rights, long grounded in English Common Law, with the principles of prior appropriation, which privileged certain water users over others based on who had begun using the water source first.

1894   The Carey Act, officially known as the *Federal Desert Lands Act*, provided 10 states up to 1 million acres of public land each if they improved the property with irrigation systems and then sold the real estate to settlers.

1899   The Refuse Act of 1899, which is Section 13 of the 1899 Rivers and Harbors Act, required all entities dumping garbage into the nation's waters to first obtain a permit from the U.S. Army Corps of Engineers. Those not obtaining the permit were subject to fines ranging from $500 to $2,500 per violation.

1901   The first federal Water Power Act was passed by Congress, which set the initial standards for regulating hydropower generation on the nation's waterways.

1902   The Reclamation Act of 1902, popularly known as the *Newlands Act*, transferred the responsibility from the states to the federal government to construct reclamation projects in the West.

1906   The Rio Grande Water Convention was signed on May 21 between Mexico and the United States, marking the first water treaty between the two countries.

1908   In the landmark *Winters v. United States* case, the U.S. Supreme Court declared that Native Americans had "implied water rights" on their reservations under the doctrine of prior appropriation. This meant that Native Americans using the water on lands they owned through treaties with the federal government were privileged over other land users because their prior appropriation rights began in "time immemorial."

1909   The Boundary Waters Treaty of 1909 was negotiated by representatives of the United States and Great Britain to govern the waters that flow over the borders between Canada and the United States.

1914   The U.S. Public Health Service set the first federal standards to ensure the safety and quality of drinking water.

1920   Congress created the Federal Power Commission to coordinate the construction of hydropower projects around the country and to regulate the distribution of the electrical power that is generated.

1922   The U.S. Supreme Court ruled on *State of Colorado v. Wyoming*, a case that helped establish how the doctrine of "prior appropriation" would be applied in interstate conflicts. As Wyoming's claims to the waters of the Laramie River predated those of Colorado's, Colorado was not allowed to divert the river's waters before they entered into Wyoming. Special dispensation was made that allowed Colorado to utilize a maximum of 15,500 acre-feet of water from the Laramie River a year.

The Colorado River Compact of 1922 was intended to equitably distribute the waters of the Colorado River by dividing the states dependent on its waters into two basins, with each basin receiving the same amount of water to share. The Upper Basin included the states of Colorado, New Mexico, Utah, Wyoming, and a small part of Arizona. The Lower Basin included the rest of Arizona, along with California and Nevada.

1923   Construction of the Hetch Hetchy Dam, now known as *O'Shaughnessy Dam*, was completed on California's Tuolomne River. The dam was bitterly fought by John Muir and the Sierra Club due to its location within Yosemite National Park.

1927   Flooding on the Mississippi River and some of its tributaries displaced approximately 700,000 people in the states of Arkansas, Illinois, Kansas, Kentucky, Louisiana, Mississippi, Missouri, Oklahoma, Tennessee, and Texas.

1928   Enacted on May 15, the Flood Control Act of 1928 authorized the construction of numerous flood control projects along the Mississippi River.

The Boulder Canyon Project Act of 1928 authorized the construction of the Boulder Dam, which after completion was renamed the Hoover Dam in honor of President Herbert Hoover.

1933   The Tennessee Valley Authority was created as part of President Franklin Delano Roosevelt's New Deal to serve parts of Alabama, Georgia, Kentucky, Mississippi, North Carolina, and Virginia. The agency presently manages 49 dams and their associated reservoirs, several nuclear plants, and approximately 290,000 acres of public land.

Other New Deal water projects commenced under the auspices of federal agencies such as the Bureau of Reclamation, the U.S. Army Corps of Engineers, and the Works Progress Administration.

1935   Hoover Dam was completed at Black Canyon on the Colorado River, at the border of Arizona and Nevada. Lake Mead, its reservoir, became the largest man-made lake in the United States.

1936   The Flood Control Act of 1936 authorized the construction of more than 800 dams and approximately 200 locks around the country. The legislation represented an effort to not only address flooding problems but also employ Americans suffering through the Great Depression.

1944   The United States–Mexico Treaty concerning the "Utilization of Waters of the Colorado and Tijuana Rivers and of the Rio Grande" was signed on February 3, 1944. The agreement detailed how the countries jointly manage the rivers that cross their shared borders and the manner through which disputes over the use of the rivers were to be settled.

The Flood Control Act of 1944 included the "Pick-Sloan Plan," which resulted in the construction of a 6-foot navigation canal between Sioux City, Iowa, and St. Louis Missouri. It also provided for the construction of five dams and other flood control measures affecting roughly 800 miles of the Missouri River and its major tributaries.

1945   Grand Rapids, Michigan, became the first city in the United States to continuously add fluoride to its public water supply to prevent tooth decay.

1948   Enacted on June 30, the Water Pollution Control Act of 1948 was designed to regulate pollution on the nation's navigable interstate waterways.

1956   The Bureau of Reclamation abandoned its attempt to construct the Echo Park Dam in the Dinosaur National Monument, located close to the Colorado—Utah border. The dam was proposed in the late 1940s as part of the Colorado River Storage Project (CRSP) but was opposed by a number of national environmental groups. In exchange for stopping the Echo Park Dam, environmentalists pledged not to oppose other dams listed as part of the CRSP. The compromise proved a mistake as the Echo Park Dam was replaced in the CRSP by the Glen Canyon Dam.

The Colorado River Storage Project Act of 1956 authorized the construction of numerous water projects, including dams, in Colorado, New Mexico, Utah, and Wyoming using the framework provided by the Colorado River Compact of 1922.

1963 *Arizona v. California* definitively gave the federal government the authority to supervise how the waters of the Colorado River would be divided among the states of Arizona, California, Colorado, Nevada, New Mexico, Utah, and Wyoming.

1964 The Water Resources Research Act of 1964 funded academic research at the nation's land-grant institutions on water issues.

1965 The Water Resources Planning Act of 1965 established a commission in every one of the states to study local river basins. The work of the respective commissions was overseen by the National Water Commission.

1966 The Clean Water Restoration Act of 1966 provided more than $3.5 billion over six years to be used for both waste treatment facilities and for research on pollution control.

1968 The Colorado River Basin Act of 1968 included the construction of an aqueduct as part of the Central Arizona Project so that Arizona could obtain its share of the Colorado River's waters.

The Wild and Scenic Rivers Act of 1968 marked a major change in national water policy because it created a program to keep all or part of rivers with cultural, natural, or recreational benefits in their original free-flowing state. Initially, 12 rivers had portions that were designated as either recreational, scenic, or wild. Approximately 170 rivers carry one of those designations today.

1969 On January 11, a Union Oil platform began spilling oil 6 miles offshore of Santa Barbara, California. Over the course of 11 days, approximately 200,000 gallons of oil was released.

Already notorious for its industrial pollution, the Cuyahoga River in Cleveland, Ohio, drew a new level of infamy when it caught on fire on June 22 for approximately 20 minutes. The environmental movement seized upon the event to highlight the impact of pollution on the nation's waters.

The National Environmental Policy Act of 1969 made it the policy of the federal government to protect both the environment and the biosphere. The legislation also created the Council of Environmental Quality, a three-person body charged with making recommendations to the president concerning federal policies impacting the environment.

1970 The Environmental Quality Improvement Act of 1970 provided the professional staffing, in the form of the Office of Environmental Quality (OEQ), for the Council on Environmental Quality.

1972 The Clean Water Act, also known as the Federal Water Pollution Control Act Amendments of 1972, was passed by Congress. It provided the federal government the primary responsibility for regulating water pollution around the country. The act became law after Congress overrode President Richard M. Nixon's veto.

The Marine Protection, Research and Sanctuaries Act of 1972 was passed to reduce the dumping of garbage and other forms of waste into the ocean.

The Great Lakes Water Quality Agreement between the United States and Canada allowed the countries to work cooperatively through the International Joint Commission to address water quality issues in all of the Great Lakes and a portion of the St. Lawrence River.

1973   Signed into law by President Richard M. Nixon on December 28, the Endangered Species Act of 1973 not only protected endangered flora and fauna from harm but also extended protections to their surrounding habitats.

1974   The Safe Drinking Water Act of 1974 enabled the Environmental Protection Agency to establish regulations to ensure that the drinking water made available to citizens met a minimum standard of cleanliness from contaminants.

1976   In the landmark case *Tennessee Valley Authority v. Hill*, the U.S. Supreme Court determined that Congress, in the Endangered Species Act, unambiguously determined that the preservation of a threatened or endangered species outweighed any other concern related to development projects.

1977   The Surface Mining and Reclamation Act of 1977 included language intended to ensure that mining activities did not result in the pollution of groundwater.

The Clean Water Act of 1977 broadens the number of pollutants regulated by the Environmental Protection Agency.

1979   In the landmark Supreme Court case *United States et al. v. State of Washington et al.*, Native Americans in Oregon and Washington obtained the right to 45 percent to 50 percent of the fish harvested on waterways passing through their reservations. That amount of fish had been guaranteed to the natives in treaties negotiated by Isaac Stevens, governor of the Washington Territory, between 1854 and 1855, but the majority American population had denied them their rightful share for more than a century.

1980   The Comprehensive Environmental Response, Compensation, and Liability Act of 1980 created the Hazardous Substances Response Trust Fund, better known as the *Superfund*.

1985   The Great Lakes Charter, which governs water diversions from the respective Great Lakes to locales outside of the Great Lakes basin, was signed on February 11 by the governors of Illinois, Indiana, Michigan, Minnesota, New York, Ohio, Pennsylvania, and Wisconsin and the premiers of Ontario and Quebec.

1986   The Water Resources Development Act not only made the Great Lakes Charter agreement binding, because states could not legally negotiate international agreements but expanded upon it by also making it nearly impossible for states within the Great Lakes basin to make intrabasin transfers, even if a transfer never crossed a state or international border.

1987   The Water Quality Act of 1987 focused on the regulation of storm water drainage emanating from factories and municipalities.

1989   The Exxon Valdez ran aground in Prince William Sound in the Gulf of Alaska the night of March 23–24, resulting in one of the largest oil spills in U.S. history. The estimated 11 million gallons of crude oil befouled more than 1,500 miles of shoreline, killed hundreds of thousands of animals, and decimated the region's commercial fishing economy.

The North American Wetlands Conservation Act of 1989 was passed to fund conservation projects impacting wetlands in Canada, Mexico, and the United States.

1990   The Oil Pollution Act of 1990 was enacted to expand the authority of the Environmental Protection Agency to both prevent oil spills and clean up those that occurred on navigable waters and shorelines.

Congress passed the Nonindigenous Aquatic Nuisance Prevention and Control Act (NANPCA) of 1990 to address the rise of invasive species in the Great Lakes, such as the Eurasian ruffe fish and the zebra mussel.

A major component of the Truckee-Carson-Pyramid Lake Water Rights Settlement Act of 1990 was the establishment of the Stampede Reservoir as a fishery to restore the populations of the Pyramid Lake cui-ui and Lahontan Cutthroat trout for the Pyramid Lake Paiutes.

1992   The Elwha River Ecosystem and Fisheries Restoration Act of 1992 was intended to restore Washington's Elwha River to a state that enabled its once prodigious anadromous fish runs to be rebuilt to their former glory. To achieve the act's goals, two dams on the river were removed between 2011 and 2013 so that the fish could arrive to their spawning grounds unimpeded.

1996   The National Dam Safety Act of 1996 was passed to mitigate the dangers of dam failures to people and property. Although woefully underfunded, the act provided some monies to improve dams in states where local funding was lacking.

2000   The Estuaries Act of 2000 called for the creation of a comprehensive plan by 2001 to improve the delicate ecosystems found where freshwater rivers flow into oceans. The projects in the plan were then enacted in the hope that 1 million acres of estuaries would be substantively improved by 2010.

2002   In recognition of the fact that many of dams in the United States were aging and thus deteriorating, Congress passed the Dam Safety and Security Act of 2002 to create a national program to protect against dam failure. The legislation also called for dam owners to ensure that their dams had adequate security, which was a direct response to the terrorist attacks of September 11, 2001.

The Great Lakes Legacy Act of 2002 charged the Environmental Protection Agency to work with other governmental entities to clean up contaminated sediment from the Great Lakes that resulted from industrial plants and mining operations.

2004   The Environmental Protection Agency, through its publication of *Evaluation of Impacts to Underground Sources of Drinking Water by Hydraulic Fracturing of Coalbed Methane Reservoirs*, determined that hydraulic fracturing, also known as *fracking*, did not threaten the nation's drinking water supply.

2005   The *Kyoto Protocol to the United Nations Framework Convention on Climate Change*, an agreement intended to reduce the emissions of greenhouse gases by industrialized countries, received enough ratifications to go into force. It was ultimately approved by 191 countries. Although President William Clinton's administration strongly supported the initiative, the U.S. Congress refused to ratify the treaty.

Hurricane Katrina made landfall on the United States' Gulf Coast on August 29, 2005, as a Category 3 hurricane on the Saffir-Simpson Hurricane Scale. Most of the damage occurred in the states of Alabama, Louisiana, and Mississippi. The storm, and calamities that followed in its wake, left hundreds of thousands of individuals displaced and caused in excess of $100 billion in damages.

2006   The Select Bipartisan Committee to Investigate the Preparation for and Response to Hurricane Katrina issued A *Failure of Initiative: Final Report of the Select Bipartisan Committee to Investigate the Preparation for and Response to Hurricane Katrina*, which concluded the impact of the storm was magnified by poor decisions made by politicians at all levels from the time before the hurricane struck to days after the immensity of the calamity was revealed.

The majority decision in the U.S. Supreme Court case *Rapanos v. United States* narrowed the definition of navigable waters that the Environmental Protection Agency used to enforce the Clean Water Act.

The United States–Mexico Transboundary Aquifer Assessment Act of 2006 authorized the U.S. secretary of the interior to work with representatives of U.S. border states and Mexico to study the aquifers located astride the United States border with Mexico.

2008   After a dike burst at the Tennessee Valley Authority's Kingston Fossil Plant on December 22, more than 1 billion gallons of toxic coal fly ash was released into Tennessee's Emory and Clinch Rivers.

2009   The Clean Water Restoration Act of 2009 was an unsuccessful attempt by Democrats in Congress to restore the Environmental Protection Agency's power to enforce the Clean Water Act, which it lost in the Supreme Court's *Rapanos v. United States* decision.

2010   On April 20, British Petroleum's (BP) Macondo well suffered a blowout that led to the sinking of the Deepwater Horizon oil rig, the death of 11 men, and an oil leak that was not sealed until September 20. The oil befouled hundreds of miles of beaches along the Gulf Coast and made a significant portion of the Gulf of Mexico unsuitable for commercial fishing.

2014   A chemical spill into the Elk River, near Charleston, West Virginia, contaminated the drinking water used by approximately 300,000 people from January 9 to 13.

According to the U.S. Geological Survey, Oklahoma averaged approximately 1.6 earthquakes a year of a magnitude of 3.0 or greater between 1978 and 1999. Beginning in 2009, Oklahoma has seen the number of earthquakes a year rise substantially. In just the first five months of 2014, Oklahoma had seen more than 140 such earthquakes. Although not definitively proven, many experts suspect that hydraulic fracturing, also known as *fracking*, is the source of Oklahoma's increased seismicity.

Between 2013 and 2014, the drought in the West resulted in the loss of more than 62,000,000,000,000 gallons of water.

More than 2,000 "Peoples Climate Marches" were held around the world in advance of the United Nation's Climate Summit. The New York City march drew an estimated 300,000 activists.

SELECTED RESOURCES

Selected Online Resources

American Rivers. 2014. "American Rivers: Rivers Connect Us." http://www.american rivers.org.

Association of Clean Water Administrators. n.d. http://www.acwa-us.org/.

CA.gov. 2014. "California Drought." http://ca.gov/drought.

Centers for Disease Control and Prevention. 2009. "Healthy Water." http://www.cdc.gov/healthywater/.

International Boundary & Water Commission, United States Section. n.d. "International Boundary & Water Commission, United States and Mexico, United States Section." http://www.ibwc.gov/home.html.

International Joint Commission (IJC). 2014. "IJC – Protecting Shared Waters." http://www.ijc.org/en_/

National Drought Mitigation Center. 2014. "Drought Risk Atlas." http://droughtatlas.unl.edu.

National Oceanic and Atmospheric Administration, Fisheries. n.d. "NOAA Fisheries." http://www.nmfs.noaa.gov.

National Resources Defense Council. n.d. "Water." http://www.nrdc.org/water/default.asp.

National Wild and Scenic Rivers System. 2007. "National Wild and Scenic Rivers System." http://www.rivers.gov.

The Nature Conservancy. 2014. "The Nature Conservance." http: www.nature.org.

Puget Sound Institute at the University of Washington Tacoma Center for Urban Waters. 2012. "Encyclopedia of Puget Sound." http://www.eopugetsound.org.

Resources for the Future. n.d. "Water." http://www.rff.org/Research_Topics/Pages/Water.aspx.

Trout Unlimited. 2014. "Trout Unlimited." http://www.tu.org.

U.S. Army Corps of Engineers. n.d. "Institute for Water Resources." http://www.iwr.usace.army.mil/.

U.S. Department of the Interior. n.d. "Water Challenges." http://www.doi.gov/whatwedo/water/index.cfm.

U.S. Department of the Interior, Bureau of Reclamation. 2014. "Reclamation: Managing Water in the West." http://www.usbr.gov.

U.S. Global Change Research Program. n.d. "GlobalChange.gov." http://www.global change.gov.

United States Department of Agriculture, Natural Resources Conservation Service. n.d. "National Water & Climate Center." http://www.wcc.nrcs.usda.gov/.

United States Department of Agriculture, National Agricultural Library. 2014. "National Invasive Species Information Center: Aquatic Species." http://www.invasivespecies info.gov/aquatics/main.shtml.

United States Environmental Protection Agency. 2014. "Water Home." http://water.epa .gov.

United States Geological Service. 2014. "Water Resources of the United States." http:// www.usgs.gov/water.

University of California, Davis, Center for Watershed Sciences. 2005. "Welcome to the Center for Watershed Sciences." http://watershed.ucdavis.edu.

Western Waters Digital Library. n.d. "Western Waters Digital Library. http://western waters.org.

The White House. n.d. "Council on Environmental Quality." http://www.whitehouse.gov/ administration/eop/ceq.

Selected Print Resources

Achenbach, Joel. 2011. *A Hole at the Bottom of the Sea: The Race to Kill the BP Oil Gusher*. New York: Simon & Schuster.

Adams, John A., Jr. 1990. *Damming the Colorado: The Rise of the Lower Colorado River Authority, 1933–1939*. College Station: Texas A&M University Press.

Albert, Richard C. 1987. *Damming the Delaware: The Rise and Fall of the Tocks Island Dam*. University Park: Pennsylvania State University Press.

Alderson, Doug. 2009. *New Dawn for the Kissimmee River*. Gainesville: University Press of Florida.

Alexander, Jeff. 2009. *Pandora's Locks: The Opening of the Great Lakes – St. Lawrence Seaway*. Lansing: Michigan State University Press.

Anderson, Robert T. 2006. "Indian Water Rights and the Federal Trust Responsibility." *Natural Resources Journal* 46, no. 2: 399–437.

Annin, Peter. 2006. *The Great Lakes Water Wars*. Washington, DC: Island Press.

Arnold, Joseph L. 1988. *The Evolution of the 1936 Flood Control Act*. Washington, DC: U.S. Army Corps of Engineers.

August, Jack L., Jr. 1999. *Vision in the Desert: Carl Hayden and Hydropolitics in the American Southwest*. Fort Worth: Texas Christian University Press.

August, Jack L., Jr. 2007. *Dividing Western Waters: Mark Wilmer and Arizona v. California*. Fort Worth: Texas Christian University Press.

Barnett, Cynthia. 2008. *Mirage: Florida and the Vanishing Water of the Eastern U.S.* Ann Arbor: University of Michigan Press.

Barnett, Cynthia. 2011. *Blue Revolution: Unmaking America's Water Crisis*. Boston: Beacon Press.

Barnett, Harold C. 1994. *Toxic Debts and the Superfund Dilemma*. Chapel Hill: University of North Carolina Press.

Barry, John M. 1997. *Rising Tide: The Great Mississippi Flood of 1927 and How It Changed America*. New York: Simon & Schuster.

Bartlett, Richard A. 1995. *Troubled Waters: Champion International and the Pigeon River Controversy*. Knoxville: University of Tennessee Press.

Becker, William H. 2004. *From the Atlantic to the Great Lakes: A History of the U.S. Army Corps of Engineers and the St. Lawrence Seaway.* Honolulu, HI: University Press of the Pacific.

Bengtsson, Lars, Reginald W. Herschy, and Rhodes W. Fairbridge, eds. 2012. *Encyclopedia of Lakes and Reservoirs.* New York: Springer.

Benke, Arthur C., and Colbert E. Cushing, eds. 2005. *Rivers of North America.* New York: Elsevier.

Bennett, Dean B. 2001. *The Wilderness from Chamberlain Farm: A Story of Hope for the American Wild.* Washington, DC: Island Press.

Billington, David P., and Donald C. Jackson. 2006. *Big Dams of the New Deal Era: A Confluence of Engineering and Politics.* Norman: University of Oklahoma Press.

Black, Maggie, and Jannet King. 2011. *The Atlas of Water: Mapping the World's Most Critical Resource.* 2nd ed. Berkeley: University of California Press.

Bogner, Stephen. 2003. *Ditches Across the Desert: Irrigation in the Lower Pecos Valley.* Lubbock: Texas Tech University Press.

Bogue, Margaret Beattie. 2000. *Fishing the Great Lakes: An Environmental History, 1783–1993.* Madison: University of Wisconsin Press.

Botts, Lee, and Paul R. Muldoon. 2005. *Evolution of the Great Lakes Water Quality Agreement.* East Lansing: Michigan State University Press.

Brewer, Thomas L. 2014. *The United States in a Warming World: The Political Economy of Government, Business, and Public Responses to Climate Change.* New York: Cambridge University Press.

Brinkley, Douglas. 2006. *The Great Deluge: Hurricane Katrina, New Orleans, and the Mississippi Gulf Coast.* New York: HarperCollins.

Brody, Samuel D., Wesley E. Highfield, and Jung Eun Kang. 2011. *Rising Waters: The Causes and Consequences of Flooding in the United States.* New York: Cambridge University Press.

Brooks, Karl Boyd. 2006. *Public Power, Private Dams: The Hells Canyon Controversy.* Seattle: University of Washington Press.

Brown, Marilyn A., and Benjamin K. Sovacool. 2011. *Climate Change and Global Energy Security: Technology and Policy Options.* Cambridge, MA: MIT Press.

Burton, Lloyd. 1991. *American Indian Water Rights and the Limits of Law.* Lawrence: University Press of Kansas.

Cech, Thomas V. 2010. *Principles of Water Resources: History, Development, Management, and Policy.* 3rd ed. Hoboken, NJ: John Wiley & Sons.

Christian-Smith, Juliet, and Peter H. Gleick. 2012. *A Twenty-First Century US Water Policy.* New York: Oxford University Press.

Clark, Ira G. 1987. *Water in New Mexico: A History of Its Management and Use.* Albuquerque: University of New Mexico Press.

Colby, Bonnie G., and Katharine L. Jacobs, eds. 2007. *Arizona Water Policy: Management Innovations in an Urbanizing, Arid Region.* Washington, DC: Resources for the Future.

Colby, Bonnie G., et al. 2005. *Negotiating Tribal Water Rights: Fulfilling Promises in the Arid West.* Tucson: University of Arizona Press.

Collins, Craig. 2010. *Toxic Loopholes: Failures and Future Prospects for Environmental Law.* New York: Cambridge University Press.

Colten, Craig E. 2014. *Southern Waters: The Limits to Abundance.* Baton Rouge: Louisiana State University Press.

Conners, John A. 2013. *Groundwater for the 21st Century: A Primer for Citizens of Planet Earth.* Granville, OH: McDonald & Woodward Publishing.

Cosens, Barbara, and Judith V. Royster, eds. 2012. *The Future of Indian and Federal Reserved Water Rights: The Winters Centennial.* Albuquerque: University of New Mexico Press.

Coyle, Kevin J. 1988. *American Rivers Guide to Wild and Scenic River Designation: A Primer on National River Conservation.* Washington, DC: American Rivers.

Crane, Jeff. 2011. *Finding the River: An Environmental History of the Elwha.* Corvallis: Oregon State University Press.

Cumbler, John T. 2001. *Reasonable Use: The People, the Environment, and the State, New England, 1790–1930.* New York: Oxford University Press.

Dalton, Meghan M., Philip W. Mote, and Amy K. Snover, eds. 2013. *Climate Change in the Northwest: Implications for Our Landscapes, Waters, and Communities.* Washington, DC: Island Press.

Daniel, Pete. 1996. *Deep'n as It Come: The 1927 Mississippi River Flood.* Fayetteville: University of Arkansas Press.

Danver, Steven L., and John R. Burch Jr., eds. 2011. *Encyclopedia of Water Politics and Policy in the United States.* Washington, DC: Congressional Quarterly Press.

DeBuys, William. 1999. *Salt Dreams: Land and Water in Low-Down California.* Albuquerque: University of New Mexico Press.

DeBuys, William. 2011. *A Great Aridness: Climate Change and the Future of the American Southwest.* New York: Oxford University Press.

DeJong, David H. 2009. *Stealing the Gila: The Pima Agricultural Economy and Water Deprivation, 1848–1921.* Tucson: University of Arizona Press.

Dempsey, Dave. 2004. *On the Brink: The Great Lakes in the 21st Century.* East Lansing: Michigan State University.

Doherty, Robert. 1993. *Disputed Waters: Native Americans and the Great Lakes Fishery.* Lexington: University Press of Kentucky.

Dolin, Eric Jay. 2004. *Political Waters: The Long, Dirty, Contentious, Incredibly Expensive but Eventually Triumphant History of Boston Harbor – A Unique Environmental Story.* Amherst: University of Massachusetts Press.

Doremus, Holly D., and A. Dan Tarlock. 2008. *Water War in the Klamath Basin: Macho Law, Combat Biology, and Dirty Politics.* Washington, DC: Island Press.

Dorsey, Kurkpatrick. 1998. *The Dawn of Conservation Diplomacy: U.S.-Canadian Wildlife Protection Treaties in the Progressive Era.* Seattle: University of Washington Press.

Dow, Kirstin, and Thomas E. Downing. 2011. *Atlas of Climate Change: Mapping the World's Greatest Challenge.* 3rd ed. Berkeley: University of California Press.

Dryzek, John S., Richard B. Norgaard, and David Schlosberg. 2011. *Oxford Handbook of Climate Change and Society.* New York: Oxford University Press.

DuMars, Charles T., Marilyn O'Leary, and Albert E. Utton. 1984. *Pueblo Indian Water Rights: Struggle for a Precious Resource.* Tucson: University of Arizona Press.

El-Ashry, Mohamed T., and Diana C. Gibbons, eds. 1988. *Water and Arid Lands of the Western United States.* New York: Cambridge University Press.

Ellerman, A. Denny, Paul L. Joskow, Richard Schmalensee, Juan-Pablo Montero, and Elizabeth M. Bailey. 2000. *Markets for Clean Air: The U.S. Acid Rain Program.* New York: Cambridge University Press.

Ellis, William E. 2000. *The Kentucky River.* Lexington: University Press of Kentucky.

Erie, Steven P. 2006. *Beyond Chinatown: The Metropolitan Water District, Growth, and the Environment in Southern California.* Stanford, CA: Stanford University Press.

Espeland, Wendy Nelson. 1998. *The Struggle for Water: Politics, Rationality, and Identity in the American Southwest.* Chicago: University of Chicago Press.

Estaville, Lawrence E. 2008. *Texas Water Atlas*. College Station: Texas A&M University Press.

Farmer, Jared. 1999. *Glen Canyon Dammed: Inventing Lake Powell & the Canyon Country*. Tucson: University of Arizona Press.

Farson, Robert H. 1977. *The Cape Cod Canal*. Middletown, CT: Wesleyan University Press.

Fowler, Don D., ed. 2012. *Cleaving an Unknown World: The Powell Expeditions and the Scientific Exploration of the Colorado Plateau*. Salt Lake City: University of Utah Press.

Fradkin, Philip L. 1995. *A River No More: The Colorado River and the West*. Expanded and Updated ed. Berkeley: University of California Press.

Frisch, Scott A., and Sean Q Kelly. 2008. *Jimmy Carter and the Water Wars: Presidential Influence and the Politics of Pork*. Amherst, NY: Cambria Press.

Gardner, Royal C. 2011. *Lawyers, Swamps, and Money: U.S. Wetland Law, Policy, and Politics*. Washington, DC: Island Press.

Garone, Philip. 2011. *The Fall and Rise of the Wetlands of California's Great Central Valley*. Berkeley: University of California Press.

Glass, Charles F., Jr. 2003. "Enforcing Great Lakes Water Export Restrictions under the Water Resources Development Act of 1986." *Columbia Law Review* 103, no. 6: 1503–1537.

Glennon, Robert. 2002. *Water Follies: Groundwater Pumping and the Fate of America's Fresh Waters*. Washington, DC: Island Press.

Glennon, Robert. 2009. *Unquenchable: America's Water Crisis and What to Do About It*. Washington, DC: Island Press.

Gold, Russell. 2014. *The Boom: How Fracking Ignited the American Energy Revolution and Changed the World*. New York: Simon & Schuster.

Green, Donald E. 1973. *Land of the Underground Rain: Irrigation on the Texas High Plains, 1910–1970*. Austin: University of Texas Press.

Green, Dorothy. 2007. *Managing Water: Avoiding Crisis in California*. Berkeley: University of California Press.

Grossman, Elizabeth. 2002. *Watershed: The Undamming of America*. New York: Counterpoint.

Grunwald, Michael. 2006. *The Swamp: The Everglades, Florida, and the Politics of Paradise*. New York: Simon & Schuster.

Harmon, Alexandra. 1998. *Indians in the Making: Ethnic Relations and Indian Identities Around Puget Sound*. Berkeley: University of California Press.

Harvey, Mark W.T. 2000. *A Symbol of Wilderness: Echo Park and the American Conservation Movement*. Seattle: University of Washington Press.

Hillstrom, Kevin. 2010. *U.S. Environmental Policy and Politics: A Documentary History*. Washington, DC: Congressional Quarterly Press.

Hird, John A. 1994. *Superfund: The Political Economy of Environmental Risk*. Baltimore: Johns Hopkins University Press.

Hundley, Norris, Jr. 1966. *Dividing the Waters: A Century of Controversy between the United States and Mexico*. Berkeley: University of California Press.

Hundley, Norris, Jr. 1982. "The Winters Decision and Indian Water Rights: A Mystery Reexamined." *The Western Historical Quarterly* 13, no.1: 17–42.

Hundley, Norris, Jr. 2001. *The Great Thirst: Californians and Water: A History*. Rev. ed. Berkeley: University of California Press.

Hundley, Norris, Jr. 2009. *Water and the West: The Colorado River Compact and the Politics of Water in the American West*. 2nd ed. Berkeley: University of California Press.

Ingram, B. Lynn, and Frances Malamud-Roam. 2013. *The West Without Water: What Past Floods, Droughts, and Other Climatic Clues Tell Us About Tomorrow*. Berkeley: University of California Press.

Jackson, Donald C. 1995. *Building the Ultimate Dam: John S. Eastwood and Control of Water in the West*. Lawrence: University Press of Kansas.

Jenkins, Jerry C., Karen Roy, Charles Driscoll, and Christopher Buerkett. 2007. *Acid Rain in the Adirondacks: An Environmental History*. Ithaca, NY: Cornell University Press.

Johnson, Rich. 1977. *The Central Arizona Project, 1918–1968*. Tucson: University of Arizona Press.

Jordan, Jeffrey L., and Aaron T. Wolf. 2006. *Interstate Water Allocation in Alabama, Florida, and Georgia: New Issues, New Methods*. Gainesville: University Press of Florida.

Kahrl, Fredrich. 2012. *Climate Change in California: Risk and Response*. Berkeley: University of California Press.

Kanazawa, Mark T. 1998. "Efficiency in Western Water Law: The Development of the Colorado Doctrine, 1850–1911." *Journal of Legal Studies* 27, no. 1: 159–184.

Karl, Thomas R., et al., eds. 2009. *Global Climate Change Impacts in the United States*. New York: Cambridge University Press.

Kromm, David E., and Stephen E. White, eds. 1992. *Groundwater Exploitation in the High Plains*. Lawrence: University Press of Kansas.

Lau, L. Stephen, and John F. Mink. 2006. *Hydrology of the Hawaiian Islands*. Honolulu: University of Hawaii Press.

Lavin, Stephen J., Fred M. Shelley, and J. Clark Archer. 2011. *Atlas of the Great Plains*. Lincoln: University of Nebraska Press.

Lawson, Michael L. 1982. *Dammed Indians: The Pick-Sloan Plan and the Missouri River Sioux, 1944–1980*. Norman: University of Oklahoma Press.

Lawson, Michael L. 2009. *Dammed Indians Revisited: The Continuing History of the Pick-Sloan Plan and the Missouri River Sioux*. Pierre: South Dakota Historical Society.

Levinton, Jeffrey S., and John R. Waldman, eds. 2006. *The Hudson River Estuary*. New York: Cambridge University Press.

Lewis, William M., Jr., ed. 2003. *Water and Climate in the Western United States*. Boulder: University of Colorado Press.

Libecap, Gary D. 2007. *Owens Valley Revisited: A Reassessment of the West's First Great Water Transfer*. Stanford, CA: Stanford University Press.

Likens, Gene E. 2009. *Encyclopedia of Inland Waters*. New York: Elsevier.

Littlefield, Douglas R. 2008. *Conflict on the Rio Grande: Water and the Law, 1879–1939*. Norman: University of Oklahoma Press.

Lowry, William R. 2003. *Dam Politics: Restoring America's Rivers*. Washington, DC: Georgetown University Press.

Malone, Patrick M. 2009. *Waterpower in Lowell: Engineering and Industry in Nineteenth-Century America*. Baltimore: Johns Hopkins University Press.

Manganiello, Christopher J. 2015. *Southern Water, Southern Power: How the Politics of Cheap Energy and Water Scarcity Shaped a Region*. Chapel Hill: University of North Carolina Press.

Margat, Jean, and Jac van der Gun. 2013. *Groundwater Around the World: A Geographic Synopsis*. New York: CRC Press.

McCool, Daniel. 1987. *Command of the Waters: Iron Triangles, Federal Water Development, and Indian Water*. Tucson: University of Arizona Press.

McCool, Daniel. 2002. *Native Waters: Contemporary Indian Water Settlements and the Second Treaty Era*. Tucson: University of Arizona Press.

McCool, Daniel. 2012. *River Republic: The Fall and Rise of America's Rivers.* New York: Columbia University Press.

McEvoy, Arthur F. 1986. *The Fisherman's Problem: Ecology and Law in the California Fisheries, 1850–1980.* New York: Cambridge University Press.

McGucken, William. 2000. *Lake Erie Rehabilitated: Controlling Cultural Eutrophication, 1960s–1990s.* Akron, OH: University of Akron Press.

McGuire, Michael J. 2013. *The Chlorine Revolution: Water Disinfection and the Fight to Save Lives.* Denver, CO: American Water Works Association.

McVoy, Christopher W., et al. 2011. *Landscapes and Hydrology of the Predrainage Everglades.* Gainesville: University Press of Florida.

Mergen, Bernard. 2014. *At Pyramid Lake.* Reno: University of Nevada Press.

Meyer, Michael C. 1984. *Water in the Hispanic Southwest: A Social and Legal History.* Tucson: University of Arizona Press.

Miike, Lawrence H. 2004. *Water and the Law in Hawaii.* Honolulu: University of Hawaii Press.

Milazzo, Paul Charles. 2006. *Unlikely Environmentalists: Congress and Clean Water, 1945–1972.* Lawrence: University Press of Kansas.

Miller, Char, ed. 2001. *Fluid Arguments: Five Centuries of Western Water Conflict.* Tucson: University of Arizona Press.

Morris, Christopher. 2012. *The Big Muddy: An Environmental History of the Mississippi and its Peoples from Hernando de Soto to Hurricane Katrina.* New York: Oxford University Press.

Moyle, Peter S., Amber D. Manfree, and Peggy L. Fiedler, eds. 2014. *Suishan Marsh: Ecological History and Possible Futures.* Berkeley: University of California Press.

Nash, Stephen. 2014. *Virginia Climate Fever: How Global Warming Will Transform Our Cities, Shorelines, and Forests.* Charlottesville: University of Virginia Press.

National Research Council. 2007. *Mississippi River Water Quality and the Clean Air Act: Progress, Challenges, and Opportunities.* Washington, DC: National Academies Press.

Norman, Emma S., Alice Cohen, and Karen Bakker, eds. 2013. *Water Without Borders?: Canada, the United States and Shared Waters.* Toronto: University of Toronto Press.

O'Neill, Karen M. 2006. *Rivers by Design: State Power and the Origins of U.S. Flood Control.* Durham: Duke University Press.

Opie, John. 2000. *Ogallala: Water for a Dry Land.* 2nd ed. Lincoln: University of Nebraska Press.

Palmer, Tim. 2004. *Endangered Rivers and the Conservation Movement.* 2nd ed. Lanham, MD: Rowman & Littlefield.

Parham, Claire Puccia. 2009. *The St. Lawrence Seaway and Power Project: An Oral History of the Greatest Construction Show on Earth.* Syracuse, NY: Syracuse University Press.

Piazza, Bryan P. 2014. *The Atchafalaya River Basin: History and Ecology of an American Wetland.* College Station: Texas A&M University Press.

Pisani, Donald J. 1984. *From the Family Farm to Agribusiness: The Irrigation Crusade in California and the West, 1850–1931.* Berkeley: University of California Press.

Pisani, Donald J. 1986. "Irrigation, Water Rights, and the Betrayal of Indian Allotment." *Environmental Review* 10, no. 3: 157–176.

Pisani, Donald J. 1992. *To Reclaim a Divided West: Water, Law, and Public Policy, 1848–1902.* Albuquerque: University of New Mexico Press.

Pisani, Donald J. 1996. *Water, Land and Law in the West: The Limits of Public Policy.* Lawrence: University Press of Kansas.

Pisani, Donald J. 2002. *Water and the American Government: The Reclamation Bureau, National Water Policy, and the West, 1902–1935*. Berkeley: University of California Press.

Pitzer, Paul C. 1994. *Grand Coulee: Harnessing a Dream*. Pullman: Washington State University Press.

Powell, James Lawrence. 2009. *Dead Pool: Lake Powell, Global Warming, and the Future of Water in the West*. Berkeley: University of California Press.

Powell, John Wesley. 2004. *The Arid Lands*. Edited by Wallace Stegner. Lincoln: University of Nebraska Press.

Prince, Hugh C. 1997. *Wetlands of the American Midwest: A Historical Geography of Changing Attitudes*. Chicago: University of Chicago Press.

Prud'homme, Alex. 2013. *Hydrofracking: What Everyone Needs to Know*. New York: Oxford University Press.

Reisner, Marc. 1986. *Cadillac Desert: The American West and Its Disappearing Water*. New York: Viking.

Reisner, Marc, and Sarah F. Bates. 1990. *Overtapped Oasis: Reform or Revolution for Western Water*. Washington, DC: Island Press.

Reuss, Martin. 2004. *Designing the Bayous: The Control of Water in the Atchafalaya Basin, 1800–1995*. College Station: Texas A&M University Press.

Riley, John L. 2013. *The Once and Future Great Lakes Country: An Ecological History*. Montreal: McGill-Queen's University Press.

Rivera, José A. 1998. *Acequia Culture: Water, Land, and Community in the Southwest*. Albuquerque: University of New Mexico Press.

Rosenzweig, Cynthia, et al., eds. 2011. *Climate Change and Cities: First Assessment Report of the Urban Climate Change Research Network*. New York: Cambridge University Press.

Rowley, William D. 1996. *Reclaiming the Arid West: The Career of Francis G. Newlands*. Bloomington: Indiana University Press.

Rowley, William D. 2006. *The Bureau of Reclamation: Origins and Growth to 1945*. Denver, CO: U.S. Bureau of Reclamation.

Sansom, Andrew. 2008. *Water in Texas: An Introduction*. Austin: University of Texas Press.

Sauder, Robert A. 1994. *The Lost Frontier: Water Diversion in the Growth and Destruction of Owens Valley Agriculture*. Tucson: University of Arizona Press.

Sauder, Robert A. 2009. *The Yuma Reclamation Project: Irrigation, Indian Allotment, and Settlement Along the Lower Colorado River*. Reno: University of Nevada Press.

Schlage, Edella, and William Blomquist. 2008. *Embracing Watershed Politics*. Boulder: University Press of Colorado.

Schneiders, Robert Kelley. 1999. *Unruly River: Two Centuries of Change Along the Missouri*. Lawrence: University Press of Kansas.

Schneiders, Robert Kelley. 2003. *Big Sky Rivers: The Yellowstone & Upper Missouri*. Lawrence: University Press of Kansas.

Schueler, Thomas R., and Heather K. Holland, eds. 2000. *The Practice of Watershed Protection: Techniques for Protecting Our Nation's Streams, Lakes, Rivers, and Estuaries*. Ellicott City, MD: Center for Watershed Protection.

Schulte, Steven C. 2002. *Wayne Aspinall and the Shaping of the American West*. Boulder: University of Colorado Press.

Shallat, Todd. 1994. *Structures in the Stream: Water, Science, and the Rise of the United States Army Corps of Engineers*. Austin: University of Texas Press.

Shapiro, Jennifer, and Barbara Warner. 2013. "Fractured, Fragmented Federalism: A Study in Fracking Regulatory Policy." *Publius: The Journal of Federalism* 43, no. 3: 474–496.

Shaw, Ronald E. 1993. *Canals for a Nation: The Canal Era in the United States, 1790–1860*. Lexington: University Press of Kentucky.

Sherk, George William. 2000. *Dividing the Waters: The Resolution of Interstate Water Conflicts in the United States*. Cambridge, MA: Kluwer Law International.

Shurts, John. 2000. *Indian Reserved Water Rights: The Winters Doctrine in Its Social and Legal Context, 1880s–1930s*. Norman: University of Oklahoma Press.

Simon, Ted. 2000. *The River Stops Here: Saving Round Valley, A Pivotal Chapter in California's Water Wars*. Berkeley: University of California Press.

Smith, Carl. 2013. *City Water, City Life: Water and the Infrastructure of Ideas in Urbanizing Philadelphia, Boston, and Chicago*. Chicago: University of Chicago Press.

Soll, David. 2013. *Empire of Water: An Environmental and Political History of the New York City Water Supply*. Ithaca: Cornell University Press.

Spencer, Robert Allan, John J. Kirton, and Kim Richard Nossal, eds. 1981. *The International Joint Commission Seventy Years On*. Toronto: Centre for International Studies, University of Toronto.

Stegner, Wallace. 1954. *Beyond the Hundredth Meridian: John Wesley Powell and the Second Opening of the West*. New York: Penguin.

Steinberg, Theodore. 1991. *Nature Incorporated: Industrialization and the Waters of New England*. New York: Cambridge University Press.

Stevens, Lawrence E., and Vicky J. Meretsky, eds. 2008. *Aridland Springs in North America: Ecology and Conservation*. Tucson: University of Arizona Press.

Stine, Jeffrey K. 1993. *Mixing the Waters: Environment, Politics, and the Building of the Tennessee-Tombigbee Waterway*. Akron, OH: University of Akron Press.

Stokes, Dale. 2014. *The Fish in the Forest: Salmon and the Web of Life*. Berkeley: University of California Press.

Sturgeon, Stephen Craig. 2002. *The Politics of Western Water: The Congressional Career of Wayne Aspinall*. Tucson: University of Arizona Press.

Summitt, April R. 2013. *Contested Waters: An Environmental History of the Colorado River*. Boulder: University Press of Colorado.

Tarlock, A. Dan. 2009. *Law of Water Rights and Resources*. Deerfield, IL: Clark Boardman Callaghan.

Taylor, Joseph E., III. 1999. *Making Salmon: An Environmental History of the Northwest Fisheries Crisis*. Seattle: University of Washington Press.

Taylor, William W., and C. Paola Ferreri, eds. 1999. *Great Lakes Fisheries Policy and Management: A Binational Perspective*. East Lansing: Michigan State University Press.

Theriot, Jason P. 2014. *American Energy, Imperiled Coast: Oil and Gas Development in Louisiana's Wetlands*. Baton Rouge: Louisiana State University Press.

Thorson, Jared E. 1994. *River of Promise, River of Peril: The Politics of Managing the Missouri River*. Lawrence: University Press of Kansas.

Ulrich, Roberta. 1999. *Empty Nets: Indians, Dams, and the Columbia River*. Corvallis: Oregon State University Press.

Van Heerden, Ivor, and Mike Bryan. 2006. *The Storm: What Went Wrong and Why During Hurricane Katrina; The Inside Story from One Louisiana Scientist*. New York: Viking.

Verchick, Robert R. M. 2010. *Facing Catastrophe: Environmental Action for a Post-Katrina World*. Cambridge: Harvard University Press.

Waldman, John. 2013. *Heartbeats in the Muck: The History, Sea Life, and Environment of New York Harbor*. Revised ed. New York: Empire State Editions.

Walton, John. 1992. *Western Times and Water Wars: State, Culture, and Rebellion in California*. Berkeley: University of California Press.

Ward, Diane Raines. 2002. *Water Wars: Drought, Flood, Folly, and the Politics of Thirst*. New York: Riverhead Books.

Ward, Evan R. 2003. *Border Oasis: Water and the Political Ecology of the Colorado River Delta, 1940–1975*. Tucson: University of Arizona Press.

Welky, David. 2011. *The Thousand-Year Flood: The Ohio-Mississippi Disaster of 1937*. Chicago: University of Chicago Press.

Wheeler, William Bruce, and Michael J. McDonald. 1986. *TVA and the Tellico Dam, 1936–1979: A Bureaucratic Crisis in Post-Industrial America*. Knoxville: University of Tennessee Press.

Whisnant, David E. 1994. *Modernizing the Mountaineer: People, Power, and Planning in Appalachia*. Revised ed. Knoxville: University of Tennessee Press.

White, Richard. 1996. *The Organic Machine: The Remaking of the Columbia River*. New York: Hill and Wang.

Wiens, John A., ed. 2013. *Oil in the Environment: Legacies and Lessons of the Exxon Valdez Oil Spill*. New York: Cambridge University Press.

Wilbur, Tom. 2012. *Under the Surface: Fracking Fortunes, and the Fate of the Marcellus Shale*. Ithaca: Cornell University Press.

Wilds, Leah J. 2014. *Water Politics in Northern Nevada: A Century of Struggle*. 2nd ed. Reno: University of Nevada Press.

Wilkinson, Charles F. 1987. *American Indians, Time, and the Law: Native Societies in a Modern Constitutional Democracy*. New Haven, CT: Yale University Press.

Wilkinson, Charles F. 1992. *Crossing the Next Meridian: Land, Water, and the Future of the American West*. Washington, DC: Island Press.

Wohl, Ellen. 2009. *Of Rock and Rivers: Seeking a Sense of Place in the American West*. Berkeley: University of California Press.

Worster, Donald. 1985. *Rivers of Empire: Water, Aridity, and the Growth of the American West*. New York: Oxford University Press.

Worster, Donald. 2001. *A River Running West: The Life of John Wesley Powell*. New York: Oxford University Press.

Yeager, Peter Cleary. 1991. *The Limits of Law: The Public Regulation of Private Pollution*. New York: Cambridge University Press.

Zimmerman, Joseph F. 2012. *Interstate Water Compacts: Intergovernmental Efforts to Manage America's Water Resources*. Albany: State University of New York Press.

INDEX

ABOUT THE AUTHOR

JOHN R. BURCH JR. earned a PhD in History at the University of Kentucky in 2005. He has authored or coauthored six books, including *Owsley County, Kentucky, and the Perpetuation of Poverty* (McFarland, 2008). Other publications include *The Encyclopedia of Water Politics and Policy in the United States* (Congressional Quarterly Press, 2011), coedited with Steven L. Danver, which was named an Outstanding Academic Title in 2012 by CHOICE: *Reviews for Academic Libraries*. He is presently serving as dean of Library Services at Campbellsville University.